LAND LAW

AUSTRALIA
LBC Information Services
Sydney

CANADA and USA
Carswell
Toronto

NEW ZEALAND
Brooker's
Auckland

SINGAPORE and MALAYSIA
Sweet & Maxwell Asia
Singapore and Kuala Lumpur

GREENS CONCISE SCOTS LAW

LAND LAW

By

PROFESSOR RODERICK R.M. PAISLEY
PH.D., LL.B., DIP.L.P., N.P.
Lecturer in Law, University of Aberdeen

EDINBURGH
W. GREEN/Sweet & Maxwell
2000

Published in 2000 by W. Green & Son Ltd
21 Alva Street
Edinburgh EH2 4PS

Typeset by YHT Ltd
Ealing, London

Printed in Great Britain by Redwood Books, Trowbridge, Wilts

No natural forests were destroyed to make this product;
only farmed timber was used and replanted.

A CIP catalogue record for this book is available from
the British Library.

ISBN 0 414 01383 2

DEDICATION

For Debbie, Victoria and Robert

PREFACE

This book is intended to promote the future developments of Scots land law amongst practitioners and students. For this purpose, the treatment is intended to be as systematic as possible so that those referring to it in respect of novel situations may find something of assistance which is rooted in our legal traditions. That is not to say that Scots property law should be unduly nationalistic, conservative or backward looking. The treatment in the book has largely ditched feudal analysis as it has been written on the threshold of a new era for property lawyers—the post-feudal world. Scots property law is a modern system and should be outward looking and willing to embrace new ideas and concepts. The footnotes in this book are intended to facilitate this and refer to authority from other jurisdictions, particularly that of South Africa, so that readers may see that Scots property law is coherent, mature and systematic, with much in common with other mixed legal systems. We have much to learn but also much to teach others. In all respects the book is intended to encourage readers to look further into the matters touched upon. Consequently, the book refers extensively to other writings and articles without which this book could not have been written. The subject matter of the book largely excludes analysis of the practice of conveyancing. Whilst the author believes that conveyancing and land law are essentially the same subject viewed from different angles, the confines of space have precluded any detailed examination of the mechanics of conveyancing. The book has therefore been crafted as a companion volume to the excellent text books on conveyancing practice such as Gretton and Reid, *Conveyancing* (2nd ed.); McDonald, *Conveyancing Manual* (6th ed.), and Halliday, *Conveyancing Law and Practice* (2nd ed.).

Many friends and colleagues assisted in the preparation of this book, and their encouragement was invaluable. The author would particularly like to thank Sheriff Douglas J. Cusine, Professor George Gretton and Scott Wortley, who read the text and made many useful suggestions. My colleagues David Carey Miller, Cornelius van der Merwe and Scott Styles have all assisted considerably by discussion and encouragement. The staff at Greens, particularly Karen Taylor and Rebecca Standing, were unfailingly helpful and supportive.

CONTENTS

TABLE OF CASES

TABLE OF STATUTES

TABLE OF STATUTORY INSTRUMENTS

CHAPTER 1

THINGS AND RIGHTS—CONCEPTS

Introduction

The subject matter of this book is land law. Nevertheless, it 1.1
should not be supposed that there is a set of particular rules which
applies exclusively to land and not to other types of property. The
law of property applies as a general theory to different types of
property including land, moveable property and incorporeal
property.[1] Many rules relating to topics such as co-ownership,
possession and the transfer of ownership are similar in respect of
the various types of property. There is, however, no absolute
identity and differences must be acknowledged. For example, the
solid physical nature of land leads to little or no room for the
application of the doctrines of *specificatio, commixtio* and *confusio.*
Given the relatively long history of civilisation in Scotland there is
comparatively little room for the application of the doctrine of
occupatio in relation to land as compared to moveables.[2] In
addition, the classification of moveables into fungibles and non-
fungibles[3] has no relevance to land except possibly in relation to the
extraction of minerals[4] and similar matter such as peat and turf.
The existence of the feudal system of landholding and statutory
provisions have also obscured the underlying consistency in the
common law to some extent.[5] Despite this, there is as much

---

1   This has been obscured for a long time since the publication of Hume's *Lectures,*
     Vols I–VI (*Stair Society,* Vols 5, 13, 15, 17, 18 and 19), originally delivered
     between 1786 and 1822. For welcome light on the subsequent obfuscation we
     must thank Professor Kenneth G.C. Reid for his brilliant exposition of the law in
     Vol. 18, *Stair Memorial Encyclopaedia,* "Rights and Things", paras 1–16. This is
     essential reading for all Scots lawyers.
2   See paras 1.23 and 3.5.
3   Gloag and Henderson, *The Law of Scotland* (10th ed.), para. 36.2; Van der
     Merwe and de Waal, *The Law of Things and Servitudes,* paras 28 and 31.
4   *Stair Memorial Encyclopaedia,* Vol. 13, para. 1639.
5   See especially the removal of the requirement of *traditio* in the sale of moveables
     now governed by Sale of Goods Act 1979, ss 17 and 18. See Vol. 18, *Stair
     Memorial Encyclopaedia,* paras 606–639.

practical as academic sense in treating the two matters together. Frequently issues of land law and moveable property arise in the same context, as, for example, in the commonest situations where a purchaser buys a house together with fixtures which are heritable and fittings which are moveable.[6] For the sake of space, however, the attentions of this book shall be confined to land law with appropriate recognition, being given to the wider context of a unitary law of property.

Sources of Law

1.2   Much of the Scottish law of property is based on Roman law. In relation to land this origin is at its clearest in relation to general matters such as the list of recognised real rights, the concepts of *traditio* and *accessio*, and many of the characteristics of the classes of servitudes recognised at common law.[7] Reliance on Civilian concepts should not in any way be taken as indicating that the Scottish law of property is overly conservative and incapable of coping with modern commercial and social conditions: rather it is the employment of Civilian principles which enables modern Scots property law to respond to changing circumstances.[8] As we shall see, even where Civilian concepts have been at their strongest in relation to servitudes, the courts have not completely turned their face against the development of the common law to recognise new rights.[9] Feudal law also provided much substance to the land law of Scotland but its influence was in decline for centuries prior to the final abolition of the feudal system of landholding at the start of the third millenium.[10] There are some remnants of the Udal legal system remaining in the Northern Isles. The survivals have some bearing on land law in that there is no feudal superior recognised by the Udal legal system and the property right in salmon fishing rights in waters within territorial limits[11] and the foreshore is not reserved

---

6   Gretton and Reid, *Conveyancing* (2nd ed.), para. 4.04.
7   Gordon, *Scottish Land Law* (2nd ed.), para. 6–106; Gretton and Reid, *Conveyancing* (2nd ed.), para. 13.01. The classes of recognised servitudes is likely to be expanded in legislation following upon Scottish Law Commission, Discussion Paper on Real Burdens, Oct. 1998, No. 106, but such expansion will be wholly consonant with Civilian principles.
8   See generally "*The Civil Law Tradition in Scotland*," Robin Evans Jones (ed.), *The Stair Society* (1995).
9   See para. 8.12.
10   Abolition of Feudal Tenure etc. (Scotland) Act 2000, ss 1–2 (to come into force on the "appointed day").
11   *Lord Advocate v. Balfour*, 1907 S.C. 1360.

to the Crown.[12] Despite the gradual importation of feudal landowning into the Northern Isles, these rights are commonly held by the adjacent landowner. The abolition of the feudal system throughout Scotland will not alter these rights.

The Scottish law of property has little in common with English law or other common law legal systems. Exceptions exist in relation to topics such as nuisance and fixtures where English notions have been imported into Scots law.[13] Similarities also exist in respect of servitudes and easements where English law and other common law legal systems have drawn on the Roman law of servitudes. Restrictive covenants in England perform largely the same functions as real conditions in Scotland but the devices are not identical. Certain judicial opinions, particularly those of Lord Jauncey, delivered in recent decisions of the House of Lords, have tended to adopt certain English notions of property law, or at least a resemblance of those notions, and it may be argued that this has not facilitated the clear development of Scots law.[14] Of late, however, there has been an encouraging sign that the House of Lords is willing to refer to other mixed legal systems to provide assistance where Scottish authority is lacking.[15] It is to be hoped that this trend will continue as it will almost certainly result in the importation of legal ideas which are more compatible with the existing structure of Scots land law. With origins and traditions which are so diverse there is no overwhelming need for Scots law to mirror every development in English law. This has been recognised in recent years with the development of a Scottish approach in relation to "keep open" clauses in leases, which is at variance with the English position.[16]

Reform

Land law is never static. Last century saw the enactment of a 1.3 major statute relative to land law approximately every 25 years. The last two decades of the last century saw land law reform being

---

12 *Smith v. Lerwick Harbour Trs* (1903) 5F. 680.
13 See paras 3.6–3.11 and 4.13–4.14.
14 *Alvis v. Harrison,* 1991 S.L.T. 64 (H.L.); *Sharp v. Thomson* 1997 S.L.T. 636, HL.
15 *Axis West Developments Ltd v. Chartwell Land Investments Ltd,* 1999 S.L.T. 1416, HL, applying the South African case *Nach Investments (Pty) Ltd v. Yaldai Investments (Pty) Ltd* [1987] 2 S.A. 820. See also Cusine and Paisley, *Servitudes and Rights of Way,* para. 12.131.
16 *Highland & Universal Properties v. Safeway Properties,* I. H. Feb. 1, 2000 (unreported); *cf.* the English position in *Co-operative Insurance Society Ltd v. Argyll Stores* [1997] 2 W.L.R. 898. See para. 7.27.

crowded out by the pressure of other parliamentary business. This became particularly acute during the latter years of the Westminster Parliament's legislative competence relative to Scottish private law. During that period so little time and importance was given to the reform of Scottish land law that Scottish lawyers were fortunate if modest, but valuable, reforms were contained in Miscellaneous Provisions Acts alongside provisions relative to matters as diverse as evidence in trials of certain sexual offences, registration of divorces and valuation of sheep stock.[17] This legislative bottleneck has highlighted the need for reform and the advent of the Scottish Parliament should enable much greater parliamentary time to be dedicated to the reform of Scottish land law. The legislative competence of the Scottish Parliament extends to enactments relative to land law provided these are not incompatible with Convention rights or Community law.[18] To the extent that land law comprises "Scots private law" the Parliament's legislative competence includes the passing of enactments relating to matters reserved to the Westminster Parliament provided the law in question relates consistently to reserved matters and otherwise.[19] The pace of statutory reform is likely to increase rapidly and continue for perhaps a decade. With the legislation relative to the abolition of the feudal system the start of this millenium has seen the most comprehensive reform of land law in a thousand years.[20] Other major reforms of Scottish land law are scheduled for the next few years to implement useful and well thought out recommendations of the Scottish Law Commission. These reforms are intended to build on feudal abolition and will begin with reform of the law relative to real conditions (relevant legislation due in 2001)[21] and the law of the tenement.[22] Increased public access to land is presently a political priority but, in contrast to feudal reform, it

---

17 Law Reform (Misc. Prov.)(Scot.) Act 1985.
18 Scotland Act 1998, s.29(2)(d). "Convention rights" and "Community law" are respectively defined in 1998 Act, s.126(1) and (9). See paras 1.4–1.7.
19 Scotland Act 1998, s.29(4). See also a similar but slightly differently worded restriction in 1998 Act, s.29(2)(c) and Sched. 4, paras 2(2)(a) and 3(1). See the discussion of the law relative to the enactment of Abolition of Feudal Tenure etc. (Scotland) Act 2000, s.70 (ownership of land by a firm) contained in Scottish Law Commission, *Report on Abolition of the Feudal System*, Feb. 1999, No. 168, para. 9.28.
20 Abolition of the Feudal Tenure etc. (Scotland) Act 2000; Scottish Law Commission, *Report on Abolition of the Feudal System* (Scot. Law Com. No. 168), Feb. 1999. Another candidate could be Registration Act 1617.
21 Scot. Law Com., *Discussion Paper on Real Burdens* (No. 106), Oct. 1998.
22 Scot. Law Com., *Report on the Law of the Tenement* (No. 162) (1998).

may be difficult to frame legislation which is universally acceptable.[23] Future reforms relative to land law may include a complete
overhaul of the system of Land Registration,[23a] the abolition of
leasehold casualties and an updating of the statutory standard
conditions incorporated into standard securities and the rights of
heritable creditors. There is obviously work to be done but the
future is bright for Scottish land law.

Human Rights

Constitutional protection of property rights is not found in all 1.4
countries.[24] Unlike some other states such as South Africa,[25]
Scotland has no written constitution containing provisions protecting rights to hold and deal with land and rights in land.
Nevertheless, it is far from the case that Scots law refuses to
recognise the value of rights to hold and deal with land and rights in
land. A major new influence on the future development of land law
in Scotland is the law relative to human rights. The effect of the
European Convention on Human Rights ("ECHR") and the First
Protocol cannot be ignored in any study of land and rights in land
since the enactment of the Human Rights Act 1998 ("the 1998
Act"). The effect of the 1998 Act is complex and only the briefest of
overviews can be given here.[26] Broadly speaking, the 1998 Act is
generally intended to give effect to the ECHR and the First
Protocol with a view to protecting individuals from abuse of power
by the state, rather than to protect them from each other.

The ECHR and the First Protocol do not form a written
constitution for Scotland, nor are they directly incorporated
wholesale into Scotland's national law by virtue of the 1998 Act.
The ECHR and the First Protocol do not generally create rights
beyond the confines of the 1998 Act except to the extent that they
will influence the development of the common law. Instead the 1998
Act merely narrates that its purpose is to give "further effect to"

---

23 *Land Reform: Proposals for Legislation*, Scottish Executive, SE1999/1, laid
before the Scottish Parliament July 1999. For an example of one view see Lynne
Raeside, *Land Reform: Proposals for Legislation*, 1999 Prop. L.B. 1–4 (Scottish
RICS response).
23a At the date of publication of this book the Bill is in progress in the Scottish
Parliament.
24 See the discussion in *Re: Certification of the Constitution of the Republic of South
Africa 1996*, 1996 (4) S.A. 744 (CC) paras 71–74.
25 1996 Constitution, s. 25. See generally D.L. Carey Miller, *Land Title in South
Africa* (1999), Chap. 6.
26 See generally Grosz, Beatson and Duffy, *Human Rights: The 1988 Act and The
European Convention* (2000).

Convention rights. The effect of the 1998 Act on the ECHR and the First Protocol is generally to constitute a form of indirect incorporation. This may be summarised as follows:

(a) The ECHR and the First Protocol cannot be regarded as paramount to legislation in all respects. Pre-existing primary legislation is not impliedly repealed by the 1998 Act if inconsistent with the provisions of the ECHR or the First Protocol. Primary and subordinate legislation, whenever enacted, must be read and given effect to so far as it is possible to do so in a way which is compatible with the Convention rights.[27] This interpretative obligation is arguably the one aspect of the 1998 Act which will have the most effect in practice. If it is not possible to give effect to this interpretative obligation in a way which is compatible with Convention rights a competent court must consider whether to make a declaration of incompatibility. In relation to civil matters the Scottish courts with power to do this are the Court of Session and the House of Lords. The effect of such a declaration is not to invalidate the legislation but to prompt a legislative response. Courts have no power to strike down legislative provisions emanating from Westminster which are incompatible with Convention rights. In stark contrast to the power of the Westminster Parliament it is provided that the legislative competence of the Scottish Parliament is limited in that any enactments must not be incompatible with Convention rights.[28] The courts have power to strike down and disapply legislation of the Scottish Parliament which is incompatible with Convention rights.[29] The compatibility of the feudal reform legislation with the ECHR was considered in the course of the framing of the Act abolishing the feudal system as this effectively deprived superiors of many rights. The Bill introduced to, and the Act eventually passed by, the Scottish Parliament omitted some provisions found in drafts of the Bill which were considered incompatible with ECHR and added other provisions to protect the rights of former superiors

---

27 1998 Act, s.3(1).
28 Scotland 1998 Act, s.29(2)(d). "Convention rights" is defined in 1998 Act, s.126(1).
29 See, *e.g. Karl Anderson v. The Scottish Ministers and the Advocate General for Scotland*, I.H. June 27, 2000, (unreported).

in an appropriate manner.[30] The proposed legislation relative to enhanced public access to the countryside has given rise to similar concerns.[31] It is of course open to the Scottish Parliament to provide a greater protection to the rights of individuals than that given by the ECHR provided it does not do so by depriving others of their Convention rights.

(b) A court or tribunal determining a question which has arisen under the 1998 Act in connection with a Convention right must "take into account" the decisions and opinions of the Strasbourg Court, Commission and Committee of Ministers, whenever made, so far as, in its opinion, they are relevant to the proceedings in which that question has arisen.[32] This is not a requirement that there should be a uniform approach throughout the states which have adopted the ECHR and in this regard one may note a point of difference with the law relating to the European Union. There is a general requirement that standards must not fall below an irreducible minimum but Scots law is free to develop an approach which is more generous in respect of an individual's human rights.

(c) There is an indirect incorporation of Convention rights via European Union law as Community law takes precedence over inconsistent national law.[33] The legislative competence of the Scottish Parliament is limited in that it cannot enact legislation which is incompatible with Community law.[34]

(d) As stated above, Convention rights are not generally part of the substantive domestic law under the 1998 Act. One significant exception to this is that it is expressly provided in the 1998 Act that no "public authority" may act in any way which is incompatible with a Convention right unless, as a result of the provisions of primary legislation, it could not have acted differently.[35] Any victim of breach may bring proceedings

---

30 Scottish Law Commission, *Report on the Abolition of the Feudal System*, (No. 168), Feb. 11, 1999, para. 4.50; Draft Bill attached to Report, (cl. 20(2) and (3), compared with Abolition of Feudal Tenure etc. (Scotland) Bill (S.P. Bill 4) introduced by Mr Jim Wallace on Oct. 6, 1999, supported by Mr Angus Mackay. See Policy Memorandum, S.P. Bill 4–PM, para. 20. Sections 19 and 20 appear to have been added to the 2000 ACt for the same reason.

31 Kay M. Springham, *Trespassing on Human Rights? The Scottish Parliament and Land Reform*, 1999 S.L.T. (News) 227–231.

32 1998 Act, s.2(1).

33 European Communities Act 1972, s.2.

34 Scotland Act 1998, s.29(2)(d). "Community law" is defined in 1998 Act, s.126(9).

35 1998 Act, s.6. "Public authority" is defined in 1998 Act, s.6(3).

against the public authority[36] and seek a range of remedies including damages.[37] This imposes a control on executive rather than legislative power and, in the context of land law, may extend to affect the actions of local authorities in compulsory acquisition of property and the exercise by the Keeper of the Registers of Scotland of his statutory discretion in relation to land registration.[38]

Relevant ECHR Provisions

1.5   The provisions of the ECHR and the First Protocol which are most directly relevant to property law include the following:

(a) Article 1, Protocol 1;
(b) Article 8.

Article 1, Protocol 1

1.6   Every natural or legal person is entitled to the peaceful enjoyment of his possessions. This guarantees in substance the right of private property.[39] It is more than a protection against deprivation in respect of a right of *dominium* in land. It extends to and includes other associated rights such as hunting and fishing rights,[40] security rights[41] and the rights of tenants.[42] It is aimed at protecting existing possessions and it does not guarantee a right to acquire future possessions.[43] The rights protected from interference include the right to carry out physical acts such as use of property,[44] the prevention of unwanted use by others,[45] and the juristic acts of sale, lease and the granting of securities.[46] Although the deprivation rule will normally apply where a formal and permanent deprivation has occurred,[47] deprivation is not confined to this. Protection may be sought against those measures which restrict the legal extent of

---

36   1998 Act, s.7.
37   1998 Act, s.8.
38   Land Registration (Scotland) Act 1979, s.4.
39   *Marckx v. Belgium* (1979) 2 E.H.R.R. 330, para. 63.
40   *Chassagnou v. France*, judgment of April 29, 1999; *Huber, Staufer, Sportanglerbund Vocklabruck & Eckhardt v. Austria* (1996) 22 E.H.R.R. CD 91.
41   *Gasus Dosier under Fordertechnik GmbH v. Netherlands* (1995) 20 E.H.H.R. 403.
42   *JLS v. Spain*, App. No. 41917/98, Decision of April 27, 1999 (Fourth Session); *Larkos v. Cyprus*, judgment of Feb. 18, 1999.
43   *App. No. 8410/78 v. Germany*, 18 D. & R. 216.
44   *Marckx v. Belgium* (1979) 2 E.H.R.R. 330.
45   *Chassagnou v. France*, judgment of April 29, 1999.
46   *Sporrong and Lonnroth v. Sweden* (1983) 5 E. H. R. R. 35, para. 62.
47   *Holy Monasteries v. Greece* (1995) E. H. R. R. 1.

property rights or those which leave the legal extent intact but merely render their exercise more difficult in practice.[48] Rent control legislation has been held not to amount to deprivation of the landlord's interest.[49] However, where legislation was enacted to permit tenants to acquire their landlord's interest in leases against the wishes of the latter this was regarded as more than mere regulation of competing legal interests and constituted redistribution and deprivation of property.[50]

The right is subject to two express limitations. First, a person may be deprived of his possessions in the public interest and subject to the conditions provided for by law. The Strasbourg Court has held that a deprivation of property effected for no reason other than to confer a private benefit on a private party cannot be in the public interest but the same act could be justified in the public interest where it had the object of securing greater social justice in the sphere of the ownership of leasehold residential property.[51] Secondly, a state has a right to enforce such laws as it deems necessary to control the use of property in accordance with the general interest. The Strasbourg Court has generally taken the approach that any such state interference must conform to the principle of proportionality and strike a fair balance between the individual and the public interest. The availability of compensation for deprivation or imposition of controls is an important element in this matter.[52]

Article 8

Everyone has the right to respect for his private and family life 1.7 and his home. Although this may not initially appear to have much to do with land law, the Strasbourg Court has given a wide interpretation to its application. For example, it may deal with issues similar to the law of nuisance. The Article has been held to require states to establish a legal regime which protects residents from exposure to noxious fumes from a waste treatment plant[53] or dust contamination from the construction of a road.[54] In other cases the court has considered matters such as the transfer of

---

48 *Chassagnou v. France, Supra.*
49 *Mellacher v. Austria* (1990) 12 E. H. R. R. 391, para. 44.
50 *James v. U.K.* (1986) 8 E.H.R.R. 116.
51 *ibid.*
52 *ibid.*
53 *Lopez-Ostra v. Spain* (1995) 20 E.H.R.R. 277.
54 *Khatun v. U.K.* (1998) 26 E.H.R.R. CD 212.

property between natural persons on death,[55] transfer of tenancies by operation of law[56] and security of tenure in residential accommodation.[57] It is possible that this approach may be developed in future to deal with issues such as access for disabled persons to public facilities.[58] The Article has been interpreted so as to refuse recognition of a right to gypsies to take up residence on land belonging to others.[59]

Property

1.8   Many Scots lawyers were surprised to read the observations of Lords Jauncey and Clyde in *Sharp v. Thomson*[60] that the term "property" is not a technical legal expression and has no definite meaning in Scots law. Its meaning, according to this view, depends on context. Whilst that approach may be easier to defend in relation to the use of the term in a statute,[61] this is far from the case generally. It is traditionally accepted that the word "property" can refer to two separate matters:

(a) The right of ownership. For clarity the right of property may be referred to as *dominium*, a term derived from Roman law.

(b) The thing, known as the *res*,[62] which is the subject of the right of ownership. In legal systems such as South Africa the law of property is known as the "law of things". This terminology brings welcome clarity to the issue.[63] The term "thing", whilst not unknown to Scots law[64] is not yet widely used perhaps because it may appear to lack sufficient dignity to identify a hugely important branch of law.

This latent confusion between the right and its object has its origin

---

55 *Marckx v. Belgium* (1979) 2 E.H.R.R. 330.
56 *X,Y & Z v. U.K.*, April 22, 1997, R. J. D., 1997–II, No. 35; 24 E.H.R.R. 143, paras 48 and 49.
57 *Larkos v. Cyprus*, App. No. 29515/95, judgment of February 18, 1999.
58 *Botta v. Italy* (1998) 26 E.H.R.R. 241, para. 32.
59 *Burton v. United Kingdom* (1997) 23 E.H.R.R. 101.
60 1997 S.L.T. 636, HL, at 643, col.1. and 645, col.2 respectively.
61 Although, even in this context, the view may be criticised, particularly where the statute is a public and general Act and not a local Act. See "Jam Today: *Sharp* in the House of Lords", K.G.C. Reid, 1997 S.L.T. (News) 79 at 80.
62 From which Latin term is derived the expression "real" property and "real estate".
63 Van der Merwe and de Waal, *The Law of Things & Servitudes* (1993 Butterworths). See *Stair Memorial Encyclopaedia*, Vol. 18, para. 3.
64 *Glasgow Corporation v. McEwan* (1899) 2F. (H.L.) 25 per Lord Halsbury L.C. at 26.

in Roman law texts and is also encountered in other legal systems.[65]

Land

In contrast to the term "property", the meaning of the term 1.9 "land" is generally accepted as varying according to context.[66] It has variously been defined as including[67] or excluding[68] the buildings thereon. More confusing, however, is the use of the term "land" to refer not only to the thing but to certain rights relating to land.[69] There is an obvious parallel with the ambiguity in the use of the word "property". Whilst this ambiguity is not often encountered in judicial statements relating to land it is much more widespread in Scottish statutes. Many of these provide definitions of terms such as "land" which are frequently stated to include both rights in land and the land itself.[70] Typical of this is the provision in the Interpretation Act 1978[71] applying to any Act[72] enacted on or after January 1, 1979[73] unless the contrary intention appears. This defines "land" as including "buildings and other structures, land covered with water, and any estate, interest, easement, servitude or right in or over land". A similar provision is to be found in the statutory instrument providing for the interpretation of Acts of the Scottish Parliament.[74] A measure of obscurity is removed in some

---

65 Van der Merwe and de Waal, *The Law of Things and Servitudes*, para. 5; Felix S. Cohen, *"Transcendental Nonsense and the Functional Approach"*, 1935 *Columbia Law Review* 809 at 815.
66 Gordon, *Scottish Land Law* (2nd. ed.), para. 4–01.
67 *Glencruitten Trs v. Love* 1966 S.L.T. (Land Ct.) 5 at 6 in the note of the court referring to *Trotter v. Torrance* (1891) 18R. 848. See also Interpretation Act 1978, s.5 and Sched.1.
68 *Glasgow City and District Railway v. MacBrayne* (1883) 10R. 894 at 902 per L.P. Inglis.
69 Such as the right to receive feu-duties see *Presbytery of Ayr, Petrs* (1842) 4D. 630. *Cf. Governors of Cauvin's Hospital, Petrs* (1842) 4D. 556.
70 Lands Clauses Consolidation (Scotland) Act, s.3; Titles to Land Consolidation (Scotland) Act 1868, s.3; Conveyancing (Scotland) Act 1874, s.3; Heritable Securities (Scotland) Act 1894, s.18; Conveyancing (Scotland) Act 1924, s.2; Sewerage (Scotland) Act 1968, s.59(1); Offshore Petroleum Development (Scotland) Act 1975, s.20(1); Water (Scotland) Act 1980, s.109(1); Town and Country Planning (Scotland) Act 1997, s.277(1). See further Cuşine and Paisley, *Servitudes and Rights of Way*, paras 1.24 and 1.25.
71 c.30, s.5 and Sched.1.
72 "Act" includes a local and personal or private Act: 1978 Act, s.21(1).
73 1978 Act, Sched. 2, para. 4. For earlier legislation see Interpretation Act 1889, s.3.
74 The Scotland Act 1998 (Transitory and Transitional Provisions)(Publication and Interpretation etc. of Acts of the Scottish Parliament) Order 1999 (S.I. 1999 No.1379), Arts 6 and 7 and Sched. 1.

statutes by the use of terms such as "interest in land", which is
usually intended to denote some of the real rights in land[75] but not
the object of the rights.[76] Additional clarity has been added by the
consequential amendments contained in the Abolition of Feudal
Tenure etc. (Scotland) Act 2000 which largely substitutes the phrase
"a real right in land" for "interest in land" where it is intended to
apply to the rights in land but not the land, and the phrase "land or
a real right in land" for "interest in land" where it occurs in earlier
legislation and is intended to denote the land itself and rights in that
land.[77]

Rights and Things

1.10   The ambiguity in the meaning of the terms "property" and
"land" mirrors the surprising width of the meaning of the term
"thing" as used in the wider law of property. The law of property is
the law of rights in things. Otherwise stated the term "thing"
denotes the subject of a right. As we shall see below[78] things may be
both corporeal and incorporeal, the latter being rights of various
types. All real rights, apart from ownership,[79] are incorporeal
things[80] which are capable of being owned. In short, there may be
rights in rights. Such an approach assists an understanding of land
law and eases analysis of issues which arise where a subordinate real
right is granted over an incorporeal right, as is the case where a
tenant grants a standard security over his lease.[81] In addition, it
emphasises a significant point – the unitary nature of property law
in the context of land law.

---

75 See commentary, 1995 Act, s.1(7) by Professor K.G.C. Reid in *Current Law
    Statutes*. This has been amended by Abolition of Feudal Tenure etc. (Scotland)
    Act 2000, s.76(1) and Sched. 12 (to come into force on the "appointed day"). See
    further Scot. Law Comm. *Report on the Abolition of the Feudal System* (No. 168,
    Feb. 1999), para. 9.5.
76 Conveyancing and Feudal Reform (Scotland) Act 1970, s.9(8) as amended by
    Abolition of Feudal Tenure etc. (S.) Act 2000 ("2000 Act"), Sched. 12, para.
    30(6); Prescription and Limitation (Scotland) Act 1973, s.1(2) and 2(2) as
    amended by 2000 Act, Sched. 12, para. 33; Land Registration (Scotland) Act
    1979, s.28(1) as amended by 2000 Act, Sched. 12, para. 39(11) (to come into force
    on the "appointed day").
77 2000 Act, s.76(1) and Sched. 12.
78 Para. 1.17.
79 *Stair Memorial Encyclopaedia*, vol. 18, para. 14, fn. 3, para. 16, fn. 10, and para.
    652; Thomas, *Textbook of Roman Law* (1976), p. 127.
80 *Stair Memorial Encyclopaedia*, vol. 18, para. 11, fn. 4, para. 16, fn. 2 and para.
    652.
81 *Stair Memorial Encyclopaedia*, vol. 18, para. 16.

Separate tenements and *iura in re aliena*

The distinction between land and rights in land is rendered more 1.11
complex by the recognition in Scots law of parts of land as separate
tenements and certain rights in land as incorporeal separate
tenements rather than as individual real rights.[82] Real rights may
be regarded as incorporeal things that are themselves capable of
ownership.[83] A separate tenement differs from an individual real
right in land in that the former is treated as if it were land itself, as if
it were a thing capable of ownership and not merely one of the *iura
in re aliena* – the real rights in or over property belonging to
others.[84] Difficulties in distinguishing the *iura in re aliena* and
separate tenements are most acute where the tenement is
incorporeal. Today the most important of the incorporeal separate
tenements recognised by Scots law is the right to fish for salmon.[85]
The *iura in re aliena* comprise all other incorporeal heritable rights,
such as heritable securities[86] and servitudes.[87]

The differences between an incorporeal separate tenement and a
ius in re aliena are in practice are twofold and may be illustrated by
reference to salmon fishings[88]:

(a) The right of salmon fishings may be held concurrently with the
right of property in the river over which the fishings are
exercised without the separate rights being extinguished by
confusion or merged. By contrast, the owner of a thing cannot
create *iura in re aliena* in his own favour. Thus a lease by a

---

82 *Cf.* the position in South Africa where the notion of a thing is restricted to
    corporeal objects. See Van der Merwe and de Waal, *The Law of Things and
    Servitudes*, paras 16 and 29.
83 *Stair Memorial Encyclopaedia*, Vol. 18, para. 10, fn. 14 and para. 16. *c.f.* the view
    expressed in Grettan, "Owing Rights and Things", 1997, *Stellenbosch Law
    Review*, 176.
84 Gloag and Henderson, *The Law of Scotland* (10th ed.), para. 36.2.
85 *Stair Memorial Encyclopaedia*, Vol. 18, para. 10(3).
86 Gretton and Reid, *Conveyancing* (2nd ed.), para. 20.31.
87 *Lean v. Hunter*, 1951 S.L.T. (Notes) 31 per Lord Mackintosh at 31; SRO ref.
    CS258/27176 (opinion of June 1, 1950), at p. 4 in the transcript; *Stewart Milne
    Group Ltd v. Skateraw Development Co. Ltd*, O.H., Aug. 10, 1995 (unreported),
    transcript available on Lexis; *MacKay v. Lord Burton*, 1994 S.L.T. (Lands Tr.) 35
    at 37; Ross, *Servitudes*, p. 15; Rankine, *Landownership*, p. 415; Gordon, *Scottish
    Land Law* (2nd ed.), para. 24–09 and 24–96; Halliday, *Conveyancing* (2nd ed.),
    Vol.2, para. 35–02; Cusine and Paisley, *Servitudes and Rights of Way*, para. 1.62.
    For a similar categorisation in other mixed legal systems such as Louisiana, see
    Yiannopoulos, *Predial Servitudes* (2nd ed.), (1997), p. 18, s.6, and South Africa,
    see *Lorentz v. Melle*, 1978 3 S.A. 1044(T) at 1049, quoted in Van der Merwe and
    de Waal, *The Law of Things and Servitudes*, para. 215, fn. 1.
88 *Stair Memorial Encyclopaedia*, Vol. 18, para. 10.

granter in his own favour or in favour of a nominee of the granter is invalid.[89] A landowner cannot grant a servitude over part of his lands and benefiting another part yet to be conveyed to a third party.[90] This may have been modified to some extent by the statutory sanction of the practice of creation of servitudes or real conditions in deeds of declaration of conditions prior to the severance of the constituent parts of the land affected by the deed of conditions.[91] If, after their creation, any of the *iura in re aliena* come to be owned by the owner of the thing affected by the right, then the right will be extinguished by confusion.[92] In relation to a servitude the authorities are inconclusive as to whether a servitude will revive if the ownership of the dominant and servient tenements are subsequently split.[93] In practice it is prudent to reconstitute the right.

(b) The right to salmon fishings, being a real right of property, is not lost by negative prescription.[94] All the *iura in re aliena* will be extinguished by negative prescription if not exercised for the appropriate period.[95]

Classification of Separate Tenements

1.12   The separate tenements recognised by Scots law may be classified in two ways[96]:

(a) "legal" and "conventional" separate tenements; and
(b) corporeal and incorporeal separate tenements.

---

89 *Kildrummy Estates (Jersey) Ltd v. IRC*, 1991 S.C. 1.
90 *Hamilton v. Elder*, 1968 S.L.T. (Sh.Ct.) 53.
91 Conveyancing (Scotland) Act 1874, s.32; *Rubislaw Land Co. Ltd v. Aberdeen Construction Group*, (unreported), briefly noted at 1999 G.W.D. 14–647, otherwise available at http://www.scotscourts.gov.uk/index1.htm per Lord Penrose; Cusine and Paisley, *Servitudes and Rights of Way*, para. 2.07.
92 *Stair Memorial Encyclopaedia*, Vol. 18, para. 9(6). For standard securities see Cusine, *Standard Securities*, para. 10.10. See further Scot. Law Comm., *Discussion Paper on Real Burdens* (No. 106, Oct. 1998), paras 5.53–5.59.
93 Erskine, *Inst.* II,ix,37; Bell, Prin., S.997; *Carnegie v. MacTeir* (1844) 6D. 1381 at 1407–1408, per Lord Medway; *Walton Bros v. Glasgow Magistrates* (1876) 3R. 1130 at 1133, per L.P. Inglis; *Stair Memorial Encyclopaedia*, Vol. 18, paras 9(6), 453 and 476; Cusine and Paisley, *Servitudes and Rights of Way*, paras 1.68 and 17.22–17.25.
94 Prescription and Limitation (Scotland) Act 1973 (c.52), s.8(2) and Sched.3(a).
95 Prescription and Limitation (Scotland) Act 1973, s.8. For servitudes see Cusine and Paisley, *Servitudes and Rights of Way*, paras 17.33–17.37.
96 *Stair Memorial Encyclopaedia*, Vol. 18, para. 209.

Legal and Conventional Separate Tenements

"Legal" separate tenements arise by implication of law. "Con- 1.13
ventional" separate tenements arise by virtue of conventional
stipulation in a conveyance either by grant or reservation. This
leads to a difference in the manner of their conveyance. Because it is
a legally implied separate tenement, where the owner of the land
dispones the river the right to salmon fishings will not pass to the
purchaser in the absence of an express conveyance.[97] A disposition
of the land with "pertinents" will be insufficient to convey those
salmon fishings[98] although it will be sufficient to convey a *ius in re
aliena* such as a servitude benefiting the subjects conveyed.[99] Similar
principles apply to a disposition of lands "together with the salmon
fishings and other rights effeiring thereto". In relation to a
conventional separate tenement such as a minerals reservation a
conveyance of the land which makes no express exception of the
minerals will be deemed to include it.[1] A conventional separate
tenement may also become a pertinent of other land and be carried
by implication in a conveyance of that land. For example, a cellar
or coal shed may pass with the house or flat which it serves.[2]

Corporeal and Incorporeal Separate tenements

Corporeal separate tenements include horizontal strata below 1.14
ground including minerals and coal, mines of silver and gold,
petroleum and natural gas. Above ground they include buildings of
more than a single storey which are divided up into separate
tenements. Where such separate tenements exist the law recognises
the problems which may arise from the special inter-relationship
created by the physical nature and proximity of the tenements. In
relation to both minerals and tenemental property the nature of the
properties is recognised at common law which generates rights of

---

97 *McKendrick v. Wilson*, 1970 S.L.T. (Sh.Ct.) 39; *Stair Memorial Encyclopaedia*,
    Vol. 18, para. 208.
98 *Stair Memorial Encyclopaedia*, Vol. 18, para. 206.
99 *Earl of Fife's Trs v. Cumming* (1830) 8S. 326; (1831) 9S. 336; Cusine and Paisley,
    Servitudes and Rights of Way, para. 1.76.
1   *Lady Bruce v. Erskine* (1716) M.9642; *Stair Memorial Encyclopaedia*, Vol. 18,
    para. 209.
2   *Stair Memorial Encyclopaedia*, Vol. 18, para. 209. *Cf.* the limits on acquiring of
    new rights of property outwith the ambit of a bounding description. See paras
    4.16–4.23.

common interest or "natural servitude" to deal with issues such as support,[3] light[4] and service media. In the tenemental situation the rights to service media recognised at common law appear to be limited to use of chimney vents,[5] down pipes and other pipes,[6] but the view has been expressed that they may extend to installation of a satellite dish.[7] These rights have been fortified to some extent by statutory provisions. Although limited in their terms, such statutory provisions permit the owner of minerals to petition the court to obtain access through the surface and other rights over the surface where these are necessary to work the minerals.[8] Similarly where a proprietor owns a flat in part of a tenement he may petition the court to obtain rights to permit the laying of cables etc. through parts of the larger building not in his exclusive ownership such as common parts.[9]

Incorporeal separate tenements include the right to fish for salmon, the right to gather mussels and oysters, the right of port, the right of ferry, the right to hold fairs and markets and teinds.[10] No issue of common interest generally arises in relation to incorporeal tenements but the abuse of the relationship between the owner of an incorporeal tenement such as salmon fishing and the owner of the land may be controlled by the prohibition of actions which are *in aemulationem vicini*.[11]

---

3 *Andrew v. Henderson and Dimmack* (1871) 9M. 554 per Lord Neaves at 255; Rankine, *Landownership*, pp. 367, 384 and 385; *Stair Memorial Encyclopaedia*, Vol. 18, paras 233, 254, 255 and 258.

4 *Heron v. Gray* (1880) 8R. 155; *Boswall v. Edinburgh Magistrates* (1881) 8R. 986; *Stair Memorial Encyclopaedia*, Vol. 18, paras 236 and 361.

5 *Gellatly v. Arrol* (1863) 1M. 592; *Todd v. Wilson* (1894) 22R. 172; *Varese v. Paisley Dean of Guild Court*, 1969 S.L.T. (Sh.Ct.) 27.

6 Gordon, *Scottish Land Law* (2nd ed.), para. 15–43; *Stair Memorial Encyclopaedia*, Vol. 18, para. 238.

7 *Stair Memorial Encyclopaedia*, Vol. 18, para. 238.

8 Mines (Working Facilities and Support) Act 1966 as amended by Mines (Working Facilities and Support) Act 1974; Gordon, *Scottish Land Law* (2nd ed.), paras 6–68–6–76.

9 Civic Government (Scotland) Act 1982, s.88; *Stair Memorial Encyclopaedia*, Vol. 18, para. 239; Gordon, *Scottish Land Law* (2nd ed.), para. 15–47.

10 This is the Scottish term for "tithes" and denotes a right of the church to share in the produce of land. The mater is arcane and is largely irrelevant in modern land law. See Gordon, *Scottish Land Law* (2nd ed.), paras 10–50–10–77. Such payments will be extinguished in terms of Abolition of Feudal Tenure etc. (Scotland) Act 2000, s.54.

11 *Campbell v. Muir*, 1908 S.C. 387; Gordon, *Scottish Land Law* (2nd ed.), paras 8–83 and 8–132; "The Civil Law Tradition in Scotland", Robin Evans Jones (ed.), *The Stair Society* (1995), Chap. 8; David Johnston, "Owners and Neighbours: From Rome to Scotland", pp. 176–197.

The State of Things – Solid, Liquid and Gas

The vast majority of things classified as heritable property are 1.15
solid in state, land and buildings being classic examples.
Certain heritable property exists in a liquid state. This class
extends to petroleum and mineral oil whilst in its natural state in
strata.[12] In certain situations water may also be heritable. Moving
water, at least where it does not exist in vast quantities, is self
evidently moveable but percolating rainwater is probably heritable
by accession.[13] Where water is standing beneath the surface of the
earth it is likely to be regarded as heritable by accession.[14] A
similar, but slightly weaker, case for the acquisition of a heritable
nature by accession may be made for water in certain pools or lochs
which lie on the surface of land.[15] No additional weight is added to
the claim to a heritable nature by the fact that water in a loch may
exist as a solid in frozen form in winter.[16] Where water or another
liquid such as gas is transported along pipelines conform to a
servitude of *aqueduct* the liquid will be regarded as moveable at
least whilst in transit. It is arguable, however, that it may be
heritable when stored as part of a servitude of inundation and
dam.[17] Where oil has been recovered from natural strata and is
stored within large terminals on land those terminals may be
heritable[18] but it is arguable that the oil contained within them is
moveable.

The fact that water moves, on one theory at least, may sometimes

---

12 Petroleum (Production) Act 1934 (c.36), s.1(1), (2) and (4) (substituted and
renumbered by the Oil and Gas (Enterprise) Act 1982 (c.23), s.18(1)); *Stair
Memorial Encyclopaedia*, Vol. 9, paras 721ff and 856ff; *Stair Memorial
Encyclopaedia*, Vol. 18, para. 210(6); Gordon, *Scottish Land Law* (2nd ed.),
paras 6–15–6–19(6); Petroleum Act 1998, ss 1–2.
13 *Crichton v. Turnbull*, 1946 S.C. 52; 1946 S.L.T. 156; *Stair Memorial
Encyclopaedia*, Vol. 18, para. 273.
14 *Stair Memorial Encyclopaedia*, Vol. 18, para. 273.
15 *Ibid.*
16 *Cf. Harvey v. Lindsay* (1853) 15D. 768 where a claim to a servitude on a frozen
loch was rejected. See Cusine and Paisley, *Servitudes and Rights of Way*, para.
3.17.
17 Bankton, *Inst.* II,vii,28; *Gairlton v. Stevenson* (1677) M.14535; *Scottish Highland
Distillery Co. v. Reid* (1877) 4R. 1118; *Williams' Trs v. Macandrew and Jenkins*,
1960 S.L.T. 246; Cusine and Paisley, *Servitudes and Rights of Way*, para. 3.80.
For a similar position in South Africa see *Stephens v. De Wet*, 1920 O.P.D. 78.
See Zimmerman and Visser, *Southern Cross: Civil Law and Common Law in
South Africa* (1996), Chap. 24; "*Servitudes*" by M.J. de Waal, at p. 809.
18 See, *e.g. Shetland Islands Council v. B.P. Petroleum Development Ltd*, 1990 S.L.T.
82.

render it an item of property which is not subject to ownership.[19] According to this view there is sufficient movement to render the water ownerless in situations such as where water is running in a natural stream.[20] The difficulty for the theory is to determine when there is a sufficient lack of movement for ownership to be possible. Water in a *stagnum* – a loch which is self-contained and from which there is no natural overflow – is probably owned by the owner of the *alveus* (loch bottom). Rainwater percolating through ground, although not totally at rest, is sufficiently still to be capable of ownership by the owner of the ground.[21] The theory must recognise an exception where water is running in a man-made system such as a pipe or mill-lade. In such a case it would seem that the water may be owned.

Heritable property existing in a gaseous state is rare. Examples include natural gas in its natural state whilst located within strata.[22] Although there is little authority on the point it seems possible to create a servitude right to permit the extraction of gases or fumes along pipelines or vents[23] and whilst they are in the course of extraction the gases or fumes may be classified as moveable. The fact that gases move renders them largely incompatible with classification as heritable property and where these gases exist in the atmosphere it is accepted that their propensity to move renders them items of property which are not generally subject to ownership.[24] Air or water which is sealed in a container is capable of ownership as moveable property.[25]

Certain of the *iura in re aliena* may be exercised only over or in liquids located above heritable property. Examples include the public right of navigation on navigable non-tidal rivers,[26] and tidal

---

19 Stair, *Inst*, II,i,5; Erskine, *Inst*. II,i,5; Bankton, *Inst*, I,iii,2; *Stair Memorial Encyclopaedia*, Vol. 18, paras 282 and 600. See para. 1.25.
20 *Stair Memorial Encyclopaedia*, Vol. 18, para. 274.
21 *Crichton v. Turnbull*, 1946 S.C. 52; *Stair Memorial Encyclopaedia*, Vol. 18, para. 273.
22 Petroleum (Production) Act 1934 (c.36), s.1(1), (2) and (4) (substituted and renumbered by the Oil and Gas (Enterprise) Act 1982 (c.23), s.18(1)); *Stair Memorial Encyclopaedia*, Vol. 9, paras 721ff and 856ff; *Stair Memorial Encyclopaedia*, Vol. 18, para. 210(6); Gordon, *Scottish Land Law* (2nd ed.), paras 6–15–6–19(6); Petroleum Act 1998, ss 1–2.
23 Cf. *Anderson v. Brattisani's*, 1978 S.L.T. (Notes) 42; Cusine and Paisley, *Servitudes and Rights of Way*, para. 3.67.
24 See para. 1.25.
25 See Van der Merwe and de Waal, *The Law of Things and Servitudes*, paras 18 and 19; Yiannopoulos, *Louisiana Civil Law Treatise*, Vol. II, 27.
26 *Wills' Trs v. Cairngorm Canoeing and Sailing School Ltd*, 1976 S.C. (H.L.) 30; 1976 S.L.T. 162; *Stair Memorial Encyclopaedia*, Vol. 18, para. 523. This suggests that the water, even though it moves, in such rivers is heritable.

waters including the territorial sea[27], and the right of common interest which permits the owners of parts of the *solum* of a non-tidal loch to boat over and fish in all the loch.[28] A servitude of access may be created not only over dry land but also over a defined stretch of water such as a canal.[29] Clearly as salmon can live only in water, a right of salmon fishing can be exercised only in that medium. A fish farming lease also permits the tenant to anchor his cages to the bed of the relevant loch or sea bed whilst maintaining his nets and associated structures in the superjacent water.[30]

Flexibility in Conveyancing Practice

The nature of a right to extract minerals has caused some 1.16 difficulties for classification in some mixed legal systems.[31] Scots law has retained a useful degree of flexibility on the matter and has permitted the right to be constituted in more than one way. A property right in minerals may constitute a separate tenement.[32] Where such minerals are worked out the owner of the tenement will retain the ownership of the spaces comprising the worked out mineral veins or subterranean chambers which may then be used for other purposes such as provision of access.[33] A small body of case law suggests that rights to extract coal,[34] sand and gravel,[35] stone or slate[36] may be constituted as servitudes. This form of right is rarely encountered in modern practice. Where such servitudes do occur

---

27 *Crown Estate Commissioners v. Fairlie Yacht Slip Ltd*, 1979 S.C. 156.

28 *Mackenzie v. Bankes* (1878) 5R. (H.L.) 192 per Lord Selborne at 202; *Stair Memorial Encyclopaedia*, Vol. 18, paras 305, 307 and 359(3).

29 See, *e.g. Tennant v. Napier-Smith's Trs* (1888) 15R. 671. Again this may suggest that the water, even though moving, is heritable although an alternative explanation is that the servitude is burdening the *solum* and the water merely physically separates the *solum* from the boats.

30 See generally *Walford v. Crown Estate Commissioners*, 1988 S.L.T. 377; *Walford v. David*, 1989 S.L.T. 876; Gordon, *Scottish Land Law* (2nd ed.), paras 8–153–8–156.

31 See, *e.g.* South Africa where it is treated as a real right but there is dispute as to whether it constitutes a *quasi* servitude or a real right *sui generis*. For discussion see *"Trojan Trilogy: III Mineral Rights and Mineral Rights Law"*, P.J. Badenhorst, 1999 Stell. L.R.96–109 at 99–102.

32 See para. 1.14.

33 *Duke of Hamilton v. Graham* (1871) 9M. (H.L.) 98.

34 *Harvie v. Stewart* (1870) 9M. 129; Gordon, *Scottish Land Law* (2nd ed.), para. 24–24; *Stair Memorial Encyclopaedia*, Vol. 18, para. 489; Cusine and Paisley, *Servitudes and Rights of Way*, para. 3.15.

35 *Aikman v. Duke of Hamilton and Brandon* (1832) 6 W. & Sh. 64; Cusine and Paisley, *Servitudes and Rights of Way*, para. 3.14.

36 *Murray v. Mags. of Peebles*, Dec. 8, 1808, F.C.; *Keith v. Stonehaven Harbour Commissioners* (1831) 5 W. & S. 234.

the right of property in the material before extraction and the spaces left after such extraction will remain with the owner of the servient tenement. The ownership of the material will pass to the dominant proprietor only when it becomes moveable upon separation from the dominant tenement.[37] When the relevant material is exhausted such servitudes will be extinguished.[38]

In contrast to the flexibility shown in relation to minerals extraction, it is not competent to create or transfer a right of salmon fishing by means of a *ius in re aliena* such as a servitude or real burden and an attempt to reserve a servitude of one tide's salmon per season has been rejected.[39] It is always possible to create a real right in and to salmon fishing rights owned by another party by means of a lease.[40] A lease of salmon fishing may be created a real right under the Leases Act 1449.[41]

Things

1.17   The things or items of property that are the subject of a right of property are classified by Scots law in various ways. There are two primary methods of classification, which are derived from Roman law,[42] as follows:

(a)   Corporeal and incorporeal property. The former comprises tangible or concrete items such as land or bars of soap, whilst the latter extends to intangible items which have no physical presence[43] such, has rights of copyright or exclusive privilege (such as the right to catch salmon) or rights arising from contract or the right to be paid a debt.[44]

(b)   Heritable and moveable property. This distinction is unsatisfactory in that it is based on two different principles. Whilst the term "moveable" indicates that the item in question is capable of being moved physically, the term "heritable" has its origins in the type of property which passed to the heir under the law

---

37   Cusine and Paisley, *Servitudes and Rights of Way*, para. 1.43.
38   Cusine and Paisley, *Servitudes and Rights of Way*, para. 2.93.
39   *Murray v. Peddie* (1880) 7R. 804; Cusine and Paisley, *Servitudes and Rights of Way*, paras 1.06, 2.49 and 3.59.
40   Gordon, *Scottish Land Law* (2nd ed.), paras 8–84–8–85.
41   *Stephen v. L.A.* (1878) 6R. 252; Gordon, *Scottish Land Law* (2nd ed.), paras 8–84 and 19–121.
42   Gaius, *Institutes*, II, 12–14; Justinian, *Institutes*, II,ii,1–3; Erskine, *Inst*, II,ii,1 and 2.
43   Erskine, *Inst*, II,2,1; Bell, *Commentaries*, II,1; Bankton, *Inst.*, I,iii,20; *Stair Memorial Encyclopaedia*, Vol. 18, para. 11.
44   *Stair Memorial Encyclopaedia*, Vol. 18, para. 652.

of succession prior to the enactment of the Succession (Scotland) Act 1964.[45] Behind the actual words used, however, there is a basic distinction between immoveable and moveable property based on the nature of the property.[46] There is a good case for recognition of this by a general abandonment of the term "heritable" in favour of "immoveable"[47], as has already occurred in limited fields such as Scottish international private law.[48]

Continuing Relevance of Distinction between Heritable and Moveable

There is a case to be made for abolishing the distinction between heritable and moveable property. Nevertheless the distinction does retain some value in modern practice. Certain real rights such as servitudes may benefit only heritable property or moveables which have become heritable by accession.[49] Certain real rights may burden only heritable property or moveables which have become heritable by accession. Examples are standard securities,[50] public rights of way[51] and servitudes. There may be a servitude of grazing over a field but not over bales of hay.[52] There may be a servitude over or in favour of land owned by a limited company[53] but not over or in favour of the assets and undertaking of a limited company not owning heritable property.[54] Certain real rights may affect moveables only, an example being the real right of pledge.[55]

1.18

---

45 Gordon, *Scottish Land Law* (2nd ed.), para. 1–01; *Stair Memorial Encyclopaedia*, Vol. 18, para. 11; Gloag and Henderson, *Law of Scotland* (10th ed.), para. 36.3.

46 Gordon, *Scottish Land Law* (2nd ed.), para. 1–01.

47 Scottish Law Commission, *Some Problems of Classification* (Consultative Memo. no.26) (1976), paras 31 and 32.

48 *MacDonald v. MacDonald*, 1932 S.C.(H.L.) 79; Civil Jurisdiction and Judgments Act 1982; Anton, *Private International Law* (2nd ed.), p. 600–601; Gordon, *Scottish Land Law* (2nd ed.), paras 1–53, 1–56–1–58.

49 Cusine and Paisley, *Servitudes and Rights of Way*, para. 1.43.

50 Conveyancing and Feudal Reform (Scotland) Act 1970, s.9(2).

51 *Cumbernauld and Kilsyth D.C. v. Dollar Land (Cumbernauld) Ltd*, 1993 S.L.T. 1318 (walkway in town centre).

52 Stair, *Inst.* II,i,34; Cusine and Paisley, *Servitudes and Rights of Way*, para. 1.43.

53 See, *e.g. North British Railway v. Park Yard Co. Ltd* (1898) 25R. (H.L.) 47; *Alba Homes Ltd v. Duell*, 1993 S.L.T. (Sh.Ct.) 49.

54 Cusine and Paisley, *Servitudes and Rights of Way*, para. 1.47. Cf. *MacDonald v. Inverness Mags*, 1918 S.C. 141 per Lord Johnston at 150; *McCulloch v. Dumfries and Maxwelltown Water Commissioners* (1863) 1M. 334; *Re Salvin's Indenture* [1938] 2 All E.R. 498; H.W. Wilkinson, *Pipes, Mains, Cables and Sewers* (6th ed., 1995), p. 5 and 21.

55 *Stair Memorial Encyclopaedia*, Vol. 18, para. 5(2); Carey Miller, *Corporeal Moveables in Scots Law*, paras 11–04–11.14.

The distinction between heritable and moveable property continues to have relevance for the purpose of aspects of the law of succession, conveyancing procedures, diligence, bankruptcy and jurisdiction. These matters will not be examined in detail in this book.[56]

Four Categories of Property

1.19   From the interaction of the classification of property in two different ways emerges four separate categories of property:

(a)   corporeal heritable property;
(b)   corporeal moveable property;
(c)   incorporeal heritable property; and
(d)   incorporeal moveable property.

Corporeal Heritable Property

1.20   Corporeal heritable property recognised by Scots law includes:

(a)   land[57]; and
(b)   things built or growing on land insofar as they accede to the land.[58]

Incorporeal Heritable Property

1.21   Incorporeal heritable property recognised at common law includes some rights, such as pensions or annuities, which appear to have little direct connection with land.[59] They shall not be discussed further in this book. Rights which are regarded as incorporeal heritable property by the common law include:

(a)   the separate tenement of salmon fishing[60];
(b)   servitude[61];
(c)   proper liferent;
(d)   the public rights over land and water, including public right of way; *I approp to call heritable?*

---

56 Gordon, *Scottish Land Law* (2nd ed.), paras 1–28–1–55.
57 Erskine, II,ii,4; Gordon, *Scottish Land Law* (2nd ed.), para. 1–03.
58 *ibid.*
59 Gordon, *Scottish Land Law* (2nd ed.), paras 1–02 and 1–03.
60 Gordon, *Scottish Land Law* (2nd ed.), para. 1–03; *Stair Memorial Encyclopaedia*, Vol. 18, para. 10(3).
61 Erskine, II,ii,5–6; Gordon, *Scottish Land Law* (2nd ed.), para. 1–03.

(e)   leases[62]; and
(f)   heritable securities (a standard security is a statutory variety of
       a common law institution).

Incorporeal Property — *Further Distinctions*

The usefulness of the distinction between incorporeal heritable   1.22
property and incorporeal moveable property has been challenged.[63]
As all real rights, apart from ownership,[64] are incorporeal things[65]
it is difficult to see how they can be physically moved or remain
incapable of movement.[66] At best it might be said the categorisation
is admittedly artificial but they may be so distinguished because of a
perceived association to some related corporeal moveable or
corporeal heritable property. This is not wholly convincing. In
place of the last two categories (c) and (d) of paragraph 1.19 it is
frequently more useful to distinguish incorporeal property according to whether the right under consideration is a real right or a
personal right.[67]

Living Things

Heritable property may be divided into non-living and living   1.23
things, although the latter category is much smaller than the
former. Living things which may be classified as heritable are
growing trees, plants and other crops which, apart from the
instance of industrial growing crops, accede to the ground in which
they are planted.[68] Industrial growing crops which require annual
seed and labour, however, do not accede and are not heritable.[69]

---

62   Gordon, *Scottish Land Law* (2nd ed.), para. 1–03; *Stair Memorial Encyclopaedia*,
      Vol. 18, para. 652. Leases are made ral by statute but they are incorporeal at
      common law.
63   *Stair Memorial Encyclopaedia*, Vol. 18, para. 11.
64   *Stair Memorial Encyclopaedia*, Vol. 18, para. 14, fn. 3, and para. 16, fn. 10;
      Thomas, *Textbook of Roman Law* (1976), p. 127.
65   *Stair Memorial Encyclopaedia*, Vol. 18, para. 11, fn. 4, and para. 16, fn. 2.
66   Van der Merwe and de Waal, *The Law of Things and Servitudes*, paras 8 and 45.
67   The subdivision of incorporeal property into heritable and moveable remains
      important for matters such as choice of diligence and calculation of legal rights in
      the law of succession. See Gordon, *Scottish Land Law* (2nd ed.), paras 1–29–1–37
      and 1–40–1–45.
68   *Stewart v. Stewart's Exrs* (1761) M. 5436; *Paul v. Cuthbertson* (1840) 2D. 1286;
      Anderson v. Ford (1844) 6D. 1315; Stair, II,i,34; Erskine, II,i,14 and 15; Carey
      Miller, *Corporeal Moveables in Scots Law*, para. 3.04; Gordon, *Scottish Land
      Law* (2nd ed.), para. 5–40; *Stair Memorial Encyclopaedia*, Vol. 18, paras 12 and
      595.
69   *Stair Memorial Encyclopaedia*, Vol. 18, para. 12.

Trees cease to be heritable when they are felled[70] and plants cease to be heritable when put into moveable pots.[71] Seaweed is heritable whilst it grows but becomes moveable when cut whether in exercise of a servitude or otherwise.[72] All animals are moveable except possibly a mussel-scalp which because of its existence as a virtually immobile mollusc attaching itself to the sea-shore with such "peculiar tenacity"[73] may be regarded as *pars soli* on an analogy with a plant.[74]

Frequently heritable living things, whether animals[75] or plants,[76] are regarded as being of such particular value to the community to merit special statutory protection. This effectively constrains the full and free exercise of the owner's right of *dominium*, particularly in relation to the aspects of that right which enable abuse and destruction. Only a brief overview of the matter in relation to trees can be set out here. A statutory licence is generally required before trees above a certain size may be felled,[77] although there are numerous exceptions to the general position.[78] Anyone (including the owner) who fells such a tree without a licence is liable to a penalty.[79] Trees or woodlands may be further protected by means of tree preservation orders.[80] A tree preservation order is enforceable against all subsequent owners of the land upon which the trees

---

70 *ibid.*
71 Stair, II,i,34; Carey Miller, *Corporeal Moveables in Scots Law*, para. 3.04.
72 *Earl of Morton v. Covingtree* (1760) M.13528; Rankine, *Landownership*, pp. 257–258.
73 *Duchess of Sutherland v. Watson* (1868) 6M. 199 per Lord Neaves at 213.
74 *Lindsay v. Roberston* (1867) 5M. 684 per Lord Benholme at 868; *Duchess of Sutherland v. Watson* (1868) 6M. 199 per Lord Neaves at 213; Carey–Miller, *Corporeal Moveables in Scots Law*, para. 3.02; William Howath, *The Law of Aquaculture*, Fishing News Books (1990), para. 15.03. In *Parker v. L.A.* (1902) 4F. 698 per Lord President Kinross at 710– 711 the alternative view was discussed as to whether the right to take mussel-scalps amounted to a separate feudal tenement. The matter was not addressed in the further proceedings in the House of Lords; see [1904] A.C. 364. *Cf.* the English position in relation to shellfish shells examined in *Bagott v. Orr* (1801) 2 B. & P. 472; *Goodman v. Mayor of Saltash* (1882) 7 App. Cas. 633.
75 For further detail in relation to shellfisheries see Gordon, *Scottish Land Law* (2nd ed.), paras 8–24–8–38.
76 For further detail in relation to trees see Gordon, *Scottish Land Law* (2nd ed.), paras 28–25 and 28–26,
77 Forestry Act 1967, s.9 as amended.
78 Forestry Act 1967, s.9(2) and (4) as amended. See also Forestry (Felling of Trees) Regulations 1979; Forestry (Exceptions from Restrictions of Felling) Regulations 1979 and the Forestry (Exceptions from Restrictions of Felling)(Amendment) Regulations 1981.
79 Forestry Act 1967, s.17, as amended.
80 Collar, *Planning* (2nd ed.), para. 9.27.

stand when it is recorded in the General Register of Sasines or the Land Register of Scotland.[81] It is an offence to cut down, uproot or wilfully destroy a tree in contravention of a tree preservation order or where the tree is situated in a conservation area.[82] In addition to these particular provisions, trees and fauna may receive protection under a series of statutory natural heritage designations, such as Natural Heritage Areas,[83] Sites of Special Scientific Interest[84] and Nature Conservation Orders[85] all of which restrict in various degrees the development or use of land. Lack of space precludes any analysis of these matters.[86]

The fact that living things grow may cause complications for landowners. A tree straddling a boundary is a particular problem. The ownership is determined by the siting of the stem of the tree and where the stem is located wholly on one side of the boundary line it is exclusively owned by the proprietor of that ground even though the roots protrude into the neighbouring property.[87] A proprietor may be ordained to cut branches[88] or roots[89] of any of his trees which encroach by protruding over the boundary line into his neighbour's property. In contrast to encroachment by non-living items such as buildings,[90] the person whose property is encroached upon may also cut such branches and roots[91] but the branches and roots severed will not be his.[92] Presumably he must offer them back to the owner before proceeding to dispose of them.

A prudent conveyancer should foresee that living things will grow. Real conditions may assist in avoiding costly and acrimo-

---

81 Town and Country Planning (Scotland) Act 1997, s.161(2). See para. 9.06.

82 Town and Country Planning (Scotland) Act 1997, ss 171 and 172; *Brown v. Michael Cooper*, 1990 S.C.C.R. 675.

83 Natural Heritage (Scotland) Act 1991, s.6.

84 Wildlife and Countryside Act 1981, s.28, as amended.

85 Wildlife and Countryside Act 1981, s.29(1).

86 For further detail see Gordon, *Scottish Land Law* (2nd ed.), paras 9–93–9–105; Collar, *Planning* (2nd ed.), paras 9.39–9.45.

87 *Heatherington v. Galt* (1905) 7F. 706; 13 S.L.T. 90; *Stair Memorial Encyclopaedia*, Vol. 18, para. 179. In this regard Scots law differs from both Roman law and the law of South Africa see respectively *Digest*, 41,1,7,13; Justinian, *Institutes*, II,1,31; H. Silberberg and J. Schoeman, *The Law of Property* (2nd ed.), 1983), p.215.

88 *Halkerston v. Wedderburn* (1781) M. 10495; *Stair Memorial Encyclopaedia*, Vol. 18, para. 175.

89 Bell, *Prin*, S.942; *Stair Memorial Encyclopaedia*, Vol. 18, para. 175.

90 Bankton, II,vii,8; *Stair Memorial Encyclopaedia*, Vol. 18, para. 179.

91 Hume, *Lectures*, Vol. III (*Stair Soc.*, Vol. 15 (1952 ed), G.C.H. Paton), Vol. 18, p. 203, citing *Geddes v. Hardie*, June 7, 1806; 18 *Stair Memorial Encyclopaedia*, Vol. 18, para. 179.

92 *Stair Memorial Encyclopaedia*, Vol. 18, para. 179.

nious neighbour disputes by expressly obliging the proprietors of trees and hedges on boundary lines to trim them failing which the proprietor on the other side of the boundary may be granted rights of access to carry out the work.[93] Similar provision is useful to augment the rights of dominant proprietors in servitudes. In this context real conditions have been used to prevent the planting of trees within a certain distance on either side of a pipeline. They have also been used to create and preserve visibility splays at the junction of a servitude road with the public road by conferring rights to cut bushes which might obscure the view[94] and to fortify and supplement rights to cut back bushes and trees encroaching from the sides to narrow the route of a servitude of access.[95] Anticipated statutory reform of real conditions is likely to require that such rights should be expressly created as servitudes in a recorded deed.[96] Negative servitudes and real conditions may preclude the growth of trees above a certain height.[97] Conversely real conditions may serve to preserve the amenity of an area by precluding the cutting of certain trees[98] or the planting of a screening belt.[99] The rights of the proprietor of trees and bushes is constrained by statutory provision conferring powers on roads authorities to require the removal of trees which overhang and obstruct the use of roads.[1]

Dry rot is a type of heritable living property which no-one wishes to own. Dry rot is an organism or fungus that has the ability to permeate and digest wood causing considerable damage to the buildings concerned. To the extent that the wood is heritable the dry rot will be so also. A purchaser will frequently seek contractual warranties from a seller of heritable property that the property is

---

93 Cusine and Paisley, *Servitudes and Rights of Way*, para. 12.113; Sara, *Boundaries and Easements*, p.202.
94 *ibid.*
95 *Stevenson v. Biggart* (1867) 3 S.L.R. 184; *Wimpey Homes Holdings Ltd v. Collins*, 1999 S.L.T. (Sh.Ct.) 19; Cusine and Paisley, *Servitudes and Rights of Way*, para. 12.95.
96 Legislation to follow upon Scottish Law Commission, *Discussion Paper on Real Burdens*, Oct. 1998, No. 106.
97 Cusine and Paisley, *Servitudes and Rights of Way*, para. 12.113; Sara, *Boundaries and Easements*, p. 202.
98 *Henderson v. Mansell*, Nov. 9, 1993 (unreported), LTS/LO/1992/41.
99 See provisions substituted by the Lands Tribunal under Conveyancing and Feudal Reform (Scotland) Act 1970, s.1(5) in *Crombie v. George Heriot's Trust* 1972 S.L.T. (Lands Tr.) 40; *Robinson v. Hamilton* 1974 S.L.T. (Lands Tr.) 2; *MacPhail v. Baksh*, Nov. 10, 1995, LTS/LO/94/42 (request for screening refused). See further Gordon, *Scottish Land Law* (2nd ed.), para. 25–29; Agnew of Lochnaw, *Land Obligations*, para. 8–05.
1 Roads (Scotland) Act 1984, ss.51, 91 and 92.

not affected by dry rot.[2] Such warranties are not always obtainable and a purchaser usually relies on such contractual or delictual remedies he may have against his surveyor should the survey fail to uncover the rot. Should the rot exist and remain undiscovered at the time of purchase the purchaser will acquire ownership of the dry rot itself when he acquires the building although it is scarcely to be regarded as a "pertinent". Whenever it exists a property owner will obviously wish to exercise the power of destruction inherent in his right of property by having eradication treatment carried out. There is no clear authority establishing a right to enter a neighbour's property to eradicate dry rot but such a right may be implied as a right of common interest in some cases.[2a] Guarantees issued by specialist firms involved will require to be assigned as they will not automatically transfer to subsequent purchasers of the affected property.[3]

The heritable right to catch salmon must be distinguished from the ownership of the salmon themselves. The right to catch salmon is a separate legal tenement.[4] The proprietor of a stretch of water in which salmon fishing is carried out or the nearest point of dry land may be different from the proprietor of the salmon fishings.[5] The salmon themselves are moveable and in their natural state are *res nullius* and remain ownerless until caught when they become the property of the captor by the doctrine of occupation.[6] Salmon in fish farm cages may be owned and usually belong to company engaged in fish farming.[7]

Special provision for growing crops is made in various statutes. For the purposes of the Requirements of Writing (Scotland) Act 1995,[8] the term "real right in land" is defined as excluding growing crops and so obligations relating to them need not be constituted in writing.[9] The definition of "goods" in the Sale of Goods Act 1979,

2 Cusine and Rennie, *Missives* (2nd ed.), para. 4.82 and 6.24; Gretton and Reid, *Conveyancing* (2nd ed.), para. 4.42.

2a *cf. Newton v. Godfrey*, June 19, 2000, unreported, noted at para. 9.31.

3 Cusine and Rennie, *Missives* (2nd ed.), para. 5.07, cl. 7.4; Gretton and Reid, *Conveyancing* (2nd ed.), para. 4.42.

4 *Stair Memorial Encyclopaedia*, Vol. 18, paras 210(1) and 322.

5 *Stair Memorial Encyclopaedia*, Vol. 18, para. 322.

6 *Stair Memorial Encyclopaedia*, Vol. 18, para. 320.

7 *ibid.*

8 1995 Act, s.1(7), as amended by Abolition of Feudal Tenure etc. (Scotland) Act 2000, s.76(1) and Sched. 10, para. 58 (to come into force on the "appointed day").

9 Gordon, *Scottish Land Law* (2nd ed.), para. 5–40.

s.61(1) includes "things attached or forming part of the land which are agreed to be severed before sale or under the contract of sale".

Property *Extra Commercium*

1.24   Certain things and rights may be classified as *extra commercium* – outwith the bounds of commerce – or *intra commercium*. This distinction is derived from Roman law[10] and is found in other mixed legal systems such as the law of South Africa.[11] In modern Scots law it denotes things "outside commerce" which are not susceptible of private ownership and things "in commerce" which are susceptible of private ownership. Scots law appears to regard things outwith commerce as falling into two sub-classifications. These are:

(a)   things not susceptible of any kind of ownership; and
(b)   things which are held in a form of public ownership.[12]

Scots law does not recognise the third sub-division of religious things (*res divini juris*) which was recognised in Roman law.[13] In Scotland private land in which a grave is located is not exempted from commerce except insofar as the rights of surviving relatives must be respected by the landowner.[14] A similar rejection of the notion is found in other mixed legal systems such as the law of South Africa.[15]

Things Unsusceptible of any kind of Ownership

1.25   This sub-class includes things which are common to mankind such as the water in the territorial sea and other running water and air in its natural state. It probably also extends to clouds and natural rainfall and this issue may arise if it becomes possible to alter weather patterns by human action.[16] This, however, does not preclude the possibility of a stratum of unoccupied airspace being capable of ownership either as a conventional separate tenement[17]

---

10   See, *e.g.* D 20 3 1 2.
11   Van der Merwe and de Waal, *The Law of Things and Servitudes*, paras 21–27.
12   See Voet, *Commentarius*, I, 8, 1.
13   See, *e.g.* D 1 8 6 2.
14   Craig, *Ius Feudale*, I,vi,11 and I,xv,3, referred to in *Welsh v. MacDonald* (1896) 2 S.L.T. 304 per Lord Moncreiff at 305; *Bankton*, I,iii,12; II,vii,194; Erskine, *Inst*, II,I,8. See para. 10.17.
15   Van der Merwe and de Waal, *The Law of Things and Servitudes*, para. 27
16   M. A. Rabie and M.M. Loubser, "Legal Aspects of Weather Modification", 1990 CILSA 177–218.
17   *Cf. Stair Memorial Encyclopaedia*, Vol. 18, para. 212.

or as part of the subjects owned by the proprietor of the subjacent ground conform to the extension of ownership *a coelo usque ad centrum*.[18] Thus a landowner may construct a new house on land owned by him provided the airspace has not been conveyed to someone else. He may also obtain interdict against the passage of the jib of a tower crane within the airspace above ground owned by him where his consent has not been obtained.[19] A statutory exception exists in respect of the overflight by aircraft. No action is to lie in respect of trespass or nuisance by reason only of flight at a height above the ground which, having regard to wind, weather and all the circumstances of the case, is reasonable.[20]

Things which are held in a form of Public Ownership[21]

Property *extra commercium* is given statutory recognition by provision of the Prescription and Limitation (Scotland) Act 1973, Sched. 3 to the effect that any right to recover property *extra commercium* is imprescriptible.[22] This must refer to the second sub-class, property held in a form of public ownership, rather than the first class of things which are unsusceptible of any form of ownership, as there is no one in respect of the first class who could seek to "recover" the property.   1.26

Some property held by local authorities or other public bodies with a statutory function[23] may be regarded as *extra commercium*. In this context the relevant property may be termed a *res universitatis*.[24] The bulk of the case law relative to this matter dates from over a century ago when the relevant authorities were usually the magistrates and town councils of Royal and other burghs. The items of property identified in this case law[25] and in the writings of the institutional writers[26] as falling within the category also reek of a different era. The items included comprise the burgh charter, town

---

18 *Glasgow City and District Railway Co. v. Macbrayne* (1883) 10R. 894 per Lord McLaren at 899; Stair, *Inst*, II,iii, 59; II,vii,7; Erskine, II,vi,1; II,ix,9; Bell, *Prin*, ss737, 940; *Stair Memorial Encyclopaedia*, Vol. 18, para. 198; F. Lyall, "The maxim *cujus est solum* in Scots law", 1978 J.R. 147.
19 *Brown v. Lee Construction Ltd.*, 1977 S.L.T. (Notes) 61.
20 Civil Aviation Act 1982, s.76; *Stair Memorial Encyclopaedia*, Vol. 18, para. 198.
21 See Voet, *Commentarius*, I, 8, 1.
22 1973 Act, Sched. 3, para. (d).
23 See, *e.g. Oswald v. The Ayr Harbour Trs* (1883) 10R. 472; (1883) 10R. 85.
24 Erskine, *Inst*, II,i,7.
25 See, *e.g. Phin v. Magistrates of Auchtermuchty* (1827) 5S. 690; *Kerr v. Mags. of Linlithgow* (1865) 3M. 370 per Lord Deas at 377; *George Donald & Sons v. Esslemont & MacIntosh Ltd*, 1923 S.C. 122 per L.P. Clyde at 131.
26 Craig, *Ius Feudale*, I,xv,11; Erskine, *Inst*, II,i,7; Mackenzie, II,i,4.

cross, town houses, the town well, the town gates and walls, the town marketplaces, public graveyards, the town hall and corporation halls, the steeple and bell, public streets, the public port and harbour and theatre. What these items have in common is that they all performed some public function, usually of a physical nature. Properties falling within this class could not be demolished and were considered inalienable.[27] That should not, however, be regarded as an absolute prohibition against legal dealings. The relevant properties could be demolished or sold if the relevant item of property ceased to perform this function and suitable replacement facilities were provided, if required.[28] In addition, the authorities indicated that the properties could not be the subject of a legal dealing such as a servitude or the grant of a heritable security if this prejudiced the performance of the public function.[29] Presumably the properties could be the subject of such legal dealings if these did not prejudice the public function. Royal and other burghs have been replaced as the unit of local government by authorities created by statute.[30] Exactly what local authority buildings or land would be regarded as *extra commercium* today remains somewhat obscure. It would seem to exclude property which is held as a mere investment and for no other functional purpose. Investments may always be replaced by other investments. In any event statutory provisions enable the obtaining of judicial sanction to the circumvention of any restriction on legal dealings arising from this doctrine.[31] There is a small body of case law dealing with the rights of modern local authorities to alienate such property.[32]

The other major class of property which could be regarded as *extra commercium* comprises certain rights held by the Crown as

---

27 See, *e.g. Trades of St Andrews v. Mags and Town Council of St Andrews*, Feb. 27, 1824, F.C.; *Anstruller v. Pollack, Gilmour & Co.* (1868) 6 S.L.R. 161.
28 *Crawford v. MacFarlane* (1870) 8M. 693; *Mags of Kirkcaldy v. Marks and Spencer Ltd*, 1937 S.L.T. 574.
29 *Oswald v. Ayr Harbour Trs* (1883) 10R. 472; (1883) 10R. 85; Gloag and Irvine, *Rights in Security*, p. 19–20.
30 Local Government (Scotland) Act 1973, ss 1(5) and 222–224; Local Government Etc. (Scotland) Act 1994, ss 15–19; Local Authorities (Property Transfer)(Scotland) Order 1995 (S.I. 1995 No. 2499); *Stirling Council v. Local Government Property Commission*, *The Times*, July 18, 1997, Lord Bonomy, O.H.
31 Local Government (Scotland) Act 1973, s.75; *Kirkcaldy District Council v. Burntisland Community Council*, 1993 S.L.T. 753, O.H.
32 *Waddell v. Stewartry District Council*, 1977 S.L.T. (Notes) 35; *East Lothian District Council v. National Coal Board*, 1982 S.L.T. 460; *Re Motherwell District Council*, Court of Session, O.H., Lord Kirkwood, March 25, 1988 (unreported); *West Dunbartonshire Council v. Harvie*, 1998 S.C.L.R. 639; 1997 S.L.T. 979; *Stirling District Council, Petrs*, Lord Penrose, May 19, 2000 (unreported).

part of the *regalia*.[33] Again, as with local authority land, the import of this classification appears to be not an absolute restriction on all legal dealings but only a ruling out of such legal dealings as are inconsistent with the purpose for which the right is held by the Crown. Prior to feudal reform, the radical infeftment of the Crown in all land within the Kingdom was regarded as completely inalienable for the purposes of securing the paramount superiority of the Crown as notional source of the feudal system.[34] At common law the Crown could alienate only by means of feu disposition. Statute has removed this restriction and after feudal reform the Crown may alienate by means of disposition.[35] The Crown's right of property in the foreshore and sea-bed are removed from commerce only to a limited extent which does not exclude that land being alienated to a subject by feu disposition (also by disposition after feudal reform) or lease.[36] The acquirer of the property right or tenant's interest cannot prevent the legitimate exercise of the recognised public rights by interdict.[37] He can, however, take appropriate legal action to seek interdict or ejection to prevent or terminate the action of a member of the public which exceeds the recognised public rights such as the building of a hut on the foreshore for the purposes of residence[38] or the removal of sand or stones from the beach.[39] In a reported case dating from as late as the nineteenth century, it was opined that the sea-bed was absolutely inalienable and could not be the subject of Crown grant whether by lease or feu.[40] By the end of the nineteenth century doubt began to be cast on this view and now the accepted opinion is that the sea-bed is *extra commercium* only to a degree similar to that of the foreshore.[41] The explanation for the development of the judicial view may lie, at least to some extent, in the fact that

---

33 See, *e.g. Agnew v. L.A.* (1873) 11M. 309 per the Lord Justice-Clerk at 332; *Lord Advocate v. Clyde Navigation Trs* (1891) 19R. 174 per Lord Kyllachy at 176; Mackenzie, II,i,4.
34 Craig, *Ius Feudale*, I,xvi,7; Erskine, *Inst*, II,vi,13; Duff, *Deeds*, p. 65, para. 49(1). In addition, a clear distinction between property and sovereignty may have led to the view that a disposition of land also comprised a surrender of sovereign right.
35 Abolition of Feudal Tenure etc. (Scotland) Act 2000, s.57.
36 See, *e.g. Agnew v. L.A., supra.*
37 See, *e.g. Earl of Morton v. Anderson* (1846) 8D. 1085; *Hope v. Bennewith* (1904) 6F. 1004.
38 *Craig v. Anderson* (1893) 1 S.L.T. 145; *Nicol v. Guthrie* (1893) 1 S.L.T. 192; *Mather v. Alexander*, 1926 S.C. 139.
39 *Campbell v. Arnett* (1893) 1 S.L.T. 159.
40 See, *e.g. Agnew v. L.A.* (1873) 11M. 309 per the Lord Justice-Clerk at 322.
41 See, *e.g. Crown Estate Commissioners v. Fairlie Yacht Slip Ltd*, 1979 S.C. 156 per Lord Dunpark at 160.

technology has over the years developed means whereby the resources of the seabed may be exploited without intrusion on, or prevention of, the legitimate and free exercise of the recognised public uses.

Property *Intra Commercium*

1.27   Things which are *intra commercium* may be further subdivided into things which are owned and ownerless property.

The vast bulk of land in Scotland is still owned by a minority of persons and legal bodies and is not evenly distributed throughout the population. This phenomenon may be a cause for legitimate political grievance but it will not be discussed further here.

An item of ownerless property is referred to as *res nullius*. In one sense there can be no such thing as ownerless property because Scots law recognises the maxim *quod nullius est fit domini regis*. This means whatever is not owned belongs to the Crown. "In legal theory the Sovereign is proprietor of all lands to which no-one else can show a title".[42] Instances of the application of the maxim include circumstances where the land has never been appropriated to private use, as is the case in respect of the vast majority of areas of sea-bed within the territorial sea (including Orkney and Shetland)[43] and some areas of foreshore[44] (this is also applicable in Orkney and Shetland, although in those islands the property right is commonly held by the adjacent proprietor).[45] An example of a new property right acquired in such a way in recent years occurred in relation to the islands of Rockall and Hasslewood Rock.[46] The maxim also applies to other heritable rights such as salmon fishings and may be utilised to justify the Crown right to mussel scalps on the alternative bases that they are fixtures attached to the sea-bed[47]

42 *Hunter v. Lord Advocate* (1869) 7M. 800 per Lord Kinloch at 911.
43 *Secretary of State for India in Council v. Sri Raja Chellikani Rama Rao* (1916) L.R. 43 Ind. App. 192; 32 T.L.R. 652; *Shetland Salmon Farmers Association (Special Case)*, 1990 S.C.L.R. 484.
44 See, *e.g. Agnew v. L.A.*, Stair Memorial Encyclopaedia, Vol. 18, paras 313–318.
45 *Smith v. Lerwick Harbour Trs* (1903) 5F. 680; 10 SLT 742; *Stair Memorial Encyclopaedia*, Vol. 18, para. 317; *Stair Memorial Encyclopaedia*, Vol. 24, para. 314.
46 D.L. Gardner, "*Legal Storm Clouds over Rockall*", 1976 S.L.T. (News) 257 and J. J. Rankin, "*Life on Rockall*", 1985 S.L.T. (News) 321; *Stair Memorial Encyclopaedia*, Vol. 18, paras 48 and 558. The Island of Rockall Act 1972 refers only to the island of Rockall.
47 *Duchess of Sutherland v. Watson* (1868) 6M. 199 per Lord Neaves at 213; *Lindsay v. Robertson* (1867) 5M. 864 per Lord Benholme at 868; Carey Miller, *Corporeal Moveables in Scotland*, para. 3.02.

or they constitute a separate tenement.[48] The maxim also applies to cases where land has in the past been held in private ownership but that ownership has failed for some reason,[49] such as where the succession to land has failed and the Crown succeeds as *ultimus haeres*.[50] A statutory version of the role applies to the property of dissolved companies.[50a]

Other Limitations on Alienation

Property which is *extra commercium* must be distinguished from property which may be owned but in respect of which restrictions on alienation arise from other sources. The origin of these restrictions are many but the most frequently encountered include the following: 1.28

(a) Restrictions on alienation which have their origin in the will of the owner of the property. These include contractual restrictions and restrictions contained in real conditions. Both forms of restriction will be examined below.[50b] Similar restrictions may apply in relation to other real rights. For example, leases frequently contain a provision limiting the tenant's freedom to assign his interest in the lease.[51]

(b) An owner cannot subdivide his land into parts which are not recognised separate tenements. Separate tenements may be legal or conventional. Unlike legal separate tenements such as salmon fishings, conventional separate tenements such as minerals reservations are included in land sold unless expressly excluded.[52] A proprietor of land cannot generally treat the ownership as a parcel of rights and alienate separately those which he wishes whilst retaining others. Generally speaking he may alienate separately only those rights which are recognised by the law as comprising a separate tenement. Thus he cannot dispone separately the rights of shooting over the land, the right of fishing in the rivers for trout or the right of farming on

---

48 *Parker v. L. A.* (1902) 4F. 698 per L.P. Kinross at 710–711. See para. 1.23.
49 *Smith v. Lerwick Harbour Trs* (1897) 5 S.L.T. 175 at 177 per Lord Kincairney; (1903), 5F. 680 per Lord Kincairney at 684; *Lerwick Harbour Trs v. Moar*, 1951 S.L.T. (Sh.Ct.) 46, per Sheriff Wallace at 48.
50 Succession (Scotland) Act 1964, s.7; *L.A. v. University of Aberdeen and Budge*, 1963 S.C. 533; Hume, *Lectures*, Vol. IV, p. 204–205.
50a Companies Act, s.654.
50b For contractual restrictions see para. 3.29. For real conditions see paras 4.4–4.6.
51 Para. 7.23.
52 *Stair Memorial Encyclopaedia*, Vol. 18, para. 209; Gretton and Reid, *Conveyancing*, (2nd ed.), para. 4.05.

the surface. Nor, it is generally considered, can he create a separate tenement in such matters by means of servitudes or real conditions.[53] Thus he may dispone the lands to A with a restriction on use limiting it to farming but, having disponed of the property right, he cannot further dispone it to B restricting his use to one of shooting. He may grant a one-third *pro indiviso* property right in the land to each of A, B and C but he cannot confer on A an exclusive right to shoot over the land by restricting B and C from such activity by means of real conditions. He may, of course, separately dispone the minerals as they may be reserved or granted as a separate tenement. This restrictive rule has been circumvented in practice by the use of leasehold rights with restricted user clauses. For example, a farmer will frequently grant a sporting lease to party A permitting him only to shoot over the ground and a concurrent lease to B permitting him only to fish for trout in the rivers and a lease to C permitting him only to crop the ground. So useful has this leasehold practice become that it has long been recognised that in relation to an agricultural lease the shooting and sporting rights are impliedly reserved to the landlord who, in turn, is free to let them out.[54] This is frequently confirmed by an express clause in the lease.[55] Where the tenanted land is a croft the reservation is acknowledged by statute.[56] Even though the rights of trout fishings[57] and shootings[58] are not themselves separate tenements they may be

---

53 See Gordon, *Scottish Land Law*, (2nd ed.), paras 8–139–8–142 and 9– 10–9–13; Cusine and Paisley, *Servitudes and Rights of Way*, paras 3.08–3.63.

54 *Welwood v. Husband* (1874) 1R. 507; *Wemyss v. Gullard* (1874) 10D. 204; *Copland v. Maxwell* (1871) 9M. (H.L.) 1; Gill, *The Law of Agricultural Holdings in Scotland* (3rd ed.), para. 11.01.

55 See, *e.g.* Gill and Fox, *Agricultural Holdings Styles* (W. Green, 1997), p. 21–22, reservation 6(h).

56 Crofters (Scotland) Act 1993 (c.45), s.5 and Sched. 2 ("The Statutory Conditions"), para. 10(h); MacCuish and Flyn, *Crofting Law*, para. 4.19.

57 Freshwater and Salmon Fisheries (Scotland) Act 1976 (c.22), s.4 (lease real under Leases Act 1449 (c.6)), reversing *Pollock, Gilmour & Co. v. Harvey* (1828) 6S. 913. See also Gordon, *Scottish Land Law*, (2nd ed.), paras 8–37 and 19–121; Scott Robinson, *The Law of Game, Salmon & Fresh Water Fishing in Scotland*, p. 230–231.

58 *Leith v. Leith* (1862) 24D. 1059; *Stewart v. Bulloch* (1881) 8R. 381 (lease made real under Leases Act 1449 (c.6)); *Palmer's Trs v. Brown*, 1988 S.C.L.R. 499; 1989 S.L.T. 128, OH (lease real under Registration of Leases (Scotland) Act 1857 (c.26)). See also Gordon, *Scottish Land Law* (2nd ed.), paras 9–01–9– 13; Scott Robinson, *The Law of Game, Salmon & Fresh Water Fishing in Scotland*, p. 35– 36.

the subject of real rights of leases.[59] Clearly the separate tenement of minerals may itself be the subject of a separate lease.

(c) Limitations on alienation may arise from registration practice. At common law there is no fixed minimum size for a piece of land which may be separately owned except that it must be sufficiently large to constitute a separate tenement. In relation to obtaining a registered title to land the Keeper is obliged to refuse applications for registration of souvenir plots.[60] In addition to this the Keeper has a statutory discretion to accept applications for registration in that he is obliged to accept applications only if they are "accompanied by such documents and other evidence as he may require". This discretion has recently been exercised to prevent the registration of certain timeshares relative to salmon fishing.[61] There is probably a corresponding discretion on the part of the Keeper to reject applications for the recording of deeds in the Sasine system[62] but plots as small as single grave plots have been accepted for registration in the Sasine system.[63] The keeper has recently indicated that the policy relating to salmon fishing timeshares should also apply to Sasine registration.[63a] The view of the keeper is not without its critics.

(d) The subdivision of certain tenancies which are subject to special codes of statutory regulation such as small land-holdings and crofts has in the past been excluded by express

---

59 *Stair Memorial Encyclopaedia*, Vol. 18, para. 208, fn. 3.
60 Land Registration (Scotland) Act 1979, s.4(2)(b).
61 Registration of Title Practice Book (2nd ed., 2000), para. 6.106.
62 McDonald, *Conveyancing Manual* (6th ed., 1997), para. 8.1.
63 See, *e.g.*, the five various Dispositions and Blench Dispositions by Trustees of the Deceased Sir James Colquhoun respectively to (1) Matthew Andrew Muirs Trustees, (2) Colin Dunlop, (3) Duncan MacFarlane, (4) Cecil Charles David Currie, and (5) Philip Grierson Keyden, respectively dated (1) Feb. 20 and 25, 1880, (2) Sep. 14 and 19, 1882, (3) Mar. 1 and 19, 1878, (4) April 1, and June 12, 1888 and (5) May 2 and 29, 1894 all recorded GRS (Dumbarton) respectively on Mar. 11, 1880, Sept. 22, 1882, Oct. 4, 1886, June 25, 1888 and June 23, 1894.
63a A.G. Rennie, "Timeshare Interests ... Salmon Fishings" (2000) 45 J.L.S.S. 39.

Land Law

statutory provision although there was some debate as to whether such provision could be waived by the landlord.[64] The present crofting legislation contains no such express provision although it may be implied in provisions restricting the crofter's assignation of his interest to "a member of his family" or "a person".[65] There is no provision in the legislation relative to crofts which specifically requires that the tenant in a croft be a natural person and not a juristic body. Nevertheless, many of the provisions of the relevant legislation presume this in that they refer to the ordinary residence,[66] death,[67] bankruptcy or family[68] of the crofter. In addition, where an existing crofter wishes to assign[69] or bequeath[70] his croft to a person[71] outwith his family[72] the purported alienation will be void unless the Crofters Commission give their consent to it. The crofter cannot sub-let his croft without the consent of the Commission.[73] The landlord of a croft is also prohibited from reletting the croft or any part of it to any person except with the consent in writing of the Crofters Commission, or with the consent of the Secretary of State (now the Scottish Ministers) if the Commission withhold consent.[74] So far as the author is aware the Commission or the Secretary of State or the Scottish

---

64 See, *e.g.*, Small Landholders (Scotland) Act 1911 (c.49), s.26(8); Crofters (Scotland) Act 1955 (c.21), s.5(2), repealed without re-enactment by Crofters (Scotland) Act 1961 (c. 58), s.2; *Mcisaac v. Orde's Trs*, 1928 S.L.C.R. 83; *South Uist Estates Ltd v. MacPherson*, 1975 S.L.C.R. App. 22; *Fea Mortification v. Cursiter*, 1966 S.L.C.R. App. 53; *Smith v. Mackenzie*, 1967 S.L.C.R. App. 59; *Campbell v. Board of Agriculture for Scotland*, 1928 S.C.L.R. 27. *Cf. Macdonald v. Wooley*, 1957 S.C.L.R. App. 79; *Niven v. Cameron*, 1939 S.L.C.R. 23; Agnew, *Crofting Law* (2000), p. 24, fn. 73, and p. 62, fn. 5.
65 Crofters (Scotland) Act 1993 ("1993 Act"), s.8(1). See also 1993 Acts, ss 10 and 11.
66 1993 Act, s.22; Agnew, *Crofting Law* (2000), p. 104.
67 1993 Act, ss 10–11 and 23(1)(b).
68 1993 Act, ss 8 and 10 and Sched.2, para. 3.
69 1993 Act, s. 8(1)(b); MacCuish and Flyn, *Crofting Law*, para. 6.04; Agnew, *Crofting Law* (2000), p. 69–70.
70 1993 Act, s.10(1); MacCuish and Flyn, *Crofting Law*, para. 7.02; Agnew, *Crofting Law* (2000), p. 71–73.
71 The term "person" is not defined in the 1993 Act but the definition supplied by the Interpretation Act 1978, s.5 and Sched. 1 (originating in the Interpretation Act 1889) includes a body of persons corporate and unincorporate.
72 Defined in 1993 Act, s.61(2).
73 1993 Act, s.27(2); MacCuish and Flyn, *Crofting Law*, para. 6.05–6.06; Agnew, *Crofting Law* (2000), pp. 113–114.
74 1993 Act, s.23(3); MacCuish and Flyn, *Crofting Law*, para. 6.03; Agnew, *Crofting Law* (2000), pp. 104–107.

Ministers have never given consent to any juristic body becoming the tenant in a croft.

(e) Limitations may arise from the nature of the real right. For example, a servitude may not be assigned separately from the dominant tenement.[75] The incorporeal nature of salmon fishings places certain limitations on the derivative rights which may be exercised even if they could be granted by the owner of the salmon fishings. It is difficult to conceive how a right of salmon fishing could be rendered subject to any of the negative servitudes (or real conditions to similar effect) or most of the positive servitudes such as fuel, feal and divot or pasturage.

(f) There are a range of statutes which impose qualifications on a proprietor's freedom to alienate. Some of these impose a right of pre-emption or reversion.[76] Although there may be a move to repeal some of these statutes[77] they remain a valuable tool in certain cases and a variant of such rights may be employed in future legislation to secure greater community control over rural land.[78] In other legislative provisions the control is more extensive. For example where a private sector landlord has purchased a house which was previously subject to a statutory right to purchase ("a qualifying house"), not only does that right to purchase survive the transfer but, in addition, the private sector landlord is unable to dispose of "less than his whole interest in a qualifying house without the consent in writing of the Secretary of State".[79]

Capacity

The law of property may be regarded as consisting of a system of   1.29
legal rules which regulates legal relationships between legal subjects

---

75 Cusine and Paisley, *Servitudes and Rights of Way*, paras 1.46 and 1.49; Van der Merwe and de Waal, *The Law of Things and Servitudes*, para. 12; *Stair Memorial Encyclopaedia*, Vol. 18, para. 652.

76 Lands Clauses Consolidation (Scotland) Act 1845, ss 120 and 121; Small Holdings Act 1892, s.11; Land Settlement (Scotland) Act 1919, s.6(5).

77 The prime candidates appear to be the pre-emptions and reversions under the Entail Sites Act 1840; School Sites Act 1841; Church of Scotland (Property and Endowments) Act 1925, s.22(2)(h) and Church of Scotland (Property and Endowments) (Amendment) Act 1933, s.9(3). See Scottish Law Commission, *Real Burdens*, Discussion Paper No. 106, Oct. 1998, paras 8.51–8.70.

78 *Land Reform: Proposals for Legislation*, Scottish Executive, SE1999/1, laid before the Scottish Parliament, July 1999.

79 Housing (Preservation of Right to Buy)(Scotland) Regulations 1993 (S.I. 1993 No. 2164), regs. 4 and 6.

with regard to a specific legal object. In the context of land law that object is the land itself or a right in the land. An important aspect of this relationship is the capacity of legal subjects to enter into and maintain that relationship. Otherwise stated this may be regarded as the capacity to hold and deal with land and rights in land. This must be considered in relation to both natural persons and juristic bodies. Natural persons are in principle able to hold and deal with land and interests in land but certain individuals may lack capacity for a variety of reasons. These exceptions are more generally examined in connection with essential validity and comprise issues such as non-age,[80] insanity, drunkenness, facility and circumvention and undue influence.[81] As regards juristic bodies legal capacity to hold and deal with land and interests in land cannot be assumed.[82] The capacity of such bodies may be established by custom, such as the Faculty of Advocates, Royal Charter[83] or Act of Parliament, as is the case with firms with a legal personality distinct from the persons who compose it, such as Scottish partnerships.[84] In respect of other bodies created under statutory procedure such as companies incorporated under the Companies Acts,[85] capacity may be regulated by the company's own constitution in terms of the memorandum of association[86] but this is qualified by certain statutory provisions generally intended to protect the interests of a party dealing with the company in good faith.[87] No party carrying out any transaction relative to land or any of the real rights in land can overlook the significance of any of these matters. They can be merely mentioned here in the briefest of outline and for detail the reader is referred to textbooks on conveyancing.

---

80 Age of Legal Capacity (Scotland) Act 1991.
81 See generally Gordon, *Scottish Land Law* (2nd ed.), paras 11–01–11–24.
82 Gordon, *Scottish Land Law* (2nd ed.), paras 11–25–11–27.
83 *Conn v. Corporation of Renfrew* (1906) 8F. 905.
84 Abolition of Feudal Tenure etc. (Scotland) Act 2000, s.70 (to come into force on the "appointed day").
85 Gordon, *Scottish Land Law* (2nd ed.), paras 1–26–11–27.
86 Companies Act 1985, ss 1–6 as amended by Companies Act 1989.
87 Companies Act 1985, ss 35, 35A, 35B and 108–112.

CHAPTER 2

REAL AND PERSONAL RIGHTS

Introduction

The distinction between real rights and personal rights is of 2.1
fundamental and primary importance to the Scottish law of
property. It is, however, not something that is readily understood
by a typical client[1] and the terminology is generally best avoided
when taking instructions from first time purchasers. In making the
distinction, Scots law largely follows Roman law and resembles
many other mixed legal systems. A real right may be known as a *ius
in rem* or *ius in re*, whilst a personal right may be referred to as a *ius
in personam*. The phrase *ius ad rem* is sometimes used to denote a
personal right to require another party to transfer a real right.
Despite institutional authority for use of such a term, it is confusing
and as it involves no more than a personal right it is best avoided.[1a]
Real rights are distinguished from personal rights according to two
separate theories.[2]

(a) According to the "personalist" theory a real right is absolute in
     that it prevails against the world at large, whilst in general a
     personal right is enforceable only against a person or a class of
     persons. In relation to personal rights these persons are under
     an obligation to the party holding the right.[3] The theory may
     be criticised on the basis that in relation to a real right there is
     no genuine universal obligation on the world at large as
     persons are restrained from interfering with the real right only
     when they come into contact with the holder of the right and
     challenge the existence or exercise of the right.[4] Furthermore in

---

1   Gretton and Reid, *Conveyancing* (2nd. ed.), para. 1.08.
1a See, *e.g.* Ersk., *Inst.* III, i,2.
2   Van der Merwe and de Waal, *The Law of Things and Servitudes*, para. 43.
3   18 *Stair Memorial Encyclopaedia*, para. 3.
4   Hume, *Lectures*, Vol.II, p. 2; Stair, *Inst.* I, i, 2; Bankton, *Inst.* II,i,1; 18 *Stair
    Memorial Encyclopaedia*, para. 3; Van der Merwe and de Waal, *The Law of
    Things and Servitudes*, para. 9.

certain cases personal rights must be respected by parties who are not the direct obligants. For example, a person who is not a party to a contractual relationship may in some circumstances be found delictually liable if he encourages one party to breach his contractual obligations.[5] The point may also be illustrated by reference to the "offside goals" rule. In certain cases where an owner makes a grant, whether of ownership or of some other real right in breach of a personal obligation not to do so, the grantee is affected by the personal obligation if he is aware of the existence of the personal obligation.[6] In other cases a person may be held liable to implement contractual obligations although he is not a contracting party. For example, in terms of the Transfer of Undertakings (Protection of Employment) Regulations 1981[7] a transfer from one person to another of an "undertaking" situated, immediately before the transfer, in the United Kingdom, or a part of an undertaking which is so situated, does not operate so as to terminate the contract of employment of any person employed by the transferor in the undertaking or part transferred, but any contract which would otherwise have been terminated by the transfer continues to have effect as if made between that person and the transferee.[8] The term "undertaking" means any trade or business provided it is in the nature of a commercial venture.[9] All the transferor's rights, powers, duties and liabilities under or in connection with the contract are transferred to the transferee without the necessity of any express novation and even if the parties purport to contract otherwise.[10] The potential liabilities which this may entail is a major issue in purchases of commercial concerns and may be the determining factor in a purchaser's decision as to whether to purchase the premises without the

---

5   *British Motor Trade Association v. Gray*, 1951 S.C. 586; *Rossleigh v. Leader Cars Ltd*, 1987 S.L.T. 355; D.M. Walker, *The Law of Delict in Scotland*, (2nd ed., 1981, W. Green & Son Ltd), p. 917–924; J.M. Thomson, *Delictual Liability* (2nd ed., 1999, Butterworths), p. 36–39. For a similar principle recognised in South Africa see *Janen v. Pienaar* (1881) 1 S.C. 276.

6   *Rodger (Builders) Ltd v. Fawdry*, 1950 S.C. 483; 18 *Stair Memorial Encyclopaedia*, para. 690 and 695–700; Gordon, *Scottish Land Law* (2nd. ed.), paras 2–35, 12–03 and 12–21. For a similar position in South Africa concerning notice and double sales see van der Merwe and de Waal, *The Law of Things and Servitudes*, para 43. See also below at para 3.30.

7   S.I. 1981 No. 1794. See Mays, "Transfer of Undertakings", 2000 S.L.P.Q. 47.

8   1981 Regs, reg. 5(1).

9   1981 Regs., reg. 2(1).

10 1981 Regs., reg. 5(2).

business or the business as a going concern together with the premises from which the business is run.

(b) According to the "classical" theory personal and real rights may be distinguished by reference to the object of the right. A real right governs the relationship between the holder of the right and the thing that is the subject of the right.[11] Personal rights govern the relationship between two persons, the holder of the right and the obligant. The theory may be criticised on the basis that real rights ultimately are enforceable against persons. For example, whilst it is true to say that a servient tenement in a servitude is burdened by the servitude,[12] that servitude will be enforceable by the dominant proprietor by raising court proceedings not against the servient land but against the servient proprietor and any other party who unlawfully interferes with the right.

Although neither theory is perfect, both do assist to some extent in identifying distinctions between real and personal rights.

Nominate Rights and Closed Systems

The personal rights and obligations in relation to land, which are 2.2 recognised by Scots law, include rights and obligations arising in both delict and contract. Delictual rights may arise in relation to both the juristic acts involved in the acquisition of land and the physical acts comprised in the use of land. For example, they extend to the delictual rights of a purchaser where there has been a negligent mis-statement by the seller as to the extent of land to be sold[13] and the rights of neighbours arising under the law of nuisance[14] and negligence.[15] As regards contract Scots law recognises the nominate contracts recognised by Roman law and also "innominate" contracts in respect which the substance is determined by the parties.[16] It therefore follows that in the context

---

11 Gordon, *Scottish Land Law* (2nd. Ed.), para. 13–02.
12 Some deeds of servitude are drafted in this way see Cusine and Paisley, *Servitudes and Rights of Way*, para. 5.32.
13 *Margaret Elizabeth Anne Smith v. Angela Cecylia Paterson*, 18 February 1986 (unreported), full text available on Lexis, O. H. Cases, Lord Davidson.
14 See generally Niall R. Whitty, *"Nuisance"*, 14 *Stair Memorial Encyclopaedia*, paras 2001–2168; Gordon, *Scottish Land Law*, (2nd. ed.), Chap. 26. See further at para. 4.13 below.
15 See, *e.g.* *Richardson v. Quercus Ltd*, 1999 S.C. 278; *Hamilton v. Wahla*, 1999 G.W.D. 25–1217 (Sh.ct.) (removal of support).
16 Cf. the rules (now superseded) concerning "innominate and unusual contracts" examined in McBryde, *Contract*, para. 27–22–27–24.

of land law, an almost infinite variety of personal rights and obligations may arise in contract. Scots law does, however, place certain limitations on the creation of such rights by imposing requirements as to formal validity. Contracts or unilateral obligations for the creation, transfer, variation or extinction of a real right in land must generally be constituted in writing.[17] The personal rights that are most frequently encountered include:

(a) the contractual rights of both seller and purchaser under missives to purchase land[18];

(b) the contractual rights of parties to an option to purchase land[19];

(c) a contractual licence to occupy land that falls short of being classified as a lease by virtue of the lack of some essential element such as payment of rent. Such licences may form part of a *locatio operis faciendi* under which a contractor is given a contractual right to occupy land during the execution of certain works on that land. These are extremely common and comprise works as diverse as agricultural works, construction contracts and civil engineering works. In the last case where the works relate to road repairs and construction speed is of the essence. To impress this fact on the contractor a modern variant of the contractual terms includes what is known as a "lane rental payment" under which the contractor pays a rental for the right to occupy the lane of the road.[20] The incentive for the contractor is that the sooner the work is done the smaller payment he makes. Such an agreement, however, is not a lease;

(d) certain leases which are not created as real rights by virtue of statute[21];

(e) the obligation of a seller or disponer under warrandice respectively in a contract of sale or in a conveyance[22];

---

17 Requirements of Writing (Scotland) Act 1995, s.1(2)(a)(i) as amended by Abolition of Feudal Tenure etc. (Scotland) Act 2000, s.76(1) and Sched. 12, para. 58 (to come into force after the "appointed day"); Gretton and Reid, *Conveyancing*, (2nd. ed.), para. 2.02.

18 See generally Cusine and Rennie, *Missives*, (2nd. ed., 1999, Butterworths/Law Society of Scotland).

19 See, *e.g.*, *Cala Management Ltd v. Corstorphine Piggeries Ltd* 1996 G.W.D. 34–2029 (OH); *Miller Homes Ltd v. Frame*, O.H., Lord Hamilton, 7 March 2000, G.W.D. 11–388.

20 MacQueen and Thomson, *Contract Law in Scotland*, (2000), para. 6.49.

21 Paras 7.04–7.19.

22 18 *Stair Memorial Encyclopaedia*, p. 701. C.f. the securing of warrandice by a standard security which is rare if not unknown. Real warrandice was abolished by Conveyancing (Scotland) Act 1924, s.14(1). See para 2.5.

(f)   the obligation on the solicitor to implement the instructions given by a client to purchase land on the client's behalf. This is apart of the contract of agency[23];

(g)   the liability of a guarantor under a performance bond relative to a tenant's obligations in a lease[24]; and

(h)   the terms of a disposition which may be enforceable between the original parties as a contract.[25] This may provide a limited means of enforcing restrictions in the disposition where they fail as real conditions.[26] These contractual rights are to be saved in terms of the legislation relating to feudal reform.[27] The matter may be altered in the proposed legislation relative to the reform of the law of title conditions.[27a]

Other less common, but equally valid, contractual rights relating to land include:

(a)   an agreement to sell heritable property on condition that the seller receives a proportion of the profit on resale[28];

(b)   an agreement that neither party should purchase lands without giving the other the option of being a joint purchaser.[29]

It should be borne in mind that the making of a contract relative   2.3 to the transfer or creation of a real right in land and the transfer or creation of a real right in land in implement thereof are distinct in law. *Traditionibus non nudis pactis dominia rerum transferuntur—*delivery, not a bare contract, transfers the ownership of things.[30] As we shall see in a later chapter, actual delivery of land is impossible and symbolical delivery has been effectively replaced by registration in a public register.[31]

The List of Recognised Real Rights

By contrast to personal obligations, parties cannot agree to create   2.4

---

23   Rennie, *Solicitors' Negligence*, (1997), paras 1.07–1.08 and 2.01 and Chap. 3.
24   *Waydale Ltd v. DHL Holdings (UK) Ltd*, 1996 S.C.L.R. 391.
25   *Marquis of Abercorn v. Marnoch's Tr.*, 26 June 1817 F.C.
26   *Kirkintilloch Kirk Session v. Kirkintilloch School Board*, 1911 S.C. 1127; 18 *Stair Memorial Encyclopaedia*, para. 392.
27   Abolition of Feudal Tenure etc. (Scotland) Act 2000, s.75.
27a See Scot. Law Comm., *Discussion Paper on Real Burdens* (No. 106, Oct. 1998), paras 7.73–7.77.
28   *Morris v. Goldrich* 1952 S.L.T. (Sh.Ct.) 86. This may be regarded as a variant of a contract of sale.
29   *Mungall v. Bowhill Coal Co.* (1904) 12 S.L.T. 80 and 262.
30   MacQueen and Thomson, *Contract Law in Scotland*, (2000), para. 1.41.
31   See paras 3.18 and 3.19.

any right which they see fit as a real right simply by entering into an agreement and designating the rights and obligations thereby created as "real rights". It is also the case that the Keeper cannot create a new type of real right merely by opening a title sheet in respect of that right or noting it on the title sheet relative to any other interest. Registration in the Land Register may create a real right only "insofar as the right or obligation is capable, under any enactment or rule of law, of being vested as a real right, or being made real or, as the case may be, of being affected as a real right".[32] Whatever the terms of any agreement or the practice of the Keeper in respect of Land Registration Scots law will countenance only a certain limited number of rights as real rights. This *numerus clausus*—a virtual closed system—is a characteristic of other mixed legal systems such as the law of South Africa.[33]

As regards land the real rights recognised by Scots law in the modern era include the following:

(a)   property (*dominium*);
(b)   proper liferent;
(c)   tenant's right in a lease;
(d)   servitude;
(e)   certain public rights such as a public right of way and a public right of navigation;
(f)   certain statutory rights; _ not as imp ·
(g)   certain exclusive privileges; ~ rare
(h)   tenant's right in a tenancy at will;
(i)   creditor's right in fixed securities and charging orders; and
(j)   possession. See para. 2.34.

Most of the various real rights outlined above will be examined further in this book but in varying degrees of depth. For the sake of brevity, only a sample of the statutory rights will be touched upon.[34] This book will not deal with the matter of exclusive privileges which, in general, are relatively rarely encountered in modern practice. In recent years these have largely been confined

---

32   Land Registration (Scotland) Act 1979, s.3(1).
33   See the approach of the law of South Africa which has a virtual *numerus clausus* of real rights see Van der Merwe and de Waal, *The Law of Things and Servitudes*, paras 8 and 45.
34   Paras 2.8–2.9 and Chapt. 10.

to monopoly rights such as fairs and markets,[35] ports and harbours,[36] public ferries[37] and the rights of Royal and other burghs.[38] Whilst the last of these have been affected by local government reorganisation and the vast array of statutory control following thereon,[39] the others are subject to a considerable overlay of statutory regulation in the public interest. As a result, it is rare for these matters to arise as a "pure" property law issue in modern times.

Alterations in the List of Real Rights

In Scotland the list of real rights is not absolutely closed and 2.5 there remains the potential for additional real rights to be added both at common law and by statute. The common law additions include:

[margin, handwritten: ? Not really breaching NC. Last to do this was Real Burden 1800s.]

(a) The expansion of the recognised class of positive servitudes to include the rights of bleaching[40] and possibly also car parking.[41] *[handwritten: Variation of content within 1 right, not new Rs - ie Typen fixierung > Zwang]*

(b) The recognition that real conditions may permit the dominant proprietor to enter on to a servient tenement and carry out activities such as road building.[42] These rights will probably be reclassified as servitudes after the statutory reform of the law of real conditions.[43] *[handwritten: Nope, now recognised as 'ancillary rights' - analogous right to S as S to O? see eg Moncrieff v Jamieson. (also serv conditions to S, 2.6 as RB to O?)]*

The major statutory additions include:

---

35 *Blackie v. Mags. of Edinburgh* (1884) 11R. 783; Gordon, *Scottish Land Law* (2nd. ed.), paras 10–44–10–46.
36 *MacPherson v. Mackenzie* (1881) 8R. 706; Gordon, *Scottish Land Law* (2nd. ed.), paras 10–04–10–22.
37 *Greig v. Mags of Kirkcaldy* (1851) 13D. 975; Gordon, *Scottish Land Law* (2nd. ed.), paras 10–23–10–33.
38 See, *e.g.*, *Grahame v. Mags of Kirkcaldy* (1882) 9R. (HL) 91.
39 See generally Local Government (Scotland) Act 1973; Local Government etc. (Scotland) Act 1994.
40 *Town of Falkland v. Carmichael* (1708) M.10916; *Jeffrey v. Duke of Roxburghe* (1755) M. 2340; (1757) 1 Pat. 632; Cusine and Paisley, *Servitudes and Rights of Way*, para. 3.12.
41 *Ronald Osborne Harris v. Wishart*, Arbroath Sheriff Court, case ref: A202/95, Sheriff J. Irvine Smith, date of judgement 23 Jan. 1997; *Murrayfield Ice Rink Ltd v. Scottish Rugby Union*, 1973 S.L.T. 99; Cusine and Paisley, *Servitudes and Rights of Way*, paras 3.45–3.52.
42 *B. & C. Group Management Ltd, Haren & Wood, Petrs*, 4 Dec. 1992, O.H., unreported.
43 Legislation to follow upon Scottish Law Commission, *Discussion Paper on Real Burdens*, No.106, Oct. 1998.

[handwritten margin note: Emphyteusis was RR in Rome]

(a)   Lease—originally regarded as a contract. Some leases which
      comply with certain essential requirements are recognised as
      real rights in terms of the Leases Act 1449[44] whilst others
      remain as contracts. Leases of freshwater fishings for one year
      or more were recognised as real rights by statute in 1976.[45]
      Other leases may be made real by recording in the Sasine
      Register or register in the Land Regster of Scotland.[45a]

(b)   Standard security—created by the Conveyancing and Feudal
      Reform (Scotland) Act 1970, P. II.[46]

(c)   Charging orders created in various statutes generally relating
      to local government.[47]

[handwritten margin note: Not a RR until attachment - if can them · A MacPh thinks jun an inter priority]

(d)   Attached floating charge security—originally introduced into
      Scots law by the Companies (Floating Charges) (Scotland) Act
      1961.[48] After various reforms[49] the effect of the charge is now
      dealt with in more recent legislation.[50]

(e)   The proposed expansion of the class of recognised servitudes to
      include the carrying out of positive activity on the servient
      tenement.[51]

---

44   C.6 Record ed. or c.18–19 12mo ed.
45   Freshwater and Salmon Fisheries (Scotland) Act 1976, s.4; Gordon, *Scottish
     Land Law*, paras 8–138 and 19–121; 18 *Stair Memorial Encyclopaedia*, para. 280.
45a Registration of Leases (Scotland) Act 1857, s.1 as amended; Land Registration
     (Scotland) Act 1979, s.2(1). See para. 7.19.
46   See Chap. 11.
47   Charging Orders (Residential Accommodation) (Scotland) Order (S.I. 1993 No.
     1516) made in terms of Health and Social Services and Social Security
     Adjudications Act 1983, s.23(5) and (6); Building (Forms) (Scotland) Regula-
     tions 1991 (S.I.1991 No. 160), Form 26 made in terms of Building (Scotland) Act
     1959, ss 10, 11, 13 and 24(1)(a), Sched. 6; Housing (Scotland) Act 1969, s.25(4)
     and Sched. 2 (repealed by Housing (Scotland) Act 1987, Sched. 24); Housing
     (Scotland) Act 1987, ss 109(5), 131, 164(4), Sched. 9 and Sched. 11, Pt IV; Civic
     Government (Scotland) Act 1982, s.108 as amended by Housing (Scotland) Act
     1987, s.339 and Sched. 23; Civil Legal Aid (Scotland) Regulations 1987 (S.I. 1987
     No. 381), reg. 40 and Sched. 4, Form 1 as amended by Civil Legal Aid (Scotland)
     Amendment (No.2) Regulations 1991 (S.I. 1991 No. 1904), reg. 9. See Gretton
     and Reid, Conveyancing (2nd. ed.), para. 4.17; McDonald, *Conveyancing
     Manual*, (6th ed.), paras 19.49 and 19.52; *County Council of Moray, Petitrs*, 1962
     S.C. 601; *Lindsay v. Glasgow D.C.*, 1998 Hous. L.R. 4.
48   "*The Coming of the Floating Charge to Scotland: and Account and an
     Assessment*", R.B. Jack in *A Scots Conveyancing Miscellany*, D.J. Cusine (ed.),
     pp. 33–46; 4 *Stair Memorial Encyclopaedia*, para. 648.
49   Gordon, *Scottish Land Law*, para. 20–214; 4 *Stair Memorial Encyclopaedia*,
     paras 649–650.
50   Insolvency Act 1986, Pt. III, Chaps II and III and Sched. 2; Companies Act 1985,
     ss 462–466. See Chap. 11.
51   Legislation to follow upon Scottish Law Commission, *Discussion Paper on Real
     Burdens*, No.106, Oct. 1998.

(f)   The possibility of creating a real right of "timeshare rights" has been suggested but there is no firm proposal as yet.[51a]

Shortening of the List of Real Rights

Conversely, the list of real rights may be shortened. Real rights which have ceased to be recognised at common law include the rights to fortalices[52] and arsenals.[53] The creation of certain real rights has been abolished by statute. Such "abolished" real rights include: | 2.7

(a)   The creation of a security over lands retained by the disponer in respect of obligations of warrandice by means of a grant of "real" warrandice after January 1 1925.[54]

(b)   The creation of a security over land or a real right in land by any means other than a standard security on or after November 29, 1970.[55] The minor exception relative to entails will be removed by the closure of the register of entails and the disentailing of all entailed land upon feudal reform.[56]

(c)   The whole feudal system of landholding comprising all estates of *dominium utile* and all other feudal estates in land (including superiorities) will cease to exist on the appointed day in terms of feudal reform. In addition any new feu grant will be incompetent. On the appointed day all estates of *dominium utile* will forthwith become ownership of the land subject to the same subordinate real rights and other encumbrances as was the estate of *dominium utile*.[57]

(d)   Kindly tenancies are abolished and replaced with ownership on

---

51a See A.G. Rennie, "Timeshare Interests in Salmon Fishings" (2000) 45 J.L.S.S. 38.

52   Craig, *Ius Feudale*, II,vii,3 and II,ix,18; Stair, II,iii,65–66; Erskine, *Inst*, II,vi,17; Bell, *Prin.*, SS.743 and 752; Ross, *Lectures*, Vol. II, pp. 167; Rankine, *Landownership*, pp. 182–248; *Orrock v. Bennet*, (1762) M. 15009; *Duke of Argyle v. Tarbert*, (1762) M. 14495.

53   Craig, *Ius Feudale*, I,xvi,9; *Commissioners of Burgh of Airdrie, Petirs* (1899) 1F. 422. Cf Highlands Services Act 1715, s.6.

54   Conveyancing (Scotland) Act 1924, s.14(1).

55   Conveyancing and Feudal Reform (Scotland) Act 1970, s.9(2) to be amended by Abolition of Feudal Tenure etc. (Scotland) Act 2000, s.76(1) and Sched. 12, para. 30(6)(a).

56   Conveyancing and Feudal Reform (Scotland) Act 1970, s.9(8)(b); Abolition of Feudal Tenure etc. (Scotland) Act 2000 ("2000 Act"), ss.50–52 (to come into force as regards ss. 50 and 51 on the "appointed day").

57   2000 Act, ss.1–2.

the appointed day as part of the legislation relative to feudal reform.[58]

(e) The *debitum fundi* in respect of the redemption sum for feu duty redeemed upon the transfer of land will cease to exist upon the appointed day in terms of the feudal reform legislation.[59]

Statutory Rights Resembling Real Rights

2.8   In addition to the statutory rights which clearly expand the list of recognised real rights, statutory provision has created a wide diversity of rights affecting land. The terminology relating to these rights varies from enactment to enactment and it is not clear whether these rights are intended to be real rights in the true sense.[59a] Many of the rights, however, seem to have been intended to be enforceable against parties in addition to the owner of the "servient" land and, at least to that extent, they resemble real rights. In modern practice many statutory rights are commonly encountered. Lack of space precludes a comprehensive survey of these provisions.[60] To illustrate the difficulty in determining whether the rights created by the statutes are real rights or some other form of right, three provisions will serve as examples:

(a) The Land Drainage (Scotland) Act 1930, s.1, permits the owner or occupier of "agricultural land"[61] to apply to a sheriff for a warrant authorising the maintenance or cleansing of a "watercourse"[62] if the owner or occupier of other land has failed to respond to a notice to take, or join in taking, the necessary steps to prevent injury. In terms of section 2 of the same Act the owner or occupier of agricultural land may apply to the sheriff for a warrant authorising the "making" of underground main drains through another person's land where the drains are necessary to prevent injury, and consent to their formation is being unreasonably withheld. After the works of cleansing or construction have been carried out it is clear that the applicant owner or his tenant and his successors may use

---

58 2000 Act, s.64.
59 2000 Act, s.13(2).
59a For statutory licences see M. Cardwell, "Milk and Livestock Quotas as Property" (2000) 4 E.L.R. 168. See also *Cay's Tr., Noter*, Peterhead Sheriff Court, Sheriff Meston, Dec. 1994.
60 For a list see Cusine and Paisley, *Servitudes and Rights of Way*, App. A.
61 Defined in 1930 Act, s.9.
62 Defined in 1930 Act, s.9.

the cleansed water course or the newly constructed drain even though there is no specific statement to this effect in the statute. The nature of the subsequent right to use the drain or watercourse is not specified in the statute but it would seem to be some form of real right. In respect of existing watercourses scoured in terms of section 1 the right may simply be a continuation of any existing right such as a servitude or right of common interest. By contrast, in terms of section 2 a wholly new drain may be laid and there may have been no prior right of any nature. In terms of section 2 the right must be a wholly new statutory creation. The owner of the ground in which such works are carried out cannot be obliged to grant a deed of servitude to convert the right, whatever it is, into a servitude.[63]

(b) The Land Drainage (Scotland) Act 1958, s.1, permits the owner or long-leaseholder[64] of "agricultural land" to apply to the Scottish Ministers for an improvement order authorising the execution of drainage works to improve the drainage of land or prevent or mitigate flooding or erosion to which the land is subject. The order may affect land other than the land of the applicant. The Scottish Ministers are given power to make the order if they are satisfied that it is appropriate to do so. The persons authorised to carry out the works are given powers of entry, inspection and survey.[65] Again, after completion of the works it is implicit that the applicant owner or tenant and their successors may use the new drainage works. The nature of the subsequent right to use the drain or watercourse is not specified in the statute but it would seem to be some form of real right. A factor which would tend to suggest this status as a real right is the power of the Scottish Ministers to certify completion of the works by certificate recorded in the Register of Sasines or Land Register of Scotland.[66] Whilst such recording would not, *per se*, create the right as a real right it would give publicity to the existence of the drains consistent with the publicity principle commonly encountered in connection with the creation of real rights.[67]

---

63 *Mackenzie v. Gillanders* (1870) 7 S.L.R. 333. See also *MacGregor v. Balfour* (1899) 2F. 345.
64 1958 Act, s.18(1).
65 1958 Act, s.11.
66 1958 Act, s.9(5).
67 Paras 3.17, 3.19, 3.22 and 3.23.

2.9 (c)   In terms of the Matrimonial Homes (Family Protection)(Scotland) Act 1981 as amended[68] an occupancy right in relation to a "matrimonial home"[69] arises where one party to a marriage owns, leases or otherwise has a right to occupy that matrimonial home and the other party to the marriage has no such right. Where husband and wife are the common proprietors of a house occupancy rights will not arise but the matter is dealt with by other special rules.[70] This situation of one spouse having title and the other having none was much more common 20 years ago when the husband typically was the breadwinner and sole earner and the wife remained as housewife without an income. At that time the title to the matrimonial home was often taken in the name of the husband only which led to the situation that the husband had the exclusive right of *dominium* in the house and the wife had a mere licence to occupy the home which was terminable at the will of the husband. This put the wife in a precarious position if domestic relations broke down. The legislation confers in certain cases occupancy rights upon the spouse without title (the "non-entitled spouse"). The Act was originally obscurely drafted but in its amended state the occupancy rights resemble real rights. The non-entitled spouse now has two rights which resemble real rights in that they can be enforced not only against the entitled spouse but also third parties. These are the rights (a) if in occupation, not to be excluded from the matrimonial home,[71] and (b) if not in occupation, to enter and occupy the matrimonial home.[72] There is some resemblance to the publicity principle[73] in the creation of the rights in that they arise automatically from the fact of marriage—the ceremony being a public fact and readily capable of ascertainment by sight of a certificate of marriage—but otherwise no process of registration is required in respect of the rights.[74] Occupancy rights are overriding interests in terms of the Land Registration (Scotland) Act 1979, s.28(1),[75] but their lack of noting on the Title Sheet does not deprive them of their enforceability as

---

68 By Law Reform (Misc. Prov.) (Scot.) Act 1985, s.13.
69 For the extensive definition see below.
70 See paras 5.6, 5.7, 5.10 and 5.11.
71 1981 Act, s.1(1)(a).
72 1981 Act, s.1(1)(b).
73 Paras 3.17, 3.19, 3.22 and 3.23.
74 See Scot. Law Comm., *Family Law*, Report No.135 (1992), paras. 11.3–11.4.
75 Definition of "overriding interest", para. (gg).

rights. The rights, however, fall short of the true nature of real rights in that they can be defeated in some cases where the property passes out of the ownership of the entitled spouse. They may be defeated where the property is transferred by sale to a *bona fide* third party purchasing the house without notice provided the entitled spouse produces either an affidavit that the property at the time of the dealing is or was not a matrimonial home in relation to which a spouse of the seller has or had occupancy rights,[76] or a renunciation of the occupancy rights or a consent to the sale which purports to have been properly granted by the non-applicant spouse.[77] In addition, the occupancy rights do not prevail in certain cases where diligence is employed. They will be defeated by an adjudging creditor of the entitled spouse or a trustee in sequestration.[78] In addition, if the right to enter the matrimonial home is not conceded by the entitled spouse it may be exercised only with leave of the court.[79] In short, the nature of the rights is anomalous and they have aptly been described as "a curious hybrid"[80] or as "quasi-real".[81] There is no entitlement on the part of an individual possessing statutory occupancy rights to require that the owner of the matrimonial home convert them into an equivalent real right by the grant of a proper liferent, although this may occur as part of an overall deal negotiated upon divorce. Still less is the non-entitled spouse entitled to a right of pre-emption in respect of the matrimonial home, they nor can demand that the entitled spouse convert their right into a right of property by conveying the house to them. This may, however, be the consequence of a property transfer order granted upon divorce.[82] The definition of the term "matrimonial home" is extensive and is as follows:[83] "any house, caravan, houseboat or other structure which has been provided or has been made available by one or

---

76 1981 Act, s.6(3)(e)(i).
77 1981 Act, s.6(3)(e)(ii).
78 Some protection is afforded by 1981 Act, s.12, and Bankruptcy (Scotland) Act 1985, s.41.
79 1981 Act, s.1(3).
80 Gordon, *Scottish Land Law* (2nd ed.), para. 14–62.
81 Gretton and Reid, *Conveyancing* (2nd. ed), para. 10.04. See *Stair Memorial Encyclopaedia*, 18, para. 10.
82 Family Law (Scotland) Act 1985, s.8(1), as amended by Law Reform (Misc. Prov.) (Scotl.) Act 1990, Sched. 8, para. 34. See Bennett, *Divorce in the Sheriff Court* (6th ed.), Chap. 7.
83 1981 Act, s.22.

both of the spouses as, or has become, a family residence and
includes any garden or other ground or building attached to,
and usually occupied with, or otherwise required for the
amenity or convenience of, the house, caravan, houseboat or
other structure but does not include a residence provided or
made available by one spouse for that spouse to reside in,
whether with any child of the family or not, separately from
the other spouse". "Caravan" is further defined as meaning "a
caravan which is mobile or affixed to the land".[84] It is clear
therefore that matrimonial homes are usually heritable but
they may in rare cases be moveable. Co-habiting unmarried
couples have considerably less extensive rights.[84a]

Primary and Subordinate Real Rights

2.10   Ownership is the primary real right. Other real rights are
generally regarded as "subordinate" rights derived from property
or as burdens on property owned by someone else.[85] They are
known as the *iura in re aliena.*[86] When a subordinate real right
comes to an end the underlying right of property will continue
unburdened. Further important differences between ownership and
the other real rights may be observed in regard to the following:

(a)   co-existence of real rights;
(b)   the derivation of real rights;
(c)   the effect of negative prescription; and
(d)   the extent of the powers of the holder.

Co-existence of Real Rights

2.11   More than one real right may exist in relation to one thing at the
one time. For example, one plot of land may be owned by A,
subject to a heritable security in favour of B, a servitude of access in
favour of C, a lease or liferent in favour of D, rights of common
interest in favour of the adjacent proprietors in respect of the
surrounding boundary structures and a public right of way. The
public right of way and a servitude of access may co-exist over the

---

84   *ibid.*
84a See J. Carruthers, "Unjustified Enrichment and the Family", 2000 S.P.L.Q. 58.
85   See the use of the terminology in Abolition of Feudal Tenure etc. (Scotland) Act
     2000, s.2(1).
86   For a similar position in South Africa see Van der Merwe and de Waal, *The Law
     of Things and Servitudes*, para. 2.

same route.[87] The same property may benefit from a servitude of access over an adjacent plot of ground. What applies to land in this regard also applies to the other separate tenements. The proprietor of a right of salmon fishings may grant subordinate real rights[88] such as a lease, standard security[89] or servitude.[90]

Although co-existence is possible it is not necessary in relation to a property right and it is in this regard that a distinction may be noted with other real rights. Only property can exist on its own—all the other real rights cannot exist on their own and must co-exist with a right of property. As they are rights affecting property belonging to another party none of the *iura in re aliena* may exist on their own. In addition, real rights such as servitude which fall within the wider class of real conditions cannot exist separately from the right of property in the dominant tenement.[91]

Although a right of property is the only real right which may exist on its own, this is encountered surprisingly rarely in practice. Most modern housing and retail developments are subject to a deed of declaration of conditions imposing a scheme of real conditions and servitudes benefiting and burdening the various parts of the development. Even where it appears to be a "stand alone" property, the purchaser may wish to acquire more than an exclusive right of property within the boundaries. A property without a servitude of access may be wholly useless and a solicitor acquiring such a property for a client may find himself sued for negligence if the client is unaware of the situation.[92]

Many real rights can co-exist in relation to the same item of property not only with different real rights but also with a real right of a similar nature. Two or more standard securities may exist in relation to the same interest in land although it is clear that the holders of such securities will wish to deal with issues of ranking and the enforcement of creditors' remedies.[93] Two or more identical

2.12

---

87 See, *e.g.*, *Smith v. Saxton*, 1927 S.N. 98; 1928 S.N. 59; *Scotland v. Wallace*, 1964 S.L.T. (Sh.Ct.) 9.
88 18 *Stair Memorial Encyclopaedia*, para. 208.
89 Conveyancing and Feudal Reform (Scotland) Act 1970 (c.35), s.9(2) and (8)(b) to be amended by Abolition of Feudal Tenure etc. (Scotland) Act 2000, s.76(1) and Sched.12, para. 30(6).
90 Cusine and Paisley, *Servitudes and Rights of Way*, para. 1.47 (salmon fishing).
91 *J.A. Mactaggart & Co. v. Harrower* (1906) 8F. 1101 at 1106 per Dean of Guild Court.
92 *Moffat v. Milne*, 1993 G.W.D. 8–572; *Watson v. Gillespie Macandrew*, 1995 G.W.D. 13–750; Cusine and Paisley, *Servitudes and Rights of Way*, para. 8–08; Gretton and Reid, *Conveyancing* (2nd. ed.), para. 1.13.
93 Cusine, *Standard Securities*, Chap. 7.

servitudes may exist in respect of the same servient tenement. For example, it is common for a single private road to be subject to a number of servitudes of access serving a multiplicity of adjacent dominant tenements. There are, however, limitations on co-existence with identical real rights as follows:

(a) Exclusive ownership may not co-exist with exclusive owner-ship.[94] In Scotland the right of ownership is an absolute right. Scots law does not admit that there may be several owners of one item of property some of whom may have better rights than others. Until recently this was obscured by the existence of the feudal system of landholding whereby several parties were regarded as co-owners in one item of land at the same time. The basic theory of this system held that all title to land was derived from the Crown which retained a title as paramount superior. Under the Crown existed mid-superiors each of whom held a right known as *dominium directum*, and lastly there was a party (known as a "vassal") who owned the property right known as the *dominium utile*.[95] Only the vassal was entitled to occupy and use the land although the right of superiority conferred several rights on the superior the most important of which in recent years was to enforce feudal real conditions. With the abolition of the feudal system in Scotland superiorities of all types will be extinguished and their rights of enforcement of feudal title conditions will disappear subject to limited preservation by various means including reallotment to a neighbouring tenement.[96]

(b) Universality of enforcement may limit co-existence with a similar right. Because a public right of way is enforceable by all members of the public it is difficult to see how more than one public right of way could exist over the same path from point A to point B at any one time. Where a public right of way for vehicles and pedestrians exists this is not usually regarded as an instance of the existence of two separate public rights of way, one for pedestrians and the other for vehicles. Only in unusual cases would such a separate analysis seem appropriate. It may

---

94 *Cf.* the special case of property rights of access and net drying etc. in relation to salmon fishing rights exercisable within the bounds of land owned by another: see *Lord Advocate v. Sharp* (1878) 6R. 108; Cusine and Paisley, *Servitudes and Rights of Way*, para. 11.32. *Cf.* also essential access to landlocked land: see *Bowers v. Kennedy*, June 28, 2000, 1st Div., unreported, but noted at 2000 G.W.D. 24–911.

95 Gordon, *Scottish Land Law*, (2nd. ed.), para. 13–03.

96 Abolition of Feudal Tenure (Scotland) Act 2000, Pt 4.

be possible for one public right of way to be created for pedestrians only by prescriptive exercise and for a second separate public right of way to exist where the proprietor of the *solum* expressly creates another public right of way by a deed perhaps for vehicles. This may be appropriate where the owner of the *solum* wishes to impose special restrictions in relation to the use by vehicles as to weight and sizes of the traffic passing.

(c) The entitlement to exclusive possession may impose practical limitations on the co-existence of certain derivative real rights. Where, for example, a proprietor grants a lease to a tenant or a liferent conferring exclusive possession on the grantee, the full and free exercise of this right would be inconsistent with the contemporaneous full and free exercise of an identical right by another party. Both tenants or liferenters simply could not occupy the subjects of the right at the same time. A similar point arises in relation to some servitudes. Where, for example, a servient proprietor confers a servitude on party A to use a drain to its full capacity, that right could not be fully exercised if another party had a similar right and simultaneously wished to exercise it. It is significant, however, that even if a "double grant" is made in these cases, one of the two competing rights is not void: rather it is left open to the grantee of the real right which has priority to seek a remedy to prevent the grant of the second real right by interdict or if it has already been granted to prevent the exercise of the second real right by interdict or to reduce the second grant. The obligation of warrandice granted by a landlord in a lease, liferent or servitude is intended to prevent such a situation arising. The granter of the relevant right personally bars himself from granting any future competing right and may be sued for damages if he grants such a right in contravention.[97] In practice some proprietors expressly derogate from this implied obligation by a number of means. First of all they may narrowly define the subjects of grant and reserve to themselves a right to deal with other subjects. This is common in practice in relation to leases where landlords make full use of restricted user clauses. For example, a landowner may grant a lease to party A permitting him only to plough the ground and a concurrent lease to B permitting him only to shoot over the ground. As has been noted above in relation to an agricultural lease the shooting and sporting

---

97 See, e.g. *Smith v. Ross* (1672) M. 16596; *Rodger (Builders) Ltd v. Fawdry*, 1950 S.C. 483. See para. 3.29.

rights are impliedly reserved to the landlord who, in turn, is free to let them out.[98] This is frequently confirmed by an express clause in the lease.[99] Where the tenanted land is a croft the reservation is acknowledged by statute.[1] The second device to permit a second grant of an identical real right in respect of the same item is frequently encountered in relation to servitudes of water supply. This is a priority of supply clause. A servient proprietor may grant A a servitude in respect of a limited supply of water and reserve to himself the right to make successive grants to C, D and E under declaration in the original grant to A that if these subsequent grants are made then B and C and D will have a priority of supply over A. In this way the granter will not be sued by A if the supply runs dry when B and C and D begin to use the water.

The Derivation of Real Rights

2.13　　It has been said that the primary status of property may be justified because all the other real rights are derived from property. As ownership or *dominium* is the "sovereign or primary real right"[2] from which all other subordinate real rights such as liferent, servitude, lease, and security derive,[3] it is clear that the holder of the right of the *dominium* may grant such subordinate real rights.

What has just been stated is subject to one qualification. If one accepts that exclusive privilege is a real right[4] it is not wholly accurate to state that all other real rights are derived from property. The true source of exclusive privilege appears to be the Sovereign right of the Crown. In the past the distinction between the Crown as feudal superior and its rights as sovereign was not clearly made in Scots law and many rights of exclusive privilege were granted in feudal form appropriate to a grant of lands. This is particularly the case where the rights were granted together with a grant of lands. Nevertheless, monopolies such as these could not be created *de novo* by a landowner unless, at least, he himself had received a grant of

---

98　*Welwood v. Husband* (1874) 1R. 507; *Wemyss v. Gullard* (1874) 10D. 204; *Copland v. Maxwell* (1871) 9M. (H.L.) 1; Gill, *The Law of Agricultural Holdings in Scotland* (3rd ed.), para. 11.01.

99　See, *e.g.*, Gill and Fox, *Agricultural Holdings Styles* 1997, W. Green, pp. 21–22, reservation 6(h).

1　Crofters (Scotland) Act 1993 (c.45), s.5 and Sched. 2 ("The Statutory Conditions"), para. 10(h); MacCuish and Flyn, *Crofting Law*, para. 4.19.

2　Erskine, *Inst*, II,i,1.

3　Gordon, *Scottish Land Law* (2nd ed.), para. 13–02.

4　Para. 2.4.

the right to do so from the Crown, frequently in the form of a Royal Charter associated with a Royal burgh or burgh of barony or regality. Once established the rights of exclusive privilege could be the subject of derivative real rights at least to the extent that they could be leased by the grantee. Such monopolies are not commonly encountered in modern practice and when they are, they are almost always of ancient origin. Another special title to which special privileges attached (including in some cases monopoly rights) was a barony title. In relation to barony titles the legislation relative to feudal reform will separate the dignity of a baron from the land itself and the former will be transmissible only as incorporeal heritable property.[5] Subject to the qualification noted, it is therefore correct to regard property as the primary real right.

The holder of a *ius in re aliena* which is itself a real right may in turn grant further subordinate real rights in certain cases. A tenant may create a standard security over the lease provided it is a long lease[6] and not otherwise excluded by the terms of the lease. A tenant may also grant sub-leases provided this is not impliedly or expressly excluded in terms of his lease.[7] A tenant may not, however, grant a servitude.[8] The dominant proprietor in a servitude may grant subordinate real rights such as standard securities[9] or lease[10] only when the same subordinate real right also affects the dominant tenement[11] but he may not render the servitude subject to another servitude.[12]

The matter may be looked at in another way by application of the maxim *nemo dat quod non habet*—no-one may grant what he himself does not possess. The phrase used in the *Digest* tends to shed a little more light on the topic—*nemo plus iuris ad alium transfere potest, quam ipse haberet.*[13] Thus a tenant may not create a

---

5   Abolition of Feudal Tenure etc. (Scotland) Act 2000, s.63 (to come into force on the "appointed day").

6   Conveyancing and Feudal Reform (Scotland) Act 1970, s.9(8); Cusine, *Standard Securities*, para. 4.03.

7   Para. 7.25.

8   Cusine and Paisley, *Servitudes*, para. 2.12. Cf. the view put forward in Gordon, *Scottish Land Law* (2nd ed.), para. 24–09–24–10 and 24–57.

9   Conveyancing and Feudal Reform (Scotland) Act 1970 Act, s.9(8); Halliday, *Conveyancing* (2nd ed.), Vol.2, para. 36–07.

10 Cusine and Paisley, *Servitudes and Rights of Way*, paras 1.55–1.61.

11 Cusine and Paisley, *Supra*, para. 1.24.

12 *Servitus servitutis esse non potest.* See *Robertson v. Duke of Atholl* (1798) 4 Pat. 54 per counsel for appellant at 60; Rankine, *Landownership*, p. 422, fn. 80; Cusine and Paisley, *Supra*, para. 13.05; Van der Merwe and de Waal, *The Law of Things and Servitudes*, para. 217(c).

13 D. 50.17.54.

new property right or transfer any existing property right. A proper liferenter may not create servitudes of an endurance greater than the liferent unless he obtains the consent of the proprietor of the land, the fiar.[14]

Derivation of Real Rights from Personal Rights

2.14   We shall see in the next chapter that the creation of many real rights involves a two-stage process. The party acquiring a real right frequently obtains a contractual right enforceable against the holder of the real right to be transferred (or against the holder of the existing real right from which a new real right is to be derived). The acquirer then converts this contractual right into a real right by some recognised public process such as possession or recording in a public register.[15] A personal right may therefore be a significant element in the creation of a real right. This situation must be distinguished from another fundamentally different situation in which the party purporting to grant a new real right or convey an existing real right is not the holder of any real right. In general the latter is not competent as real rights cannot be derived from personal rights with the result that the holder of a mere personal right in respect of a plot of land has no power to grant real rights in respect of it. This is another application of the maxim *nemo dat quod non habet*. A limited number of apparent exceptions exist as follows:

(a)   the uninfeft proprietor;
(b)   the doctrine of accretion;
(c)   power of attorney; and
(d)   consent to transfer.

2.15   As we shall see, not all of these are true exceptions.

2.16   **Uninfeft Proprietor** The instance of the uninfeft proprietor is to a limited extent a true exception to the application of the maxim *nemo dat quid non habet*. To the extent that it exists the exception has been created by statute. An uninfeft proprietor (the feudal reform legislation abandons feudal wording and prefers the neutral terminology "person with uncompleted title")[16] is one who has a right to land but no complete title. A person who is uninfeft has no

---

14   Cusine and Paisley, *Servitudes and Rights of Way*, para. 2.92.
15   Paras 3.16–3.21.
16   Abolition of Feudal Tenure (Scotland) Act 2000, s.76(1) and Sched.12, para. 15.

real right in the land[17] and, strictly speaking, is not a proprietor at all.[18] Nevertheless, the expression "uninfeft proprietor" is used to denote a person who has received a delivered disposition or other conveyance (such as a confirmation or a transfer by statutory provision) in his favour which has not been recorded in the General Register of Sasines or registered in the Land Register of Scotland. Such a person has it in his power to convert his existing right into a real right by the presentation of the conveyance for recording or registering or, if this is not possible because it is a general conveyance,[19] by the presentation of a notice of title for recording or registering.[20] The power will be extended in the feudal reform legislation to permit deduction of title from persons having no recorded or registered title.[21] This will be of considerable assistance to local authorities having right to lands originally granted to Royal burghs in terms of charters granted prior to the creation of the Sasine register.

Whilst his title remains uncompleted an uninfeft proprietor may not create new real rights in the lands in respect of which he is the uninfeft proprietor unless an exceptional case exists. Certain statutory provisions permit an uninfeft proprietor to create certain real rights where the deed of creation is recorded in the General Register of Sasines or registered in the Land Register of Scotland. Such cases are limited to instances where (a) the relevant deed contains a deduction of title clause in statutory form, or (b) where the deed relates to a registered interest if sufficient mid-couples or links between the uninfeft proprietor and the person last infeft are produced to the Keeper on registration in respect of that interest in

17 Unless, of course, the notion of "beneficial interest" as referred to in *Sharp v. Thomson*, 1997 S.L.T. 636 (HL) may be regarded as a type of real right. This is highly controversial and, in the author's view, spurious. See para. 3.23. See also *Burnett's Trs v. Grainger*, 2000 S.L.T. (Sh. Ct) 116.
18 Gordon, *Scottish Land Law* (2nd ed.), para. 13–04; 18 *Stair Memorial Encyclopaedia*, para. 645.
19 Such as a will conveying all the testator's heritable property to a named party without specifying what that property is or the act and warrant of a trustee in bankruptcy vesting the property of the bankrupt in the trustee. See Gretton and Reid, *Conveyancing* (2nd ed.), para. 24.02.
20 Conveyancing (Scotland) Act 1924 (c.27), s.4(1), Sched. B, Form 1. Refinements have been added in the case of registration in the Land Register of Scotland: see Land Registration (Scotland) Act 1979, ss.3(6) and 15(3) (to be amended by Abolition of Feudal Tenure, etc. (Scotland) Act 2000, s.76(1) and Sched. 12, para. 39(3)(c) and 39(6)(b)); 18 *Stair Memorial Encyclopaedia* para. 645, fns 9 and 10.
21 Abolition of Feudal Tenure etc. (Scotland) Act 2000, s.6.

land.[22] A specific statutory exception exists for a standard security.[23] A more general statutory provision relates to certain types of deeds rather than types of real rights.[24] The provision is primarily aimed at deeds which transfer existing real rights[25] but insofar as it relates to a "disposition of land"[26] it may be applied to the creation of new real rights such as proper liferents and servitudes.[26a] The statutory provision will probably extend to a disposition granting or reserving a proper liferent. To benefit from the provision an uninfeft proprietor wishing to create a servitude probably requires to ensure that the right is granted not in a separate deed but is either granted in a disposition of the dominant tenement or reserved in a disposition of the servient tenement.[27] Deduction of title cannot be used in the grant of a long lease.[28] Deduction of title clauses are wholly inappropriate to the creation of new real rights by means involving no recording or registration and, on principle, the uninfeft proprietor should have no title to create real rights by such methods.[29] An uninfeft proprietor may avoid any difficulty by completing title by means of the expeding of a notice of title.[30] As regards standard securities a creditor will

---

22 Land Registration (Scotland) Act 1979, s.15(3), to be amended by Abolition of Feudal Tenure etc. (Scotland) Act 2000, s.76(1) and Sched. 39(6).

23 Conveyancing and Feudal Reform (Scotland) Act 1970, s.12 and Sched.2, nn. 2 and 3; Cusine, *Standard Securities*, para. 4.13.

24 Conveyancing (Scotland) Act 1924, s.3. 18 *Stair Memorial Encyclopaedia*, para. 644, fn. 13 and para. 645.

25 The deeds listed in 1924 Act, s.3, in addition to a "disposition of land" are "an assignation, discharge or deed of restriction of a heritable security", but whilst these may transfer or extinguish a real right, they do not create new real rights. See 18 *Stair Memorial Encyclopaedia*, para. 104 and para. 449, fn. 6.

26 The term "disposition" is not defined in the 1924 Act or any of the earlier statutes referred to for definitions. The term "land" or "lands" (under the qualification that it shall not include securities: 1924 Act, s.2(1)(a)) is defined by virtue of the reference in the 1924 Act, s.2(1), in 1874 Act, s.3, to be amended by Abolition of Feudal Tenure etc. (Scotland) Act 2000, s.76(1) and Sched. 12, para. 9(2), including "all subjects of heritable property which prior to the day appointed by order made under section 69 of the Abolition of Feudal Tenure etc. (Scotland) Act 2000 were, or might be, held of a superior according to feudal tenure".

26a For servitutes granted in separate deeds see Gretton, "Servitudes and Uninfeft Proprietors", 1997 S.L.P.Q. 90–92.

27 Cusine and Paisley, *Servitudes and Rights of Way*, paras 4.08 and 6.12; Gretton and Reid, *Conveyancing* (2nd ed.), para. 24.07. For a similar position in relation to real conditions see 18 *Stair Memorial Encyclopaedia*, para. 388, fn. 10.

28 Gretton and Reid, *Conveyancing* (2nd ed.), para. 24.07.

29 See Kenneth G.C. Reid, "Jam Today: *Sharp* in the House of Lords", 1997 S.L.T. (News) 79 at 80–81.

30 1924 Act, s.4; Gretton and Reid, *Conveyancing* (2nd ed.), para. 24.02.

usually insist that the proprietor complete title first. The provision permitting deduction of title in standard securities is rarely, if ever, used and has been described as "virtually a dead letter".[31]

Accretion If a party wishes to transfer a right of property or other subordinate real right to a second party or to create a real right to that second party he will usually insure that he has title to do so. Nevertheless, even if the first party has no title all is not lost and has no right or title at the date of the grant, the defect may be remedied by the operation of the doctrine of accretion.[32] This occurs when the first party subsequently requires title. No new conveyance to the second party is necessary.[33] Two bases of the doctrine are possible. If the granter includes in the original conveyance a grant of absolute warrandice[34] or a conveyance of his whole right and title in and to the property conveyed[35] the law in either case regards him as falling under an obligation to grant a second conveyance to fortify the title. Accretion simply elides this necessity of further conveyancing. At the time of the original *a non domino* grant the granter may have had no title at all or a mere personal right to the land or real right in question. This, however, does not amount to an example of a real right derived from a personal right. What occurs is that accretion works by means of legal fiction. The granter is deemed to have owned the property and to have had a real right therein at the time of the original grant.[36]

2.17

Representation There is no requirement in Scots law that a party wishing to transfer a right of property, transfer an existing subsidiary real right or create a new subsidiary real right must do so in person. Juristic acts may be carried out on behalf of others in certain cases. This is known as representation. Various instances are recognised by Scots law, such as representation by guardian in cases where a child is under 16. Judicial factors may represent parties who are unable to manage their affairs. Probably the most common instance of representation is where a principal appoints an agent to act. A suitably authorised agent may grant dispositions, grant assignations, standard securities, deeds of servitude and other

2.17

---

31 Gretton and Reid, *Conveyancing* (2nd ed.), paras 20.08 and 24.07.
32 18 *Stair Memorial Encyclopaedia*, para. 677. See this text at para. 7.03.
33 Stair, *Inst*, III,ii,1 and 2; Erskine, *Inst.*, II,vii,3; Bankton, III,ii,16–18; Bell, *Prin*, ss.881–882.
34 Stair, III,ii,2; Erskine, II,vii,3.
35 *ibid.*
36 18 *Stair Memorial Encyclopaedia*, para. 677.

appropriate deeds. This has been recognised in statute in relation to incorporated companies.[37] The right of the agent under the power of attorney is a personal right and he has no real right in the property to which a deed executed by him relates. That said, deeds granted by him within his authority clearly may create new subsidiary real rights. This is not an instance of a real right being derived from a personal right: rather the acts of the agent are attributed to his principal and the newly created subsidiary real right is derived from the real right possessed by the principal. A crucial issue in such circumstances is the extent of the authority of the agent.[38]

2.19 **Consent to Transfer** In some cases a party with a contractual right to obtain a grant of a disposition of an existing property right or an assignation of an existing subsidiary real right or the grant of a new subsidiary real right does not wish to obtain the grant in his own favour. Instead the party may wish the right to be granted in favour of a third party. A clause in the existing contract may expressly provide for this by requiring the proprietor of land to grant a disposition in favour of the nominee of the purchaser. The party to the contract frequently indicates his consent to the disposition in favour of the nominee by executing the disposition as "consenter".[39] This has the effect of confirming that the consenter acknowledges that the disposition may be regarded as implementing his wishes and as personally barring the consenter from objecting to the grant in favour of the nominee. The title of the nominee is not derived from the personal rights of the consenter under the contract: rather it is derived directly from the granter's existing real right.

The Extent of the Powers of the Holder

2.19   Property confers upon the holder the most extensive of rights in respect of the thing which is the subject of the right. The traditional

---

37 Requirements of Writing (Scotland) Act 1995, s.7(7) and Sched. 2, para. 3(1).

38 *Danish Dairy Co. v. Gillespie* 1922 S.C. 656 (no ostensible authority of solicitor in relation to a lease). See also *Cowan v. Stewart* (1872) 10M. 735; *Brodt v. King*, 1991 S.L.T. 272; *MacGregor v. Balfour* (1899) 2F. 345; *Robson v. Chalmers Property Investment Co. Ltd*, 1965 S.L.T. 381; Cusine and Paisley, *Servitudes and Rights of Way*, paras 4.30–4.31.

39 McDonald, *Conveyancing Manual*, (6th ed.), paras 7.4 and 12.16. In many other cases the consenter is the holder of a subordinate real right or statutory right which would otherwise preclude the transferee or grantee enjoying his right to the full.

definition of ownership in Civilian systems has been the right of use, enjoyment and abuse (*ius utendi, ius fruendi, ius abutendi*).[40] This states the matter in the abstract. As we shall see below restraints on the full and free exercise of a right of property arise from various sources and it is rare for the proprietor to be able to exercise these rights to the full. Leaving aside such restrictions and considering the matter in the abstract assists in demonstrating the more extensive nature of a proprietor's rights when compared to the holder of some of the other real rights.

(a) The holder of a proper liferent does have a right of use and enjoyment of the liferented subjects but must exercise his right *salva rerum substantia*, without encroaching on the substance.[41] The point is made by Paul in the *Digest: usufructus est ius alienis rebus utendi fruendi salva rerum substantia.*[41a] An exception is made in relation to minerals in that it has been recognised that a liferenter is entitled to dig out minerals by opening quarries and pits for domestic consumption and for the purposes of a landed estate, at least where these were in existence at the start of the liferent.[42]

(b) The holder of a servitude is entitled to carry out only such activities as are permitted by the particular servitude. For example, a servitude of access will entitle the dominant proprietor to a right of passage and nothing else. He will not be entitled to lay service media in *solum* of the road over which the servitude of access may be exercised except possibly where the service media are ancillary to the right of passage such as would be the case with drains to keep surface water off the road itself. If the dominant proprietor wishes to lay service media to facilitate a development on the dominant tenement he will require to obtain a servitude of *aqueduct* and variants thereof. Certain activities are wholly beyond the powers of the holder of a servitude of any sort because they are inconsistent with the underlying right of property. The right to erect buildings on a property is clearly an incident of the right of *dominium* relating to that property but a right to erect buildings on ground disponed has been rejected as a servitude

---

40 18 *Stair Memorial Encyclopaedia*, para. 5.
41 Gordon, *Scottish Land Law* (2nd ed.), paras 17–01 and 17–36.
41a *Digest* 7,1,1.
42 See, *e.g, Dick's Trs v. Baillie* (1891) 19R. 220. See para. 6.8.

and a real burden.[43] Lesser structures to be used for a particular purpose may, however, be acceptable. In relation to the servitudes of dam or drain and septic tank has the dominant proprietor has a right to construct the relevant structure comprising the dam or septic tank on the servient tenement.

(c) A tenant in a lease is entitled to use and enjoy land within the terms of the user and other clauses in the lease. It is rare for a tenant to have the right to destroy the leased subjects. One example where this may be permitted is where a building is leased and the tenant is given express power to demolish the building for the purposes of constructing a new development— possibly on an entirely different scale from the existing building. Destruction of the leased subjects is also inherent in the proper exercise of the tenant's right in a minerals lease where part of the heritable subjects is broken up and converted into moveable aggregates.

Duration of the Right

2.21 That property is the most extensive real right is true not only in respect of what the holder of the right is entitled to do but also as regards the period of endurance of the right. Property is a real right with perpetual endurance.[44] By contrast, most subordinate real rights (apart from most servitudes[45]) have a limited endurance. Liferents usually terminate upon the death of the liferenter but the right may be created for a fixed or uncertain period which may be less than the holder's lifetime.[46] Leases granted on or after June 7, 2000 have a maximum fixed term of 175 years.[47]

The Effect of Negative Prescription[47a]

2.21 Most real rights prescribe after 20 years if they have subsisted for a continuous period of 20 years unexercised or unenforced and

---

43 *Scottish Temperance Life Assurance Co. v. Law Union and Rock Insurance Co.*, 1917 S.C. 175 per Lord Dundas at 183.
44 Subject of course to reversions and pre-emptions, but these effect a transfer of a property right, not its extinction. Extinction of property is rare, and true examples are positive prescription, statute, destruction of the thing, separation from the land and loss of territory respectively discussed in paras 3.13, 3.36, 3.41, 3.43 and 3.44.
45 Cusine and Paisley, *Servitudes and Rights of Way*, paras 2.89–2.98.
46 Gordon, *Scottish Land Law* (2nd ed.), para. 17–26.
47 Abolition of Feudal Tenure (Scotland) Act, s.67.
47a See generally Johnston, *Prescription and Limitation* (1999, W. Green), Pt I.

without any relevant claim having been made in relation to them.[48]
Two rights are specifically declared by statute to be imprescriptible.
These are the ownership of land[49] (it has been suggested that this
may also include a right of proper liferent[50]) and a right of a tenant
in a lease which has been registered in the Register of Sasines or the
Land Register of Scotland.[51] A right of access to land which would
otherwise be landlocked may be a right of property and not a
servitude and therefore will not prescribe negatively.[52] Although
there is no express exception for this in the relevant legislation, it
has been said that negative prescription does not apply to
extinguish a public right of navigation.[53] The legislation also
exempts from negative prescription an ill-defined class of rights
which are known as *res merae facultatis*.[54] It has been held that the
right to make a road on another party's property falls within this
class, but the case is controversial.[55] It seems at least arguable that
this right is a servitude or a real condition which would negatively
prescribe. Much may depend on the manner in which the clause is
framed. Rights which are more appropriate to the classification as
res merae facultatis appear to be rights which are inherent in, and
exercisable within the geographical extent of, other real rights. For
example, the right to enjoy or use land is inherent in the right of
property. An owner of a field will not lose the right to build on it
merely because he or his predecessor in title has not built on it for
20 years.

Terminology

Not all rights which have the adjective "real" attached to them 2.23
are real rights in the strict sense of that term. Scots law recognises a
class of obligations relating to the use of heritable property which

---

48 Prescription and Limitation (Scotland) Act 1973, s.8.
49 1973 Act, s.8(2) and Sched.3, para. (a).
50 Gordon, *supra*, para. 17–70.
51 1973 Act, s.8(2) and Sched.3, para (b).
52 *Bowers v. Kennedy*, 1st Div., 28 June 2000 (unreported but briefly noted at 2000
     G.W.D. 24–911). See also *Lord Advocate v. Sharp* (1878) 6R. 108; Cusine and
     Paisley, *Servitudes and Rights of Way*, para. 11.32.
53 *Will's Trs v. Cairngorm Canoeing and Sailing School Ltd*, 1976 S.C. (H.L.) 30 per
     Lord Wilberforce at 126.
54 1973 Act, s.8(2) and Sched. 3, para. (d).
55 *Smith v. Stewart* (1884) 11R. 921; Cusine and Paisley, *Servitudes and Rights of
     Way*, para. 14.18.

are known as "real conditions" or "real burdens".[56] Those terms
are largely interchangeable but confusion arises because they can
have several meanings. At their broadest the terms denote a family
of various assorted rights including servitudes, rights of common
interest and real conditions enforceable by neighbours. A narrower
meaning comprises only real conditions enforceable by neighbours
against neighbours.[57]

Even if one's attention is confined to the narrower meaning of
"real condition" it is possible to make further distinctions which
assist in identifying which of these rights are real rights in the strict
sense of the term. At common law real conditions may be
categorised into three groups as follows according to their
content[58].

(a) Obligations requiring the servient proprietor to do something.
     An example is the obligation to build a house or a pig sty on
     the servient tenement within a period of time. The obligation is
     not a real right in the strict sense of the term as it may be
     enforced not against the rest of the world but only against the
     proprietor for the time being of the dominant tenement. Future
     statutory reform may of course alter this position and such
     alteration could prove useful where the property is occupied on
     a long lease and the landlord/proprietor is unknown or
     difficult to identify.

(b) Obligations requiring the servient proprietor to refrain from
     doing something. An example is an obligation not to alter
     existing buildings on the servient tenement. The nature of the
     obligation at common law is a little less clear. Insofar as the
     substance of the obligation coincides with any of the existing
     recognised negative servitudes it will be enforceable as a real
     right not only against the servient proprietor but against any
     person infringing the right. This will remain the case even if the
     obligation resembles a recognised negative servitude subject to
     limited qualifications.[59] In other cases there is some authority
     suggesting that a real condition imposing a negative obligation
     may be enforced against the servient proprietor and tenants

---

56 The Scottish Law Commission has invited views as to whether the term "real
    burden" should be changed to some other name and, if so, what that other name
    should be: Scot. Law Commission, *Discussion Paper on Real Burdens* (Oct. 1998,
    no. 106), para. 9.16, proposal 63.
57 See Chap. 9.
58 18 *Stair Memorial Encyclopaedia*, para. 391.
59 *Braid Hills Hotel v. Manuels*, 1909 S.C. 120; Cusine and Paisley, *Servitudes and
    Rights of Way*, para. 14.12.

occupying the servient land[60] but there is no suggestion that it is enforceable directly against others at common law.

(c) Obligations requiring the servient proprietor to permit the dominant proprietor to carry out some sort of activity within the servient tenement. An example is the right of the dominant proprietor to park a car on a certain part of the servient tenement or to place (and thereafter use) a private electricity cable in a neighbour's property. There is again obscurity as to the nature of these obligations at common law. There may be a strong ground on the basis of convenience to regard them as real rights in the strict sense and enforceable against the whole world. Statutory reform of this matter is imminent and is likely to stifle development of the common law on this matter. That aside, had common law development continued it might have been possible that the courts would deal with the issue by declaring that such rights could be recognised servitudes and therefore always were real rights in the strict sense.[61] In any event the law may be reformed by statutory provision. After such reform the obligations falling into this third division of real conditions are likely to be regarded as servitudes proper.

The enforceability of obligations falling into any of these classes 2.24 may be altered by statute. Put another way, statute may convert a burden which, at common law, is enforceable only *in personam* against servient proprietors, into a right enforceable *in personam* against an expanded class of persons or even into a right enforceable *in rem*. An example of the former has occurred in relation to standard securities. A creditor under a standard security who is in lawful possession of the security subjects is liable for all the obligations of the proprietor which relate to their management and maintenance.[62] As mentioned above, statutory reform may enable real conditions to be enforced against a wider class of persons including the proprietor of the servient tenement and his tenant. This would constitute an expansion of the class of persons against whom the right is enforceable *in personam*: it would not be a transformation of the rights into real rights in the strict sense.

---

60 See, *e.g.*, *Colquhoun's Curator Bonis v. Glen's Tr.*, 1920 S.C. 737; 18 *Stair Memorial Encyclopaedia*, para. 413.
61 Cusine and Paisley, *Servitudes and Rights of Way*, para. 1.06; Paisley, "*Development Sites, Interdicts and the Risks of Adverse Title Conditions*", 1997 S.L.P.Q. 249–273 at 251–256 and 262–263.
62 Conveyancing and Feudal Reform (Scotland) Act 1970, s.20(5)(b). Cf. *David Watson Property Management v. Woolwich Equitable Building Society*, 1992 S.L.T. 430, HL.

Classification of Real Rights

2.25   Real rights in land may be classified with regard to certain characteristics in various ways as follows:

(a)   common law rights and statutory rights;
(b)   differences in the identity of the holders and granters of the rights;
(c)   classifications for limited purposes may be made in various statutes; and
(d)   differences in the manner of creation of real rights. This will be explored in the next chapter.

Common Law Rights and Statutory Rights

2.25   Real rights may be classified by reason of whether they arise from statute or common law.

(a)   Real rights recognised at common law include property, proper liferent, the classic types of servitude and public rights of way.
(b)   Real rights recognised by statute include lease, standard security, attached floating charge, and the proposed expansion of the class of recognised servitudes to include the carrying out of positive activity on the servient tenement.

The Holder of the Right

2.26   The real rights in land may be classified according to the party entitled to the right as follows:

(a)   Rights held without restriction. These include property, standard security and proper liferent.
(b)   Rights held by persons in their capacity as the owner of another piece of land. At common law these include servitudes and probably also real conditions in so far as they are rights *in rem*. A few peculiar property rights also fall into this category. The rights ancillary to a right of salmon fishing such as the right of access over adjacent land, the slaying of fish and the drying of nets on adjacent land including banks of rivers may be a peculiar form of property right which may not be separated from the salmon fishing right.[63] Kindly tenants are to be abolished under the legislation relative to feudal reform and converted into a form of ownership. Prior to their

---

63   *Lo. Ad. v. Sharp* (1878) 6R. 108; Cusine and Paisley, *Servitudes and Rights of Way*, para. 11.32.

abolition certain rights of salmon fishing effeired to some or all of the tenancies. After abolition of kindly tenancies these rights of salmon fishing are to be inseverable from ownership of the land in question.[64] A right of commonty, a rare form of co-ownership, may be owned only as an inseverable pertinent of adjoining land.[65]

(c) Rights held by the public at large. These include public rights of way and certain public rights in respect of the foreshore and seabed and public rights of navigation.[66] The general public may comprise natural persons (including incomers such as Ulster Scots who come to live in Scotland) and juristic bodies. It has been judicially observed that a incorporated company has no title to enforce a public right of way but it is suggested that observation is wrong unless the power to raise such an action is excluded in the company's memorandum and articles of association.[67] In many cases the right of limited companies to enforce public rights of way has been judicially recognised.[68] It is the duty of local authorities to "assert" public rights of way.[69] The meaning of the term "assert" is obscure[70] but it clearly includes the raising of proceedings to seek declarator of the public right of way.[71] There have been some complaints that local authorities have not been sufficiently enthusiastic in relation to the implementation of their duties in this regard but very few of these complaints have ever been upheld by the Commissioner for Local Administration.[72] Local authorities generally have more pressing demands on their time and finances than to raise a multiplicity of legal actions in relation to public rights of way.

(d) Rights held by a limited class of members of the public or a limited class of juristic bodies. At common law these include

---

64 Abolition of Feudal Tenure etc. (Scotland) Act 2000, s.64. See *Royal Four Towns Fishing Association v. Assessor for Derbyshire*, 1956 S.C. 379 for the earlier position.
65 18 *Stair Memorial Encyclopaedia*, para. 37.
66 See Chap. 10.
67 *North British Ry Co. v. Park Yard Co.* (1898) 25R. 1148 per Lord (Ordinary) Low at 1153. See Cusine and Paisley, *Servitudes and Rights of Way*, para. 23.03.
68 See, e.g. *Scottish Rights of Way and Recreation Society Ltd. v. MacPherson* (1888) 15R. (H.L.) 68.
69 Countryside (Scotland) Act 1967, s.46, as amended by Countryside (Scotland) Act 1981, s.7.
70 Cusine and Paisley, *Servitudes and Rights of Way*, para. 19–04.
71 *Alston v. Ross* (1895) 23R. 273; *Renfrew District Council v. Russell*, 1994 G.W.D. 34–2032.
72 J. Rowan-Robinson, *Review of Rights of Way Procedure*, paras 4.2.4.–4.2.5.

rights to graves enforceable by the relatives of the interred[73] and community rights arising from the rights of Royal burghs which are enforceable not by the general public as a whole but by an ill-defined group of burghers—now virtually impossible to define given the reorganisation of local government.[74] Certain statutory rights are conferred on a limited class of persons. For example, occupancy rights in respect of matrimonial homes are limited to "non-entitled" spouses.[75] This clearly excludes juristic bodies from entitlement to such rights as they cannot marry. The power to acquire statutory wayleaves in relation to the provision of services such as electricity[76] and gas[77] is limited to the relevant statutory undertaker. The entitlement to the creditor's interest in a charging order is limited to the body named in the relevant statute—typically a local authority.[78] Conservation burdens may be enforced only by conservation bodies.[79]

(e) Rights capable of being held only by the Crown. Prior to the abolition of the feudal system such rights included the paramount superiority which was regarded as inalienable.[80] As that superiority is to be abolished in terms of feudal reform and the Crown will soon have the capacity to convey land by disposition,[81] these rights are now restricted to the Crown's title to hold certain public rights in trust for the general public[82] such as public rights of recreation in the foreshore and navigation on the territorial sea, and also, possibly, public rights of way.[83] Maritime burdens may be enforced only by the Crown.[84]

---

73 See Chap. 10.
74 *ibid.*
75 Para. 2.9.
76 Electricity Act 1989, Pt 1 and Sched. 4, para. 6; 9 *Stair Memorial Encyclopaedia*, paras 643–658; Gretton and Reid, *Conveyancing*, (2nd ed.), para. 4.16.
77 Gas Act 1986, s.9(3)(a), as amended by Gas Act 1995, s.10(1) and Sched. 3, para. 3, and Sched. 3, para. 1(1) as amended by Gas Act 1995, s. 10(1) and Sched. 3, para. 56; 9 *Stair Memorial Encyclopaedia*, paras 874–879; Gretton and Reid, *Conveyancing*, (2nd ed.), para. 4.16.
78 See *Chap.* 11.
79 See para. 9.8.
80 Craig, *Ius Feudale*, I,xvi,7; Erskine, *Inst.*, II,vi,13; Duff, *Deeds*, p. 65, para. 49(1); 18 *Stair Memorial Encyclopaedia*, para. 42, fn. 4.
81 Abolition of Feudal Tenure (S). Act 2000, s.59.
82 See Chap. 10.
83 *ibid.*
84 See para. 9.8.

It should be remembered that there may be some matter personal to a particular party which restricts the extent of the rights which may be held by such a party. For example, in relation to leases, some statutes confer a particular set of additional rights on particular types of tenants and not others. It is a requirement for an assured tenancy that the tenant be an individual and leases to companies are outwith the coverage of assured tenancy protection.[85] Landlords wishing to rent out for periods of less than six months without providing security of tenure to their tenants still utilise these devices.[86]

The Holder of the Right and Alienation

The identification of those parties who may be the holder of a particular real right is another way of ascertaining the transmissibility of that real right. Rights of property and rights in security are generally freely alienable. A proper liferent cannot be assigned the effect of substituting another party as liferenter.[87] However, a liferenter may assign his liferent to the limited extent of allowing the assignee the enjoyment of the liferented property—this usually constitutes an assignation of the right to the income of the liferented property—during the original liferenter's lifetime.[88] The alienation of a servitude is partly restricted in that it may be alienated only together with the dominant tenement to which it is attached.[89] As public rights of way and public rights of navigation are already enforceable by all members of the public the issue of their transmissibility does not arise.

The distinction between the real rights which may be held without restriction and those which may be held by a limited class of persons is sometimes obscured by virtue of conventional provision restricting the class of persons to whom other real rights may be alienated or which limits such class to the persons who own another item of heritable property. For example, in the case of leases assignation of the tenant's interest may be expressly

2.28

---

85 Housing (Scotland) Act 1988, s.12(1)(a); *Hilton v. Plustitle* [1988] 3 All E.R. 1051.

86 Robson and Halliday, *Residential Tenancies* (2nd ed.), paras 2–57 and 5–10.

87 Stair, II,vi,7; Erskine, II,ix,41; *Ker's Trs v. Justice* (1868) 6M. 627.

88 Ersk., II,ix,41; *Scottish Union and National Insurance Co. v. Smeaton* (1904) 7F. 174.

89 *J.A. Mactaggart & Co. v. Harrower* (1906) 8F. 1101 at 1106 per Dean of Guild Court; Van der Merwe and de Waal, *The Law of Things and Servitudes*, para. 12; 18 *Stair Memorial Encyclopaedia*, para. 652.

prohibited[90] or limited to a class of potential tenants (such as companies which are members of the same group of companies). The assignation of a tenant's interest in a lease may also be limited by conventional stipulation referring to the ownership of an adjacent plot of ground. For example, many leases of small items such as lock-up garages for cars may expressly permit free assignation to the successive owners of a particular house but otherwise prohibit assignation altogether.[91]

The Granter of the Right

2.29   Real rights may be classified according to the granter of the right. In most cases all that is relevant is that the real right sought to be created may competently be derived from the real right held by the party seeking to grant it. Otherwise stated, a real right may be created by any holder of another sufficiently extensive real right. For example, the general rule is that any proprietor of land may grant a lease. A few real rights, however, are more restricted in the identity of the party who may grant them. Floating charges may be granted only by incorporated companies[92] and a limited number of other juristic bodies such as an industrial and provident society[93] and a European Economic Interest Grouping.[94] It follows that floating charges exist invariably in relation to the land held by such bodies although there remains a theoretical possibility that the land may be transferred to another party after the charge has attached and remain subject to the charge.[95] Leases attracting the protection of the crofting legislation may be granted only by landlords in respect of lands within the crofting counties or by the Crofters' Commission in default of such a grant where it is required by

---

90   18 *Stair Memorial Encyclopaedia*, para. 652. See para. 7.24.
91   Para 7.24.
92   Companies Act 1985, s.462(1).
93   Industrial and Provident Societies Act 1967, s.3, as substituted by the Companies Consolidation (Consequential Provisions) Act 1985, s.26.
94   Gordon, *Scottish Land Law* (2nd ed.), para. 20–205.
95   The concatenation of events required to allow this to happen would be bizarre. First the company would require to grant two floating charges with a receiver being appointed under one and not the other and the company would also require to be in liquidation. This liquidation would mean that the charge without the receiver would have attached (Companies Act 1985, s.463(1) prospectively amended by Companies Act 1989, s.140). The receiver under the other charge would require to sell the heritable property without the consent of the other charge holder and without the sanction of the court. (Insolvency Act 1986, s.61(1), leaving the other charge undischarged and attaching to the property (4 *Stair Memorial Encyclopaedia*, para. 710).

statute by the Crofters' Commission.[96] The crofting counties do not extend to the whole of Scotland but include only Argyll, Caithness, Inverness, Orkney, Ross and Cromarty, Sutherland and Shetland.[97]

Statutory Classification of Real Rights

Real rights may be classified in a statute in any manner that the 2.30 legislature deems fit. The definitions sometimes have specific meanings attributed to them whilst others are lacking in this regard leaving the application of a particular statutory provision unclear. Even where the same terminology is used in two statutes, the accepted canons of statutory construction make it unsafe to assume that the meaning appropriate to one Act may be applied to the other.

Land Registration

One of the most important statutory frameworks for the 2.30 classification of real rights is contained in the Land Registration (Scotland) Act 1979. At first reading the two key terms defined in that Act appear to be, respectively, "interest in land" and "overriding interest". The term "interest in land" is defined[98] as meaning "any estate, interest, servitude or other heritable right in or over land,[99] including a heritable security[1] but excluding a lease which is not a long lease".[2] The term "overriding interest" is a term defined by statute[3] as the right or interest over any "interest in land" of any of the following:[4]

(a) the lessee under a lease which is not a long lease;[5]

---

96 Crofters (Scotland) Act 1993, s.23(5). See para. 7.06.
97 Crofters (Scotland) Act 1993, s.3(1).
98 1979 Act, s.28(1). In terms of Abolition of Feudal Tenure etc. (Scotland) Act 2000, s.76(1) and Sched. 12, para. 39(11), the definition will be altered on the appointed day to read as follows: "(a) any right in or over land, including any heritable security or servitude but excluding any lease which is not a long lease; and (b) where the context so admits, includes the land".
99 1979 Act, s.28(1) further defines "land" as including "buildings and other structures and land covered with water".
1   1979 Act, s.28(1) assigns to the term "heritable security" the same meaning as is contained in Conveyancing and Feudal Reform (Scotland) Act 1970, s.9(8).
2   The term "long lease" is defined in 1979 Act, s.28(1).
3   Land Registration (Scotland) Act 1979, ss.3(1) and 28 as amended. The definition is subject to 1979 Act, ss.6(4) and 9(4).
4   Keeping the lettering of 1979 Act, s.28(1).
5   The term "long lease" is further defined as a lease exceeding 20 years with an additional provision relating to leases with obligations to renew beyond 20 years.

(b)   the lessee under a long lease who, prior to the commencement of the 1979 Act, has acquired a real right to the subjects of lease by virtue of possession of them;

(c)   a crofter or cottar within the meaning of section 3 or 28(4) respectively of the Crofters (Scotland) Act 1955,[6] or a landholder or statutory small tenant within the meaning of section 2(2) or 32(1) respectively of the Small Landholders (Scotland) Act 1911;

(d)   the proprietor of the dominant tenement in a servitude;

(e)   the Crown or any government or other public department, or any public or local authority, under any enactment or rule of law, other than an enactment or rule of law authorising or requiring the recording of a deed in the Register of Sasines or registration[7] in order to complete the right or interest;

(ee) the operator having a right conferred in accordance with paragraph 2, 3 or 5 of Schedule 2 to the Telecommunications Act 1984 (agreements for execution of works, obstruction of access, etc.);

(ef) a licence holder within the meaning of Part 1 of the Electricity Act 1989 having such a wayleave as is mentioned in paragraph 6 of Schedule 4 to that Act (wayleaves for electric lines), whether granted under that paragraph or by agreement between the parties;

(eg) a licence within the meaning of Part 1 of the Electricity Act 1989 who is authorised by virtue of paragraph 1 of Schedule 5 to that Act to abstract, divert and use water for a generating station wholly or mainly driven by water;

(eh) insofar as it is an interest vesting by virtue of section 7(3) of the Coal Industry Act 1994, the Coal Authority;

(f)   the holder of a floating charge whether or not the charge has attached to the interest;

(g)   a member of the public in respect of any public right of way or in respect of any right held inalienably by the Crown in trust for the public;

(gg) the non-entitled spouse within the meaning of section 6 of the Matrimonial Homes (Family Protection) (Scotland) Act 1981;

(h)   any person, being a right which has been made real, otherwise than by the recording of a deed in the Register of Sasines or by registration; or

---

6   This Act has been repealed and substantially re-enacted in the Crofters (Scotland) Act 1993.

7   This denotes registration in the Land Register of Scotland: see 1979 Act, s.28(1), definition of "the register", and 1979 Act, s.1(1) and (3).

(i) any other person under any rule of law relating to common interest or joint or common property, not being an interest constituting a real right, burden or condition entered in the title sheet of the interest in land under section 6(1)(e) of the 1979 Act or having effect by virtue of a deed recorded in the Register of Sasines.

For the purposes of the 1979 Act it is declared that "overriding interest" does not include any subsisting burden or condition enforceable against the interest in land and "entered" in its title under section 6(1) of the 1979 Act.

Scheme of 1979 Act

Whilst the term "interest in land" refers only to real rights, not all 2.32 of the rights defined as "overriding interests" are real rights. Nevertheless, a closer examination of the statute discloses that the class of rights comprised in the terms "interest in land" and "overriding interest" are not mutually exclusive. Furthermore, the two definitions, by themselves, do not provide the key to the scheme of the 1979 Act. The reason for this is that the 1979 Act does not adopt a conceptual approach.[8] A clear analysis of the 1979 Act requires a stepping back from the statutory definitions and the imposing of a wholly different framework on the rights effected by the 1979 Act. This framework requires the division of all real rights into three types as follows:[9]

(a) those in respect of which a separate title sheet may be issued ("Primary Interests"[10]);
(b) those which are, or may be,[11] registered or noted on the title sheet of another real right—the Primary Interest to which they relate.[12] ("Secondary Interests"); and
(c) those in respect of which a separate title sheet cannot be issued and which may not be registered or noted on the title sheet of another real right ("Tertiary Interests").

Examples of Primary Interests are the right of *dominium* in relation 2.32 to land or a right of salmon fishings and the right of a tenant in a

---

8 Gretton and Reid, *Conveyancing* (2nd ed.), para. 8.03, fn. 9.
9 This terminology is not used in the 1979 Act and acknowledgement is properly due to Gretton and Reid, *supra*, para. 8.03, where a division is made into two types.
10 1979 Act, s.5(1)(a) and the definition of "interest in land" in s.28(1).
11 See the noting of "overriding interests" in 1979 Act, s.4(a) and (b).
12 1979 Act, s.5(1)(b) and the definition of "interest in land" in s.28(1).

long lease in relation to land or salmon fishings. There is a statutory definition of "long lease" which confines the meaning of that term to (a) a "probative lease"[13] exceeding 20 years, or (b) a "probative lease" which is subject to any provision whereby any person holding the interest of the granter is under a future obligation, if so requested by the grantee, to renew the lease so that the total duration could (in terms of the lease, as renewed, and without any subsequent agreement, express or implied, between the persons holding the interests of the granter and the grantee) extend for more than 20 years.[14]

Examples of Secondary Interests are standard securities, liferents, real burdens, servitudes and incorporeal heritable rights (other than the right to salmon fishings)[15] but excluding Tertiary Interests.

Tertiary Interests are confined to the rights of a lessee under a long lease which is not a long lease and a non-entitled spouse within the meaning of the Matrimonial Homes (Family Protection)(Scotland) Act 1981, s.6.[16] The Keeper will, however, add a note that there is no subsisting occupancy rights of spouses of former owners if he is satisfied that this is the case.[17] Such a note neither creates new occupancy rights nor extinguishes such rights if they do exist but is generally taken as imposing liability on the Keeper under his statutory indemnity if it is inaccurate.[18]

The importance of the categorisation—which is not express in the 1979 Act—is to enable the functioning of the scheme of creation of title by registration with the accompanying benefits of the Keeper's indemnity. Details of this scheme should be sought in a textbook on conveyancing.[19] For present purposes, however, it should be noted that none of the foregoing three categories precludes the creation of certain real rights as "overriding interests" without registration in the Land Register. For example, a servitude may be created by

---

13 In terms of the Requirements of Writing (Scotland) Act 1995, s.14(1) and Sched. 1(1) in relation to a document executed after 1 August 1995 this denotes a reference to a document in relation to which 1995 Act, s.6(2) applies.

14 1979 Act, s.28(1), definition of "long lease".

15 See definition of "incorporeal heritable right" in 1979 Act, s.28(1) to be amended by Abolition of Feudal Tenure etc. (Scotland) Act 2000, s.76(1) and Sched 12, para 39(11).

16 1979 Act, ss. 6(4) and 9(4).

17 Land Registration (Scotland) Rules (SI 1980: 1413), rule 5(j); Gretton and Reid, *Conveyancing*, (2nd. Ed.), para 10.23.

18 Notwithstanding the terms of 1979 Act, s.2(3)(h). Land Registration (Scotland) Rules (SI 1980: 1413), rule 7; Registration of Title Practice Book, (2nd. Ed.), (2000), para 2.13.

19 See, e.g. Gretton and Reid, *Conveyancing*, (2nd. Ed.), (1999); Registration of Title Practice Book, (2nd. Ed.), (2000).

exercise for the prescriptive period of twenty years.[20] The various methods of original acquisition of title are examined in the next chapter.

Possession[21]

For centuries there has been a debate as to whether possession is 2.34 a real right or a mere fact. This debate is more academic than practical and the treatment here shall concentrate on certain important consequences of possession. The mere fact of possession of heritable property confers upon the possessor a right not to be deprived of possession except by voluntary surrender or court order. Although the right to possess heritable subjects, is inherent in many other real rights such as property or proper liferent the right not to be dispossessed may arise independently from the existence of these other real rights. It may therefore be available to any member of the public possessing no other real right who is simply in possession of heritable subjects, such as a squatter. Unlawfulness of possession is, however, relevant in a question with the person rightfully entitled to possession and a squatter may be dispossessed by him. The rightful possessor is entitled not only to recover his property but to an accounting of the income in the period during which property was unlawfully withheld. Where the possession by the unlawful possessor was in good faith that good faith will entitle him to resist a claim to pay to the lawful possessor any of the actual income produced as the law takes the view that it will not protect the interests of a party which he has jeopardised by tardiness. Where the possession was in bad faith the unlawful possessor is liable for "violent profits" which are generally calculated as double the rent which the property would produce on the open market.[22]

In relation to heritable property possession is relevant in respect of the acquisition of a number of rights as follows:

(a) the creation of real rights by means of a public act following upon a contractual stage[23];

(b) the creation of real rights by means of exercise for the period of positive prescription[24];

---

20 Prescription and Limitation (Scotland) Act, 1973, s.3(1)(a).
21 This is a complex area of law and only a very brief note of certain aspects will be given here. For an outstanding treatment of the issue generally see 18 *Stair Memorial Encyclopaedia*, paras. 114–192.
22 Stair, IV,xxix,3.
23 Paras 3.16–3.20.
24 Para. 3.12.

(c) the obtaining of protection against rectification of the Land Register[25]; and

(d) the entitlement to a possessory judgment. A person who has possessed land for a period of at least seven years on a prima facie title has an entitlement to an award of interim possession without consideration of the merits of any competing rights to possession.

---

25 Land Registration (Scotland) Act 1979, s.9(1).

CHAPTER 3

CREATION AND EXTINCTION OF REAL RIGHTS

Introduction

A distinction may be drawn between original and derivative 3.1
acquisition of real rights. Original acquisition is where a party
acquires a real right which previously had no existence at all or
where a party acquires a new right which has the effect in law of
extinguishing the right of a previous holder of a similar right.
Derivative acquisition occurs where a right already exists and is
held by a party who transfers it to another. Obviously the issue of
derivative acquisition cannot arise where a right is not alienable
such as is the case with public rights of way.[1]

Property—Methods of Original Creation

Despite the unitary nature of Scots property law, the immoveable 3.2
physical nature of land means that some of the doctrines by which a
title to moveable property can be originally acquired have little
relevance to land law. These include the doctrines of *specificatio*
(specification), *commixtio* (commixtion) and *confusio* (confusion).
In relation to property rights in land the principal methods by
which a real right may be originally acquired include the following:

(a) *occupatio* (occupation);
(b) *accessio* (accession);
(c) positive prescription;
(d) registration of title in the Land Register of Scotland. This is
     unique to land law and has no relevance to moveable property;
     and
(e) creation by statute.

Methods of Creation—Differences with Subsidiary Real Rights

A significant difference between the right of property and many 3.3

---

1   Para 2.28.

subordinate real rights may be seen in that the original acquisition of a right of property does not always involve the grant of a deed with a public act such as registration or possession following thereon. This is of course required for prescriptive possession to follow a Sasine recorded deed but in relation to the Land Register a deed is merely the method of persuading the keeper to issue a title sheet to create the property right. By contrast, the primary method of creation of many of the subordinate real rights such as liferent, lease and servitude is by grant of a deed with a public act following thereon. Indeed in relation to a standard security the grant of a deed with subsequent recording or registration is the only method of creating the real right.[2] This has the effect that many of the methods of creation of property are "involuntary" in the sense that they involve no granter. The term "involuntary" where it is employed in relation to the creation of subsidiary real rights may also have this meaning, as would be the case if the right were created by positive prescription,[3] but it may also denote a situation where a granter is obliged to grant a deed against his will. Examples of the latter form of involuntary creation may be found in certain statutory obligations relative to leases,[4] standard securities[5] and servitudes.[6]

Certain subsidiary real rights may be described as "tacit" rights in that they arise by implication of law from the topographical or architectural features encountered in a particular location. These may be contrasted with "acquired" rights which are those which fall to be acquired by some positive means such as exercise over a number of years. These "tacit" rights include:—

(a) Rights of common interest. The most common situations in

---

2   Conveyancing and Feudal Reform (Scotland) Act 1970 ss.9(2), (3) and 11(1) to be amended by Abolition of Feudal Tenure (Scotland) Act 2000, s.76(1) and Sched. 12, para. 30(6) and (8).
3   See, *e.g.*, positive servitudes and public rights of way created by prescription in terms of Prescription and Limitation (Scotland) Act 1973, s.3.
4   See the grant of a crofting lease in terms of Crofters (Scotland) Act 1993, s.23(5), discussed at paras 2.23 and 7.06. *Cf.* the power of the sheriff to grant renewals of certain long leases under Land Registration (Scotland) Act 1979, s.22A.
5   See, *e.g.*, Civil Legal Aid (Scotland) Regulations 1987 (S.I. 1987: No. 381), reg. 40(3), substituted by the Civil Legal Aid (Scotland) Amendment (No.2) Regulations 1991 (S.I. 1991 No. 1904), reg. 9.
6   Town and Country Planning (Scotland) Act 1997, s.277(1); Cusine and Paisley, *Servitudes and Rights of Way*, para. 1.25.

which rights of common interest arise are tenemental build-ings,[7] mutual boundary walls[8] and naturally sloping ground.[9] In the first situation a range of rights exists in respect of different parts of the building which are as diverse as a right of support, a right of shelter and the right to light. As regards naturally sloping ground there may be a common interest or a "natural right" of drainage permitting the higher proprietor to drain his land by surface or underground drains on to his neighbours' lower land. Other rights of this type arise in different situations and these are examined in more detail later in this book.[10]

(b) Public rights of navigation in tidal waters.[11] Tacit rights do not include the public right of navigation in non-tidal waters, the existence of which depends on the establishment of user from time immemorial.[12] Similarly the public right to use river banks for purposes ancillary to navigation are not tacit rights but fall to be acquired by other means—usually a demonstra-tion of use from time immemorial.[13]

(c) Public rights of navigation and whitefishing on the foreshore[14]

(d) The modern judicial tendency is to treat other public rights over the foreshore, such as the *ius spatiandi* (recreation), as tacit rights.[15]

From a property lawyer's point of view the importance of these "tacit" rights is that they highlight the importance of a site visit when a property is being purchased. It is unlikely that any of these rights will be evidenced in the Sasine-recorded titles or by express reference in the Title Sheet. They may be impossible to identify by other extrinsic evidence available at "desk top" level. Whilst it is may be a relatively simple matter to identify the possibility that rights of common interest exist in relation to a building described in the sales particulars as "second floor flat right", it will often not be possible without visiting the site to check the details of site gradients 3.4

---

7   18 *Stair Memorial Encyclopaedia*, paras 232–239.
8   *Thom v. Hetherington* 1988 S.L.T. 724; 18 *Stair Memorial Encyclopaedia*, paras 225–226.
9   18 *Stair Memorial Encyclopaedia*, paras 340 and 342.
10 Chap. 10.
11 18 *Stair Memorial Encyclopaedia*, paras 516 and 523,
12 *Wills' Trs v. Cairngorm Canoeing and Sailing School Ltd*, 1976 S.C. (H.L.) 30.
13 Hume, *Lectures*, Vol. IV, pp. 244–245; 18 *Stair Memorial Encyclopaedia*, para. 528.
14 18 *Stair Memorial Encyclopaedia*, paras 524–525.
15 *Marquis of Bute v. McKirdy and McMillan*, 1937 S.C. 93; *Burnet v. Barclay* 1955 J.C. 34; 18 *Stair Memorial Encyclopaedia*, para. 526.

which might give rise to natural drainage rights. The contours shown on the most detailed Ordnance Survey maps simply do not provide sufficient information, and photographs produced by clients or surveyors may prove deceptive.

It is significant that these tacit rights arise only in relatively well-established situations in which certain topographical or architectural features exist. Such features are not privately known facts: rather they are capable of objective ascertainment by any interested party. Thus the creation of the rights complies with the publicity principle encountered in the creation of many real rights.[16]

Occupatio

3.5   The doctrine of *occupatio* enables a party to acquire a right of property in an ownerless thing by taking possession of it. The doctrine is of considerable importance in relation to the acquisition of moveable property. It continues to be relevant in relation to territorial disputes in international law. It has, however, only a very restricted application to land in Scottish domestic law in recent years because all land in Scotland has been claimed. It has been used to justify the claim of the Crown in respect of a title to the islands of Rockall and Hasslewood Rock.[17] The doctrine of *occupatio* is linked to creation of property rights by sovereign right. This is a specialty reserved to the Crown. The Crown is deemed to have a title to the whole of Scotland by virtue of its being sovereign. Such a right is subject to all extant property rights of subjects with the result that where no title of another party may be shown to exist the land in question belongs to the Crown.[18]

Accessio

3.6   Accession occurs when two items of property are joined or connected with the result that one item is regarded as having become subsumed in the other. The item which is subsumed is known as the accessory and the item into which it is subsumed is known as the principal. Accession has no relevance to incorporeal property. There are various recognised instances of *accessio* but not all are of relevance to land. The first recognised variant, accession of moveables to moveables, has obviously no relevance to land. Those which have relevance to land are:

---

16 Para. 3.19.
17 Para. 1.27. For further details see J. Fisher, "Rockall" (Geoffrey Bles, 1956).
18 18 *Stair Memorial Encyclopaedia*, para. 48.

(a)   accession of moveables to land;
(b)   accession of land to land; and
(c)   accession by fruits.

*Accession—Moveables to Land (*naedificatio*)*

Corporeal moveable property which is attached to land may   3.7
become part of the land by accession. The item so attached is
known as a "fixture". Accession may occur by reason of natural
causes but accession because of human acts is far more common.
The classic example is a permanent heritable building attached to
land which at one time would have been a load of moveable bricks
and cement. Where a moveable item is attached to heritage it is then
owned by the owner of the heritage to which it is attached.[19] There
is usually a direct physical connection between the fixture and the
ground to which it is attached, as is illustrated in the common
example of a building erected on ground. That direct connection,
however, is unnecessary and a satellite dish fixed to the roof of the
house will accede to the ground under the house. There can, of
course, be no accession across separate tenements. Where an aerial
is attached to the wall of one flat in a tenement building it will
belong to the owner of that wall and not the owner of other flats in
the building or the owner of the *solum* of the building.

Accession operates independently of the will of the parties
involved. They may not contract out of the operation of the
doctrine.[20] Still less will it be excluded by an intent implied from
their legal relationship—the fact that the tenant has attached the
accessory is irrelevant to the issue of accession.[21] It may, however,
be excluded by statute. Thus, certain fixtures in an agricultural
holding remain the property of the tenant[22] and public sewers are
vested in the sewerage authority not in the owner of the land in
which they are located.[23]

Accession has three effects. First, the accessory becomes part of
the principal and ceases to have a separate existence. Secondly,
where the accessory is moveable and the principal is heritable the
accessory ceases to be moveable and becomes heritable. Thirdly, the
title of the owner to the accessory whilst it was separate is
extinguished and the owner of the principal owns both. Where the

---

19   *Brand's Trs. v. Brand's Tr.* (1876) 3R. (H.L.) 16.
20   *Shetland Islands Council v. BP Petroleum Development Ltd,* 1990 S.L.T. 82.
21   *Brand's Trs. v. Brand's Tr.* (1876) 3R. (H.L.) 16.
22   Agricultural Holdings (Scotland) Act 1991, s.18.
23   Sewerage (Scotland) Act 1968, ss 16 and 16A.

principal is held in common ownership the accessory will become
owned in the same way.[24] The separation of the principal and
accessory at a later stage does not entail the reversion of the right of
ownership in respect of the accessory to the former owner.[25] The
separation results in the accessory reverting to its moveable state.

Objective Conditions for Accession

3.8   Various writers indicate a differing number of requirements for
accession to take place. This text shall adopt the analysis that there
are three objective conditions for accession.[26] Usually all three must
be met to a sufficient extent before accession takes place.

(a)   First, there must be some physical connection—usually a
      physical attachment—between the land and the fixture. The
      firmer the physical attachment the greater the likelihood that
      this requirement will have been met. Most houses meet the
      requirement because foundations have been dug into the
      ground. Lesser physical bonds will suffice in other cases.
      Wallpaper pasted on a wall attaches to the wall. In other
      instances the sheer mass of the accessory imposes such a
      considerable weight on the subjacent land that it is regarded as
      qualifying as a fixture.[27]

(b)   Secondly, the item attached must be subordinate in function to
      the land or building to which it is attached and serve the
      purposes of that land or building. Storage heaters attached to
      the wall of the house in which they are attached are usually
      fixtures in that they are intended to heat the house.[28] Speakers
      for a music stereo system are not fixtures in a normal
      residential property even though they may be attached to a
      wall by metal brackets. The matter may be different if the
      speakers are part of a sound system in a concert hall or other
      building intended for public functions. In some cases this
      subordination will be sufficient to compensate for a lack of a
      high degree of actual attachment. On this basis the front door
      key of a house is regarded as heritable even though it is not
      chained to the house or hidden under the door mat.

(c)   Thirdly, the attachment must be more than temporary and

---

24 Bell, *Prin*, s.1076.
25 *Cf. Scottish Discount Co. Ltd v. Blin*, 1985 S.C. 216 per Lord (Ordinary) Murray
    at 226.
26 See 18 *Stair Memorial Encyclopaedia*, paras 579–584.
27 *Christie v. Smith's Exx*, 1949 S.C. 572.
28 *Fife Assessor v. Hodgson* 1966 S.C. 30.

usually it is permanent. Where an item has been specially adapted for a particular room this may indicate that it is to remain there permanently. The converse is also true—where a room has been specially adapted for an item of machinery, such as by the installation of special foundations, this may indicate that the machinery is a fixture.[29]

Possible Subjective Conditions for Accession

Two additional factors are sometimes mentioned as having relevance in the context of accession. These are intention and custom. 3.9

The intention of the parties is clearly a subjective factor which is sometimes mentioned in the context of accession. Evidence of what the parties intended or could be deemed to have intended given their legal relationship was rejected as irrelevant in the House of Lords in *Brand's Trs v. Brand's Trs.*[30] The actual intention of the parties is still regarded as irrelevant. The decision of the First Division of the Court of Session in *Scottish Discount Co. Ltd v. Blin*[31] indicates that in some cases the deemed intention of the parties arising from their legal relationship may be relevant. Thus the fact that the item attached was a moveable thing being acquired under a contract of hire purchase was regarded as tending to indicate that accession was not intended. This is contrary to the position in *Brand's Trs.* It introduces a subjectivity into the law of accession which may cause considerable difficulty.[32] That said, the criteria identified in *Scottish Discount Co. Ltd v. Blin* have been applied in at least one subsequently reported case.[33]

A factor which is rarely taken into account in deciding whether accession has taken place is the custom of the district.[34] Exactly why this should be relevant is difficult to determine. It may be that the custom of a district may indicate the wider framework of the legal relations of the parties and have a bearing on their presumed intent. If that is the case it may be open to a similar criticism to that applied to the decision in *Scottish Discount Co. Ltd v. Blin.*[35] Having said that, it may be argued that the custom of a district

---

29 *Scottish Discount Co. Ltd v. Blin*, 1985 S.C. 216.
30 (1876) 3R. (H.L.) 16.
31 1985 S.C. 216.
32 *Cf.* the similar position in South African law examined in Van der Merwe and de Waal, *The Law of Things and Servitudes*, para. 145.
33 *Taylor Woodrow Property Co. Ltd v. S.R.C.*, 1996 G.W.D. 7–397.
34 See, *e.g.*, *Campbell v. McCowan*, 1945 S.L.T. (Sh.Ct) 3.
35 1985 S.C. 216.

should be capable of objective ascertainment without reference to the intention of the parties. Unfortunately the case law on the matter is scant and the discussion in published writings sheds little light on the matter.[36]

Accession—Land to Land

3.10   Accession of land to land occurs as a result of alluvion. This applies to the imperceptible but permanent alteration of boundaries of land with water features such as the sea, lochs and rivers. Where the water permanently recedes or soil or sand is added to the land by deposits borne by the water, the additional dry area or the additional material accedes to the existing dry land. Conversely, where the water permanently increases its extent the ownership of the subsumed land becomes part of the existing *alveus*. Typical cases of alluvion include transmission of soil from one bank of a river to another, the retreat or advance of tidal and non-tidal waters and the formation of islands in rivers or lochs. Alluvion may occur as a result of natural events or human acts.[37] Sudden and violent alterations in the boundary caused by events such as storms are not alluvion but avulsion. Avulsion does not result in any change in the ownership of the relevant land.

It may be possible that in rare cases alluvion occurs in situations where there is no boundary of land with water. Consider the case of a ploughed and harrowed field which is subject to strong winds. The top soil may be blown off to some extent and the soil dust deposited in a neighbouring field. Whilst this will not extend the lateral boundaries of the existing fields it will imperceptibly alter the quantity of soil contained in the various fields. It seems to follow that the soil dust ceases to be owned by the proprietor of the field from which it came and becomes the property of the owner of the field in which it is deposited. Presumably if the wind changes direction and the dust is blown back there is the possibility of a series of excambions repeated *ad infinitum*.

Rights of Compensation and Severance

3.11   For the loss of his property the owner of the accessory may have

---

36 Rankine, *Landownership*, pp. 130–131; Gordon, *Scottish Land Law* (2nd. ed.), para. 5–15.

37 *Smart v. Dundee Magistrates* (1796) 3 Pat. App. 606. *Cf. Stirling v. Bartlett*, 1992 S.C.L.R. 994. For complications with the Land Register see R. Rennie, "Alluvio in the Land Register: Shifting Sands and the Thin Red Line", 1996 S.L.T. (News) 41.

two separate remedies. These are a right to monetary compensation and a right to severance.

Monetary compensation may be due to the owner of the accessory by the owner of the principal. This is the case where the act of accession was carried out by the act of the owner of the principal in which case the amount of the compensation, failing agreement between the parties, is the value of the accessory. Accession in bad faith may allow a claim in reparation which may result in a greater amount of compensation. Where the accession is carried out by the owner of the accessory there is no claim for compensation. Where the accession is carried out by a third party matters are more complex. The third party may be liable to pay the compensation to the owner of the accessory and it is also possible that the owner of the principal may be liable to the extent of his enrichment. The claim for compensation is a personal right and, where it relates to the owner of the principal, is enforceable only against the party holding the property right in the principal as at the date of the accession. No claim can be made against the singular successor in title of that party.[38]

The owner of the accessory may have a right of severance in certain cases. If such a right exists and it is lawfully exercised, the right of property in the accessory reverts to the owner prior to accession (or his assignee). In certain cases the right of severance arises by virtue of law. Such is the case where a liferenter attaches fixtures for the purposes of his trade. A tenant has a similar right at common law[39] and this has been fortified and expanded by statute in relation to agricultural fixtures.[40] At common law the tenant has a right to remove the fixtures during the lease and within a brief period thereafter, the length of which may be regulated by the term of the lease. The right of removal is enforceable against the original landlord and his successors in title. In some cases rights of severance are expressly conferred by the relevant deed. These are common in deeds of servitude relative to pipelines and septic tanks where the servient proprietor not only grants a right on the dominant proprietor to remove the structure at the termination of the servitude but imposes an obligation on him so to do. There is some doubt if rights of severance created by agreement are enforceable against singular successors of the owner of the principal. Where, at the time of the accession, the owner of the

---

38 *Beattie v. Lord Napier* (1831) 9 S. 639.
39 *Brand's Trs v. Brand's Trs* (1876) 3R. (H.L.) 16.
40 Agricultural Holdings (Scotland) Act 1991, s.18.

principal was also the owner of the accessory, that party will remain free to sever the accessory unless he has obliged himself not to do so in terms of a contract or subordinate real right. Thus a landlord who constructs a building on his ground and thereafter leases it cannot sever the building during the currency of the lease without the consent of the tenant. Similarly in a standard security there is an obligation falling on the debtor "not to demolish . . . any buildings or works forming part of the security subjects".[41]

Accession by Fruits

3.12   Accession by fruits differs from other forms of accession in that the accessory is produced by the principal. It is confined to living things and for this reason its application to heritable property is much more restricted than in relation to moveable property. Because only a very restricted class of animals may be regarded as heritable the application of the doctrine in relation to land is confined to plants. Growing trees, plants and other crops, apart from industrial growing crops, accede to the ground in which they are planted.[42] Industrial growing crops which require annual seed and labour, however, do not accede and are not heritable.[43] Trees do not require annual seed and labour and therefore do accede to the ground.[44] Trees cease to be heritable when they are felled[45] and plants cease to be heritable when put into moveable pots.[46] The severance does not affect the ownership of the items which continue to be owned by the owner of the principal except possibly where the principal was lawfully possessed and the fruits harvested by someone else. Examples of the exceptional case occur in relation to a liferenter who is entitled to the fruits,[47] and in relation to a tenant although the latter's right is more restricted unless established by a suitably expansive clause in the lease itself.[48]

---

41   Conveyancing and Feudal Reform (Scotland) Act 1970, s.11 and Sched. 3, Standard Condition 2(b).
42   *Stewart v. Stewart's Exrs* (1761) M. 5436; *Paul v. Cuthbertson* (1840) 2D. 1286; *Anderson v. Ford* (1844) 6D. 1315; Stair, II,i,34; Erskine, II,i,14 and 15; Carey Miller, *Corporeal Moveables in Scots Law*, para. 3.04; Gordon, *Scottish Land Law* (2nd. ed.), para 5–40; 18 *Stair Memorial Encyclopaedia*, paras 12 and 595.
43   18 *Stair Memorial Encyclopaedia*, para. 12.
44   *Paul v. Cuthbertson* (1840) 2D. 1286.
45   18 *Stair Memorial Encyclopaedia*, para. 12.
46   Stair, II,i,34; Carey Miller, *Corporeal Moveables in Scots Law*, para. 3.04.
47   Chap. 6.
48   Ersk., II,vi,22.

Positive Prescription

Positive prescription may be regarded as a means of original 3.13
acquisition of a right of *dominium* and other subordinate real rights
in land including proper liferent, lease, standard security, positive
servitude and public right of way.[49] As negative servitudes are not
capable of exercise they are generally regarded as incapable of
acquisition by positive prescription.[50] In any event it may soon be
incompetent to create new negative servitudes.[51]

Where prescription relates to the right of exclusive property (or
involves any acquisition of the exclusive right to an existing
subordinate real right upon a competing title) then upon acquisition
of the new right the earlier title of the former owner is
extinguished.[52] Existing subordinate real rights which burdened
the existing property right (or other existing real right acquired) are
not extinguished.[53] So where a party acquires a right of property to
a plot of land by means of possession following upon the recording
of an *a non domino* disposition that property will remain burdened
by any servitudes which affected the ground prior to the creation of
his title. Where positive prescription relates to the creation of a new
subordinate real right the underlying property right and other
existing subordinate rights are not extinguished but are thereafter
burdened with the new subordinate real right. So when a servitude
is created by positive prescription the ownership of the servient
tenement does not change and any existing securities, leases or
public rights of way are not discharged.

Another view[54] is to the effect that in these circumstances positive
prescription does not create a new title of ownership at all but
merely creates an irrebuttable presumption that the title upon
which the possessor holds, whatever it happens to be, is
"unchallengeable" but otherwise innominate. One may surmise
that the title comprises a real right but this remains obscure. This
theory also leaves open the possibility that the party who held the

---

49 Prescription and Limitation (Scotland) Act 1973, ss 1–3 and 15(1).
50 Bell, *Prin*, S. 994; Cusine and Paisley, *Servitudes and Rights of Way*, para. 10.02.
    Cf. Gordon, *Scottish Land Law* (2nd ed.), para. 24–42.
51 Scottish Law Com., *Discussion Paper on Real Burdens* (No. 106, Oct. 1998),
    paras 2.42–2.50.
52 18 *Stair Memorial Encyclopaedia*, para. 674.
53 They may of course be extinguished by negative prescription (1973 Act, s.8) but
    the period for positive prescription (10 or 20 years dependant on the right or
    property affected—1973 Act, ss 1–3) and negative prescription may not
    necessarily coincide in any particular case.
54 Johnston, *Prescription and Limitation*, paras 14.01–14.15.

property title prior to positive prescription operating is still the owner. This has two rather inelegant consequences. First, such an owner is excluded from exercising all rights of ownership by the party with the "unchallengeable" title even though the property right has not been extinguished. Secondly, the right of the party with the "unchallengeable" title to sell the subjects and grant subordinate real rights in respect of them must be questionable if he is not the owner, but it is clear that the title of other parties deriving rights from the party with the "unchallengeable" title are also "unchallengeable" by the owner. Whilst acknowledgement must be given to the existence of the second approach it is generally ignored in conveyancing practice and will not be adopted in this book.

In the application of the law of positive prescription distinctions must be made between real rights which can be created without a recorded or registered deed, Sasine-recorded titles and Land Registered interests.

(a) Certain real rights such as servitudes and public rights of way may be created without the necessity of any deed recorded in the Sasine register or a title registered in the Land Register of Scotland. Special statutory provision is made for the constitution of such rights in that exercise of the right for a period of 20 years is required.[55] In each case the possession must be open, peaceable and without judicial interruption.

(b) As regards those real rights requiring the recording of a deed in the Sasine Register, the simplest case to examine is a right of property. For positive prescription to run there are two requirements. First there must be a "foundation writ"—a deed recorded in the Sasine register which is sufficient in its terms to constitute a title to the land.[56] If there is no foundation writ then no length of possession will suffice.[57] There is no requirement that the deed itself is valid but the invalidity must not be apparent from the face of the deed and it cannot be forged.[58] Secondly, the registration of the deed has to be followed by exclusive possession for 10 years.[59] The period is extended in respect of an interest in the foreshore or salmon fishings where a party seeks to establish a title by prescription

---

55 Prescription and Limitation (Scotland) Act 1973, s.3(2) and (3).
56 1973 Act, s.1(1)(b).
57 *British Railways Board v. Sykes*, 18 December 1985 (unreported); D.J. Cusine (ed.), *Halliday Opinions*, Opinion Number 117, pp. 499–502.
58 1973 Act, s.1(1A).
59 1973 Act, s.1(1)(a).

Handwritten marginal notes:

1. Orig title is essentially extinguished on this view, as need not necessarily be balanced with acquis on on side

2. While point is that law acts as if good title in every future a ⇒ more a recognit that there isn't some platonic LR in the sky but that (hist) had to go by evidence + 20 yrs.

in a question involving the Crown as owner of the *regalia*.[60] The possession has to be "open, peaceable and without judicial interruption" and referable only to the foundation writ.[61] There is no requirement that the possession be in good faith— indeed if an *a non domino* deed is recorded by or on behalf of the party exercising possession it is difficult to see how it could be. Possession includes civil possession.[62]

(c) Positive prescription has no application to the creation of real rights in so far as they are interests in land in respect of which a Title Sheet has been issued because the title is created by the issuing of that Title Sheet.[63] Even where the Keeper's indemnity has been excluded the title is still created at that time without necessity of showing possession for a subsequent period of time.[64] Where indemnity has been excluded, however, the title remains open to rectification by the Keeper on the application of the person who would have been the proprietor but for the issuing of the Land Certificate.[65] In appropriate cases rectification may lead to a Title Sheet being cancelled. If, however, possession for the appropriate period follows upon the issuing of a Title Sheet with excluded indemnity then the title becomes "exempt from challenge" and invulnerable to rectification.[66] The proprietor may then apply to the Keeper to have the exclusion from indemnity removed.[67] The difference as to the application of the law of prescription in relation to Land Registered titles with exclusion of indemnity and those with no exclusion of indemnity is not

---

60 1973 Act, s.1(4). The special case of allodial land also requires 20 years possession, see 1973 Act, s.2. This will be replaced by Abolition of Feudal Tenure, etc. (Scotland) Act 2000, s.76(1) and Sched. 12, para. 33(2).

61 *Hamilton v. McIntosh Donald*, 1994 S.L.T. 212; 1994 S.L.T. 793; R.Rennie, "*Possession: nine tenths of the law*", 1994 S.L.T. (News) 261.

62 1973 Act, s.15(1).

63 1973 Act, s.1(1)(b). There is no similar provision for registration in the Land Register for servitudes: see 1973 Act, s.3.

64 Land Registration (Scotland) Act 1979 ("1979 Act"), s.3(1)(a); 18 *Stair Memorial Encyclopaedia*, para. 673; *Scottish Enterprise v. Ferguson*, 1996 G.W.D. 26–1522 (OH); *Kaur v. Singh*, 1997 S.C.L.R. 1075; 1999 S.C. 180; *Stevenson-Hamilton's Exrs v. McStay*, 1999 S.L.T. 1175; *Wilson v. Keeper of the Registers of Scotland*, 1999 S.C.L.R. 872.

65 Land Registration (Scotland) Act 1979, s.9(3)(a)(iv) has no limitation on the persons who may apply but some limitations may be imposed by the courts: see *Stevenson–Hamilton's Exrs v. McStay, supra Wilson v. Keeper of the Registers of Scotland, supra.*

66 1973 Act, s.1(1)(b).

67 Registration of Title Practice Book (2nd ed., 2000), para. 7.34.

entirely satisfactory as it is possible in a limited number of
cases to rectify titles even where indemnity has been issued.[68]
In such cases the power to rectify exists until extinguished by
the long negative prescription.

Registration of Title

3.14   Recording of a title in the Sasine Register does not create a title
to the land therein described. Recording of the deed in the Sasine
register is a necessary but not a sufficient condition of obtaining a
real right—it is not a sufficient title because the deed may be void.[69]
In the Sasine system title flows from the recorded deed and if the
party granting that deed has no right the deed will be *a non domino*
and no title will be created until the recording of the deed is
followed by exercise of the right for the prescriptive period.[69a] By
contrast, when a title is registered in the Land Register of Scotland
title does not flow from the deed, it flows from the register. Upon
registration a statutory title is created in favour of the person
named in the title sheet in respect of the particular interest to which
that title sheet relates.[70] This title is based on statute and is quite
distinct from any title which might previously have been conveyed
by any prior Sasine or Land Registered titles. The exercise of the
Keeper's discretion to accept a particular application for first
registration often acts to the advantage of the applicant by granting
in his favour a Land Certificate conferring upon him a statutory
title where such a title may not be warranted by the prior Sasine
titles and the possession following thereon. Frequently the Keeper
exercises his statutory discretion to clear up minor irregularities in
Sasine titles. The statutory title is created whether or not the Keeper
issues full indemnity or a restricted form of indemnity.

There are various methods whereby information may be inserted
into the Title Sheet of an interest in land. These are "registration",[71]

---

68 1979 Act, s.9(3)(a)(i) to (iii).
69 Gretton and Reid, *Conveyancing*, (2nd ed.), para. 8.02.
69a A similar situation may arise where the deed is recorded without the authority of
the disponee.
70 Land Registration (Scotland) Act 1979, s.3(1)(a); 18 *Stair Memorial Encyclopaedia*, para. 673; *Scottish Enterprise v. Ferguson, supra*; *Kaur v. Singh*, 1997
S.C.L.R. 1075; 1999 S.C. 180; *Stevenson-Hamilton's Exrs v. McStay*, 1999 S.L.T.
1175; *Wilson v. Keeper of the Registers of Scotland*, 1999 S.C.L.R. 872.
71 1979 Act, ss 1–5.

"rectification",[72] "noting,"[73] and "entering".[74] "Registration" has the effect of creating a real right.[75] "Noting" does not create a real right but merely allows additional information to be added to the register although noting may disclose the existence of a real right created by other means such as possession.[76] "Entering" is a term with a wider meaning which appears to include both registration and noting. As registered interests are stated to be "subject to" matters entered in the title sheet[77] this suggests that matters entered may themselves be real rights. "Rectification" permits the Keeper to insert, amend or cancel any inaccuracy in the register and clearly extends to remedying a fault where something should previously have been registered, noted[78] or entered. Whether rectification creates a real right will depend on the nature of the process which should previously have been carried out and which is now to be remedied. The use of these four terms without any comprehensive statement of their effect in the statute adds to the confusion within the scheme of the 1979 Act. One of the most important areas of obscurity relates to servitudes. It has been suggested that a servitude may be "registered" in the title of the dominant tenement but may only be "noted" in the title of the servient tenement.[79] If this is correct then there is an unexpected consequence. A servitude cannot be created a real right by a reservation in a disposition of a servient tenement where that disposition induces a first or subsequent registration of the property right in the servient tenement, except by exercise of the right after the registration of the property right in the servient tenement in the name of the disponee.[80] As negative servitudes cannot be exercised they cannot be made real by insertion in the title of the servient tenement. The way out of the difficulty appears to treat all such servitudes as "subsisting real burdens or conditions" affecting the interest in the servient tenement with the result that the servitude may be entered in the

---

72 1979 Act, s.9.
73 1979 Act, ss6(4) and 9(3)(a)(i); Land Registration (Scotland) Rules 1980, r. 13.
74 1979 Act, ss6, 13(3)(g) and 28(1); Land Registration (Scotland) Rules 1980, r. 4, 5, 6, 7, 8 and 13.
75 1979 Act, s.3(1).
76 1979 Act, s.6(4).
77 1979 Act, s.3(1)(a). See also the reference to "entry" in 1979 Act, s.9(3A).
78 1979 Act, s.9(3)(a)(i).
79 *Registration of Title Practice Book* (2nd ed., 2000), para. 6.51.
80 Exercise is preserved as a method of creating a real right by 1979 Act, s.3(2), but it cannot create the right as real until there are two tenements in separate ownership, *i.e.* after registration of the servient tenement in the ownership of the disponee. See Cusine and Paisley, *Servitudes and Rights of Way*, para. 6.31.

Title Sheet that interest.[81] Whilst it is relatively easy to regard
servitudes as "real burdens and conditions",[82] it is arguable that the
servitudes which the parties to the disposition wish to create are not
"subsisting" until after registration of the property right in the
servient tenement in the name of the disponee. Despite this infelicity
of expression it is submitted that this is a better approach than that
which holds that a servitude may only be noted in the title of the
servient tenement. In any event, whichever approach is adopted, the
problem may be lessened with the reform of the law relative to title
conditions which is likely to require registration of a servitude
and a real burden in the title of both dominant and servient
tenements.[83]

Statutory Process

3.15   The creation of title in terms of the Land Registration process
may be viewed as one example of creation of title by statutory
provision or process. Other particular examples may occasionally
be found in local statutes. These have been enacted from time to
time over the last two centuries almost as a matter of last resort to
clear up problems in titles where this would otherwise be
impracticable by normal conveyancing techniques. The problem
common to most of these situations is that no certain evidence
could be obtained as to the true owner of a particular piece of
ground and the statutory provision creates a new title to fill the gap.
One general statutory provision which appears to have been
enacted to serve a similar purpose is that under the Roads
(Scotland) Act 1984 which provides that where a public road is
"stopped up" by the roads authority ownership of the former road
vests in the frontagers. Unfortunately this vesting is stated to be
"subject to the prior claim of any person by reason of title".[84] As
there always will be someone, be it the Crown or another party,
who has right to the *solum*, this has the effect of removing the
possibility that the statutory provision could create a title. The
provision, however, may have a limited useful effect where the
frontager subsequently applies to the Keeper for a first registration
of the title to the relevant part of the *solum*. The statutory provision

81 1979 Act, s.6(1)(e).
82 Cusine and Paisley, *Servitudes and Rights of Way*, para. 11.07. *Cf.* 1979 Act,
    s.12(3)(g) and (l).
83 Scot. Law Com., *Discussion Paper on Real Burdens* (No. 106, Oct. 1998), paras
    7.1–7.5.
84 Roads (Scotland) Act 1984, s.115; 20 *Stair Memorial Encyclopaedia*, para. 613;
    Gretton and Reid, *Conveyancing* (2nd. ed.), para. 4.13, fn. 40.

may be a factor of assistance to the Keeper in the decision to exercise his discretion positively and to issue to the frontager a Land Certificate without exclusion of indemnity. The new title in such a case is, however, created by the Land Registration process and not the process under the Roads Act. As regards areas which are not yet operational for the Land Register a frontager seeking a title to the *solum* in such a case usually proceeds to record in the Sasine Register an *a non domino* disposition. Whilst title to the subjects will be acquired only if the recording of the deed is followed by exclusive possession for the prescriptive period the frontager may be able to find a title indemnity provider who is willing to issue a suitable policy for the intervening period. The statutory provision will be a factor in the decision of the insurer as to whether the risk is insurable.

The Manner of Transmission

Derivative acquisition involves transfer of an existing real right. 3.16 Transfer of a real right is either voluntary or involuntary. Voluntary transfer is far more common and involves the consent to the transfer of both the transferor and the transferee. Involuntary transfer involves only the consent of the transferee. The transferor does not consent to such transfer. Examples of involuntary transfer include transfer (a) on death or presumed death; (b) on bankruptcy; (c) by means of compulsory acquisition; (d) in implement of a court order; and (e) in implement of a statutory obligation. Involuntary transfer will not be considered further in this book and reference may be made to the undernoted text.[85]

Conveyancing and Real Rights

There is a two-stage process in relation to the derivative 3.17 acquisition (transmission) of the right of property and the subordinate real rights. A similar two-stage process also applies to the original acquisition (creation) of some, but not all, of the subordinate real rights. This two-stage process does not apply to the original acquisition of property. Where the two-stage process applies, it comprises the following. First, there is a contractual stage usually known only to the parties to that contract. The time when this occurs is usually known only to the parties and in practice may be obscured slightly by the practice of sending settlement items

---

85   Gordon, *Scottish Land Law* (2nd ed.), paras 12–96–12–124.

under cover of a letter stating that the contents are to be held as "undelivered" and only later is mutual delivery agreed by telephone and confirmed by letter.[86] Secondly, there is a stage which almost invariably involves some act which publicises the existence of the right to the general public.[87] The timing of this event should be capable of precise determination by third parties and this enables the application of the common law rule governing all real rights—*prior tempore potior jure*—meaning earlier by time, stronger by right. In a competition between real rights an earlier date of creation gives a priority.[88] Deeds recorded or registered on the same day rank equally regardless of the actual time of delivery of the deed to the registers.[88a] A problem in this regard may arise in relation to the statutory powers of the courts to rectify deeds creating or transferring real rights.[89] The effect of the court order may be retrospective and lead to the creation or transfer of a real right at the original date of the grant and this may lead to difficulty where there has been no prior awareness of the mistake requiring rectification beyond the parties to relevant deed.[90] The court, however, has power to modify this rule where third parties have acted in reliance on the unrectified deed.[91]

The transmission of existing property rights and existing subordinate real rights and the creation of subordinate real rights

---

86   "*Settlement Cheques Sent to be held as Undelivered*" (1998) 43 J.L.S.S. 47 (Oct.); 1999 J.L.S.S., letter, p. 12; Gretton and Reid, *Conveyancing* (2nd ed.), paras 2.11, fn.22 and 2.14.

87   Gordon, *Scottish Land Law* (2nd ed.), para. 12–03. For the "publicity principle" in South African law see Van der Merwe and de Waal, *The Law of Things and Servitudes*, paras 7 and 10.

88   Gretton and Reid, *Conveyancing* (2nd ed.), para. 20.21. For a similar position in South Africa see Van der Merwe and de Waal, *The Law of Things and Servitudes*, para. 44.

88a Titles to Land Consolidation (Scotland) Act 1868, s.142; Land Registration (Scotland) Act 1979, s.7(2).

89   See, *e.g.*, the rectification of a disposition in *Alistair Mortimer Robertson v. James Robertson and Jeffrey John Robertson*, Banff Sheriff Court, case ref. B170/88 (unreported). A disposition had been granted on 11 April 1988 and recorded in the Sasine register on 8 November 1988. The words "do hereby dispone to and in favour of the said Alistair Mortimer Robertson" had been omitted. The disponers had been sequestrated subsequent to the grant. The action was raised against the granters but not the trustee in bankruptcy. The warrant to cite defenders was dated 15 December 1988 but there was no appearance on behalf of the defenders. The decree was granted 17 February 1989 and extracted 1 February 1989.

90   Law Reform (Misc. Prov.)(Scot.) Act 1985 ("1985 Act"), s.8(4); Gretton and Reid, *Conveyancing* (2nd ed.), para. 17.13.

91   1985 Act, s.9(4) and (5).

is a major branch of the law of property known as "conveyancing". Given that about 40 per cent of the business of many firms of solicitors comprises conveyancing, its significance is obvious.[92] Unfortunately the essential link between conveyancing and property law may have been obscured for decades after the middle of the nineteenth century with the enactment of a series of statutes intended to simplify the process of transmission of property.[93] It could be argued that the impression given by some of the subsequent legal comment[94] tends to indicate a view that these statutes represented a complete code which could be divorced from underlying principles of property law. If that indeed was the case then it was a blind alley for the development of Scottish property law from which it has now escaped following a renewed interest in the Civilian roots of Scots property law,[95] the imminent abolition of the feudal system[96] and the rediscovery of the unitary nature of Scottish law of property.[97]

Examples of the Two-Stage Process

Common examples of how the two-stage process of acquisition 3.18 applies are as follows:

(a) As regards transmission of an existing real right the simplest case is the right of *dominium*. This right is normally transferred by means of a deed known as a "disposition" granted by the existing proprietor. A disposition differs from an assignation which is used in relation to the transfer of many subordinate real rights. No intimation to a third party follows upon the delivery or recording of a disposition. The distinction between a conveyance of a property right and an assignation has unfortunately been obscured by the use of loose language in certain deeds such as the form of the Schedule Conveyance commonly employed in many compulsory acquisitions.[98] The

---

92 A measure of the importance of the topic may be assessed from the volume of the highest quality scholarly analysis given to it. See, *e.g.*, Halliday, *Conveyancing* (2nd ed.); Gretton and Reid, *Conveyancing* (2nd. ed.); McDonald, *Conveyancing Manual* (6th ed.); Cusine, *Standard Securities*.
93 See, *e.g.*, Titles to Land (Consolidation) Act 1868; Conveyancing (Scotland) Act 1874; Conveyancing (Scotland) Act 1924.
94 See, *e.g.*, Begg, *The Conveyancing Code* (1876, Bell & Bradfute).
95 See, *e.g.*, T.B. Smith, *A Short Commentary on the Law of Scotland* (1962).
96 Abolition of Feudal Tenure etc. (Scotland) Act 2000.
97 The most important writing in this regard is clearly 18 *Stair Memorial Encyclopaedia*.
98 Lands Clauses Consolidation (Scotland) Act, 1845, s.80 and Sched. (A).

statutory words of grant in that deed are "sell, alienate, dispone, convey, *assign* and make over" even though the function of the deed is primarily that of a disposition. In any event the use of the word "dispone" is not required in any disposition or conveyance—even a Schedule Conveyance— provided the deed contains any other word or words importing conveyance or transference or present intention to convey or transfer.[99] In the normal situation of a "voluntary" sale a disposition is used. Although there is no statutory form of such a deed a well recognised style has evolved from centuries of practice. The granter of the deed is commonly under a contractual obligation to grant the disposition in terms of pre-existing missives. The conclusion of this contract does not effect the transfer of the property right. The contract comprised in the missives usually contains many clauses relative to a considerable number of matters ancillary to transfer of the property right. There is usually a specific clause, however, requiring the seller to deliver a valid disposition in favour of the purchaser or his nominees to the purchaser on the date of settlement. The grantee named in the disposition ("the disponee") does not become the owner of the property until the disposition is recorded in the General Register of Sasines (or, where appropriate, registration in the Land Register of Scotland).[1] Mere delivery of the disposition is insufficient to transfer ownership of land.[2] Separate tenements, even if they consist of incorporeal rights such as the right to fish for salmon, are transferred by disposition rather than assignation and intimation.

(b) Most subordinate real rights are incorporeal rights which are transferred by the use of a deed known as an assignation rather than a disposition. An exception exists in relation to an existing servitude which is transferred by a disposition because it cannot be transferred separately from the property right in the dominant tenement to which it is attached.[3] The more common

---

99 Conveyancing (Scotland) Act 1874, s.27; Cusine and Paisley, *Servitudes and Rights of Way*, para. 5.30.

1   Abolition of Feudal Tenure etc. (Scotland) Act 2000, s.4, to come into effect on the appointed day.

2   *Cf. Sharp v. Thomson* 1997 S.L.T. 636, HL. See also *Burnett's Tr. v. Grainger*, 2000 S.L.T. (Sh.Ct.) 116.

3   18 *Stair Memorial Encyclopaedia*, para. 657; Cusine and Paisley, *Servitudes and Rights of Way*, para. 1.46. The same applies to real burdens despite the decision in *Marsden v. Craighelen Lawn Tennis and Squash Club*, 1999 G.W.D. 37-1820. See Reid and Gretton, *Conveyancing*, (1999), pp. 10 and 59–61.

case of the use of an assignation is exemplified in relation to the tenant's right in a lease. The assignation is granted by the existing tenant and delivered to the assignee. At that stage the assignee has a mere contractual right in a question with the assignor.[4] As the lease contains personal rights enforceable against the landlord the assignation is intimated to the landlord.[5] The tenant should proceed to take possession of the leased subjects. If the lease is a recorded (or registered lease) the assignation is also recorded in the Sasine register (or registered in the Land Register of Scotland as appropriate).[6] Whilst registration in either of these registers has the effect of intimation to the landlord,[7] the taking of possession of the subjects of lease does not,[8] neither does registration for preservation.[9] In a manner similar to dispositions the form of assignations has largely arisen from practice. There are, however, a few instances of statutory styles of assignations such as those relating to recorded leases[10] and standard securities.[11] The creditor's interest in a floating charge is transferred by means of assignation and intimation to the owner of the property falling within the charge. Such an assignation does not require to be notified to the Registrar of Companies.[12] This can give rise to problems as it may be difficult to establish who is the holder of a floating charge from time to time.[13] The change should be entered in the company's own register of charges[14] following intimation but the penalty for a failure to do this is a monetary penalty and does not involve invalidation of the assignation.

(c) As regards creation of subordinate real rights, dispositions or assignations are not generally employed: rather the deed used

---

4   Ersk., *Inst*, II,v,3.
5   18 *Stair Memorial Encyclopaedia*, para. 657.
6   Registration of Leases (Scotland) Act 1857, s.3(1); Land Registration (Scotland) Act 1979, s.2(4)(a).
7   *Edmond v. Gordon* (1858) 20D. (H.L.) 5; 3 Macq. 116 (bond and disposition in security).
8   *Yeoman v. Elliot and Foster*, 2 Feb. 1813 F.C.
9   *Tod's Trs v. Wilson* (1869) 7M. 1100 (trust).
10 Registration of Leases (Scotland) Act 1857, s.3 and Sched. (A).
11 Conveyancing and Feudal Reform (Scotland) Act 1970 ("1970 Act"), s.14 and Sched. 4, Forms A and B.
12 After the coming into force of the amending provisions of the Companies Act 1989 it may be required to be so notified: see Companies Act 1985, s.401 (substituted by the Companies Act 1989, s.96).
13 4 *Stair Memorial Encyclopaedia*, para. 667.
14 *ibid.* para. 667.

is one which specifies the nature of the right created. For example, a standard security is a special deed which is executed by the proprietor of the security subjects. The two possible forms of the deed are prescribed by statute.[15] Upon delivery to the creditor a contract exists between the proprietor of the security subjects and the creditor.[16] Only when the standard security is recorded in the General Register of Sasines or registered in the Land Register of Scotland (as appropriate) will the security be created as a real right.[17] Similarly, when a lease is executed by the landlord and tenant there is a contract of lease but the tenant's right does not become a real right until he takes possession or the lease is recorded or registered.[18]

The Second Public Stage

3.19 The public act in the second stage of transfer of a property right or an existing subordinate real right or the creation of a new subordinate real right in heritable property operates largely as the legal equivalent of the delivery of corporeal moveable property. This was clearly apparent in the transfer of land by means of symbolical delivery on the ground in question before the removal of that requirement in 1845.[19]

In modern Scots law the public act varies in relation to different real rights as follows:

(a) registration of the deed of creation in a public register; and
(b) taking possession of the subject of the right or exercise of the right.

It is important to note that these two methods of creating real rights are consonant with the "publicity principle" because the existence of the real right is brought to the attention of the general public. Nevertheless, it is not actual knowledge of the existence of the right which binds the general public. Where a real right is created by either registration or possession the public will be bound by it even though they have no actual knowledge of the right. As

---

15 1970 Act, s.9(2) and Sched.2.
16 Scott C. Styles, "Rights on Security", in A.D.M. Forte (ed.), *Scots Commercial Law* (1997), Chap. 6, p. 198.
17 1970 Act, s.11(1).
18 Paras 7.12–7.19.
19 Infeftment Act 1845, s.1; Gordon, *Scottish Land Law* (2nd. ed.), para. 2–33. After the public registration of instruments of Sasine was made compulsory in 1617 an unregistered instrument was of no effect. See *Young v. Leith* (1847) 9 D. 932, aff'd (1848) 2 Ross L.C. 103, H.L.

regards registration in the General Register of Sasines and the Land Register of Scotland, these are public registers and the general public may be deemed to have knowledge of their contents. It is more difficult, albeit not impossible, to sustain an argument that there is such constructive knowledge in respect of possession or exercise of the right, particularly where possession or exercise is not exclusive or constant. Conversely, where a right has not yet been made real by either of the above two methods actual knowledge of its existence as a potential real right will not bind a party, such as a singular successor to the right of *dominium* who wishes to challenge it. This commonly occurs in relation to a lease in respect of which a document of lease has been executed and delivered but which has not yet been created as a real right when the landlord's interest is transferred.[20]

Registration in Public Registers

For rights in land the most important registers are the General Register of Sasines and the Land Register of Scotland with a subsidiary role being provided by the Company Charges Register. Registration in the Books of Council and Session or Sheriff Court Books does not create real rights.[21]

Dominium, proper liferent,[22] and a standard security[23] are among those real rights created only by registration of a deed in the General Register of Sasines in an area where the Land Register of Scotland is not yet effective.[24] Such registration is an alternative to possession in relation to the creation of real rights such as servitudes (both positive and negative) and long leases.[25] For many transactions resulting in the creation or transfer of real rights the Register of Sasines ceases to have effect when a registration county becomes an "operational area" under the Land Registration system.[26] The rules for the continued efficacy of the Sasine Register are complex and details can be sought in the undernoted texts.[27]

3.20

---

20 *Birkbeck v. Ross* (1865) 4M. 272 per Lord Barcaple at 276; *Johnston v. Monzie* (1760) 5 Brown's Supp. 877; 13 *Stair Memorial Encyclopaedia*, para. 315.
21 McDonald, *Conveyancing Manual* (6th ed.), para. 4.7.
22 Gordon, *Scottish Land Law* (2nd ed.), para. 17–05. See Abolition of Feudal Tenure etc. (Scotland) Act 2000, s.65, to come into effect on the appointed day.
23 Conveyancing and Feudal Reform (Scotland) Act 1970, s.9(1)–(3) and s.11(1).
24 Johnston, *Prescription*, para. 15.10.
25 Registration of Leases (Scotland) Act 1857 (c.26), s.2.
26 1979 Act, ss 3(2) and 8.
27 See *Registration of Title Practice Book* (2nd ed.), para. 2.15; Gordon, *Scottish Land Law* (2nd ed.), para. 13–23.

Where a registration county becomes an "operational area" the general rule is that most deeds transferring or creating "interests in land" are registerable in the Land Register of Scotland.[28] This term "interest in land" is defined as meaning "any estate, interest, servitude or other heritable right in and over land, including a heritable security[29] but excluding a lease which is not a long lease".[30] In an operational area possession shall cease to be a means of creating a real right to the tenant's right in a long lease[31] but remains an option for positive servitudes.[32] In operational areas the tenant's right in a lease which is not a long lease is still made real by possession by the tenant regardless of whether any other interest in the land is registered in the Land Register.

In relation to land the company charges register has relevance only where an incorporated company grants a standard security or floating charge which may affect land. Where a company incorporated under the Companies Acts grants a standard security that security must be registered not only in the Land Register of Scotland or Sasine Register (as appropriate) but also the charges register within 21 days of its registration in the Sasine Register or Land Register of Scotland (or such longer period as is sanctioned by the court),[33] failing which the security will be void as against a future liquidator, a future administrator and any creditor.[34] The exact meaning of this phraseology is obscure but it effectively means that the security is null though the debt remains a valid debt.[35] Timeous registration of a charge in the register of charges is evidenced by a certificate issued by the Registrar of Companies.[36]

Similar provisions relating to registration apply to a floating charge but there is a significant difference in the date from which

---

28 1979 Act, ss 2 and 8; Johnston, *Prescription*, para. 15.10.
29 This term is defined by reference to Conveyancing and Feudal Reform (Scotland) Act 1970, s.9(8).
30 The definition will be amended by Abolition of Feudal Tenure etc. (Scotland) Act 2000, s.76(1) and Sched. 12, para. 39(11). The term "long lease" is defined in 1979 Act, s.28(1), as being a lease exceeding 20 years or which could exceed 20 years by reason of an obligation to renew.
31 1979 Act, s.3(3)(a).
32 1979 Act, s.3(2). The reforms of the law relating to title conditions may lead to a requirement to register deeds of servitudes in the titles of both servient and dominant tenements. See Scot. Law Com. *Discussion Paper on Real Burdens* (No. 106, Oct. 1998), para. 7.5.
33 Companies Act 1985, s.420. The sanction of the court may be given subject to conditions.
34 Companies Act 1985, s.410.
35 Gretton and Reid, *Conveyancing* (2nd ed.), para. 28.05.
36 Companies Act 1985, s.418.

the time limit within which the charge must be registered in the company charges register runs. This date is not from the date of registration in the Sasine or Land Register (because that is incompetent in respect of a floating charge) but from the last date of the execution of the charge.[37]

Possession

Taking possession of the subject of the right or exercise of the right is a method of creating some real rights. Those rights which may be so created include short leases and positive servitudes.[38] The Scottish Law Commission has proposed that positive servitudes which are created expressly in writing should become real rights only on registration.[39] Negative servitudes cannot be created as real rights in this way because they cannot be possessed and reform of the law relative to title conditions may result in the creation of new negative servitudes becoming incompetent in any event. To create a tenant's right in a long lease as a real right, possession remains an alternative to recording in the Sasine Register outwith operational areas for the Land Register.[40] As mentioned above, in an operational area for the Land Register possession shall cease to be a means of creating a real right to the tenant's interest in a long lease.[41]   3.21

The usefulness of possession as a method of publicising the creation of a real right has a major drawback. As regards publicity possession is at its best where the possession is exclusive, continuous and at a high level of intensity. Such is likely to be the case in relation to the tenant's right in a lease of subjects such as a residential house in an urban area. As regards other leasehold subjects the possession may be intermittent and involve a low level of activity, particularly if the lease itself contains a suitably restrictive user clause. For example, where a lease relates to a right of shooting over a large moor the permitted activity is never exercised in a continuous way and a member of the public may visit the subjects when the right is not being exercised. As regards other real rights such as servitude of access the possession is likely to be

---

37 For companies incorporated in Scotland see Companies Act 1985, s.419(5) prospectively amended by Companies Act 1989, s.103.
38 Gordon, *Scottish Land Law* (2nd ed.), para. 24–26ff.
39 Scot. Law Com., *Discussion Paper on Real Burdens*, (No. 106, Oct. 1998), paras 7.3 and 7.5, proposal 37(2).
40 Leases Act 1449; Registration of Leases (Scotland) Act 1857 (c.26), s.2. For the degree of possession required see *Millar v. McRobbie*, 1949 S.C. 1.
41 1979 Act, s.3(3)(a).

desultory and intermittent. A member of the public may visit the servient tenement when the servitude is not being exercised and have no indication that the right exists. The difficulty in relation to servitudes will be elided if reform is enacted to require registration of deeds whereby servitudes are created.[42] This will of course have no effect in relation to the continuation of the rules relative to the creation of a positive servitude by exercise for the prescriptive period.[43]

No Public Act

3.22   Difficulties arise where the method of creation of a real right involves no public act. This is an acute problem in relation to two real rights and a theoretical problem in relation to one other. These are respectively:

(a) floating charges;
(b) negative servitudes; and
(c) public rights of way.

Floating Charges

3.23   A floating charge creates a personal right on the part of the creditor when the deed is delivered.[44] This remains personal even after registration of the charge in the register of charges[45] and becomes real only if the charge attaches following the appointment of a receiver or the liquidation of the company.[46] For any party dealing with a company there are certain problems in this area.

(a) First, although registration in the register of charges is intended to publicise to members of the public that a floating charge has been created[47] it is an imperfect means of doing this because the time of creation as a real right does not coincide with that publicity. The creditor has a period of 21 days after

---

42 Scot. Law Com., *Discussion Paper on Real Burdens* (No. 106, Oct. 1998), para. 7.5.
43 Prescription and Limitation (Scotland) Act 1973, s.3(1)(a).
44 *AIB Finance v. Bank of Scotland*, 1995 S.L.T. 2; Gretton and Reid, *Conveyancing* (2nd ed.), para. 28.12.
45 18 *Stair Memorial Encyclopaedia*, para. 5, fn. 5 and para. 8.
46 Companies Act 1985 (c.6), s.463(1); Insolvency Act 1986 (c.45), s.53(7); Scott C. Styles, "Rights on Security", in A.D.M. Forte (ed.), *Scots Commercial Law* (1997), Chap. 6, p. 198. Gretton and Reid, *Conveyancing* (2nd ed), paras 28.09 and 29.06. See also *National Commercial Bank of Scotland Ltd v. Telford Grier Mackay & Co. Ltd Liquidators*, 1969 S.C. 181.
47 4 *Stair Memorial Encyclopaedia*, para. 657.

execution of the floating charge within which to register it in the register of charges. During that period it is possible that only the company and the creditor in the floating charge will be aware of its existence.

(b) Secondly, a floating charge becomes a fixed charge when it "attaches" or "crystallizes".[48] This occurs when the company goes into liquidation[49] or a receiver is appointed to the company under the floating charge.[50] Neither of these is an event which can readily be discovered by the public immediately upon the happening of the event. A company "goes into liquidation" when it passes a winding-up resolution or when an order for its winding up is made by the court at a time when it has not already passed such a resolution.[51] The appointment of a receiver is extra-judicial. The chargeholder merely executes an "instrument of appointment" appointing a receiver to run the company. The fact of receivership does not appear in the personal register or the register of insolvencies but only in the companies register.[52] A copy of the instrument of appointment must be delivered to the Register of Companies within seven days, but failure incurs a fine, not invalidation.[52a] The problems for a purchaser from the company in this area have been lessened to some extent by the decision of the House of Lords in *Sharp v. Thomson*.[53] In that case it was held that an item of heritable property is released from the ambit of a floating charge as soon as a selling company delivers a disposition to a purchaser. The case, however, throws up a problem for purchasers from a receiver. If an item of property is subject to a delivered, unregistered disposition, that item of property may still belong to the company but will fall outwith the property attached by the charge. Ironically this problem

---

48 The two terms have identical meanings. The first term is used in the Companies Act 1985 but the latter is widely used. See 4 *Stair Memorial Encyclopaedia*, para. 659; Gretton and Reid, *Conveyancing* (2nd ed.), paras 28.09 and 29.06.

49 Companies Act 1985 (c.6), s.463(1), prospectively amended by Companies Act 1989 (c.40), s.140(1) from a day to be appointed under s.215(2). See 4 *Stair Memorial Encyclopaedia*, para. 659.

50 Insolvency Act 1986 (c.45), ss 53(7) and 54(6); *Forth & Clyde Construction Co. Ltd v. Trinity Timber & Plywood Co. Ltd*, 1984 S.C. 1 per Lord President Emslie at 10; *National Commercial Bank of Scotland Ltd v. Telford Grier Mackay & Co. Ltd Liquidators*, 1969 S.C. 181 (liquidation case predating receivership).

51 Insolvency Act 1986, s.247(2); 4 *Stair Memorial Encyclopaedia*, para. 659.

52 Gretton and Reid, *Conveyancing* (2nd. ed.), para. 29.06.

52a Insolvency Act 1986, s.53(2). See para. 11.27.

53 1997 S.C. (H.L.) 66; 1997 S.L.T. 636; 1997 S.C.L.R. 328; Gretton and Reid, *Conveyancing* (2nd ed), paras 11.31 and 28.09.

arises because of a further breach of the publicity principle
arising because of the partial discharge of the attached charge
by a deed known only to a few persons. This, however, appears
to be a risk which conveyancing practitioners and the Keeper
regard as acceptable.[54]

Negative Servitudes

3.24   Negative servitudes may be created by delivery of an unrecorded
deed[55] and involve no possession or exercise which may put
purchasers of the servient tenement or anyone else on notice of its
existence.[56] They are regarded as an anomaly in the law which is not
to be lightly extended.[57] The reforms of the law relative to title
conditions presently being considered by the Scottish Law
Commission may result in it being no longer possible to create
negative servitudes. If this reform occurs it is likely that their place
will be taken by real burdens imposing negative restraints.[58] These
will be evident upon a search in either the dominant or servient
tenement.

Public Rights of Way

3.25   In theory the same difficulty with the lack of a public act may
arise in relation to the case of a public right of way created by
express grant in an unrecorded deed. It has been commented that
there is no authority for saying that exercise of the right by the
public is essential in such circumstances to create the right as a real
right.[59] If this is correct it may give rise to problems if the public
right of way is conferred on certain conditions which impose a
positive duty on the public, as the right may be created without any
exercise to indicate the general public's acceptance of those
conditions. Given that the vast majority of public rights of way

---

54   *"From the Registers"*, 1997 J.L.S.S. 507; *Registration of Title Practice Book* (2nd
     ed., 2000), para. 5.37; Gretton and Reid, *supra*, para. 29.06.
55   Gordon, *Scottish Land Law* (2nd. ed.), para. 24–29. See, *e.g.*, *Mearns v. Massie*
     (1800) Hume 736.
56   Cusine and Paisley, *Servitudes and Rights of Way*, para. 6.31.
57   *Sivright v. Wilson* (1828) 7S. 210 per Lord Gillies at 213; Cusine and Paisley,
     Servitudes and Rights of Way, para. 1.31; Gloag and Henderson, *Law of Scotland*
     (10th ed.), para. 40.27.
58   Scot. Law Com., *Discussion Paper on Real Burdens* (No. 106, Oct. 1998), paras
     2.49–2.50.
59   18 *Stair Memorial Encyclopaedia*, para. 498. See this text, para. 10.04.

are created by exercise for the prescriptive period[60] this does not create a major problem in practice.

Protection During the Intervening Period

In relation to real rights there is usually a time gap between the 3.26 creation of the contractual right and the real right on the part of the acquiring party. The existence of this time gap causes a difficulty in conveyancing practice because the purchaser of a plot of land almost invariably pays the purchase price in exchange for delivery of the disposition. That is the universal requirement of missives in standard form. Similar situations arise in relation to a tenant acquiring a lease or a bank lending on the security of a standard security. In all cases the acquiring party will have delivered his cash or cheque to the granter of the right but will have received in exchange only a personal right. The acquiring party remains at risk for a number of reasons.

(a) First, the granter may have already made or intends to make another grant to a third party which will be created real before the acquiring party's right is made real.[61] Where this involves two competing rights of exclusive property or lease this will result in the acquiring party obtaining no title. Where it involves two securities it will result in the acquiring party obtaining a security but one which is postponed in ranking. Where the grant to the third party is another subsidiary real right such as a servitude, the right obtained by the acquiring party may be subject to that servitude right.

(b) Secondly, the granter may be insolvent and if a trustee in bankruptcy, liquidator, receiver or administrator is appointed the acquiring party may find he is unable to prevail against the title of that insolvency practitioner or the rights of creditors.

Conveyancing practice has evolved several methods of managing this situation although none of them exclude the risks altogether. Full details of how these methods work in practice should be sought in a textbook on conveyancing and only an outline will be given here. The main legal devices employed are as follows:

(a) practical steps to make the gap period as short as possible;
(b) letters of obligation;
(c) the warrandice of the granter;

---

60 Prescription and Limitation (Scotland) Act 1973, s.3(3).
61 18 *Stair Memorial Encyclopaedia*, para. 684.

    (d)   the "offside goals" rule; and

    (e)   reliance on *Sharp v. Thomson* or "trust" clauses.

Shortening the Gap Period

3.27   Steps may be taken to shorten the gap period. These are largely practical matters. Whilst the public registers and stamp office remain located only in Edinburgh some delay in transporting the deed to Edinburgh is inevitable if the settlement takes place elsewhere. A period of a week between settlement and recording is not unusual in residential conveyancing practice. Settlement does not, however, require to take place where the property is located. What are known as "presentation book" settlements sometimes occur where a risk to a purchaser is perceived as being particularly acute. These are settlements at a place in Edinburgh, possibly in or near the public registers. Once the settlement occurs the deed is promptly stamped and recorded—usually within a matter of hours. In extraordinary cases the stamp office may be prepared to accept the presenting agent's obligation to pay stamp duty and written confirmation of this arrangement may be sufficient to permit the Keeper to accept the deed for recording. Where a bank is giving a loan to a company and in return is obtaining a floating charge and standard security it may seek to elide the risks of the gap period by other means. It may require the granting and registration of the floating charge to be completed before the money is drawn-down. On the draw-down date the standard security is delivered but the bank will have already a form of security for the money advanced in the form of the floating charge. There is therefore no gap period without a form of security. This practice is available only to creditors taking security from a company.

Letter of Obligation

3.28   The bringing down of reports and interim reports on search in the Sasine, Land and company charges registers may provide some objective evidence to show that the seller has not granted a competing real right which has already been recorded or is the subject of an application for registration. With the limitations of present technology these searches are never fully up to date and there still will remain a brief gap before settlement although the increasing use of increasingly sophisticated computer technology by the Registers of Scotland will tend to limit the risk. The massive investment of time and effort by the Registers of Scotland in this regard is to be commended. There will also be a gap after settlement before the title of the acquiring party is made real. To provide the purchaser with some protection in respect of these two gap periods the seller's solicitor may issue a letter of obligation.[62] By granting this letter of obligation the seller's solicitor grants his personal obligation, *inter alia*, that no prejudicial or competing deed granted by the seller will be recorded or given effect to in the Sasine or Land Registers. In effect the selling solicitors are acting as guarantors for their client. To a certain extent the solicitor's obligation may be covered by the solicitor's professional indemnity insurance.[63] It is therefore a valuable personal right on the part of the purchaser. There are usually a number of express limitations on this personal obligation. The primary one is that it is a temporary and not a permanent obligation and is usually stated to relate only to a period of 14 days after settlement. Secondly, the obligation usually does not cover the granting of rights which can be made real by possession. In respect of the company charges register the obligation given by the selling solicitor under current practice is on behalf of the selling company only.[64] If the selling company is insolvent the obligation is probably worthless.

Warrandice of the Granter

In most transactions a party granting a deed relative to the creation or transfer of a real right undertakes an obligation known as warrandice. In the simplest of situations involving the purchase of a property right in a plot of land the obligation is contained in the missives and the disposition. Warrandice comprises various warranties and obligations on the part of the granter. Most of these will be outlined in the following paragraphs on guarantee of title and the details of the technicalities may be sought in textbooks on conveyancing. In the context of competing rights, however, one obligation has direct relevance. This is the obligation on the part of the seller that he will not by future acts prejudice the title conferred in the transferee.[65] The obligation will be breached by grant of a second disposition in respect of the property[66] or the grant of a second standard security.[67] The warranty runs from the date of conclusion of missives so in respect of grants made before then which have either already been made real or have not yet been made

3.29

---

62 McDonald, *Conveyancing Manual* (6th ed.), paras 33.44–33.52; Gretton and Reid, *Conveyancing* (2nd. ed.), paras 9.26–9.27.
63 Rennie, *Letters of Obligation*, 1993 J.L.S.S. 431–433.
64 Gretton and Reid, *Conveyancing* (2nd. ed.), para. 28.10.
65 18 *Stair Memorial Encyclopaedia*, para. 706.
66 *Smith v. Ross* (1672) M. 16596; *Rodger (Builders) Ltd v. Fawdry* 1950 S.C. 483.
67 *Trade Development Bank v. Crittal Windows Ltd*, 1983 S.L.T. 510.

real, the grantee will require to rely on some of the other warranties inherent in warrandice. The normal remedy for breach of warrandice is damages. An obligation in warrandice is merely a personal obligation and is worthless where the granter is a man of straw.

The "Offside Goals" Rule

3.30   An owner of property may oblige himself expressly as a matter of contract not to alienate except to a certain named party or to give a certain named party a pre-emption.[68] This express obligation is commonly found in options to purchase.[69] As we have seen above[70] a similar obligation against a double sale is comprised within a grant of warrandice where the owner of the property has contracted to sell the property to a certain party or has delivered a disposition to that party. In certain circumstances a purported alienation may be voidable and any acquisition of a real right following thereon reducible at the instance of the party in whose favour the obligation not to alienate has been granted.[71] This is known as the "offside goals" rule. It can apply not only to give protection against second grants adverse to the transfer of a property right[72] (whether in respect of a second disposition or the grant of an adverse subordinate real right such as a standard security[73]) but also to second grants which are adverse to the grant of the subordinate real rights such as servitude.[74] The application of the doctrine has met resistance in relation to standard securities.[75] It does not operate to protect the grant of personal rights which cannot become real rights against adverse grants of other real rights.[76]

    The following are the requirements for the application of the offside goals rule:

(a)   the granter must be under an antecedent obligation not to make the second grant;

---

68 *Matheson v. Tinney*, 1989 S.L.T. 535; *Roebuck v. Edmunds* 1992 S.C.L.R. 74.
69 *Davidson v. Zani* 1992 S.C.L.R. 1001.
70 Para. 3.29.
71 18 *Stair Memorial Encyclopaedia*, paras 600, 690 and 695–700.
72 *Rodger (Builders) Ltd v. Fawdry*, 1950 S.C. 483.
73 *Trade Development Bank v. Crittall Windows Ltd*, 1983 S.L.T. 510.
74 *Greig v. Brown* (1829) 7 S. 274.
75 *Scotlife Home Loans (No.2) Ltd v. W. & A. S. Bruce*, Sh.P. J.J. Maguire, Q.C., 4th Sept. 1994 (unreported), overruling the sheriff's judgment of 17th June 1994, Dunfermline Sheriff Court. See also *Scotlife Home Loans (No.2) Ltd v. Muir*, 1994 S.C.L.R. 791 and *Leslie v. McIndoes Trs* (1824) 3 S. 48.
76 *Wallace v. Simmers*, 1960 S.C. 255.

(b) the second grant must breach the terms of that obligation;
(c) prior to the creation of his right as a real right the grantee in the second grant must know of the existence of the existing obligation or the second grant must not be for value. A grantee is deemed to know of the contents of relevant deeds or entries in the Sasine or Land Register.[77]

The usual remedy sought by the party entitled to the antecedent obligation is to reduce the second grant. This is common in respect of a double sale. In other cases it is more appropriate to have the grantee in the second grant held bound by the antecedent obligation. For example, where the antecedent obligation relates to the grant of a subordinate real right such as a servitude and the second grant is a disposition of the property right in the servient tenement it is more convenient to have the grantee in that disposition declared bound by the servitude.[78] Although the "offside goals" rule may be described as "an equitable solution" to the problem of double grants,[79] it is not an instance of equitable rights (in the English sense) trumping legal rights and creates no "equitable" real right or *quasi*-real right on the part of the party entitled to the antecedent personal obligation.

Sharp v. Thomson

It is possible to construct an argument that the delivery of a 3.31
disposition may confer on the grantee a "beneficial interest" which protects the grantee in the period before the recording of the deed in the Sasine Register or registration of the interest in the Land Register of Scotland.[80] This protection may, according to this theory, prevail against a receiver in an attached floating charge[81] or, even more controversially, against a trustee in bankruptcy appointed to the estate of the granter.[82] The law is currently the subject of a divergence of views, but if the notion of a "beneficial interest" is ultimately accepted as part of Scots law it is possible that the "beneficial interest" created by the delivery of such a

---

77 *Trade Development Bank v. Warriner and Mason (Scotland) Ltd*, 1980 S.C. 74. See also para. 3.19.
78 *Greig v. Brown* (1829) 7S. 274.
79 18 *Stair Memorial Encyclopaedia*, para. 695.
80 *Cf.* McDonald, *Conveyancing Manual* (6th ed.), para. 4.1.
81 *Sharp v. Thomson*, 1997 S.L.T. 636, H.L., per Lord Jauncey.
82 *Burnett's Tr. v. Grainger*, 2000 S.L.T. (Sh.Ct.) 116; *Inglis v. Mansfield* (1835) 1 Sh. and McL. 203 per Lord Brougham at 338–339; *Brock v. Cabbell* (1830) 8 S. 647 aff'd (1831) 476.

disposition is a form of temporary real right which fills the gap between the contractual stage and the public creation of a real right. This is highly controversial and, in the author's view, totally spurious. At its widest the decision in *Sharp v. Thomson*[83] may be regarded as authority on the construction of the phrase "property and undertaking" where used in the Companies Acts to indicate those things falling within the ambit of a floating charge and to exclude the subjects of a delivered disposition from that definition.

Declaration of Trust

3.32   Recently a practice has arisen in which an express trust clause is inserted in a disposition. The theory is that in the period between the delivery of the disposition and its recording the disponer will hold the property in trust for the disponee. The intention is to protect the disponee against the disponer's insolvency and to preclude the disponer from making a second grant. The intention is presumably that the trust terminates when the grantee's right is made real by registration. More recently there has been a trend in practice to insert a clause stating that the trust will come to an end at a particular time—usually coinciding with the time limit in the accompanying letter of obligation. It is open to argument whether this clause really does create a trust.[84] If it does, however, there is some protection for the grantees as beneficiaries. Creditors of a trustee are unable to attach trust property.[85] Those who acquire from a trustee in bad faith may have their rights reduced at the instance of the beneficiaries. This is an application of the offside goals rule which has been fortified by statute.[86] This is not an instance of a temporary real right as the beneficiary's right in a trust is not a real right.[87] One writer has suggested calling this right a *ius ad rem* or a personal right of property[88] but this phraseology has not met with judicial acceptance.[89]

---

83 1997 S.L.T. 636, HL.
84 A.J.M. Steven and S. Wortley, "*The Perils of a Trusting Disposition*", 1996 S.L.T. (News) 365; Gretton and Reid, *Conveyancing* (2nd ed.), para. 11.31.
85 *Heritable Reversionary Co. Ltd v. Millar* (1892) 19R. (H.L.) 43; Bankruptcy (Scotland) Act 1985, s.33(1)(b); *Bank of Scotland v. Liquidators of Hutchison, Main & Co.*, 1914 S.C. (H.L.) 1.
86 Trusts (Scotland) Act 1961, s.2. The requirement for good faith is controversial and one reading of the 1961 Act, s.2 suggests it is not necessary. See further K. Reid, "Trusts nd Floating Charges", 1987 S.L.T. (News) 113.
87 18 *Stair Memorial Encyclopaedia*, para. 10(1).
88 Mclaren, *Law of Wills and Succession* Vol. II, para. 1527.
89 *Johnston v. MacFarlane*, 1987 S.C.L.R. 104.

Statutory Protection

The Scottish Law Commission has proposed the introduction of 3.33 a statutory priority period of 14 days during which a purchaser can register a disposition and create a real right unaffected by the seller's insolvency.[90] This does not deal with the issue of second adverse grants.

Guarantee of Title

A person who wishes to acquire a real right frequently does so in 3.34 the context of a conveyancing transaction. In this context the acquiring party may have the benefit of several personal rights which, to various extents, guarantee the proper creation of the real right. In outline these are as follows:

(a) The warrandice granted by the granter in missives and the disposition (or standard security, deed of servitude or lease as the case may be). Subject to special as qualification the seller's obligations under this warrandice comprise three warranties to the following effects: (i) the title is absolutely good; (ii) there are no subordinate real rights; (iii) there are no unusual real conditions; and there is an obligation on the seller not to carry out any future acts prejudicial to the title.[91]
(b) In respect of Land Registered interests the Keeper may issue a state indemnity.[92]
(c) Where there are certain defects in title which have been discovered in the course of a title examination the acquiring party may be able to obtain a title indemnity from a firm of professional private title insurers
(d) Where title contains defects which were not discovered in the course of a title examination the acquiring party may be able to recover from his solicitor. That solicitor may be liable if a client fails to obtain a real right because of the solicitor's negligence.[93]

Real Rights—Manner of Extinction

The important instances of extinction of real rights include: 3.35

---

90 Scot. Law Com., *Discussion Paper on Diligence against Land*, (No. 107, 1998), paras 2.39–2.60.
91 18 *Stair Memorial Encyclopaedia*, paras 702–714.
92 Land Registration (Scotland) Act 1979, ss 9 and 12.
93 Rennie, *Solicitors' Negligence*, Chap. 6.

(a) negative prescription;
(b) positive prescription;
(c) abolition by statute;
(d) expiry of term;
(e) renunciation;
(f) irritancy;
(g) confusion;
(h) destruction of the thing;
(i) separation from land;
(j) loss of territory.

Certain of these matters, including positive and negative prescription, have already been examined above.[94] The others are briefly outlined below.

Abolition by Statute

3.36   Statute may provide for the extinction of property and any of the other real rights. It may do so by provision extinguishing rights without further process.[95] More common, however, are provisions which establish a procedure for the extinction of real rights usually involving notice to the entitled party, a form of hearing before a court or tribunal and payment of compensation. Typical of the latter are the provisions of Part I of the Conveyancing and Feudal Reform (Scotland) Act 1970 which enable "land obligations" (including servitudes) to be varied or discharged by application to the Lands Tribunal. Compulsory purchase may also extinguish servitudes and real burdens affecting the lands acquired.[95a]

Expiry of Term

3.37   Some real rights such as property are perpetual and expiry of term has no relevance to their extinction. Where a real right exists only for a period of time it will terminate at the end of that period. For example a proper liferent will terminate at the death of the liferenter or any earlier date specified in the grant.[96] A lease will terminate at the ish date provided a suitable notice has been timeously sent to prevent continuation of the right by means of tacit

---

94 Paras 2.22 and 3.13.
95 *E.g.* the extinction of public rights of navigation in Paisley Corporation (Cart Navigation) Order Confirmation Act 1971, Sched., para. 4. See also Abolition of Feudal Tenure etc. (Scotland) Act 2000, ss 2 and 64.
95a See paras 8.25 and 9.26.
96 Gordon, *Scottish Land Law* (2nd. ed.), paras 17–65–17–66.

relocation. Certain other real rights such as servitudes and public rights of way are normally perpetual but they may be created for a limited period of time if created by express grant containing a suitable limitation as to duration.[97] It remains undecided whether tacit relocation applies to extend servitudes originally granted expressly for a limited duration.[98]

Renunciation

Any *ius in re aliena* will be extinguished when the party entitled to 3.38 the right renounces it in favour of the party owning the real right subject to that *ius in re aliena*. There are some specialities in relation to the renunciation of liferents which will be outlined later in this book.[99]

A separate issue arises as to whether the holder of the *ius in re aliena* has a right to renounce unilaterally. A servitude may be renounced in whole or in part by the dominant proprietor without the consent of the servient proprietor unless the grant provides otherwise.[1] Similarly the creditor in a proper liferent,[2] a standard security and floating charge may renounce in whole or in part the security without the consent of the debtor. The tenant in a lease may not renounce his lease unilaterally without the consent of the landlord unless the lease contains a "break" clause.[3] Where a real right is to be renounced the renunciation should be in writing.[4] Unless there is a contrary requirement in the document creating the original real right or in statute (as is the case with a standard security),[5] there is no prescribed form for a renunciation of a real right. Some statutes provide a form of discharge which may be used but is not prescribed.[6]

Irritancy

Irritancy is a remedy which may be available to the landlord in a 3.39 lease where it is implied by law in relation to non-payment of rent

---

97 Cusine and Paisley, *Servitudes and Rights of Way*, paras 2.89–2.92.
98 Cusine and Paisley, *supra*, para. 2.92.
99 Para 6.11.
1   Cusine and Paisley, *supra* paras 12.141, 14.62 and 17.02.
2   Gordon, *Scottish Land Law* (2nd. ed.), para. 17–69.
3   Para 7.39.
4   Requirements of Writing (Scotland) Act 1995, s.1(2)(b).
5   Conveyancing and Feudal Reform (Scotland) Act 1970, s.17 and Sched. 4, Form F.
6   Registration of Leases (Scotland) Act 1857, s.13 and Sched. (G).

by the tenant[7] and may be limited, varied or extended to other obligations of the tenant by a suitable conventional provision. In relation to servitudes,[8] proper liferent[9] or a public right of way, a remedy of irritancy is not implied by law but may be conferred respectively on the servient proprietor, fiar and proprietor of the *solum* provided suitable drafting is employed. The remedy of irritancy in favour of superiors in respect of property rights was abolished as part of the abolition of the feudal system of landholding.[10]

Confusion

3.40   *Confusio* is a term which may denote two entirely separate matters. First it may denote the mixing of liquids which results in the mixture being owned in common by the owners of the separate liquids.[11] This has no relevance to land or rights in land. Secondly, it denotes the means of extinction of the certain subordinate real rights when the right and the right from which it is derived come to be owned by the one party. This second doctrine applies to contractual rights, rights in land such as real conditions enforceable *in personam*[12] and certain real rights. The real rights which may be extinguished in this way at common law are the *iura in re aliena* which include proper liferents[13] and servitudes[14] but in the latter case the rule is likely to be altered by statutory reform.[15]

Confusio does not apply to a right of property because it is not derived from any other right and there are no two separate rights which can come into the same ownership. In theory *confusio* could apply to public rights such as public rights of way. A landowner will never be able to enforce a public right of way against himself. Nevertheless, as public rights of way remain enforceable by all members of the public by *actio popularis*,[16] the doctrine will never be applicable until either the population of Scotland is reduced to a

---

7   *Nisbet v. Aikman* (1866) 4M. 284; Agricultural Holdings (Scotland) Act 1991, s.20; Gordon, *Scottish Land Law* (2nd. ed.), para. 19–59.
8   Cusine and Paisley, *Servitudes and Rights of Way*, paras 1.80 and 12.179.
9   Gordon, *Scottish Land Law* (2nd. ed.), para. 17–67.
10 Abolition of Feudal Tenure etc. (Scotland) Act 2000, s.53.
11 18 *Stair Memorial Encyclopaedia*, para. 564.
12 Gordon, *supra*, para. 23–18.
13 *Martin v. Bannatyne* (1861) 23D. 705; Gordon, *supra*, para. 17–68.
14 Gordon, *supra*, paras 24–96–24–98; Cusine and Paisley, *supra*, paras 17.22–17.31.
15 Scot. Law Com., *Discussion Paper on Real Burdens* (No. 106, Oct. 1998), paras 5.53–5.59.
16 Chap. 10.

single individual who owns all the land therein, or the whole land in Scotland is nationalised together with all rights to enforce public rights of way.

Destruction of the Thing

If the land which is the subject of a real right is destroyed, the real right in it will be extinguished. Actual destruction rarely happens to land in Scotland because the country is usually not subject to violent acts of nature. It is, however, possible for small coastal areas of land to fall into the sea and a right of property and all subsidiary real rights in this land could be extinguished in this way. More normal occurrences are less dramatic. Where a building is demolished the proprietor of that building will still retain a right of property in the airspace previously occupied by that building. Similarly, where an owner of a minerals reservation digs out the minerals and removes them he will retain ownership in the worked-out space. Unless the terms of the grant require otherwise, a servitude in favour of a particular plot of ground is not extinguished simply because the building standing on the dominant tenement is subsequently demolished. The servitude will continue to exist for buildings which are constructed on the subjects as part of a redevelopment project.[17] Where the subjects of lease are destroyed the parties to the lease may regard it as having come to an end by virtue of the doctrine of *rei interitus*. The option of both landlord and tenant to do so is frequently varied by contrary provision in terms of a commercial lease. In relation to usufruct of a house the Roman law rule was that the right would come to an end if the house was destroyed.[18] The rule in Scots law in respect of proper liferent is less strict and where a house subject to a liferent is destroyed, either the fiar or the liferenter have a right to rebuild it.[19] This may be expressly confirmed in the deed of grant.

Destruction can also apply to rights and lead to the termination not only of that right but also other rights deriving therefrom. For example, where a lease is terminated by irritancy all subordinate real rights deriving from the lease such as a security over the tenant's interest will be terminated.[20] Statute may provide otherwise

3.41

---

17 *Irvine Knitters Ltd v. North Ayrshire Cooperative Society Ltd*, 1978 S.C. 109.
18 D. 7.4.5–12. see para. 6.11.
19 Ersk, II,ix,60; Bell, *Prin*, S.1063.
20 For this reason lenders seek special protection when lending on the security of a lease. See Ross and McKichan, *Drafting and Negotiating Commercial Leases in Scotland* (2nd. ed.), para. 12.7.

Land Law

and ensure the continuance of existing derivative rights: such has been the case in relation to the termination of interposed leases,[21] kindly tenancies,[22] and *dominium utile*.[23]

Cessation of Purpose

3.42   A disposition or deed of conditions may impose real conditions which restrict the purposes for which a property may be used. Feudal irritancy having been abolished,[23a] the right of property will not come to an end when the permitted use ceases. It is still possible, however, that a right of reversion or pre-emption may exist under which the property must be transferred to the party holding that right if a particular use ceases. The efficacy of such rights has been limited by statute[24] and may be further constrained.[25] When exercised, the effect of such rights is to transfer a property right rather than to extinguish it.

Where a real right other than a right of property is created for a certain purpose it may terminate when that purpose is achieved or ceases to be capable of achievement. For example, where a servitude is granted for the purposes of constructing a particular building it will cease to exist when the building is erected. Difficult questions may arise as to whether the performance of the act specified in the stated purpose has been rendered incapable of performance on a temporary or permanent basis. Such may be the case in respect of a servitude of access for the purposes of maintenance. Where subsequent building works render maintenance unnecessary it is possible that the servitude may be "suspended" during the endurance of the subsequent building works but it may not be fully extinguished and may revive when these works are demolished.[26] Payment of the underlying debt or performance of the underlying obligation will discharge the security.[27] A lease may contain an express clause indicating that the property is let only for the purpose of carrying out certain specified activity on the subjects of let and when such activity ceases

---

21 Land Tenure Reform (Scotland) Act 1974, s.17(2).
22 Abolition of Feudal Tenure etc. (Scotland) Act 2000, s.64(2).
23 2000 Act, s.2(1). This will, of course, be immediately replaced with ownership.
23a 2000 Act, s.53.
24 Conveyancing Amendment (Scotland) Act 1938, s.9; Land Tenure Reform (Scotland) Act 1974, s.12.
25 Scot. Law Com., *Discussion Paper on Real Burdens* (No. 106, Oct. 1998), paras 8.1–8.69.
26 *Gray v. Macleod*, 1979 S.L.T. (Sh.Ct.) 17.
27 *Cameron v. Williamson* (1895) 22R. 293.

the lease will terminate *ipso facto*. Alternatively the landlord or tenant may be given an option to terminate the lease when the relevant activity ceases.

Separation from Land

In the treatment of the doctrine of accession it has been noted   3.43 that in certain cases the right of property in the accessory may be extinguished when the accessory is separated from the principal.[28] In other cases certain subordinate real rights confer on the grantee the right to extract material from land in such a way as to convert it into a moveable product. Frequently encountered instances include a minerals lease under which the tenant extracts material such as stone, and servitudes of fuel, feal and divot in which the dominant proprietor extracts turf and peat. In both cases the material to be extracted belongs to the owner of the land whilst the material forms part of the land but upon extraction the ownership of that proprietor is extinguished. After extraction the material is moveable and belongs to the party entitled to the right.[29]

Loss of Territory

Given the attempts to outlaw aggressive war in international law   3.44 one would trust that this will remain of historic interest only. The two principal losses of territory suffered by Scotland have been that of Berwick to the English and Rathlin to the Ulster Scots.[30] These lands are now respectively subject to English and Northern Irish law and all property rights conferred by Scots law have been extinguished.[31] It remains possible, however, that part of the Kingdom of Scotland could secede or part of the territory could be given away by voluntary act. Presumably any modern treaty would make express provision for acquired property rights. In this respect one should note that the island of Rockall is subject to a territorial claim by the Irish republic but there is no sign that the land is to be surrendered by Scotland.

---

28 Para 3.11.
29 Cusine and Paisley, *Servitudes and Rights of Way*, para. 1.43.
30 This may be of greater cultural significance than might at first be thought. It is reputed to be the location of the cave in which Robert the Bruce saw the persistent spider inspiring him to return to the Scottish mainland and defeat the English.
31 The Wales and Berwick Act 1746 (20 Geo.2, c.42), s.3. There is no statute relative to Rathlin.

Extinction and Marketability

3.45   Where a real right, particularly one of the *iura in re aliena*, is originally created by a method which involves recording or registration in a public register it is not necessary for its extinction that the method of its extinction involves an entry in the same public register effecting an acknowledging of its extinction. The Keeper, however, may note the discharge of an overriding interest in the Land Register with a view to making it as comprehensive as possible.[32]

Nevertheless, where such an express entry is lacking it may be difficult to convince a purchaser of any right of property or other interest which bears to be affected by that real right, that the title to the right of property is marketable. "Marketability" varies according to the general requirements of the market and conveyancing practice in this regard will change from time to time. Nevertheless, at present it is clearly advantageous to have an express recorded discharge of a real burden or a servitude which has been expressly constituted by recorded deed.[33] The same applies to standard securities even though the underlying personal obligation has been discharged.[34] In current practice it is acceptable to acquire an ex-local authority house from the first purchaser without an express discharge of the standard security in favour of the local authority where this relates to the first purchaser's obligation to repay the discount and the period for repayment has expired.[35]

The disadvantage of many methods of extinction of real rights is that they require the determination that a particular set of facts exist at a certain time before the relevant legal doctrine may be applied. In modern commercial practice many purchasers (and their banks) are not prepared to take a view on this matter and, instead, prefer to insist that the seller put the matter beyond doubt by having the matter judicially declared. The Lands Tribunal have no jurisdiction to discharge land obligations which have already been discharged by other doctrines such as *confusio* or loss of interest to enforce and they cannot issue an order for the purposes of permitting the applicant to record the extract and clear the public

---

32 Land Registration (Scotland) Act 1979, s.6(1)(g); *Registration of Title Practice Book*, (2nd. ed.), (2000), para. 5.72.
33 Cusine and Paisley, *Servitudes and Rights of Way*, para. 17.04.
34 *Cameron v. Williamson* (1895) 22R. 393. Cusine, *Standard Securities*, para. 10.03.
35 Housing (Scotland) Act 1987, s.72(5).

record.[36] It may be that such a jurisdiction will be conferred upon the Lands Tribunal as part of the reform of the law relative to real conditions.[37]

---

36 *McCarthy & Stone (Developments) Ltd v. Smith*, 1995 S.L.T. (Lands Tr.) 19; *Geddes v. Cluny Trs*, 25 Jan. 1993; LTS/LO/1992/23 (right of pre-emption); Agnew of Lochnaw, *Land Obligations*, para. 3–18. For a similar position in England see *Re Purkiss's Application* [1962] 1 W.L.R. 902 per the Master of the Rolls at 908.
37 Scot. Law Com., *Discussion Paper on Real Burdens* (No. 106, Oct. 1998), Pt 6.

Chapter 4

PROPERTY

Introduction

4.1   The right of ownership is potentially the most extensive right in respect of an item of property.[1] It therefore follows that no two or more persons may hold simultaneously a full right of ownership in the same piece of land. The examples of co-ownership and the various rights of beneficiaries and trustees in land falling within the trust are not exceptions to this principle.

Definitions of Ownership

4.2   It is difficult to identify a satisfactory comprehensive definition of the right of property but incidents of it may be observed in a brief review of definitions which have been offered in various contexts. The right of property has been defined by Erskine as "the right of using and disposing of a subject as our own, except in so far as we are restrained by law or paction".[2] Many of these restrictions will be detailed in the later chapters of this book. Lord Halsbury L.C. addressed the issue by reference to the holder of the right[3]: "A person who is entitled to exclude anyone else, and who is himself entitled to enjoy and possess a thing, must be, in any ordinary sense of the term, the proprietor." The traditional definition of ownership in Civilian systems has been the right of use, enjoyment and abuse (*ius utendi, ius fruendi, ius abutendi*).[4] Whilst they shed some light on ownership, most of these definitions do not take analysis particularly far and they may be regarded as of no more than limited assistance.

---

1   Van der Merwe and de Waal, *The Law of Things and Servitudes*, para. 9.
2   Erskine, *Inst.*, II,i,1. See also Stair, *Inst.*, II,i,2B.
3   *Glasgow Corporation v. McEwan* (1899) 2F. (H.L.) 25 at 26.
4   18 *Stair Memorial Encyclopaedia*, para. 5.

Powers of Owner

The right of ownership may be analysed by reference to the 4.3 specific rights of the owner in relation to the thing owned. This should not be taken to suggest that the term ownership is itself meaningless except to denote a basketful of lesser rights. A right of property of land confers upon the owner the following particular rights:

(a) the right to carry out juristic acts such as alienation and the grant of subsidiary real rights over the land; and

(b) the right to carry out physical acts in relation to the land such as use, enjoyment and possession of the land and to exclude others from doing so.

Limitations on Juristic Acts

A proprietor of land may usually transfer his right of property to 4.4 others, subdivide it and grant derivative real rights such as a lease, a proper liferent and standard security all as he sees fit. There are, however, various limitations on the exercise and existence of the right to carry out such juristic acts and some of these have already been noted above in the context of property *intra commercium* and *extra commercium*,[5] warrandice and second grants.[6] Other restrictions may exist where a property is co-owned.[7] This paragraph will examine restrictions on juristic acts imposed by real conditions.

Any attempt to create as real conditions obligations which are "repugnant to the common legal notion of property" will fail.[8] Obligations of this sort are invalid as real conditions.[9] This class of invalid real conditions includes obligations which purport to prohibit the exercise of juristic acts such as disponing a right of property, granting a lease[10] and the seeking of a division and sale where property is held in common. It is, however, possible to impose qualified restrictions on the exercise of juristic acts. Two particular types of qualified restrictions are enforceable. These are:

(a) pre-emptions; and

(b) limitations on subdivision.

---

5   Paras 1.24–1.28.
6   Paras 3.29 and 3.30.
7   Chapter 5.
8   *Moir's Trs v. McEwan* (1880) 7R. 1141 per Lord Young at 1145.
9   18 *Stair Memorial Encyclopaedia*, para. 391.
10 *Moir's Trs v. McEwan* (1880) 7R. 1141 per Lord Young at 1145

Pre-emptions

4.5   A pre-emption does not entirely deprive the proprietor of his
right to dispone the property but limits his right to do so. In current
practice the most frequently encountered form of pre-emption
declares that the proprietor shall have no power to alienate the
property unless he has first offered to sell the same to the party
entitled to the pre-emption. Whilst such rights remain competent,
statute has progressively limited the circumstances under which
such rights may be exercised.[11] More restrictions may be enacted in
the context of reform of the law relative to title conditions.[12] A
disposition in breach of a right of pre-emption may be reduced by
the party entitled to the pre-emption[13] but he may not force the
proprietor to sell to him unless the terms of the clause are suitably
expansive.[14] Such an expansive clause is more an option to
purchase than a pre-emption, and is rare. Where a pre-emption is
also a land obligation the servient proprietor may apply to the
Lands Tribunal for its variation or discharge.[15] Pre-emptions in
favour of superiors may be reallocated to another tenement in terms
of feudal reform legislation.[15a]

Limitations on Subdivision

4.6   The right to subdivide land feudally will be removed as part of
the abolition of the feudal system.[16] What remains competent is
geographical subdivision and it is to this alone that this paragraph
will refer. Subdivision is basically the sale of an existing plot of land
in more than one unit or the sale of a part with the retention of the
remainder. The right of subdivision of a property may be restricted
by means of real conditions imposed in conveyances of land or
deeds of declaration of conditions. In such cases the party entitled
to enforce the condition may interdict a threatened transaction
which violates the title condition, and completed transactions which

---

11 Conveyancing Amendment (Scotland) Act 1938, s.9, as amended by Conveyan-
     cing and Feudal Reform (Scotland) Act 1970, s.46, and Land Tenure Reform
     (Scotland) 1974, s.13.
12 Scot. Law Com., *Discussion Paper on Real Burdens* (No. 106, Oct. 1998), paras
     8.1–8.69.
13 *Matheson v. Tinney*, 1989 S.L.T. 535.
14 *Roebuck v. Edmonds*, 1992 S.L.T. 1055.
15 *MacDonald, Applicant* 1973 S.L.T. (Lands Tr.) 26; *Banff and Buchan Dist. C. v.
     Earl of Seafield's Estate*, 1988 S.L.T. (Lands Tr.) 21; Gordon, *Scottish Land Law*
     (2nd ed.), para. 25–03.
15a See para. 9.8.
16 Abolition of Feudal Tenure etc. (Scotland) Act 2000, s.2(3).

violate the restriction may be reducible at the instance of the party entitled to enforce the title condition, but the transaction is not void. A limitation on subdivision commonly occurs in two types of situations. First, a number of sites may be conveyed for the purposes of the construction of a single house with a large garden. To avoid the lowering of the tone of the neighbourhood by the building of additional houses in the gardens of any of the sites or the conversion of a house into flats, the titles to each site contains not only a restriction on change of use and a prohibition on future development but also a restriction on subdivision.[17] The second example relates not to a single site but two smaller sites linked by function. Where a house is conveyed together with a garage or bin store located on an adjacent or neighbouring site a real condition in the heritable title to the bin store or garage and house may stipulate that each may not be conveyed separately from each other. There seems to be little doubt that such restrictions are valid in both types of cases.

The Right of Use and Enjoyment

The right of use, enjoyment and possession in the abstract will permit the owner to use his property in any manner he sees fit. He may build dens of iniquity or temples of righteousness, sow and reap crops, or do nothing at all if he pleases. So stated the definition bears little relation to real life. The right of property may be (and usually is) limited by agreement and invariably is restricted by the common law and statute especially where it tends to injure the rights of others or exposes them to danger.[18] Such limitations derogate from the "absolute" nature of the right.[19] So numerous are these limitations that it would be futile to attempt a complete list here. Nevertheless, some of the more commonly encountered limitations are as follows:

4.7

(a) limitations on geographic extent;
(b) limitations arising because of extent of legal share;
(c) limitations arising from agreement;
(d) statutory limitations; and
(e) common law limitations such as nuisance.

Limitations on geographic extent will be examined in the context

---

17 See, *e.g. Girls School Company Ltd v. Buchanan*, 1958 S.L.T. (Notes) 2; *Williamson and Hubbard v. Harrison*, 1970 S.L.T. 346.
18 Bell, *Prin.*, s. 939.
19 Bell, *Prin*, s.939; 18 *Stair Memorial Encyclopaedia*, para. 195.

of boundaries later in this chapter.[20] Limitations arising from extent of legal share will be examined in the context of co-ownership in the following chapter. The others will be examined in the following paragraphs after a brief note concerning subordinate rights.

Limitations on Subordinate Rights conferred by Proprietor

4.8   For simplicity, these five types of limitation will be outlined in this book only in respect of the actual exercise of a right of *dominium* by the proprietor. Nevertheless it should be noted that they all limit the full and free exercise of any of the subordinate real rights such as lease or servitude by which the proprietor of land confers the right on others to use his land. For example, a servitude may be exercised only within the geographic extent of the servient tenement,[21] it may be limited by conventional servitude conditions,[22] a dominant proprietor requires to comply with statutory limitations on the exercise of his right and it is no defence to an action of interdict based in nuisance to assert that the party creating the nuisance is entitled not to a right of property but to a mere right of servitude.[23] In addition, to avoid the possibility of liability falling on the proprietor on the basis that he has permitted the carrying out of activity otherwise excluded by any of the four types of limitations listed (a), (c), (d) and (e) above, the proprietor will often insert an express clause imposing an obligation on the grantee of the subsidiary real right to comply with those limitations. For example, in a lease the subjects of lease will be accurately defined to an area equal to or smaller than the area owned by the landlord and the lease may contain a clause requiring the tenant (a) to comply with existing title provisions, and servitudes, (b) to comply with all relevant statutory provisions, and (c) to avoid activity which may constitute a nuisance.[24]

Limitations arising from Agreement

4.9   Limitations on the free use of a right of property may be merely contractual as where a builder enters into a contractual agreement with another builder that he will not develop a particular plot of ground for a period of years. Such contractual limitations will not

---

20 Paras 4.16–4.23.
21 Cusine and Paisley, *Servitudes and Rights of Way*, paras 2.22 and 12.143–12.147.
22 Cusine and Paisley, *Servitudes and Rights of Way*, Chap. 14 and 15.
23 *Cloy v. T.M. Adams & Sons*, 2000 S.L.T. (Sh.Ct.) 39.
24 Ross and McKichan, *Drafting and Negotiating Commercial Leases in Scotland* (2nd ed.), Style P1, p. 268, cl. 5.9.

bind the singular successor of the proprietor. Real conditions, such as real burdens and rights of common interest, may impose limitations on use which are enforceable *in personam* against the proprietor and his successors in title. For example, a servient proprietor may be subject to an obligation to use his property for a specific use only. The grant of any subordinate real right will almost invariably create a limitation on use. For example, where a servitude is granted the servient proprietor will be precluded from carrying out any activity which is inconsistent with the free and full use of the servitude.[25]

Statutory Limitations

The statutory provisions limiting the activity which may be 4.10 carried out by a proprietor are legion and only a mere indication of their importance can be noted here. For example, the sale of alcohol from a property requires a statutory licence.[26] Planning permission is required for any significant building work and for certain changes of use. For the purposes of planning law there are various defined types of use, known as Use Classes, and a change of use within a Use Class does not require planning permission.[27] The obtaining of planning permission does not absolve the proprietor from the requirement of obtaining other statutory permissions which are required under other statutes. For example, construction or demolition of many types of building requires a building warrant.[28] Use of land as a caravan site requires permission.[29] The right of destruction may be limited by statute. For example, demolition of a building within a conservation area requires permission.[30] Outwith a conservation area a proprietor must obtain permission to demolish a listed building[31] or an ancient monument.[32]

Occupiers' Liability

A statutory duty of care rests on the occupier or party in control 4.11

---

25 *Rattray v. Tayport Patent Slip Co.* (1868) 5 S.L.R. 219 per Lord Deas at 219.
26 Licencing (Scotland) Act 1976.
27 Town and Country Planning (Use Classes)(Scotland) Order 1997 (S.I. 1997 No. 3061)(as amended).
28 Building (Scotland) Act 1959, s.6(1); Gretton and Reid, *Conveyancing* (2nd ed.), paras 4.23–4.28.
29 Caravan Sites and Control of Development Act 1960.
30 Planning (Listed Buildings and Conservation Areas) (Scotland) Act 1997, s.66.
31 Town and Country Planning (Scotland) Act 1997, s.26 (definition of "development").
32 Ancient Monuments and Archaeological Areas Act 1979, s.2.

of premises to show care for persons entering those premises in respect of dangers arising from the state of the premises or anything done or omitted to be done on them.[33] Under the statute the duty falls on the person who in the circumstances of any case has the right and the means to protect the visitor from the particular danger in question. The duty usually will fall on the person in actual occupation of the premises such as a tenant. The person in occupation may not, however, be the person in control and in such a case the duty will fall on the person in control. The dangers covered by the reference in the statute to the state of the premises include structural defects in buildings, the existence of poisonous shrubs, unfenced holes in the ground and unprotected machinery upon which children would play. The reference to things done on the premises may extend to the keeping of dangerous animals such as dogs or bulls. The reference to omissions may include failures to lock doors and place lights near dangerous holes. The standard of care required of the occupier under the statute is that of the reasonable, prudent man and the degree of care is "such care as in all the circumstances of the case is reasonable". As a result an occupier may be required to fence a quarry where it is close to a public road but not where it is located at such a distance from any public place that the public are not likely to come near it.[34] A high degree of care would fall on local authorities or private companies who provide play areas for children to which parents are invited to send children unaccompanied.[35] An occupier may to some extent restrict, modify or exclude his obligations to any person by agreement.[36] Where an occupier gives express notice of a danger to a person who voluntarily accepts it, the defence of *volenti non fit iniuria* will be available.[37] Where premises are used for a business purpose any purported exclusion of liability will be subject to the application of the Unfair Contract Terms Act 1977.[38] Where premises are occupied by virtue of a tenancy under which the landlord is responsible for maintenance or repair of the premises the landlord has the same duty of care towards persons or property as would be imposed on an occupier under the Act but only in respect of dangers arising from faulty maintenance or repair.[39]

---

33 Occupiers' Liability (Scotland) Act 1960 ("1960 Act"), s.2.
34 *Melville v. Renfrwshire C. C.*, 1920 S.C. 61; *Black v. Cadell* (1804) M. 13905.
35 *Plank v. Stirling Mags*, 1956 S.C. 92.
36 1960 Act, s.2(1).
37 1960 Act, s.2(3).
38 1977 Act, S.16, as amended.
39 1960 Act, s.3.

Common Law Limitations

Two doctrines may be invoked at common law to restrict the 4.12 activity carried out by a landowner. These are (a) the law of nuisance, and (b) the rules prohibiting behaviour *in aemulationem vicini*. For any particular landowner the rules are both a hindrance and a protection. They may restrict his undertaking of undesirable activity but may protect him from his neighbour's unacceptable actions.

Nuisance[40]

Nuisance may be defined as use of land which occasions material 4.13 and intolerable interference with the enjoyment or use by another party of his land or property.[41] The import of the law of nuisance is sometimes summed up in the maxim *sic utere tuo ut alienum non laedas*. The maxim serves little to clarify the issues and provides no evidence of any Roman origins of the law of nuisance. The maxim has been imported into Scots law as a less than helpful product of the law of England.

Nuisance occupies a broad area of law. There may be some overlap with the rules relating to encroachments. An attempt at distinction may be made in that it may be possible to categorise encroachment as some activity which interferes with the legal extent of a landowner's right of property—as is the case with the construction of a building that overhangs the boundary line—whilst nuisance may centre on the interference with the full and free exercise of the activity which the landowner may wish to carry out on his land—as may be the case where a neighbour causes smoke to billow out over a landowner's garden. The distinction may be difficult to apply in practice to items such as tree roots causing damage to buildings across the boundary line. Perhaps the greatest area of obscurity lies in relation to the removal of a right of support. The removal of support has, from time to time, been regarded as a breach of a natural servitude or right of common interest or even as a subject of the delict of negligence, but more recent authority has suggested that it may be actionable in nuisance.[42]

Nuisance may be committed in an infinite variety of ways and the

---

40 The most comprehensive and authoritative statement of the law of nuisance in recent years is that of Niall R. Whitty in 14 *Stair Memorial Encyclopaedia*, para. 2001. The author acknowledges his debt to this magnificent work.

41 *Watt v. Jamieson*, 1954 S.C. 56 per Lord President Cooper at 57–58.

42 *Lord Advocate v. Reo Stakis Organisation Ltd*, 1980 S.C. 203.

wrongdoer's actions or use of his land need not be unusual.[43] The relevant question is deciding whether any activity occasions material and intolerable interference with the enjoyment or use by another party of his land or property? The answer is to be determined from the point of view of the victim of the harm rather from the point of view of the alleged wrongdoer. This does not, however, import a non-objective standpoint: the matter will be judged by reference to the standards of ordinary inhabitants of the locality and not persons who are overly sensitive.[44] In deciding whether an invasion of an interest in the use and enjoyment of land is more than reasonably tolerable and thus a nuisance, the courts will undertake a balancing exercise taking into account various factors. These include (a) the gravity of harm suffered by the complainer, and (b) the defender's conduct.

In evaluating the gravity of harm suffered by the complainer the courts may take into account the following factors:

(a) The type of harm. This will include physical damage to land and buildings and interference with the enjoyment of land.
(b) The extent of the harm. In general harm will not be actionable as a nuisance unless it is material.
(c) The suitability of the particular use or enjoyment invaded to the character of the locality. For example, interference with the comfortable enjoyment of a dwellinghouse in a residential area is more likely to occasion a nuisance in a residential area than in an industrial area even though the harm to each house may be identical.
(d) The sensitivity to harm of the persons or property affected. In general ultra-sensitivity of persons or property will be disregarded. The standard of tolerability is that of the average reasonable person in the particular locality.
(e) The burden on the complainer of taking protective measures. If trivial measures are able to minimise the effect of any conduct complained of, that conduct is not likely to be regarded as a nuisance. A proprietor, however, will not be required to do what is unreasonable to minimise the effect. For example, a house owner will not be required to keep his windows shut or to install double glazing to minimise the effect of noise.[45]

In evaluating the defender's conduct in causing or failing to abate

---

43 *Maguire v. Charles McNeil Ltd*, 1922 S.C. 174.
44 *Maguire v. Charles McNeil Ltd*, 1922 S.C. 174.
45 *Webster v. L. A.*, 1984 S.L.T. 13.

a nuisance the courts may take into account the following factors:

(a) The primary purpose of the conduct causing the harm. Most nuisances are unintentional but where the conduct of the defender is aimed at causing harm to the complainer it is more likely to be regarded as a nuisance. It is no defence to an action of nuisance that the activity of the defender is for the public benefit or provides employment for a large number of persons.[46]

(b) The suitability of the defender's conduct to the character of the locality. The more inappropriate the activity of the defender to the locality the greater chance that it will be accounted a nuisance.

(c) The practicability of remedial measures. The easier it is to take remedial measures the more likely that the conduct of the defender will be regarded as a nuisance.

It is a defence to an action of nuisance to show that the party 4.14 complaining has consented expressly or impliedly to the nuisance.[47] The right to object to a nuisance may also be lost by the expiry of the 20-year period of negative prescription.[48] It is no defence to an action that the defender will suffer loss if he has to desist from the activity complained of[49] or that the public is benefited by the activity.[50] In some cases actions of nuisance may be excluded by statute.[51]

Title to sue in an action of nuisance probably extends to any party having a real right in a plot of land which confers upon them a right to possess the subjects affected by the nuisance. Thus a proprietor has title and this remains the case where he has granted a lease and is not in actual possession of the leased subjects.[52] The owner of a right of salmon fishings may seek interdict against pollution of the water.[53] A *pro indiviso* property owner has title to seek interdict against a nuisance which threatens the common property.[54] A tenant has title to raise actions of declarator, interdict

---

46 *Ben Nevis Distillery (Fort William) Ltd v. North British Aluminium Co. Ltd*, 1948 S.C. 592.
47 *Hill v. Dixon* (1850) 12D. 508.
48 Prescription and Limitation (Scotland) Act 1973, s.8.
49 *Shotts Iron Co. v. Inglis* (1882) 9R. (H.L.) 78.
50 *Duke of Buccleuch v. Cowan* (1866) 5M. 214.
51 Civil Aviation Act 1982, ss 76 and 77.
52 *Adam v. Alloa Police Commissioners* (1874) 2R. 143.
53 *Countess of Seafield v. Kemp* (1899) 1F. 402; *Duke of Richmond v. Lossiemouth Burgh* (1904) 12 S.L.T. 166.
54 *McCulloch v. Wallace* (1846) 9D. 32.

or damages relating to nuisances affecting the leased subjects.[55] It may be that any lawful possessor of land has a title to sue at common law and it is possible that a statutory title exists in relation to occupancy rights of non-entitled spouses.[56] There appears to be no authority to confirm that the dominant proprietor in respect of a servitude can raise an action of nuisance but this appears to be consonant with principle at least where the servitude is positive in nature. There may be circumstances where the right presently enjoyed by means of a negative servitude should be so protected also. Consider the case of the right obtained by a negative servitude of prospect or view enjoyed by A over B's land. If the view is obscured by the actings not of B but of C (as may be the case if C lets smoke or dust billow out over the land of B) then A can presently enforce the servitude directly against C because it is a real right. After the anticipated reform of the law of real conditions a right of view such as that under consideration is likely to be capable of creation only by real condition.[57] In such a case it is unlikely that the real condition will be enforceable against C with the result that A may require to rely on the law of nuisance for his remedy. Members of the public have a title to raise an action by means of *actio popularis* to prevent nuisances which interfere with their rights to passage along a public right of way or a public street.[58] A statutory title to raise actions of nuisance arises where the duty to maintain particular subjects, such as a road, is imposed on a body or person.[59]

The primary remedies for nuisance are interdict, declarator and damages. Self-help appears to be competent but is probably inadvisable because of the possibility of physical conflict.

Behaviour in Aemulationem Vicini

4.15   The doctrine of *aemulatio vicini* has survived in Scots law. Its role is to provide protection for a landowner where the law of nuisance is unable to apply. It may be resorted to where the proprietory rights of the parties are not clearly established (which may be the case if there is an ongoing boundary dispute or an unresolved claim in respect of the existence of a positive servitude) or where the

---

55 *Johnston v. Constable* (1841) 3D. 1263.
56 Matrimonial Homes (Family Protection) (Scotland) Act 1981, s.2(1)(b); 14 *Stair Memorial Encyclopaedia*, para. 2134.
57 Scott. Law Com. *Discussion Paper on Real Burdens*, (No. 106, Oct. 1998), paras 2.42–2.50.
58 *Ogston v. Aberdeen and District Tramways Co.* (1896) 24R. (H.L.) 8.
59 *Elgin County Roads Trs v. Innes* (1886) 14R. 48.

conduct of a party causes *damnum absque iniuria*—loss without breach of legal duty. In respect of the latter type of case the two most common cases where the doctrine of *aemulatio vicini* is applied are abstraction of percolating water[60] and "spite fences" intended to block out light.[61] The doctrine applies where the motive of the party carrying out the act is merely to cause harm to the landowner although such activities as the erection of a fence may be perfectly legitimate if the motive was not directed at the detriment of the interests of another.

Limitations on Extent—Boundaries

Determination of boundaries of property is vital in many 4.16 disputes relating to land. A proprietor of land may not exercise any rights of property outwith his boundaries, although if he is entitled to any of certain rights, collectively known as "pertinents", these may in some cases be exercisable outwith the boundaries and over the land of other parties. In conveyancing practice the determination of the boundary lines is a skilled task which can only be briefly outlined here.[62] Much litigation relative to property law relates to the maintenance of boundary structures, the exercise of servitudes and other rights outwith the boundaries, trespass and encroachment. As the issue of the location of boundaries is central to all of these it is to this topic that we shall now pass. Trespass and encroachment will be examined at the end of this chapter[63] with maintenance of boundary structures and exercise of servitudes being outlined in Chapter 9.[64]

Pertinents

The significance of boundaries is qualified to some extent by the 4.17 recognition of certain rights as pertinents. The term "pertinents" denotes rights which stand in a subsidiary and ancillary relationship to a piece of land and generally pass together with a grant of that land by implication and without necessity of express enumeration.

---

60 Bankton, *Inst.*, I,x,40 and IV,xlv,112; *Milton v. Glen-Moray Glenlivet Distillery Co. Ltd* (1898) 1F. 135.
61 *Dunlop v. Robertson* (1803) Hume 515; *Glassford v. Astley* (1808) M. "Property" App. No. 7; Hume 516n; *Ross v. Baird* (1829) 7S. 361. See para. 4.25.
62 See further Gordon, *Scottish Land Law* (2nd ed.), paras 4.01–4.50; Halliday, *Conveyancing Law and Practice* (2nd ed.), Vol. 2, paras 33.05–33.14; Gretton and Reid, *Conveyancing*, (2nd ed.), paras 12.10–12.15.
63 Paras 4.28–4.30.
64 See Chap. 9.

As a general rule modern dispositions, particularly those intended for registration in the Sasine register, add the words "together with the parts and pertinents" after the main body of the description of the lands conveyed. The words are still found in dispositions which induce registration in the Land Register of Scotland even though it is provided by statute that the registration of an interest in land carries with it "any right, pertinent or servitude, express or implied, forming part of" the relevant interest.[65] The term "parts" is commonly associated with the term "pertinents" but the words are not synonymous. The former term indicates the principal land itself as contained within its boundaries, the fixtures such as houses and buildings, the right to physically enjoy the land and to carry out juristic acts in respect of it.

Legally separate tenements such as salmon fishing cannot pass as a pertinent of the land adjacent to them.[66] Apart from that exclusion pertinents may comprise a variety of rights as follows:

(a) Rights which, whilst they exist, cannot be severed from the benefited lands. These comprise real conditions such as servitudes, real burdens and rights of common interest.[67]

(b) In relation to tenemental property the common stair and passage is presumed to be the common property of each of the flats benefited thereby and the relevant share therein passes as a pertinent of right of exclusive property in each flat.[68] This presumption can be rebutted by the terms of the titles. The calculation of the extent of the share is sometimes problematic but this should not cause significant difficulties in practice at least whilst the tenement remains intact.[69]

(c) It is possible for an area of land to be regarded as a pertinent of other land in some cases. A small area of contiguous land is more likely to be regarded as a pertinent than a large part of land which is discontiguous. Certain Sasine-recorded title deeds contain an express statement that another area of ground is a pertinent. This is relatively common in relation to bin stores and the flat which they serve, where a clause in the disposition frequently precludes separate conveyances of the

---

65 Land Registration (Scotland) Act 1979, s.3(1)(a).
66 Para 1.11 *Cf. McKendrick v. Wilson*, 1970 S.L.T. (Sh.Ct.) 39. See the exceptional case of salmon fishings attached to land which used to be a kindly tenancy in terms of Abolition of Feudal Tenure etc. (Scotland) Act 2000, s.64(3).
67 Chap. 9.
68 *WVS Premises Ltd v. Currie*, 1969 S.C. 170.
69 18 *Stair Memorial Encyclopaedia*, para. 231.

two items.[70] It is more difficult to acquire a pertinent by prescription only given the rule that acquisition of land beyond the stated boundary is inconsistent with a bounding description.[71] This effectively rules out acquisition of a property right in other land as a pertinent where the title is registered in the Land Register of Scotland. However, a general description in a title recorded in the Sasine register may be habile to the acquisition of a property right in other land separate from the core of the title as a pertinent. In addition, possession for the prescriptive period may lead to the acquisition of servitudes beyond the boundary line even of a bounding or Land Registered title.[72]

The Location of the Boundary Lines

In respect of property rights in land the boundary lines will be 4.18 determined by a construction of the terms of the titles. As writing is required for the creation, transfer, variation or extinction of most real rights otherwise than by the operation of a court decree, enactment or rule of law,[73] questions of the location of boundaries are therefore largely questions of interpretation of terms of the deeds which describe the lands over which rights are claimed. Even where a right of property is created by prescription this may occur only where the possession follows upon the recording of a deed which is sufficient in respect of its terms (and containing a habile description of the land) to constitute in favour of the acquiring party a title in the particular land.[74] Where a real right may be created by exercise for the prescriptive period alone without the necessity of a prior deed, as is the case with a positive servitude,[75] the measure of the right is determined by the extent of the possession conform to the maxim *tantum praescriptum tantum possessum*.[76] This applies to all aspects of the right including the location of the extent of the servient tenement and the location of the boundaries thereof. The issue frequently arises in relation to the

---

70 Para. 4.6.
71 *Cooper's Trs v. Stark's Trs* (1898) 25R. 1160.
72 *Beaumont v. Lord Glenlyon* (1843) 5D. 1337.
73 Requirements of Writing (Scotland) Act 1995, ss.1(2)(b) and 1(7).
74 Prescription and Limitation (Scotland) Act 1973, s.1(1)(b).
75 Prescription and Limitation (Scotland) Act 1973, s.3(2).
76 Cusine and Paisley, *Servitudes and Rights of Way*, para. 15.29.

width of roads over which a servitude right of access has been established.[77]

Boundaries—Land Certificate

4.19   The determination of horizontal boundaries is a relatively simple task in relation to interests in land registered in the Land Register of Scotland because that system of registration is a map-based system. A plan based on the most recent edition of the Ordnance Survey map showing the boundaries of each interest in land is entered in the title sheet[78] and attached to the relevant Land Certificate issued in respect of each interest in land. It is relatively rare (but competent) for a supplementary plan to be attached to a Title Sheet indicating the vertical boundaries of a plot of ground. Whilst the Ordnance Survey map is a considerable improvement on much of the earlier practice in relation to the Sasine Register, some tolerance must still be allowed for map scaling.[79] The Keeper's indemnity is qualified to account for this.[80] The Keeper is able to supplement the information as to a boundary line by the use of a verbal description or by a system of arrows but again the information given in this respect is usually not guaranteed.[81]

Boundaries—Sasine Titles

4.20   Sasine titles relied heavily upon verbal descriptions particularly where the title was drawn up prior to 1934. Up to that date no record of plans appended to deeds was kept at the Sasine Register except insofar as the parties could lodge a duplicate plan in terms of statutory provision dating from 1924.[82] Many titles recorded in the Sasine Register since 1934 have plans attached to them but the parties are generally free to determine the scale of such plans and they may be declared to be "demonstrative", meaning the plan is not guaranteed to be accurate. In addition many plans identify the boundaries of the site but fail to give sufficient details as to location

---

77 *E.g. Fraser v. Bruce*, Stonehaven Sheriff Court, 16 December 1987 and 27 January 1988 (unreported.), case ref. A80/87 where the dominant proprietor was able to establish a servitude of access over a road 10 feet wide, but not in respect of the same road to an extent of 13 ft 6 in. wide.
78 1979 Act, s.6(1)(a).
79 *Registration of Title Practice Book* (2nd ed., 2000), para. 4.26.
80 1979 Act, s.12(2)(d).
81 Land Registration (Scotland) (Amendment) Rules 1988 (S.I. 1988 No. 1143); McDonald, *Conveyancing Manual* (6th ed.), para. 13.30.
82 Conveyancing (Scotland) Act 1924, s.48; McDonald, *Conveyancing Manual* (6th ed.), para. 8.13.

of the site. As a result many plans attached to Sasine titles are much less useful than they could be and frequently require to be supplemented by the terms of the verbal description which invariably accompanies them in the text of the deed. Where the terms of the verbal description are inconsistent with the plan attached to the deed there are considerable difficulties. There is a body of case law on this subject from which it is difficult to extract a single governing principle.[83]

Verbal descriptions found in Sasine titles fall into two types: general and bounding. The term "particular" description is sometimes equiparated with a bounding description.[84] General descriptions may be illustrated by examples such as "the lands of Kilnaslee" and "the moss and muir of Mullaghfurtherland". Clearly these descriptions are general and the location of the boundaries around these lands must be established by evidence of actual possession or of topographical features (such as natural boundaries indicated by the lie of the land)[85] all of which is extrinsic to the titles. Bounding descriptions, by contrast, contain specific detail of the boundaries and no proof is needed of the extent of the lands. The distinction between bounding and general descriptions appears simple enough but there are two difficulties in its application. First of all a description may be bounding in some respects and not in others in that it may contain specific details of some boundaries only. Secondly, it is always a matter of degree as to whether a description contains sufficient detail in relation to a particular boundary to be accounted a bounding description. This may lead to some surprises. For example in one case a specification of an area by reference to a plan and approximate measurements was regarded as leaving room for reference to the existence of a row of trees to denote the exact line of the boundary.[86] Such a case tends to emphasise the value of a site visit which unfortunately the pressures of modern conveyancing practice has ruled out at least as a regular occurrence. Even where a title does contain a bounding description the measurements stated therein are frequently accompanied by the qualification "or thereby". This allows a certain

---

83 Gordon, *Scottish Land Law* (2nd. ed.), para. 4–08; McDonald, *supra*, para. 8.15.

84 *Beneficial Bank plc v. McConnachie*, 1996 S.C. 119, relating to Conveyancing and Feudal Reform (Scotland) Act 1970, Sched. 2, no. 1, reversed in relation to standard securities by Abolition of Feudal Tenure etc. (Scotland) Act 2000, ss 76(1), 77(2) and (3) and Sched. 12, para. 30(23)(a).

85 *Whitsun v. Ramsay* (1813) 5 Pat. App. 664; *Lumsden v. Gordon* (1870) 42 Sc. Jur. 530.

86 *Hetherington v. Galt* (1905) 7F. 706.

latitude in the application of the measurements but it will always be a question of circumstances what that latitude will be.[87]

Title Presumptions

4.21   As has been indicated above, many Sasine titles contain a verbal description of the property which is of an imprecise nature and may not define the exact line of one or more of the boundaries. In such cases the proprietor of land may have resort to certain legal presumptions. These presumptions are rebuttable by contrary provisions in the titles.[88] The most commonly encountered of these are as follows:

(a)   Where a property is stated to be "bounded by" a road the boundary is presumed to be the mid-line of the road if the road is a public road[89] and the near edge of the road where it is a private road.[90]

(b)   Where a loch forms the boundary of land the presumption is each of the proprietors of the land bordering it have an exclusive right of property in the bed opposite their lands.[91] This is of course without prejudice to the existence of rights of common interest to enable each bordering landowner to fish and boat in the water.[92]

(c)   Where land is bounded by a river the presumption is that the boundary is the *medium filum* of the river.[93] Where, however, the river is both tidal and navigable the presumption does not apply as the *alveus* is, in the absence of any other title, part of the Crown's property.[94]

(d)   Where subjects are described as bounded by a wall the presumption is that the wall is excluded. Where, however, the wording is "enclosed by" a wall the presumption is that the wall is included.

---

87   *Hetherington v. Galt* (1905) 7F. 706; *Young v. McKellar Ltd*, 1909 S.C. 1340; *Griffin v. Watson*, (1962) 78 Sh.Ct.Rep. 134; Halliday, *Opinions*, D.J. Cusine (ed.), pp. 202–206, No. 45.
88   *Houston v. Barr*, 1911 S.C. 134.
89   *Mags of Ayr v. Dobbie* (1898) 25R. 1184.
90   *Argyllshie Commissioners v. Campbell* (1885) 12R. 1255.
91   *Mackenzie v. Bankes* (1878) 5R. (HL) 192; *Waugh v. Wylie* (1885) 23 S.L.R. 152.
92   Chap. 9.
93   *Menzies v. Marquis of Breadalbane* (1901) 4F. 55.
94   Bell, *Prin.*, s.648; *Orr Ewing & Co. v. Colquhoun's Trs* (1877) 4R. 344; 4R. (H.L.) 116.

Vertical Boundaries

It is rare for Sasine title deeds or the Title Sheet to specify the 4.22
vertical boundaries of land with any detail. As regards vertical
boundaries the normal rule is that a proprietor owns the minerals
below his ground and the airspace above consonant with the maxim
a coelo usque ad centrum. He may therefore prevent encroachments
into airspace by machines such as tower cranes.[95] The upward
extent of ownership has become debatable since the advent of
aviation and the use of space with the result that any theory
asserting infinite nature of the upward boundaries is questionable.[96]
The general rule of vertical ownership is varied where minerals
under a site have been split off as a separate tenement and are held
on a separate title or where flats on different storeys within a single
building are owned by different owners. Where airspace is split off
above urban buildings the modern practice is to specify the height
above the natural ground at which the slice of airspace begins. Such
precision is not common in relation to tenemental flats and in such
a case the boundary above and below a tenement flat is presumed to
be the mid-line of the joists.[97] Again this may be altered by
provision in the titles to contrary effect where there are special
features such as mezzanine floors.

Boundary Agreements

Agreements and plans entered into and executed in accordance 4.23
with the provisions of the Land Registration (Scotland) Act 1979,
s.19, may resolve certain discrepancies as to common boundaries
between adjoining lands whether held on Sasine- or Land-registered
titles. There are three preconditions set out for the applicability of
the whole of section 19.[98] First, the section can apply only "where
the titles to adjoining lands disclose a discrepancy as to the common
boundary". This refers to the line of the boundary rather than
discrepancies as to other matters such as maintenance obligations.
Secondly the proprietors of those lands must "have agreed to . . .
that boundary". Thirdly, the proprietors of those lands must "have
executed a plan of . . . that boundary". The term "land" is broadly
defined in the 1979 Act so as to permit the application of the section
to buildings and other structures and land covered with water.[99]

---

95 *Brown v. Lee Construction Ltd*, 1977 S.L.T. (Notes) 61.
96 14 *Stair Memorial Encyclopaedia*, para. 2028.
97 Bell, *Prin.*, s.1086; *Dickson v. Morton* (1824) 3S. 310.
98 1979 Act, s.19(1).
99 1979 Act, s.28(1).

Although the horizontal limit of adjoining estates is the boundary to which section 19 agreements are by far and away most frequently applied, there is no restriction as to the plane or angle at or in which the common boundary is to lie. Combining this possibility with the express extension of the definition of "land" to buildings and other structures,[1] the common boundaries to which the section could apply include the common boundary forming the vertical limits of adjoining properties such as flatted dwellinghouses in a tenement block or the limits of various layers of mineral strata running at whatever plane or angle they are to be found.

Until recently the commonly accepted view[2] was that a section 19 agreement and plan enabled the proprietors of the adjacent lands to regularise two forms of discrepancy between the common boundaries: first, a discrepancy indicated in the titles such as a competition of title or overlap, and secondly, a discrepancy as to the occupational common boundary observed on a comparison between the tiles and an inspection of the site or by reference to the current Ordnance Survey plan.[3] A strict reading of the terms of section 19 may support the first application only and this appears to be confirmed by recent indications given by the Keeper.[4] Any difficulty in such a narrow application is frequently elided by a generous exercise by the Keeper of his discretion to create a statutory title where none previously existed.[5]

There are difficulties in the application of the statement in section 19 to the effect that when the plan is recorded or registered it will be binding on all parties having an interest in the lands.[6] It is unclear what this means in relation to the holders of subordinate real rights such as heritable creditors or tenants. A narrow meaning would suggest that it requires them to respect any transfer of ownership of a disputed strip effected by a section 19 agreement but more expansively it may be intended partially to discharge their subordinate real right. To cap it all the holder of a short lease is not automatically bound by a section 19 agreement because of a defect in the definition section in the 1979 Act.[7] The prudent course is to have all such parties consent to the agreement and declare in the deed the effect of their consent.

---

1   *ibid.*
2   See, *e.g.*, 18 *Stair Memorial Encyclopaedia*, paras 219 and 220.
3   The information in such a map is, of course, itself based on a survey of the site.
4   *Registration of Title Practice Book* (2nd ed., 2000), para. 6.64.
5   Para. 3.14.
6   1979 Act, s.19(2) and (3).
7   1979 Act, s.28(1) "interest in land".

The alteration of the boundary line by the use of section 19 depends entirely on agreement. If the parties fail to agree it has no application. In rare cases a proprietor who wishes to force the issue of an alteration of the boundary line may have recourse to the March Dykes Act 1669. The Act probably applies to rural land only where there are no existing fences or walls or where the existing boundary structures are unsuitable. The party wishing to alter the line of the boundary must petition the court. If successful, relevant parts of land on either side of the boundary are adjudged to the other party. Title is completed by the recording of the decree in the Sasine Register or registration in the Land Register of Scotland as appropriate. This is a limited form of compulsory acquisition and a party who suffers loss from the adjustment is entitled to compensation.

Boundary Structures

The issue of the location of the line of a boundary is in one sense   4.24 entirely distinct from the issue of the maintenance rights and obligations existing in respect of a boundary structure.[8] Yet the two issues are inextricably interlinked because the nature and extent of those rights and obligations largely depends on the location of the boundary structure in relation to that line. The obligations of maintenance largely arise at common law although they have been varied in the special cases to which the March Dykes Act 1661 applies. Examination of rights and obligations in relation to boundary structures may conveniently be set out under a number of headings:

(a)   structure located entirely within one plot;
(b)   structure located on boundary line; and
(c)   statutory provisions and fences.

Boundary Structure Located within One Plot

A proprietor is generally free to erect a boundary structure within   4.25 his own land. Any wall so erected will belong to him exclusively and he may demolish it at will. He may be restrained from erecting such a wall by planning constraints, title conditions or, if the fence is intended merely as a spite fence, by the rules precluding behaviour

---

8   See, *e.g.*, *McClymont v. McGibbon*, 1995 S.L.T. 1248 where it was observed that the erection of a boundary fence "to the satisfaction of X" related to the creation of the boundary structure and did not allow X to determine the line of the boundary.

in aemulationem vicini. It is difficult to prove that a boundary fence or wall intended to preserve privacy is a spite fence.[9]

Except in relation to the cases where the March Dykes Act 1661 applies (or where there is a separate contractual arrangement) the person erecting such a fence cannot recover the cost from the owner of the adjacent landowner. The 1661 Act applies only to plots of land extending to more than five acres in rural areas. It enables the proprietor of land wishing to erect a wall to recover one half of the cost from the adjoining proprietor. This liability is personal and does not transmit against successors in title.[10] Prior to starting work the party wishing to erect the wall must either obtain the consent of the neighbouring proprietor or the sanction of the court. To be successful in the latter forum the cost of fencing must be reasonable when compared to the advantage accruing by the completion of the project. The advantage must be mutual though it need not be equal.[11] Any wall erected in pursuance of an order under the 1661 Act must be built on the applicant's land as the Act does not sanction encroachment.[12]

Where a wall is located wholly within the property of one party it is usually his sole responsibility to maintain it. It is competent, but rare, for a real condition to impose an obligation on the owner of one tenement to repair a wall or fence on another tenement or to contribute to its maintenance. An obligation to share in the maintenance of such a wall may fall on an adjacent proprietor in terms of the March Dykes Act 1661 where the wall was or could have been erected in terms of that statute or has been treated as such a wall from time immemorial.[13]

Boundary Structure Located on Boundary Line

4.26   In two cases a proprietor may obtain a right to erect a wall on the midline of his boundary with half of it located on his land and the other half within the land of his neighbour. These are, first, where the right is conferred by a validly created real burden affecting the title of his neighbour, and secondly, where the works are sanctioned by the special rules relative to common gables. Real burdens will be examined in a later chapter.[14]

---

9   *Dunlop v. Robertson* (1803) Hume 515; *Ross v. Baird* (1829) 7S. 361; *Glassford v. Astley* (1808) M. "Property", App. No. 7. See para. 4.15.
10   Bankton, *Inst.*, I,x,153.
11   *Earl of Peterborough v. Garioch* (1748) M. 10497.
12   *Graham v. Irving* (1899) 2F. 29.
13   *Strang v. Steuart* (1864) 2M. 1015 (affd (1886) 4M. (HL) 5).
14   Chap. 9.

A common gable is the shared division wall located between two connected buildings which are intended to be in separate ownership or occupation. The classic case is the wall between two semi-detached houses. Special rules were evolved to deal with a practice of building, common in the eighteenth century, whereby the plot on one side of the intended mutual gable was developed by one builder and the other by another builder. As this practice has largely disappeared because of the dominance of the building market by larger builders who usually control both plots, these special rules are rarely applied today. In summary the rules permitted the first builder to build the wall to the extent of one half on his neighbour's land and to recover half the cost from him when the neighbour came to tie into that wall for the purpose of developing his own land. All these obligations run with the land.[15]

After its construction, a wall erected on the mid-line of a boundary line will be owned exclusively by each proprietor up to the mid-line.[16] Each half is subject to rights of common interest in favour of the other half. These rules govern alterations, maintenance and repairs. Each of the owners is obliged to maintain his side of the wall and may not carry out any activity which would undermine the strength and stability of the wall as a whole.[17]

Statutory Provisions and Fences

There is no general obligation on a landowner to fence his land 4.27
just because he stocks it with animals such as sheep.[18] The matter may be otherwise if the animals pose a danger to the public in which case there may be a duty to fence arising under the Occupiers' Liability (Scotland) Act 1961. Statutory obligations to fence may fall upon the owners of certain property used for particular functions such as railways.[19] Roads authorities have statutory power to erect fences along or near roads and footpaths.[20]

More commonly encountered statutory provisions relative to fences are contained in the Civic Government (Scotland) Act 1982. These place on owners of certain open spaces set apart for the use

15 *Wallace v. Brown*, 21 June 1808, F.C.
16 *Thom v. Hetherington*, 1988 S.L.T. 724.
17 *ibid.*
18 *Robertson v. Wright* (1885) 13R. 174; *Forest Property Trust v. Lindsay*, 1998 G.W.D. 31–1581; Animals (Scotland) Act 1987, ss 1–4.
19 Railways Clauses Consolidation (Scotland) Act 1845, ss 60–65; *A.R. Mathers & Sons v. British Railways Board*, Aberdeen Sheriff Court, Sheriff Douglas J. Risk, 25 February 1982 (unreported).
20 Roads (Scotland) Act 1984, ss 28 and 29.

by the owners or occupiers of two or more separate properties the duty of maintaining these and any boundary walls or fences.[21] These provisions are restricted largely to urban areas by the reference to "populous places".[22] In addition, a local authority may, by notice in writing, require the owner or owners of any building to bring the building into a reasonable state of repair, regard being had to its age, type and location.[23] The term "building" is defined sufficiently widely to include a boundary wall or fence.[24] The local authority is empowered by notice to carry out necessary works themselves if the owners fail to do so and recover the cost from them.[25]

Trespass and Encroachment

4.28   Trespass is transient intrusion into the land of another as may be occasioned by straying animals or children. Where the intrusion is permanent or semi-permanent it is classified as encroachment as may be the case if a party erects a building partly on the land of his neighbour. In both cases the essence of the intrusion is use of another's land without right or justification. A proprietor of land may seek interdict to prevent encroachment or trespass on his land or obtain damages where interdict is not available. As a result the law of trespass and encroachment, like nuisance, serves both to restrict the actions of a landowner and to protect him. It is a double edged sword.

Trespass

4.29   The transient intrusion into the land of another party may constitute a trespass even without proof of actual damage to the land. Where the party entering the land of another has the right to do so or he is justified on other grounds there can be no trespass. For example, the proprietor of land may grant permission to others to enter his land either verbally or in writing. Such permission constitutes a personal licence usually revocable at the will of the landowner. In certain cases the permission to enter the land of another may constitute a real right as is the case where a dominant proprietor entitled to exercise a positive servitude has a right to enter onto the servient tenement. In innumerable cases entry to

---

21 1982 Act, s.95.
22 1982 Act, s.95(1).
23 1982 Act, s.87(1).
24 1982 Act, s.87(2); 18 *Stair Memorial Encyclopaedia*, para. 226(6).
25 1982 Act, s.99.

property is justified under statute. The landowner's remedies in respect of trespass include interdict in relation to a future trespass, self-help in relation to an ongoing trespass and damages for injury or damage to property caused by the trespassing party. There is a special regime of remedies in respect of trespassing animals.[26]

Encroachment

Encroachment takes many forms. It includes the building of a wall on another's land, the projection of a sign over that land or even the deposit or failure to remove moveables from the land of another.[27] The first two examples commonly occur between neighbours. The last instance is of particular relevance where property changes hands and the seller fails to redd out the building. 4.30

There is no encroachment where the owners of the property (and all others who have rights to occupy the subjects such as tenants) have consented to the works complained of. Consent may be written, verbal or implied from inaction.[28] There is, however, a continuing debate as to whether such consent is personal to the party giving it or whether in some or all cases the consent also binds singular successors.[29] With such doubts it would be prudent for a party wishing to make a quasi-permanent encroachment to seek to acquire the property right in the land encroached upon or, alternatively, to obtain a subordinate real right to provide a defence to encroachment. For example, a suitably extensive servitude of stillicide will enable a house to be erected tight up against the boundary even though this causes rainwater to discharge into the neighbouring property.[30] In other cases encroachments such as pipes may be justified on the basis of an order granted under statutory provisions.[31]

A landowner may seek interdict to prevent encroachment on his land which is threatened and the remedy is still available even if building works have started but they have not been substantially completed. In such a case the landowner may also seek an order to

---

26 Animals (Scotland) Act 1987. In trivial cases a remedy of interdict may be refused. See *Winans v. Macrae* (1885) 12 R. 1051.
27 Hume, *Lectures*, Vol. III, pp. 204–205; *S.R.C. v. Persimmon Homes (Scotland) Ltd*, 1996 S.L.T. 176.
28 *Duke of Buccleuch v. Edinburgh Mags* (1865) 3M. 528.
29 J.M. Halliday, "*Aquiescence, Singular Successors and the Baby Linnet*" (1977) 22 J.R. 89.
30 Erskine, *Inst*, II,ix,9; Bell, *Prin.*, s.941.
31 Land Drainage (Scotland) Act 1930, ss 1 and 2; Land Drainage (Scotland) Act 1958, s.1; Civic Government (Scotland) Act 1982, s.88. See para. 2.6.

demolish the partially completed building and restore the land. Where the encroachment is completed the landowner upon whose land the encroachment is built may wish to consider extra-judicial remedies such as self-help. There are practical drawbacks to such an approach. The appropriateness of the remedy cannot be determined until the ownership of the encroaching structure or item is known. That is a difficult matter upon which there is little authority.[32] In addition, any unilateral action may lead to fights on site. The safer course of action is to seek the remedy of removal through the courts.

In principle a landowner should always be entitled to have an encroachment removed. The courts, however, have a discretion to withhold this remedy in appropriate cases and, in lieu thereof, to award damages as a form of compensation.[33] The remedy is more likely to be withheld where the encroachment is slight and the party encroaching had proceeded in good faith in the belief that he had the right to do what he did.[34] The courts will also consider the balance of benefit and burden and where the encroachment is absolutely necessary for some reasonable use of the encroaching party's other land it is more likely to be allowed to remain.[35] Delay in acting may be a major factor in refusing remedy.[36] Even where an order requiring removal of an encroachment is refused, this does not settle the entire matter between the parties. No property is transferred so the issue of the ownership of the encroaching structure remains and the encroaching party will not be able to pass a valid and marketable title to a purchaser until he obtains this title by other means.

---

32 *Hetherington v. Galt* (1905) 7F. 706; 18 *Stair Memorial Encyclopaedia*, para. 179.
33 *Jack v. Begg* (1875) 3R. 43; *S.R.C. v. Persimmon Homes (Scotland) Ltd, supra.*
34 *Forbes v. Inverurie Picture House Ltd* (1936) 53 Sh.Ct.Rep. 43; *Stockton Park (Leisure) Ltd v. Border Oats Ltd*, 1991 S.L.T. 333.
35 *Anderson v. Brattisani's*, 1978 S.L.T. (Notes) 42.
36 *Sclater v. Oddie* (1881) 18 S.L.R. 495.

CHAPTER 5

CO-OWNERSHIP

Introduction

More than one person may have a right of property in the same 5.1
item of heritable property as an undivided whole. This is known as
pro indiviso or undivided ownership and may also be referred to as
co-ownership. In this form of ownership the individual parts of the
item owned are not individually attributed. Thus, where two parties
own a two-bedroom house on a *pro indiviso* basis they each do not
have the exclusive ownership in one bedroom: rather each bedroom
(and all the other parts of the house) are owned in common.

Co-ownership is frequently a source of many disputes between
the co-owners[1] and for that reason many lawyers take the view that
the less items which are held in common, even in relation to
tenemental property, the better.[2] The law provides special rules to
provide regulation of the interests of the parties and to avoid undue
prejudice to each co-owner. These special rules place some
limitations on the full and free exercise of a single co-proprietor's
use and management of the whole common property and his
carrying out juristic acts in relation to it.[3] Such limitations arise by
operation of law because of the existence of common property and
may be classified as "overriding interests".[4] They will bind a co-
proprietor and his successors in title though they are not expressly
disclosed at length in the Sasine titles or the Land Certificate. A
purchaser of the burdened interest will be sufficiently warned,
however, of the existence of these limitations by virtue of the
content of the dispositive clause of the relevant deed or the property

---

1 *Communio est mater rixarum*—co-ownership is the mother of disputes. For an
extreme example see *Baxter v. H.M.A.*, 1998 S.L.T. 414. For a similar general
position in South Africa see Van der Merwe and de Waal, *The Law of Things and
Servitudes*, para. 208.
2 Gretton and Reid, *Conveyancing* (2nd ed.), para. 30.04, referring to *Rafique v.
Amin*, 1997 S.L.T. 1385.
3 Paras 5.5. and 5.6 *et seq.*
4 Land Registration (Scotland) Act 1979, s.28(1)(i).

section of the Title Sheet to the effect that the interest conveyed or registered (as the case may be) is a mere *pro indiviso* property right and not an exclusive property right.

It is equally possible for the subordinate real rights to be held on a *pro indiviso* basis. For example, unless it is excluded by the terms of the lease or by statutory provision,[5] a tenant's right in a lease may be held by two or more tenants. Where the dominant tenement is owned by co-proprietors both will be entitled to exercise the servitude. An action of division and sale, in theory, may be available in respect of the tenant's interest in a lease but so far as the writer is aware there are no cases in which the procedure has been invoked in relation to such an interest. In any event the terms of the lease itself may render such an action of no avail. For simplicity's sake, this chapter will concentrate on the situation where co-ownership relates to the right of *dominium*. Common property may be acquired originally or derivatively although the latter is much more common.

ownership.

Types of Co-ownership

5.2   If one employs the term "co-ownership" in a wide sense it may be asserted that up to the end of the twentieth century Scots law recognised four types. These are:

(a) feudal landownership which recognised the concurrent existence of the *dominium directum* and the *dominium utile*[6];
(b) commonty;
(c) joint property; and
(d) common property.

The first of these, which may be regarded as co-ownership only of a very peculiar sort, is to be abolished as part of feudal reform and will disappear within a few years.[7] The second relates almost exclusively to areas in the neighbourhood of burghs or private estates over which the inhabitants exercise grazing or peat cutting rights. A right of commonty, like a servitude, is held as an inseparable pertinent of a plot of adjoining land. Given the activities usually carried out on the land this has rendered it

---

5   Para 1.27.
6   18 *Stair Memorial Encyclopaedia*, paras 38 and 49.
7   Bell, *Lectures on Conveyancing*, Vol. I (3rd ed.), p. 562; Green's *Encyclopaedia*, Vol. 14, para. 616; Abolition of the Feudal Tenure etc. (Scotland) Act 2000, ss 1–2 following upon Scot. Law Com., *Report on the Abolition of the Feudal System* (No. 168).

difficult to distinguish any remaining examples of the right from servitudes of grazing and fuel, feal and divot. With changes in agricultural techniques and division under statutory procedure[8] it is infrequently encountered in modern practice.[9] Scots law does not acknowledge a division of ownership where trusts exist and, although the trustees are recognised as having the real right of ownership in the property, the right of the beneficiaries is a mere personal right and not a species of beneficial or equitable ownership.[10]

Terminology and Badly Expressed Deeds

Despite the frequency of their occurrence the terminology 5.3 distinguishing the last two types of co-ownership identified above as (c) and (d) was not clearly established until the middle of the nineteenth century.[11] The words used in many conveyancing deeds are unhelpful. Until recent years many dispositions adopted formulae in the *addenda* to the description of the subjects conveyed such as "all rights of joint or mutual property"[12] which could refer only to common property. Even today a title held in common property by two individuals is frequently referred to as a title in "joint" names.[13]

It is unfortunately the case that many titles, particularly deeds of declaration of conditions, are obscurely worded and it is sometimes unclear whether the draftsman intended to create a right of common property or some other lesser right. Views differ as to whether a right of common interest may be created expressly or whether it arises only by operation of law.[14] If the former view is correct there may be some difficulty in interpreting a grant of "a

---

8   Division of Commonties Act 1695 (c.69) Record ed. and c.38 12mo ed.
9   18 *Stair Memorial Encyclopaedia*, para. 37; *cf. Macandrew v. Crerar*, 1929 S.C. 699 where it was held that the right was common property and not commonty. For recent litigation initiated in 1999 relating to a commonty see *Orkney Builders Ltd v. Kenneth Grieve*, Kirkwall Sheriff Court, case ref: A98/99.
10   18 *Stair Memorial Encyclopaedia*, para. 40.
11   *Cargill v. Muir* (1837) 15 S. 408; *Banff Magistrates v. Ruthin Castle Ltd*, 1944 S.C. 36 at 68 per L.J.-C. Cooper; 18 *Stair Memorial Encyclopaedia*, para. 17.
12   See, *e.g.*, Disposition by Lawrence McDonald Chalmers and others to Lawrence McDonald Chalmers dated 15 May and recorded BRS (Aberdeen) 2 June 1924 (folio 163).
13   18 *Stair Memorial Encyclopaedia*, para. 17.
14   For the view that it arises only by operation of law see 18 *Stair Memorial Encyclopaedia*, paras 22, 358 and 362. For a view that it may arise by express stipulation see Gordon, *Scottish Land Law* (2nd ed.), para. 24–05 and Chap. 15. See para. 9.28.

right in common" without further specification. The meaning of the term may depend on the physical structure to which the wording relates. It has been held that the term denotes common property when applied to the common access to a town house which is subdivided into two units.[15] The courts have taken a different view in earlier case law relating to different physical structures such as the area in front of tenement flats[16] or gardens in ornamental squares.[17] To avoid evasion of any future recasting of the law of servitudes and real conditions it may be necessary to provide expressly by statute that a right of common interest may not be created by express provision in a deed.

Distinctions—Joint and Common Property

5.4   The main distinctions between joint and common property may be summarised as follows:

(a)   Common property is much more frequently encountered than joint property. Joint property exists only in limited circumstances. These are (i) trust ownership and (ii) ownership by unincorporated associations. Joint property cannot be created by express use of the words "joint property" in other situations.[18] In the standard case of a property such as a matrimonial home owned by a husband and wife the ownership is common property[19] even if the title contains a survivorship clause and despite the special rules provided by statute for matrimonial property.[20] Joint property and common property can co-exist at different levels in complex situations. For example, common property exists where a trust owns a one-half *pro indiviso* share in a field and the other *pro indiviso* half share is owned by an individual. If there are two or more trustees the title of each trustee to the one-half *pro indiviso* share of the whole field is itself a right of joint property.

(b)   In common property each of the co-owners has a *pro indiviso*

---

15   *WVS Office Premises Ltd v. Currie*, 1969 S.C. 170; 1969 S.L.T. 254; 18 *Stair Memorial Encyclopaedia*, para. 22. *Cf. McCallum v. Gunn*, 1955 S.L.T. (Sh.Ct.) 85.

16   *Johnston v. Whyte* (1877) 4R. 721.

17   *George Watson's Hospital Governors v. Cormack* (1883) 11R. 320.

18   *Banff Magistrates v. Ruthin Castle Ltd*, 1944 S.C. 36; 18 *Stair Memorial Encyclopaedia*, para. 34.

19   See, *e.g., Eunson v. The Braer Corporation*, 1999 S.L.T. 1405.

20   Matrimonial Homes (Family Protection) (Scotland) Act 1981 (c.59), as amended. See 18 *Stair Memorial Encyclopaedia*, para. 27. See paras 5.6, 5.7 and 5.10.

share in the whole.[21] The undivided shares held by each of the co-owners need not necessarily be equal and the parties are free to specify in the deeds creating the co-ownership whatever fractions they please provided, of course, the total shares created add up to 100 per cent of the whole. Two parties are not limited to half shares each. A well drafted deed relating to common property will specify the extent of the share conveyed. It is arguable that a disposition which fails to specify the extent of the share conveyed lacks sufficient precision to render the disposition effectual.[22] The geographic extent of the property right is clear[23] but the fraction which the share conveyed bears to the whole of the common subjects may fluctuate depending on how many subdivisions are made of the common subjects.

(c) In common property each share is legally separate from the shares held by the other co-proprietors. The general rule is that each of the co-proprietors may carry out certain juristic acts in relation to their separate share. Thus each of them may sell, bequeath,[24] or dispone (gratuitously or for a consideration) their share[25] or subdivide into smaller *pro indiviso* shares[26] their own share or grant a right of security over it without the consent of any of the other proprietors. Many banks and major building societies have considerable reservations in relation to lending on the security of *pro indiviso* shares in a plot of heritable property. Not only are such properties difficult to value but certain of the remedies of the heritable creditor, such as the power to enter into possession[27] and

---

21 *Eunson v. The Braer Corporation*, 1999 S.L.T. 1405 per Lord Gill at 1408.
22 18 *Stair Memorial Encyclopaedia*, para. 22.
23 Given the geographic precision, Land Registration (Scotland) Act 1979, s.4(2)(a) should not apply. *Cf.* Gretton and Reid, *Conveyancing* (2nd ed.), para. 12.10. The provisions relative to the Keeper's discretion in 1979 Act, s.4(1) are applicable.
24 Provided always there is no extant survivorship destination which the parties are contractually bound not to evacuate. This obligation may arise expressly or impliedly, albeit the latter is much more common: see *Perrett's Trs v. Perrett*, 1909 S.C. 522; 1909 1 S.L.T. 302; *Brown's Trs v. Brown*, 1943 S.C. 488; 1944 S.L.T. 215; *Hay's Tr. v. Hay's Trs*, 1951 S.C. 329; 1951 S.L.T. 170. See generally G.L. Gretton, "*Destinations*" (1989) 34 J.L.S.S. 299.
25 Bell, *Prin*, s.1073. This is not affected by an extant survivorship destination see *Steele v. Caldwell*, 1979 S.L.T. 228, OH; *Smith v. MacKintosh*, 1989 S.C.L.R. 83; 1989 S.L.T. 148.
26 *Menzies v. Macdonald* (1854) 16D. 827; 18 *Stair Memorial Encyclopaedia*, para. 28.
27 Conveyancing and Feudal Reform (Scotland) Act 1970, S.C. 10(3).

lease[28] may be less than fully effective. Although there are certain limitations on the type of juristic act which each co-proprietor may carry out in relation to his share,[29] the right of each co-owner to alienate his property is not limited by any right of pre-emption in favour of any of the other co-owners[30] unless this is expressly created in the titles. As regards common property the share in the property is owned by the owner in his own right and no question of automatic transfer of ownership upon resignation from an office will arise. The *pro indiviso* share of the deceased in relation to common property will form part of his estate on death unless the title contains a survivorship clause in which case it will accress to the party named in the survivorship clause. It follows from the above that a *pro indiviso* proprietor has no right to dispone or carry out other juristic acts in respect of the shares of the other co-proprietors[31] except to the extent that sufficient authority to do so has been delegated to him.[32]

(d) In joint property there are no separate shares. Instead, the title to the property is held by the trustees for the time being or, as the case may be, by the members of the unincorporated association.[33] In relation to joint property the co-proprietors cannot separately carry out juristic acts. A trustee may not grant a security over property in joint ownership in respect of his private debts. Ownership of joint property continues only for so long as the owner remains as trustee or a member of the unincorporated association as the case may be. Upon resignation or death of a joint owner the right of property will accress automatically to the remaining trustees or members of the association.

(e) The management of joint property is dealt with by rules of trust property for which the reader is directed elsewhere[34] whilst the details of the applicable rules of common property are outlined below.

---

28 1970 Act, s.20(3) and (4) and S.C. 10(3).
29 Para. 5.11.
30 For a similar position in South Africa see Van der Merwe and de Waal, *The Law of Things and Servitudes*, para. 211.
31 *McLeod v. Cedar Holdings Ltd*, 1989 S.L.T. 620.
32 For an example of authority given by all co-proprietors to one co-proprietor to lease the common property, see *Grozier v. Downie* (1871) 9M. 826.
33 18 *Stair Memorial Encyclopaedia*, para. 20.
34 See, *e.g.*, Wilson and Duncan, *Trusts, Trustees and Executors* (2nd ed., 1995).

Management of Common Property

A clear statement of the rules of management relating to common 5.5
property is bedeviled by the fact that the relevant passage in Bell's
Principles appears to set out two general rules which are difficult,
although not wholly impossible, to reconcile.[35] On the one hand,
Bell asserts that the view of a majority of common proprietors will
prevail over a minority. He equally maintains that the consent of all
co-proprietors must be obtained in respect of acts of management
with the result that any one co-owner has a veto. The first of these
rules has not been upheld or dismissed by the courts but the latter
has been frequently affirmed.[36] It has been suggested[37] that a
reconciliation of the two rules is possible on the basis that
unanimity is required in respect of three matters. First, the raising
of court action against third parties, secondly, the granting of
subordinate real rights conferring a right to possess the whole of the
property held in common such as a lease or a positive servitude, and
thirdly, the carrying out of non-necessary repairs to the common
property. Majority decision, it has been suggested, may permit
changes to the use of the item held in common property. Attractive
though it is, no court decision has yet affirmed this approach. In
relation to practice, conveyancers will obviously wish to adopt a
safety-first approach and will probably insist upon unanimity
unless it can be demonstrated that there is clear authority for the
efficacy of majority decisions in any particular case.

Common law recognises that any requirement of unanimity may
be confirmed or removed by express provision in the titles. Where
this is contained in the form of a real condition in a deed of
declaration of conditions, such a provision may bind singular
successors.

Where the requirement as to unanimity results in complete
deadlock any of the co-proprietors may apply for judicial
regulation[38] or the appointment of a judicial factor.[39] There is no
reported case in which the former has been granted[40] and the latter

---

35 Bell, *Prin*, ss 1072, 1075 and 1077.
36 See, *e.g.*, *Johnston v. Craufurd* (1855) 17D. 1023 per Lord Ivory at 1025; *Murray v. Johnstone* (1896) 23R. 981 per Lord Moncreiff at 990.
37 18 *Stair Memorial Encyclopaedia*, para. 23.
38 18 *Stair Memorial Encyclopaedia*, paras 23 and 30.
39 18 *Stair Memorial Encyclopaedia*, paras 23 and 31.
40 See *Menzies v. Wentworth* (1901) 3F. 941; 9 S.L.T. 107; 18 *Stair Memorial Encyclopaedia*, para. 30.

is resorted to only in exceptional cases.[41] Nevertheless, no person is obliged to remain a co-owner against his will. It is always open for a co-proprietor to end his link with his co-proprietors by disponing his share to them or a third party. Should such voluntary disposal prove unobtainable any proprietor may seek a termination of the association by means of an action of division and sale.[42]

Use of Common Property

5.6   Subject to contrary agreement[43] between the co-owners and subject to the special rules relative to "matrimonial homes"[44] the use of common property is governed by four principles:

(a)   Each common proprietor is entitled to use every part of the item which is subject to common ownership.[45] No common owner may take exclusive possession of the whole or any part of that property without the consent of the other co-proprietors.[46] If commonly owned land is tenanted each co-owner is entitled to receive a share of the rents proportionate to his share. There is no recognised servitude of exclusive possession[47] and it would be incompetent to confer on a *pro indiviso* proprietor such an exclusive right by means of a real condition. This has caused some difficulty with salmon fishing timeshares where the parties seek to register *pro indiviso* property rights and a deed of conditions in the Land Register.[48] This does not appear to rule out the possibility of *pro indiviso* proprietors entering into contractual arrangements permitting one of their number to have exclusive possession for a limited period in respect of all or part of the co-owned subjects. In one case which concerned salmon fishings owned by two *pro indiviso* proprietors the court assumed the validity

---

41   See, *e.g.*, *Mackintosh, Petrs* (1849) 11D. 1029; *Morrison* (1857) 20D. 276; *Bailey v. Scott* (1860) 22D. 1105; *Allan* (1898) 6 S.L.T., OH; *affd* (1898) 6 S.L.T. 152; 18 *Stair Memorial Encyclopaedia*, para. 30.

42   18 *Stair Memorial Encyclopaedia*, paras 23, 32 and 33.

43   There are some limitations on the extent to which the principles may be varied: see paras 5.8 and 5.11.

44   See paras 5.6, 5.7 and 5.10.

45   Ersk, *Inst*, II,vi,53.

46   *Bailey v. Scott* (1860) 22D. 1105 per Lord Benholme at 1109. A similar rule exists in South Africa, see *Swart v. Taljaard* (1860) 3S. 35; *Sauerman v. Schultz*, 1950 4 S.A. 455 (O); *Milne v. Abdoola*, 1955 2 S.A. 187 (D).

47   *Leck v. Chalmers* (1859) 21D. 408; Cusine and Paisley, *Servitudes and Rights of Way*, para. 3.77.

48   Para. 1.28(c).

of an agreement between the proprietors allowing exclusive
fishing on alternate weeks.[49] A similar approach is seen in
South Africa where the owners of a farm owned in common
may agree as to how many cattle may be grazed by each co-
owner[50] or which portions of the farm may be cultivated by
each co-owner.[51] There is considerable tension between this
approach and that which denies the possibility of co-
proprietors granting a lease to one of their number.[52]

(b) Each co-owner may make only "ordinary" use of the
property.[53] What amounts to an ordinary use may depend
both on the nature of the property in question and on the
recent history of use. Unfortunately reported case law is
scant[54] but the matter may be illustrated by reference to an
access. Where a common entrance hall leads to a number of
properties it has been held that such an entrance may not be
used for storing material such as a bicycle, a bath chair,[55]
crates, domestic rubbish or agricultural manure unless sanctioned by clear prior use.[56] Where an access has been used for
pedestrian access only and the topography indicates that the
route is not suitable for vehicular traffic no single co-
proprietor is free to use the access for vehicles.[57] It is *a fortiori*
the case that a co-proprietor may not convert a common
garden area into an access route.[58] The ordinary use of
common property as an access will include ancillary activity
required to facilitate access. In one case the court permitted the
installation of a small name plate on a gate across an access
route owned in common. The permission was limited to the

49 *Bailey's Exrs v. Upper Crathes Fishing Ltd,* 1987 S.L.T. 405, OH.
50 Grotius, 3 28 5; Voet 10 3 9; Van Leeuwen *RHR* 4 29 2; *Cens For* 1 4 27 8; Van
    der Keessel *Prael ad Gr* 3 28 5; *Oosthuyzen v. Plessis* (1887) 5 S.C. 69; *Glas v.
    Nefdt* 1931 T.P.D. 18 at 23; Van der Merwe and de Waal, *The Law of Things and
    Servitudes,* para. 211.
51 *Swart v. Taljaard* (1860) 3S. 354; *Strydom v. Tiran* (1873) 3 Buch. 83; *Glas v.
    Nefdt* 1931 T.P.D. 18 at 23; Van der Merwe and de Waal, *The Law of Things and
    Servitudes,* para. 211.
52 Para. 5.11.
53 Bell, *Prin,* s.1075. See para. 8.06.
54 Further illustration of the same principle may be found in South Africa see Van
    der Merwe and de Waal, *The Law of Things and Servitudes,* para. 209.
55 *Carmichael v. Simpson,* 1932 S.L.T. (Sh.Ct.) 16.
56 *Wilson v. Pattie* (1829) 7S. 316.
57 *Mitchell v. Brown* (1826) 5S. 56.
58 *Riddell v. Morisetti,* 1994 G.W.D. 38–2238; 1997 GWD 5–177, relating to
    proceedings on 19 Oct. 1994, 19 Jan. 1996 and 22 Nov. 1996, all available on
    Lexis.

disclosure of the name and profession of one of the common
proprietors who had a business at the end of the mutual access
lane but not the advertisement of the business.[59] The decision
may be justified on the basis that the sign was a direction sign.
On similar principles a co-proprietor may install drains to
carry away surface water which might destroy the surface of
the access and disrupt traffic. He may not install drains for
other purposes such as sewerage disposal unless, possibly, he
can demonstrate that drains for such other purposes are
commonly installed under accesses of the nature under
consideration, as might be the case where the access serves a
modern commercial, retail or residential development. It
remains open to the parties to define "ordinary" and permitted
uses by means of a real condition in a deed of declaration of
conditions affecting all the shares. Again there is little reported
case law on this matter but it has been held that a *pro indiviso*
proprietor may not erect temporary sheds or shops on ground
where a real condition required it to be kept unbuilt upon in all
time coming and used as a pleasure ground.[59a]

(c)   No co-proprietor may obtain an excessive benefit at the
expense of the other co-proprietors. What amounts to
"excessive" benefit may depend on the nature of the property,
the total number of co-proprietors and the size of share held by
the party alleged to be taking the excessive benefit. According
to one judicial view a co-owner with a large *pro indiviso* share
should be able to make a greater use of the co-owned property
than another co-owner with a smaller share.[60] According to
this view, where the co-owned property is an access road, a co-
owner with a three-quarters *pro indiviso* share should be able to
make more extensive use than another co-owner with a quarter
share. There are, however, contrary judicial views so the matter
cannot be regarded as settled.[61] It is open to the parties to
create express limitations on the burden which may be imposed

---

59   *Barkley v. Scott* (1893) 10 Sh.Ct.Rep. 23.
59a *Parlane v. Duncan* (1881) 18 S.L.R. 561. *cf. Stewart v. Marshall* (1894) 31 S.L.R.
     912.
60   *Menzies v. Macdonald* (1856) 2 Macq. 463 at 473, HL, per Lord Cranworth L.C.;
     George Watson's Hospital Governors v. Cormack (1883) 11R. 320 at 323 per Lord
     McLaren (*affd.* (1883) 11R. 320, IH).
61   *Menzies v. Macdonald* (1854) 16D. 827 at 856 per Lord Deas (*affd* 1856) 2 Macq.
     463, HL); *Menzies v. Wentworth* (1901) 3F. 941 per Lord Kinnear at 959; 9
     S.L.T. 107 at 110–111.

by each *pro indiviso* proprietor by means of real conditions created in the title of the relative share of the subjects.

(d) A co-owner may communicate his right of use to third parties[62] although he may not create a lease conferring exclusive possession of the whole subjects on the grantee. Where a third party has the right of use communicated to him, the burden of his use will be attributed to the share of the co-owner from whom his right derives. It follows that a co-owner may not permit parties to whom he has communicated a benefit to use his *pro indiviso* share to an extent which exceeds his legitimate share of the benefit.[63] It is *a fortiori* the case that the party to whom the *pro indiviso* property right has been communicated may not carry out acts which the owner cannot lawfully carry out.

(e) "Ordinary" use of a "matrimonial home"[64] commonly owned by a husband and wife or matrimonial homes owned by the spouses in common with one or more third parties clearly includes the occupancy of that property by either of the spouses for residential purposes. Under statutory provision either spouse may apply to the court for an order to regulate the exercise of occupancy rights.[65] In suitable cases the court may exclude the other spouse from the matrimonial home.[66] If one spouse conveys his or her *pro indiviso* share in the matrimonial home to a third party without the written consent of the other spouse[67] the third party will acquire no right to

---

62 *George Watson's Hospital Governors v. Cormack* (1883) 11R. 320 at 323 per Lord McLaren (*affd.* (1883) 11R. 320, IH).
63 *Bailey's Exers v. Upper Crathes Fishing Ltd*, 1987 S.L.T. 405, OH.
64 This is defined in 1981 Act, s.22, as amended by Law Reform (Misc. Prov.)(Sc.) Act 1985 (c.73), s.13(10). The term means any house, caravan, houseboat or other structure which has been provided or has been made available by one or both of the spouses as, or has become, a family residence. It includes any garden or other ground or building attached to, and usually occupied with, or otherwise required for the amenity or convenience of, the house, caravan, houseboat or other structure. Excluded from the definition is a residence provided or made available by one spouse for that spouse to reside in, whether with any child of the family or not, separately from the other spouse.
65 1981 Act, s.3(1)(d).
66 1981 Act, s.4, amended by Law Reform (Misc. Prov.) (Sc.) Act 1985, s.13(5). See 10 *Stair Memorial Encyclopaedia*, paras 863 and 864.
67 For the form of consent see 1981 Act, s.6(3)(a)(i) applied by 1981 Act, s.9(2); Matrimonial Homes (Form of Consent)(Scotland) Regulations 1982 (S.I. 1982 No. 971). Consent may be dispensed with under 1981 Act, s.7 (applied by 1981 Act, s.9(2) and amended by the Family Law (Scotland) Act 1985 (c. 37), s.28(2), Sched. 2, and the Age of Legal Capacity (Scotland) Act 1991 (c. 50), s.10(1), Sched. 1, para. 37).

occupy the matrimonial home.[68] This will usually result in one spouse having exclusive occupation of the matrimonial home – a position which is a significant alteration to the common law position.

(f) One *pro indiviso* proprietor may obtain a <u>remedy under the law of nuisance in suitable cases</u> where the offending activity is carried out by another co-owner. The introduction of excessive heat into a flue in a common gable separating dwellinghouses may be interdicted on this basis.[68a]

Alterations, Improvements and Repairs

5.7   Subject to contrary agreement by means of real conditions the issue of alterations, improvements and repairs is governed by the following principles:

(a) Each common proprietor has a right to veto the carrying out of any alterations to the common property.[69] Put another way, all common proprietors must consent to any alteration to the common property before it may be carried out. Where a co-proprietor does consent to an alteration his consent will bind singular successors. Whilst such consent should be given in writing it need not be created as a real condition. The right of veto may be subject to a *de minimis* exception.[70] Where an alteration has not been consented to and has not yet been carried out it may be prevented by interdict.[71]

(b) An exception to the requirement of unanimity exists in relation to necessary repairs. A single co-proprietor may instruct necessary repairs without the consent of his co-proprietors[72] and, probably also, without consulting them in advance.[73] The instructing party may then recover a proportion of the cost

---

68   1981 Act, s.9(1)(b).

68a *Wilsons v. Brydone* (1877) 14 S.L.R. 667.

69   Bell, *Prin*, s.1075; *Anderson v. Dalrymple* (1709) M. 12831; *Reid v. Nicol* (1799) M. "Property", App. No. 1; *Taylor v. Dunlop* (1872) 11M. 25.

70   *Barkley v. Scott* (1893) 10 Sh.Ct.Rep. 23 commented on in 18 *Stair Memorial Encyclopaedia*, para. 25.

71   *Riddell v. Morisetti* 1994 G.W.D. 38–2238; 1997 GWD 5–177 relating to proceedings on 19 Oct. 1994, 19 Jan. 1996 and 22 Nov. 1996, all available on Lexis.

72   Bell, *Prin*, s.1075 approved in *Deans v. Woolfson* 1922 S.C. 221; 1922 S.L.T. 165. Cf *Murray v. Johnstone* (1896) 23R. 981 per Lord Moncreiff at 990.

73   *Rennie v. McGill* (1885) 1 Sh.Ct.Rep. 158. Cf *Homecare Contracts (Scotland) Ltd v. Scottish Midland Co-operative Society Ltd* 1999 GWD 23–1111.

from his co-proprietors, conform to the size of their respective shares.[74] Despite the strength of the position of the instructing party in this regard it is clearly prudent to seek the consent of the other co-proprietors not only as to the necessity of the repairs but also the cost of the repair works themselves. There is institutional authority to the effect that necessary repairs may include rebuilding a totally destroyed building.[75] Nevertheless it is perhaps more prudent to assume that such extensive works would be beyond the class of works permitting unilateral action if only for the reason that a replacement building constructed according to modern techniques is unlikely to resemble the replaced building in all respects.[76]

(c) At its simplest and strictest a repair is intended to maintain property in its existing condition and should exclude improvements. Alterations are works which may deteriorate the state of the property or improve it (although one would hope the latter would be more frequent) and should be excluded from the definition. Nevertheless, matters are not as simple as that in practice and in many cases it may be difficult to distinguish between an alteration and a repair. It is common for access areas and doors to tenemental buildings to be owned in common by the various flat owners. It has been held that each proprietor may veto the installation of a door entry system on the front door.[77] In different circumstances where there is a higher risk of vandalism and crime it may be possible to argue that a different decision should be reached on the basis that the door entry system is essential to maintain the property in its existing state. A pragmatic approach is to be seen in a decision which took into account the fact that a property would no longer be insured by the existing insurers unless certain works were carried out. The court construed the term "repair" in a deed of conditions so as to permit a co-proprietor to carry out works to a lift even though these works were new and did not

---

74 *Rennie v. McGill* (1885) 1 Sh.Ct.Rep. 158; *Miller v. Crichton* (1893) 1 S.L.T. 262, OH; W.M. Gloag, *The Law of Contract* (2nd. ed., 1929), p. 323.

75 Bell, *Prin*, s.1075.

76 See the view expressed in 18 *Stair Memorial Encyclopaedia*, para. 25; *Deans v. Woolfson*, 1922 S.C. 221; 1922 S.L.T. 165.

77 *Addis v. Whittingehame Court Block 2 Residents' Association*, Sheriff M. Sischy, Glasgow Sheriff Court, 25 Sept. 1990, case ref: A2989/1988 (unreported).

constitute a replacement and thereafter to recover a proportion of the cost from a co-proprietor who objected.[78]

(d) A statutory variation of the common law position relative to repairs, alterations and improvements exists where the co-owned property comprises a "matrimonial home".[79] In respect of the statutory provisions dealing with division and sale the matrimonial homes affected include not only those owned in common by the husband and wife but also those owned by a husband and wife in common with one or more third parties.[80] Without the consent of the other spouse either spouse is entitled to carry out such non-essential repairs or improvements to the matrimonial home as the court considers to be appropriate for the reasonable enjoyment of the spouse's occupancy rights.[81] Improvements are defined to include alterations and enlargements.[82] Recovery of expense in carrying out such repairs or improvements may be dealt with by court order and the court may apportion the expenditure incurred having regard to the respective financial circumstances of the spouses.[83] These statutory rules cannot be excluded by means of contract, real condition or otherwise.

Variation of Position by Real Conditions

5.8 The normal rules relative to use and management of common property may be varied to some extent by real conditions whether in the form of servitudes, real burdens or rights of common interest.

(a) Real burdens are frequently employed to impose a more detailed regime of maintenance and repair than that which is envisaged by the common law.[84] They are also used to regulate use to some extent.[85] The method of imposition of the obligations is frequently a deed of conditions which relates to

---

78 *McLay v. Bennett and Bennett*, Edinburgh Sheriff Court, Sheriff Principal Gordon Nicholson; briefly noted at 1998 G.W.D. 16–810; "*Conveyancing – What Happened in 1998*". Reid and Gretton The University of Edinburgh. Faculty of Law, p. 9 and commentary p. 94.

79 As defined in statute: see para. 2.9.

80 Matrimonial Homes (Family Protection) (Scotland) Act 1981, s.19. See 18 *Stair Memorial Encyclopaedia*, para. 27, fn. 4.

81 Matrimonial Homes (Family Protection) (Scotland) Act 1981, s.2(4)(a).

82 1981 Act, s.2(9).

83 1981 Act, s.2(4)(b).

84 *E.g. Wells v. New House Purchasers Ltd*, 1964 S.L.T. (Sh.Ct.) 2; *McNally and Miller Property Co. v. Mallinson*, 1977 S.L.T. (Sh.Ct.) 33.

85 Para. 5.6.

the whole subjects. Where the various *pro indiviso* property rights are held separately from any other property the dominant and servient tenements will be the *pro indiviso* shares themselves and there will be a regime of mutually enforceable real conditions with each share simultaneously forming a benefited and burdened tenement in respect of the real burdens.[86] Frequently, however, the *pro indiviso* shares are linked in some way with the ownership of various neighbouring tenements in the exclusive ownership of each of the parties. Such would be the case, for example, where an ornamental square in common ownership of the immediately neighbouring property owners was surrounded by exclusively town houses.

(b) Common interest generally arises by implication of law in certain situations the absence of regulation by real conditions.[87] It may limit the free exercise of the rights of one *pro indiviso* property owner by conferring certain rights on others. The types of situations in which common interest arises tend to be those where the *pro indiviso* property right is held together with exclusive ownership of some property in close proximity. Typical examples include tenemental buildings containing flats in separate ownership and items such as the common passageway and roof in common ownership, the shared ornamental gardens within squares of residences or offices and similar cases. Nevertheless, common interest may also exist where there is no exclusive property in the ownership of the various co-owners in close proximity. The content of the rights and obligations will vary according to the nature of the property and, in particular circumstances, has been held to extend to rights of access, rights to light and rights of support. Where the various *pro indiviso* property rights are held together with an exclusive property right in surrounding land, as is the case in many ornamental squares, the dominant tenement will be the exclusively owned house or office and the servient tenement will be the *pro indiviso* property rights of the other proprietors.

(c) Where a positive servitude (such as access) is to burden the co-owned property the whole of that property comprising all the shares will be the servient tenement. Any number less than all of the co-owners cannot burden the co-owned property with a

---

86 The matter has never been directly considered by the courts but appears to have been assumed in *Wilson's Trs v. Brown's Exers* (1907) 15 S.L.T. 747, OH. See 18 *Stair Memorial Encyclopaedia*, paras 26 and 411.

87 See further Chap. 9.

positive servitude.[88] This rule is sometimes circumvented in practice where, by means of a deed of conditions, all the common proprietors have irrevocably delegated authority to a single *pro indiviso* proprietor or a body of such proprietors to grant such servitudes.[89] There are, however, limitations on the efficacy of such a device, particularly in relation to singular successors.[90]

Division and Sale

5.9   As with Roman law[91] and other mixed legal systems such as South Africa[92] and Sri Lanka,[93] Scots law does not imprison co-owners in a regime of common property. Quite apart from his right to sell his own share,[94] each co-owner in common property is entitled to apply to the court to have the property divided proportionately amongst all the co-owners or, if such physical division is impracticable, to have the entire property sold and the proceeds divided.[95] Subject to the exceptional cases noted below,[96] the entitlement of each co-proprietor to a division and sale is absolute.[97] A co-proprietor is entitled to a division and sale even though his share is small when compared to the shares of others or could have been readily sold as a *pro indiviso* share without the sale of the other's shares. There is no obligation on co-proprietors to attempt to agree the terms of any division or division and sale before the court will grant an appropriate remedy.[98] Nevertheless it would be prudent for the party seeking the division or division and sale to make such an attempt if only because an agreed solution is almost certainly quicker than a forced solution and the conveyancing costs incurred by him in connection with the entering into of an

---

88 *Grant v. Heriot's Trust* (1906) 8F. 647; *Fearnan Partnership v. Grindlay*, 1990 S.L.T. 704; Cusine and Paisley, *Servitudes and Rights of Way*, para. 4.11.
89 Cusine and Paisley, *Servitudes and Rights of Way*, para. 4.11.
90 Cusine and Paisley, paras 4.11 and 4.26–4.28.
91 G. MacCormack, "The *Actio Communi Dividundo* in Roman and Scots Law", in A.D.E. Lewis and D.J. Ibbetson (eds), *The Roman Law Tradition* (1993).
92 Van der Merwe and de Waal, *The Law of Things and Servitudes*, para. 212–213.
93 G.L. Peiris, "*Servitudes and Partition*", in *The Law of Property in Sri Lanka* (1977), pp. 158–376.
94 Para. 5.4.
95 Craig, *Jus Feudale*, II,8,35,41; Stair, I,vii,15; Bankton, I,viii,36,40; Ersk, *Inst*, III,iii,56; Bell, *Prin*, ss 1079–1082.
96 Para. 5.10.
97 *Upper Crathes Fishings Ltd v. Bailey's Exers*, 1991 S.C.L.R. 151; 1991 S.L.T. 747.
98 The position is otherwise in South Africa: see Van der Merwe and de Waal, *The Law of Things and Servitudes*, para. 212.

agreement are likely to be less than the irrecoverable expenses of a successful court action.

An action of division and sale may be raised in the Court of Session or the relevant sheriff court.[99] Only where property is indivisible will the court order it to be sold. Property will be considered indivisible if it is impossible to divide the property in such a manner as to give each co-proprietor a *pro rata* share or if such a division can be carried out only by adversely affecting the value of the whole property.[1] The application of this twofold test renders the vast majority of instances of common property indivisible. Unless indivisibility is admitted by the parties[2] it will require to be determined by a proof[3] or by reference to a person of skill.[4] The method of sale may be by public roup or by private bargain,[5] the latter being more common in modern practice. The method selected will be that which will yield the highest price in any particular case.[6] There is some authority to support the proposition that a party seeking division and sale may also conclude for warrant to purchase the shares of the other co-owners.[7] Given that the whole object of the procedure is to obtain the highest price it may be that this will be granted only if there is no evidence that a higher price will be obtained on the open market. Sale on the open market will also resolve difficulties arising where more than one co-proprietor applies for warrant to purchase the shares of the others. Upon sale the proceeds of sale are divided in proportion to the shares held by the respective co-owners or, alternatively, in accordance with any agreement entered into between the parties.

Limitation on Division and Sale

The absolute right of a *pro indiviso* proprietor to obtain a division 5.10 and sale in respect of the common property may be limited in various ways as follows:

---

99 Sheriff Courts (Scotland) Act 1907 (c. 51), s.5(3); I.D. Macphail, *Sheriff Court Practice* (2nd ed., 1999), paras 23–37ff.
1 See *Thom v. MacBeath* (1875) 3R. 161.
2 *E.g. Brock v. Hamilton* (1857) 19D. 701.
3 *E.g. Bryden v. Gibson* (1837) 15S. 486. *Cf. Thom v. MacBeath* (1875) 3R. 161 at 165 per Lord Gifford.
4 *E.g. Upper Crathes Fishings Ltd v. Bailey's Exers*, 1991 S.C.L.R. 151; 1991 S.L.T. 747.
5 *Campbells v. Murray*, 1972 S.C. 310; 1972 S.L.T. 249.
6 *The Miller Group Ltd v. Tasker*, 1993 S.L.T. 207. *Cf. Berry v. Berry (No.2)* 1989 S.L.T. 292.
7 *Scrimgeour v. Scrimgeour*, 1988 S.L.T. 590, OH. *Cf. Berry v. Berry (No.2)*, *supra*. See 18 *Stair Memorial Encyclopaedia*, para. 33.

(a) The right may be excluded by contract but this will not bind singular successors. The contract will require to be precisely worded to deprive a co-proprietor of such a right and a contract not to carry out other juristic acts such as sale, lease or evacuation of a special destination will not suffice. It is *a fortiori* the case that the right to seek a division and sale is not affected by the mere existence of a survivorship destination.[8]

(b) In appropriate circumstances a co-proprietor may be personally barred from insisting on division and sale.[9] Such personal bar will not bind singular successors.

(c) Limitations may be imposed by means of common interest. Common interest in some cases may preclude resort to an action of division and sale by any of the owners without the consent of the others.[10] The aim in such cases is to preserve the co-owned property for the purposes to which it is dedicated. Such cases include essential access areas owned in common, such as staircases in tenements, common access roads serving modern developments and shared gardens.[11]

(d) Where the co-owned property comprises a "matrimonial home"[12] co-owned by a husband and wife, statutory rules limit, but do not wholly exclude, the right of each of the spouses to apply for a division and sale. In respect of the statutory provisions dealing with division and sale the matrimonial homes affected are limited to those owned in common by the husband and wife and do not include those owned by a husband and wife in common with one or more third parties.[13] The court has discretion (i) to refuse to grant a right to division and sale, or (ii) to postpone the granting of decree for such period as it considers reasonable in the circumstances which may include a period occurring after the marriage has been ended by divorce,[14] or (iii) it may grant decree subject to such conditions as it may prescribe. Statute

---

8   *Dunsmore v. Dunsmore*, 1986 S.L.T. (Sh.Ct.) 9. *Cf. Allan v. MacPherson* (1928) Sh.Ct.Rep. 63. The latter case appears to be wrongly decided see 18 *Stair Memorial Encyclopaedia*, para. 28, fn. 2

9   *Upper Crathes Fishing Ltd v. Bailey's Exers*, 1991 S.C.L.R. 151 at 152, 1991 S.L.T. 747 at 749 per L.P. Hope; *Bush v. Bush*, 1999 S.L.T. (Sh.Ct.) 22.

10 Bell, *Prin.*, s.1082.

11 *Grant v. Heriot's Trust* (1906) 8F. 647 at 665 per Lord McLaren; 18 *Stair Memorial Encyclopaedia*, para. 26.

12 As defined in statute: see para. 2.9.

13 Matrimonial Homes (Family Protection) (Scotland) Act 1981, s.19. See 18 *Stair Memorial Encyclopaedia*, para. 27, fn. 4.

14 *Hall v. Hall*, 1987 S.C.L.R. 38; 1987 S.L.T. (Sh.Ct.) 15.

confirms that in the exercise of its discretion the court is to have regard to all the circumstances of the case and, in a rather otiose list, confirms a range of matters which are included in this.[15] Although there have been a number of decided cases on the matter there is as yet no consensus as to how the discretion conferred on the court is to be exercised.[16]

Limitation on Juristic Acts

The right of each co-proprietor to carry out juristic acts in relation to his own share has been noted above.[17] This right is subject to some limitations as follows: **5.11**

(a) A co-proprietor's rights to carry out juristic acts is limited by the application of the maxim *nemo dat quod non habet*.[18] A single co-proprietor cannot validly confer any right on a third party which purports to confer exclusive possession on a third party.[19]

(b) A co-proprietor cannot contract with himself. On this basis it has been held that co-proprietors even if they all act together cannot grant a lease to one of their own number.[20] This decision is not beyond criticism as it may be argued that the debtor and creditor in such a lease are not the same[21] and it seems inconsistent with the approach which permits the co-proprietors to contract with each other to regulate the use of the co-owned property.[22] In practice the difficulty is avoided

---

15 Matrimonial Homes (Family Protection) (Scotland) Act 1981, s.10 (applying s.3(3)(a)–(d)).

16 See, *e.g.*, the contrasting approaches in *Hall v. Hall*, 1987 S.C.L.R. 38; 1987 S.L.T. (Sh.Ct.) 15; *Berry v. Berry*, 1988 S.C.L.R. 296; 1988 S.L.T. 650, OH; *Rae, v. Rae* 1991 S.C.L.R. 188; 1991 S.L.T. 454.

17 Para. 5.4.

18 No-one may confer a right which he does not himself possess. See also paras 2.13 and 2.14.

19 18 *Stair Memorial Encyclopaedia*, para. 28, fn. 14. *Cf.* the position in South Africa discussed in *Kelly v. Kirkwood* (1857) 3 S. 5 (lease); Van der Merwe and de Waal, *The Law of Things and Servitudes*, para. 211, fn. 4.

20 *Barclay v. Penman*, 1984 S.L.T. 376; *Clydesdale Bank plc v. Davidson*, 1996 S.L.T. 437.

21 18 *Stair Memorial Encyclopaedia*, para. 28. The position in South Africa supports the criticism and recognises the validity of such a lease. Indeed in that jurisdiction a co-owner enjoys a preferential right to lease the common property from all the common owners if he is prepared to pay the rent required. See Grotius, *Inleidinge* 3 28 4–5; Voet 10 3 8; Van der Keessel, *Thes Sel*, 772–773; *Pretorius v. Botha* 1961 4 S.A. 722 (T) at 726.

22 Para. 5.6.

by the co-proprietors granting a lease to a third party who immediately sub-leases to the single co-proprietor. It may be argued that the same theoretical difficulty should arise where co-proprietors wish to grant a servitude over the common property in favour of a dominant tenement exclusively owned by one of their number. It is submitted that in this respect there is also sufficient difference between the creditor and debtor.[23] In any event, even if the servitude were to be regarded as invalid such a grant could be regarded as a declaration by the common proprietors as to what they regard as an acceptable or ordinary use of the common property and enforceable on that basis.[24]

(c) There are certain limitations arising from the special statutory regulation of matrimonial homes.[25]

(d) As in relation to exclusive rights of property,[26] real conditions cannot generally be used to restrict the performance of juristic acts but qualified restrictions, such as the creation of a right of pre-emption in favour of another co-proprietor or a third party, will be enforceable.[27]

Legal Proceedings – Title to Sue

5.12   The general rule is that legal proceedings affecting one *pro indiviso* share only must be raised by the owner of that share and a co-proprietor has no title to raise legal proceedings in respect of matters affecting only another share.[28] Actions relating to the whole common property must be raised by all the owners acting together. Thus where land is leased and the landlords are common proprietors they must all join in an action of removing[29] or recovery of rent.[30] Nevertheless, where a particular *pro indiviso* share is adversely affected by the actions of a third party, whether they constitute trespass or encroachment[31] or a delict,[32] the relevant *pro*

---

23 Cusine and Paisley, *Servitudes and Rights of Way*, para. 2.07.
24 Para. 5.6.
25 See paras 5.5, 5.6, 5.7 and 5.10.
26 Para. 4.4.
27 Para. 4.4.
28 *Eunson v. The Braer Corporation* 1999 S.L.T. 1405.
29 Ersk., *Inst.*, II,vi,53; *Murdoch v. Inglis* (1679) 3 Brown's Supp. 297; *Johnston v. Craufurd* (1855) 17D. 1023.
30 *Schaw v. Black* (1889) 16R. 336.
31 *Johnston v. Craufurd* (1855) 17D. 1023; *Lade v. Largs Baking Co. Ltd* (1863) 2M. 17; *Laird v. Reid* (1871) 9M. 699. See also 18 *Stair Memorial Encyclopaedia*, paras 29 and 141.
32 *Eunson v. The Braer Corporation, supra.*

indiviso proprietor is not disabled from raising procedings in respect of his own share merely because other *pro indiviso* shares have also been adversely affected by the activity.

Timeshares

Timeshares usually involve various people having the right to the 5.13 exclusive use of land or salmon fishings for fixed periods of time. Arrangements intended to last for a limited period of time may be set up by the use of leases[33] but the arrangement frequently is intended to last in perpetuity. In Scotland they may be created by various legal devices but, given the limitations on the possibility of a co-owner having exclusive occupation of the co-owned property even for a limited time, they do not usually involve co-ownership of any sort.[34] The most commonly encountered methods of creating a timeshare in Scotland is for the real right of property in the item subject to the timeshare to be held either by a trustee and for the persons purchasing timeshares to be beneficiaries of that trust or, alternatively, by a limited company in which the timeshare purchasers hold shares. Statute provides for a cooling-off period in relation to the entering into of agreements to purchase timeshares and related loan agreements.[35] For the statute to apply, the agreements must be entered into between parties one of whom is in the United Kingdom at the time of contracting or, alternatively, the agreement must be governed by the law of one of the jurisdictions within the United Kingdom to some extent.

---

33 Gordon, *Scottish Land Law*, (2nd ed.), para. 19–13.
34 See paras 1.28(c) and 2.6.
35 Timeshare Act 1992 (c. 35), ss 2 and 5; Timeshare (Cancellation Notices) Order 1992, (S.I. 1992 no. 1942).

CHAPTER 6

PROPER LIFERENTS, TENANCIES AT WILL AND KINDLY TENANCIES

Introduction

6.1   Liferent is the right to the use or income of property for the duration of the lifetime of the holder or some shorter period as is determined in the deed of constitution. It may affect both moveables[1] and heritage but the former will not be discussed further here. It should be noted, however, that it is common for liferents in relation to a domestic house to affect the furniture in that house as well.[2]

The party creating the liferent is known as the "constituent".[3] The party entitled to the use of the liferented subjects without encroaching on the substance is the "liferenter" and the party entitled to the substance on termination of the liferent is known as the "fiar". In relation to a trust or improper liferents there are also trustees who hold the property right in the subjects whilst the liferent endures. No trustees exist in relation to proper liferents. The exact manner and the identity of the person to which the right of fee devolves will be determined by the construction of the express clause in the grant known as the "destination". The interpretation of these clauses is a matter of considerable technicality which is beyond the scope of this book.[4] Because liferents, particularly proper liferents, are rare in modern practice, they will receive a relatively brief treatment in this book.

Proper and Improper Liferents

6.2   Two types of liferent are recognised in Scotland—proper and

---

1   18 *Stair Memorial Encyclopaedia*, para. 534(2).
2   *Cochran v. Cochran* (1755) M. 8280; 2 *Bell's Illustrations*, p. 141.
3   Stair, *Institutions*, II,vi,8.
4   See 13 *Stair Memorial Encyclopaedia*, paras 1622–1629.

improper.[5] Improper liferents are sometimes termed "trust" or "beneficiary" liferents.[6]

(a) Proper liferent is one of the real rights recognised by Scots law.[7] The right of the party entitled to the liferent is less than full *dominium*. In principle he must exercise his right without encroaching on the substance of the thing which is subject to the right—*salva rerum substantia*.[8] Nevertheless, the right of liferent comprises certain aspects which resemble the greater right of ownership in the extent of the rights of use and the power to carry out certain juristic acts. For example a proper liferenter may enforce rights of common interest against a neighbouring proprietor[9] and, by analogy, he may enforce servitudes and rights constituted as real conditions. So extensive are these rights that the liferenter has been termed "*interim dominus* or proprietor for life".[10] Proper liferent may have developed from the personal servitude known in Roman law as *usufruct*.[11]

(b) Improper liferent is merely the beneficial interest under a trust and the beneficiary has no real right in the land. The real right of ownership rests with the trustees[12] who hold the property for two classes of beneficiary, the liferenter and the fiar.[13] It follows that an improper liferent may be constituted only by the creation of a trust. For details of these the reader is referred to authorities on trusts as they will not be examined in detail here. It should be noted, however, that an improper liferent is a much more flexible device than a proper liferent and is more commonly encountered in modern practice.[14]

Further Classifications of Liferents

Two further classifications of liferents may be made: 6.3

---

5 Gordon, *Scottish Land Law* (2nd ed.), para. 17–02.
6 See, *e.g.*, Gordon, *Scottish Land Law* (2nd ed.), para. 17–02.
7 18 *Stair Memorial Encyclopaedia*, paras 5(3) and 74.
8 Gordon, *Scottish Land Law* (2nd ed.), para. 17–01. See this text, para. 2.20(a).
9 *Cyril Newton v. Agnes Godfrey*, June 19, 2000, Sheriff Smith, Stranraer Sheriff Court (unreported, case ref. A118/98). The author thanks Tony MacAndrew, solicitor in Stranraer, for this reference.
10 Erskine, *Institute*, II,ix,41, approved in *Miller v. Inland Revenue*, 1928 S.C. 819 per L.P. Clyde at 829.
11 Justinian, *Institutes*, II,vii; Erskine, *Inst.*, II,ix,39.
12 18 *Stair Memorial Encyclopaedia*, paras 5(3) and 74.
13 13 *Stair Memorial Encyclopaedia*, para. 1603.
14 13 *Stair Memorial Encyclopaedia*, para. 1609.

(a) Legal and conventional liferents.[15] Legal liferents arise by virtue of law whilst conventional liferents are created by the granting of a deed. The two principal legal liferents are the widow's terce and the widower's courtesy which affect land in the estate of the pre-deceasing spouse. As these rights cannot be claimed in respect of any death occurring after 10 September 1964[16] they shall not be discussed further here. Because of this time limitation the distinction between legal and conventional liferents has been described as "obsolescent".[17] This is not entirely accurate as there are other rights which may be regarded as "legal" liferents. For example, where the site of a croft house is purchased by the existing crofter then that person and his spouse may enjoy any right of peat cutting which they enjoyed prior to the purchase as crofting tenants. This statutory right is a form of legal liferent as it exists whether or not it is stated in the subsequent conveyance of the croft house[18] and terminates on the death of the last survivor of the husband and wife.[19]

(b) Alimentary and non-alimentary.[20] An alimentary liferent is a special category of improper liferent which is intended to provide for the maintenance of the liferenter in a manner which also protects the liferenter from his or her own improvidence. A proper liferent may not be created as an alimentary liferent.[21] No person may create an alimentary liferent of his own property in his own favour.[22] In relation to such a liferent there are two main limitations which secure this protection. First, the liferented subjects may not be attached by the liferenter's creditors (except creditors for alimentary debts[23]).

---

15 Gordon, *Scottish Land Law* (2nd ed.), para. 17–03.
16 Succession (Scotland) Act 1964, ss 10(1) and 33(1).
17 Gloag and Henderson, *Laws of Scotland* (10th ed., 1995), para. 47.2.
18 *Macleod v. Viscount Thurso*, 1982 S.L.C.R. 125.
19 Crofters (Scotland) Act 1993, s.17(6), replacing Crofting Reform (Scotland) Act 1976, s.6(6).
20 Gordon, *Scottish Land Law* (2nd ed.), para. 17–04.
21 *Forbes's Trs v. Tennant*, 1926 S.C. 294; Gordon, *supra*, para. 17–32.
22 The rule for men arises from the common law, see, *e.g.*, *Ker's Tr. v. Justice* (1866) 5M. 4; *Ord Ruthven v. Drummond*, 1908 S.C. 1154. For women the exceptional cases in which such a device was permitted at common law have been removed by statute insofar as the contract is entered into after 24 July 1984: see Law Reform (Husband and Wife) (Scotland) Act 1984, s.5(1)(b).
23 *Earl of Buchan v. His Creditors* (1835) 13S. 1112; *Lord Ruthven v. Pulford & Sons*, 1909 S.C. 951; *Maitland v. Maitland*, 1912 1 S.L.T. 350.

Secondly, the beneficiary may not assign, terminate or vary the alimentary liferent except with court approval.[24] In an alimentary liferent the trustees must be independent from the beneficiary.[25] To establish an alimentary liferent it is not necessary to use the word "alimentary" although it is prudent to do so to avoid future dispute as to the proper construction of the deed. It is sufficient to indicate an alimentary nature of the right granted if the deed employs terminology confirming that the right is granted "for the maintenance" of the holder or if it restricts the legal dealings of the holder and excludes the diligence of creditors.[26]

Creation of Liferent

An improper liferent relating to land is created in the same 6.4 manner as any trust relating to heritage. A proper liferent may be constituted in various ways. First, the constituent may convey the fee to another and reserve the liferent to himself. Secondly, the constituent may convey the fee to one party and the liferent to another. Both these types of proper liferents are known as simple liferents. Thirdly, the constituent may retain the fee and confer the liferent on another. This is known as a liferent by reservation. Where a liferent of heritage is granted it will be made real not by delivery of the deed but by recording of the deed in the General Register of Sasines (or Land Register as the case may be).[27] Where a liferent is reserved the constituent need take no further steps to create his liferent as a real right because the law deems the real right of the liferenter to spring from the original title. The transfer of the right of fee, however, remains to be made real by registration in the normal fashion.

Restrictions on the Creation of Liferents

As regards heritage there are two statutory regimes which restrict 6.5 the creation of liferents. Their applicability depends on the date of

---

24 Gordon, *supra*, (2nd ed.), paras 17–01 and 17–32; Trusts (Scotland) Act 1961, s.1(4).
25 *McCallum v. McCulloch's Trs* (1904) 7F. 337.
26 *Chambers' Trs v. Smiths* (1878) 5R. (HL) 151; *Dewar's Trs v. Dewar*, 1910 S.C. 730; *Arnold's Trs v. Graham*, 1927 S.C. 353. The exclusion of the diligence of creditors alone may be insufficient, see *Douglas Gardiner & Mill v. Mackintosh's Trs*, 1916 S.C. 125.
27 Abolition of Feudal Tenure etc. (Scotland) Ast 2000, s.65, to come into force on the appointed day.

execution of the relevant deed. The regimes apply (a) to liferents created prior to 25 April 1968 and (b) to liferents created on or after 25 April 1968.

(a)   As regards liferents created prior to 25 April 1968 the relevant provisions are contained in the Entail Amendment Act 1848, ss 47 and 48.[28] It is undecided whether the latter section applies only to proper liferents leaving the former, which relates to "trusts", to deal with improper liferents.[29] For a liferent to be competent the liferenter must be alive at the date of the execution of the relevant deed. Where a liferenter was not alive at the date of execution of the deed he is entitled to the fee upon obtaining a court decree to that effect.

(b)   As regards liferents created on or after 25 April 1968 the governing provision is the Law Reform (Miscellaneous Provisions)(Scotland) Act 1968, s.18. If the person to whom the liferent is granted is conceived after the date upon which the deed comes into operation then that person is given an absolute interest in the property in question on the date on which he becomes entitled to the liferent interest. The date of operation of the deed is usually the date of execution of an *inter vivos* deed but in respect of a *mortis causa* deed it is the date of death of the granter.

(c)   The anti-accumulation provisions relating to trusts generally also apply to trust liferents but have no application to proper liferents.[30]

Duration of the Right

6.6   In the absence of special provision a liferent will endure for the lifetime of the party entitled thereto. It may, however, be created for a fixed period[31] or uncertain period which is shorter than the lifetime of the holder such as the marriage of the liferenter.[32] An irritancy clause may be inserted in a grant or reservation of a proper liferent which may result in the early termination of the liferent in a case of breach by the liferenter of the stated prohibition. No remedy of irritancy is implied by law in relation to a proper liferent.

The assignation of a proper liferent is not competent but the

---

28 To be amended by Abolition of Feudal Tenure etc. (Scotland) Act 2000, s.76(1) and (2) and Sched. 12, paras 5(5) and (6) and Sched. 13, P 1.
29 *Lord Binning, Ptr*, 1984 S.L.T. 18.
30 See Wilson and Duncan, *Trust, Trustees and Executors* (2nd ed., 1995), Chap. 9.
31 *Campbell v. Wardlaw* (1883) 10R. (H.L.) 65 per Lord Blackburn at 66.
32 *Kidd v. Kidd* (1863) 2M. 227.

liferenter may assign the right to use the liferented subjects during the original liferenter's lifetime. If such assignation is competent the right to use enjoyed by the assignee will terminate when the liferent terminates. Such assignation may be precluded by an express exclusion of the right and such a prohibition is frequently fenced with an irritancy clause.

The Terms of the Grant

Deeds creating liferents have a notoriety for ambiguity. This arises largely because many of such deeds are *mortis causa* deeds which may have been drafted in the absence of legal advice. Many cases interpreting deeds creating liferents are decided on their own special facts and provide little authoritative guidance for the modern property lawyer or conveyancer.[33] Only broad principles may be gleaned from the morass of decided cases. These may be summarised as follows:

6.7

(a) The law does not recognise an interest intermediate between those of liferent and fee.[34] This has the direct consequence that certain purported qualifications of the fee may be invalid.[35] In other circumstances certain qualifications of a purported grant of fee may reduce that grant to one of liferent only. The distinction is easy to make in the abstract but horrendously difficult to apply as a matter of practice.

(b) With suitable drafting the liferenter may be given certain rights which would not be conferred on him by law. These include the right to borrow on the security of the land itself and not merely his interest in the land. A liferent may be granted with certain limitations but in some grants these restrictions may be so extensive as to give rise to doubts as to whether the right conferred is a liferent or a mere personal right. A reference to a right to "use" or "occupancy" in the absence of the employment of the word "liferent" tends to indicate a personal right[36] although this is not conclusive.[37] If no funds are provided for the maintenance of the property this tends to indicate that the burden of maintenance will fall on the occupier of the property

---

33 Gordon, *Scottish Land Law* (2nd ed.), para 17–09.
34 *Cochrane's Exrx v. Cochrane* 1947 S.C. 134; Smith, *Short Commentary*, p. 487.
35 *Johnston v. Johnstons* (1903) 5F. 1039; *Ironside's Exr v. Ironside's Exr*, 1933 S.C. 116; *Cochrane's Exr v. Cochrane*, 1947 S.C. 134.
36 *Clark* (1871) 9M. 435; *Johnston v. Johnston* (1904) 6F. 665; *Miller v. Inland Revenue*, 1928 S.C. 819.
37 *Milne's Tr. v. Milne*, 1920 S.C. 456.

and points to a liferent even though the term "liferent" is not employed.[38]

(c) In principle it would appear to be competent to restrict the use of the liferented subjects and impose both negative restraints and certain positive obligations on the liferenter. Some restraints would be enforceable by the fiar. Although there is no clear authority on the matter these devices would appear to be a form of real condition where they occur in relation to a proper liferent.

Rights to Use Liferented Subjects

6.8 The liferenter has the right to actual possession of the liferented subjects conform to the terms of the liferent.[39] Where he is in such actual possession the liferenter will be civilly possessing the liferented subjects on behalf of the proprietor—the trustee in an improper liferent or the fiar in a proper liferent.[40]

A cardinal rule of any liferent is that the liferenter is entitled to use the subjects but must enjoy them without diminishing the substance thereof. It is clear, however, that an exception to this general rule is recognised in the case of mines and quarries where these existed, and exploitation had begun, prior to the start of the liferent. These can be enjoyed by the liferenter who may continue to extract minerals even though the extraction of minerals must diminish the subjects of the right.[41] Subject to any qualification in the deed of constitution the liferenter has the right to enjoy the "fruits" of the subjects of liferent: in other words he may be entitled to the income but not the capital.

The rights of the liferenter and fiar are most easily illustrated by reference to the commonly encountered examples of a domestic house and a farm.

(a) As regards a domestic house the principal right of the proper liferenter is to occupy the house and any lands effeiring thereto. As he may not encroach upon the substance the liferenter may not rip the roof off the house or undermine the foundations by excessive DIY work. If the property is let, the liferenter is entitled to the rents.

(b) As regards arable farms the liferenter is entitled to any crops

---

38 *Johnstone v. Mackenzie's Trs*, 1912 S.C. (H.L.) 106; *Montgomerie-Fleming's Trs v. Carre*, 1913 S.C. 1018.
39 18 *Stair Memorial Encyclopaedia*, para. 127.
40 18 *Stair Memorial Encyclopaedia*, para. 121.
41 *Wardlaw v. Wardlaw's Trs* (1875) 2R. 368.

sown by him on the property and to the rents of any fields or farm property let. As regards stock-rearing farms the liferenter is obliged to maintain the stock if they were originally stocked at the start of the liferent.[42] Where there is timber growing on a farm the liferenter has no general right to cut it[43] but he is entitled to ordinary windfalls and he is entitled to cuttings at the normal time of coppice wood.[44]

In exchange for the right to use the liferented property the proper 6.9 liferenter must bear the burdens attendant on those subjects such as local taxation, water and electricity charges and other yearly payments chargeable on the land or directly referable to its use.[45] In general the liferenter is obliged to preserve the subjects by means of ordinary repair necessary to keep the subjects in a tenantable condition but is not liable for ordinary wear and tear or accident. It seems competent to supplement these obligations by means of express real conditions enforceable by the fiar against the liferenter. A liferenter who makes improvements to the subjects is presumed to do this for his own benefit and cannot recover the value thereof from the fiar.[46] The same principles are generally applied to trust liferents subject always to variation in the trust deed.

Juristic Acts

In a proper liferent the liferenter has a real right in the land and is 6.10 able to grant subsidiary real rights such as servitudes[47] or leases which have an endurance equal to or less than the liferent itself but may grant rights extending beyond this duration only with the consent of the fiar. As regards a trust liferent the position of the liferenter is completely different. Having no real right himself, he has no power to create derivative real rights[48] except insofar as the power to do so is delegated in terms of the trust deed from the party holding the real right—the trustee. In relation to a trust liferent the power to grant leases is held by the trustees unless excluded by the

---

42 *Rogers v. Scott* (1867) 5M. 1078.
43 Stair, *Inst.*, II,iii,74; Erskine, *Inst.*, II,ix, 56 and 58; Bell, *Prin*, s.1046.
44 *MacAlister's Trs v. MacAlister* (1851) 13D. 1239. *Cf. Marquess of Breadalbane's Trs v. Pringle* (1854) 16D. 359.
45 Erskine, *Inst*, II,ix,61.
46 Erskine, *Principles*, II,ix,33; Bell, *Prin*, ss 1061.
47 18 *Stair Memorial Encyclopaedia*, para. 449.
48 *Miller v. Inland Revenue*, 1928 S.C. 819 per L.P. Clyde at 829; 13 *Stair Memorial Encyclopaedia*, para. 1634.

trust deed.[49] Additional powers may be obtained by trustees upon application to court.[50]

Termination of Proper Liferents

6.11   Proper liferents may be terminated in various ways as follows:

   (a)   Death of the liferenter. This is the most common means by which a liferent is ended. In rare cases the original deed of constitution specifies the length of the liferent by reference to the lifetime of another party, in which case the liferent continues after the earlier death of the liferenter.

   (b)   Renunciation by the liferenter. The effect of renunciation of a liferent depends on whether or not the fee has vested. If it has, the fiar is free to take possession of the subjects when the liferent is renounced. If the fee has not vested the outcome depends on the provisions of the deed constituting the liferent. In some cases the deed permits accelerated vesting which will terminate the liferent. This, however, is relatively rare. In the more common case there will be no possibility of immediate extinction of the liferent as the fee has not vested. Instead what emerges is a type of "shadow liferent"[51] and the terms of the deed must again be construed to identify the party entitled to it.[52]

   (c)   Confusion or consolidation. When the same party holds both fee and liferent the liferent is extinguished by consolidation. In practice the matter is frequently confirmed by a deed styled "deed of renunciation" or "minute of consolidation" where the liferented subjects comprise only heritage. Although there is some authority to suggest that such a practice is necessary,[53] this requirement is not supported by basic principle. In any event, even if the practice is technically ineffective it does assist in relation to evidential matters.

   (d)   The occurrence of a stated event. It is possible to create a liferent which is either terminable at the option of the fiar upon the happening of particular event or one which terminates automatically upon the happening of a particular event. Where

---

49 Trusts (Scotland) Act 1921, s.4(1)(b).
50 Trusts (Scotland) Act 1921, s.5.
51 G.L. Gretton, "*Vesting, Equitable Compensation and the Mysteries of the Shadow Liferent*", 1988 S.L.T. (News) 149.
52 13 *Stair Memorial Encyclopaedia*, para. 1657.
53 *Young's Trs v. Mair's Trs*, 1914 S.C. 893. *Cf.* 13 *Stair Memorial Encyclopaedia*, para. 1650.

such an approach is adopted it is best to choose an event which is capable of objective ascertainment by reference to public facts or records—such as the marriage of the liferenter[54]—failing which the liferent should contain a mechanism for the happening of the event to be certified by an independent third party.

(e) Destruction of the subjects. In relation to usufruct of a house the Roman law took the approach that the right would terminate if the house was destroyed.[55] Scots law is less harsh in respect of proper liferent and where a house subject to a liferent is destroyed either the fiar or the liferenter have a right to rebuild it.[56] In some cases a right of compensation will be available to the liferenter where this is impracticable.[57] This may be expressly confirmed in the deed of grant.

(f) Prescription. As a real right in land a proper liferent does not prescribe.[58] If, however, the liferenter is not infeft because he has not made up title the right remains personal and will be extinguished by prescription if not enforced for 20 years.[59]

Termination of Trust Liferents

Negative prescription cannot terminate the rights of beneficiaries 6.12 in trust liferents as the rights of beneficiaries are declared imprescriptible by statute.[60] Special rules apply to the termination of alimentary liferents which generally cannot be renounced after acceptance without the approval of the court in terms of statutory provision.[61] Trust liferents are terminable in any of the other ways in which proper liferents are terminable and, in addition, by the following means:

(a) Under statute the court may approve an arrangement to vary or revoke all or any of the purposes of a trust and this includes an arrangement to terminate a liferent.[62]

(b) At common law the courts could require the trustees to denude

---

54 See, *e.g.*, *Kidd v. Kidd* (1863) 2M. 227.
55 D.7.4.5–12. See para. 3.41.
56 Ersk, *Inst.*, II,ix,60; Bell, *Prin.*, s.1063.
57 *Maclennan v. Scottish Gas Board*, 1985 S.L.T. (Notes) 2.
58 Prescription and Limitation (Scotland) Act 1973, s.8(2) and Sched.3, para. (a). See para. 2.17.
59 Prescription and Limitation (Scotland) Act 1973, s.8(1).
60 Prescription and Limitation (Scotland) Act 1973, s.8(2) and Sched.3, para. (e).
61 Trusts (Scotland) Act 1961, s.1(4).
62 Trusts (Scotland) Act 1961, s.1(1).

in favour of the liferenter where it was certain that the trust purpose relative to the fee would fail.[63]

Kindly Tenancies

6.13   The Crown's (or King's) kindly tenants of Lochmaben are a peculiar form of landholding occuring only in or around the four villages of Hightae, Smallholm, Heck and Greenhill, near Lochmaben in Dumfriesshire.[64] These rights will be abolished as a separate form of landholding as part of the scheme of abolition of the feudal system. The right of a kindly tenant will be converted to ownership.[65] The rights will retain a peculiarity in that any right of salmon fishing presently pertaining to the tenancies will attach to the newly created rights of property as an inseparable pertinent.[66]

Tenancies at Will

6.14   The term "tenancy at will" has a number of meanings. In this context, however, it is applied to a form of title to occupy land which exists in some villages in some areas of Scotland such as the north east, the highlands and certain parts of Lanarkshire such as Leadhills.[67] Under the arrangement the occupier (otherwise known as "the tenant at will") builds a house on ground provided by the landowner. The arrangement is usually reduced to writing but the document is rarely preserved by registration in a public register. The occupier is required to pay rent and may be removed only on failure to do so. Although described as "a form of building lease",[68] and "a perpetual lease",[69] the lack of an ish date may mark this right out as an arrangement which is something other than a lease. The right appears to be a real right, recognised as such by ancient local custom forming part of common law and not by statute, although statute confers on the tenant at will is granted certain specific additional rights.[70] These include the right to acquire his landlord's interest upon payment of compensation determined either by agreement or by the application of a statutory

---

63 See, *e.g.*, *Beith's Trs v. Beith*, 1950 S.C. 66.
64 18 *Stair Memorial Encyclopaedia*, para. 72; Gordon, *Scottish Land Law*, (2nd ed.), para. 19–15.
65 Abolition of Feudal Tenure etc. (Scotland) Act 2000, s.64(1) and (2).
66 Abolition of Feudal Tenure etc. (Scotland) Act 2000, s.64(3).
67 Gordon, *Scottish Land Law* (2nd ed.), para. 19–16.
68 *ibid.*
69 18 *Stair Memorial Encyclopaedia*, para. 72.
70 Land Registration (Scotland) Act 1979, ss 20–22.

mechanism.[71] Common law recognises the right of the tenant to alienate his tenancy at will by *inter vivos* and *mortis causa* deed.

---

71 Land Registration (Scotland) Act 1979, s.22(3).

CHAPTER 7

LEASES

Introduction

7.1   A lease is a right to use or possess land or other heritable subjects in exchange for a recurring payment known as a rent.[1] The term "lease" is also applied to the document embodying the rights and obligations of the parties. Leases of heritable property were formerly referred to as "tacks" or "assedations".

The tenant's right in many, but not all, leases is one of the real rights recognised by the law of Scotland.[2] This "real" quality is conferred by statute and does not arise at common law.[3] Especially in the twentieth century there has been a substantial raft of legislation which has conferred additional rights on tenants in particular types of leases. These additional rights are collectively known as "security of tenure". In recent years the tenants for whom such legislation has been enacted include those who occupy: (1) dwelling houses[4]; (2) shops[5]; and (3) agricultural tenancies[6] and crofts.[7] These provisions are outlined here but are too detailed to be examined in this book and reference may be made to the specialist texts noted in the footnotes. As a result of this statutory overlay the clear identification of the rights and responsibilities of tenants and landlords is notoriously complex.

---

1   Gordon, *Scottish Land Law* (2nd ed.), para. 19–01.
2   18 *Stair Memorial Encyclopaedia*, para. 5(5). See para. 2.4.
3   Paras 7.12–7.19.
4   Housing (Scotland) Act 1987 and Housing (Scotland) Act 1988; Robson and Halliday, *Residential Tenancies* (2nd ed., 1998).
5   Tenancy of Shops (Scotland) Act 1949 as amended by Tenancy of Shops (Scotland) Act 1964; McAllister, *Scottish Law of Leases* (2nd ed.), Chap. 8; *McMahon v. Associated Rentals Ltd*, 1987 S.L.T. (Sh.Ct.) 94.
6   Agricultural Holdings (Scotland) Act 1991; Gill, *Agricultural Holdings* (3rd ed., 1997).
7   Crofters (Scotland) Act 1993; Agnew, *Crofting Law* (2000).

Social and Commercial Value of Leases

Leases have an enormous role to play in facilitating social and 7.2
economic development in Scotland. For the tenant, a lease generally
enables him to obtain the use of land without the capital outlay of
outright purchase. For the landlord, the land is an investment in
that he may obtain a return, in the form of rent, from land which he
does not personally use.[8] The importance of leases has been
enhanced by their flexibility. Scots law has permitted the parties to
a lease considerable freedom to determine the terms and conditions
of their legal relationship. In relation to commercial property, the
law of Scotland has been subject to considerably less statutory
intervention than in England. In general the landlord in Scottish
commercial property has a much freer hand than his English
counterpart.[9] Modern leases vary considerably and the occasional
attempt by practitioners to gain acceptance for a standard form of
lease even on a modest scale has generally foundered at an early
stage. On the one hand, one may encounter leases of very short
duration, perhaps even days, with a high rent and terms which
greatly restrict the activity which the tenant may carry out. On the
other hand, there are those leases which confer on the tenant a right
which virtually equates with ownership. These are ground leases,
enduring perhaps for hundreds of years, imposing the minimum of
restrictions on the tenants and granted for an initial payment,
known as a grassum, with a nominal rent payable thereafter. Of
late, Scots law has somewhat restricted this flexibility in an attempt
to mark out a clearer distinction between leases and ownership.
Significant in this regard are the legal implication of an unwaivable
term in certain long leases[10] to the effect that the subjects may not
be used as or part of a private dwellinghouse[11] and the imposition
of a general 175-year limitation on leases granted after the
commencement of provisions contained in the legislation relative
to feudal reform.[12]

---

8   Gordon, *supra*, para. 19–01.
9   Gordon, *Scottish Land Law* (2nd ed.), para. 19–02.
10 Extensively defined in Land Tenure Reform (Scotland) Act 1974, s.8(4) and
    subject to exceptions in s.8(5).
11 Land Tenure Reform (Scotland) Act 1974, s.8(1).
12 Abolition of Feudal Tenure etc. (Scotland) Act 2000, s.67, in force on June 9,
    2000.

Land Law

Title to Grant a Lease

7.3   A proprietor of land must be infeft to grant a lease of the land. A lease is not a deed in which title may be deduced.[13] Accretion will apply to rectify a lease which was granted *a non domino*.[14] A proper liferenter may grant a lease with a duration no longer than that of the liferent. Where a creditor in a standard security is in lawful possession of the security subjects he may let those subjects or any part thereof for a period not exceeding seven years. He may let the subjects or a part of them for a longer period only if he receives the warrant of the court.[15] Where sub-leasing is permitted in terms of a lease, a tenant may grant a sub-lease for a period not greater than the term of his own lease.

Legal Essentials of a Lease—Scheme of Analysis

7.4   It is simplest to distinguish leases into two types as follows:

(a)   leases at common law in respect of which the tenant's right is not a real right under statute;

(b)   leases in respect of which the tenant's right is a real right by virtue of statute.

Although as indicated above, there are many leases in respect of which the tenant has been granted additional rights by virtue of statute, such security of tenure has not fundamentally altered the division of leases into those which are real rights and those which are mere personal rights. By and large, security of tenure is limited to leases in respect of which the tenant's right is already a real right by virtue of general legislation.

All leases, whether they benefit from statutory fortification or not, are contractual in origin and confer contractual rights and obligations enforceable between the landlord and tenant. It is important therefore to identify what are the essentials of a contract of lease at common law before confirming what sort of contract of lease may be converted into a real right. Thereafter one may determine the classes of lease in relation to which additional security of tenure is given to the tenant.

---

13 Para. 2.17.
14 *Neilson v. Menzies* (1671) M. 7768; 18 *Stair Memorial Encyclopaedia*, para. 677. See this text, para. 2.17.
15 1970 Act, s.20(3) and (4) and Sched. 3, S.C. 10(4).

Contracts of Lease at Common Law

The common law requires certain essentials before there will be a   7.5
contract of lease. Without these, the parties cannot create a lease
even if they use the term "lease" to describe their arrangement.[16] It
is equally irrelevant that the parties are referred to as "landlord"
and "tenant".[17] Although the use of the phrase "do hereby lease" is
not essential to create a contract of lease,[18] it would be rare in
modern practice for parties wishing to create such a legal
relationship to fail to use these or similar words, especially where
the relevant deed has been drafted with the benefit of legal advice. A
contract purporting to grant a right of occupancy of land which
fails in any of the essentials of a lease may still be valid at common
law as a contractual licence.[19] In some agreements for the
occupancy of land the parties describe their relationship as a
"licence" but the courts will not regard this description as
determinative of the relationship between the parties: instead they
will look at the whole circumstances in deciding whether there is a
lease or a licence.[20] An agreement for hostel accommodation is not
a lease.[21]

Essentials of Lease at Common Law

Before a lease can exist as a contract the parties must have   7.6
reached *consensus in idem* in respect of certain essentials. The
essentials of a contract of lease at common law are as follows:

(a)   The parties, namely, the landlord and tenant.
(b)   The subjects.
(c)   A rent.
(d)   A term.

Where the parties have not agreed on one or more of the essential
elements of a lease then as a general rule the court cannot impose its
own determination to supply the defect.[22]
   The entering into of a lease and the reaching of *consensus in idem*

---

16   *Broomhill Motor Co. v. Assessor for Glasgow*, 1927 S.C. 447; Gordon, *Scottish Land Law* (2nd ed.), para. 19–12.
17   *Brand & Son v. Bell's Trs* (1872) 11M. 42; *Mann v. Houston*, 1957 S.L.T. 89.
18   *Mackintosh v. May* (1895) 22R. 345.
19   Gordon, *supra*, para. 19–14; 18 *Stair Memorial Encyclopaedia*, para. 195.
20   *Scottish Residential Estates Development Co. Ltd v. Henderson* 1991 S.L.T. 490; *Brador Properties Ltd v. British Telecommunications plc*, 1992 S.C. 12.
21   *Denovan v. Blue Triangle (Glasgow) Housing Association Ltd*, 1999 Hous. L.R. 97 (Sh.Ct.); *Conway v. Glasgow City Council*, 1999 S.C.L.R. 248.
22   Hume, *Lectures*, Vol. II, p. 57.

on the essential elements are generally the voluntary acts of the landlord and tenant. Put another way, it is a general rule that a proprietor of land is free to decide whether or not to grant a lease and a tenant cannot be forced to take a lease. There are very few limited statutory exceptions to this because compulsory acquisition powers generally relate to the acquisition of property or servitude rights and rarely relate to the obtaining of leasehold rights. The most widely used of the statutory powers under which a proprietor may be obliged to grant a lease relates to crofting tenancies. Where a croft is vacant the proprietor may be obliged by the Crofters' Commission to submit letting proposals and where this is not done timeously the Commission may proceed to do so themselves. Any lease granted by the Commission in terms of this provision shall have effect in all respects as if it had been granted by the landlord.[23] Another significant provision confers on a heritable creditor in lawful possession of the security subjects the power to let the security subjects.[24] The duration of such leases is limited to a term not exceeding seven years except with the consent of the sheriff. As the debtor and not the heritable creditor will be the landlord in such a lease this may be regarded as an example of a lease granted without the immediate voluntary act of the proprietor, although he may originally have created the standard security by voluntary act.[25]

Parties

7.7   A lease is fundamentally a contract between a landlord and a tenant. No-one may contract with himself.[26] There must be two parties before there is a lease—the landlord and tenant. It is possible, however, to have a lease between one party acting in two capacities such as an individual on the one hand and the same party acting as a trustee on the other hand. Although the logic of the decision establishing the general rule is not entirely free from criticism it has been held that common proprietors may not grant a lease to one of their number.[27] The converse case is where a single landlord grants a lease to a number of co-tenants of which he is one. This possibility appears to be accepted by Scots law[28] but some

---

23 Crofters (Scotland) Act 1993, s.23(5).
24 1970 Act, s.20(3) and Sched. 3, S.C. 10(4).
25 For the rare case of involuntary creation of standard security: see para. 3.3.
26 *Kildrummy Estates (Jersey) Ltd v. IRC*, 1991 S.C. 1. For difficulties with this case see para. 1.11.
27 *Clydesdale Bank plc v. Davidson*, 1998 S.C. (H.L.) 51.
28 *Pinkerton v. Pinkerton* 1986 S.L.T. 672.

reservations have been expressed about the reliance which may be placed on the decision confirming the point.[29]

A lease is competent between distinct legal *persona* even if one party has the right to control the actions and existence of the other.[30] Such arrangements are common for income management and tax purposes where a company frequently grants a lease to another company in the same company group. Such devices are also used to avoid the conferring of security of tenure on tenants in agricultural leases because the landlord has the ability to bring the existence of the tenant, and thereby the lease, to an end. For this purpose, leases in favour of a limited partnership in respect of which the landlord is the limited partner are commonly employed.[31]

When a lease is to be granted, difficulties can arise where an individual wishes to take the tenant's interest in the name of a limited company owned by him. The landlord, by contrast, may wish the lease to be entered into by the individual with a view to obtaining the covenant of someone without limited liability. Problems may arise where the documentation remains incomplete when entry is taken by the tenant when the identity of the tenant remains unclear. The acceptance of rent by the landlord in the form of a cheque drawn on the company's bank account may make it difficult for him to assert that the individual is the tenant. The golden rule should be that no entry to the premises should be given until the documentation is complete. If the individual is still insistent that he wishes the company to be the tenant, a compromise may be reached whereby the landlord can obtain fortification of the covenant by means of a guarantee granted by the individual in respect of the leasehold obligations.[32] Whether the liability of the individual under the guarantee is limited or unlimited will largely depend on the negotiating strengths of the parties in the prevailing market conditions.

Subjects of Lease

A lease must have an item of heritable property as its subject. 7.8 This may either be land, the right to salmon fishings or something which has become heritable by annexation such as a building or part of a building. Where a document purports to create a lease in

---

29 McDonald, *Conveyancing Manual*, (6th ed.), para. 26.3.
30 *ibid.*
31 *Dickson v. MacGregor*, 1992 S.L.T. (Land Ct.) 83; *Macfarlane v. Falfield Investments Ltd*, 1996 S.C.L.R. 826.
32 See, *e.g.*, *Waydale Ltd v. DHL Holdings (U.K.) Ltd*, 1996 S.C.L.R. 391.

respect of a moveable thing it is more properly classified as a contract of hire. Close reading of the relevant documentation may be required in some cases to identify the subjects of the right. A contract relative to the use of a mobile home may be a contract of hire but if the contract relates to the use of the site of the mobile home it may be a lease.[33] It is possible to have a lease of mineral rights even though they involve the removal of part of the subjects of lease and their conversion into moveable items such as stones or aggregate which can be carted away.[34]

Broadly speaking, if a property or right in land can be disponed it can also be leased. Two rights, however, may be leased separately from the land over which the right is exercised even though they cannot be disponed separately. These are rights to fish for fish other than salmon and rights to shoot game over land.

Any lease must properly identify the property which is subject to the lease. This requires attention to the same matters as have been identified in relation to the description of subjects in a disposition of the property right such as boundary lines and pertinents.[35]

Rent

7.9   The doctrine of consideration as developed in English law has no place in Scots law.[36] Nevertheless, it is sometimes stated that an essential of a contract of lease is a consideration.[37] This means that a lease must have a rent. The rent may be nominal.[38] A party who is permitted to occupy ground without payment of a rent may be entitled to do so by some other form of contractual licence but it is not a lease. The rent, however, need not be money. It may be produce of the subjects let. For example in relation to fish farm leases a tenant is sometimes required to pay a rent consisting of a quantity of fish.[39] It may consist of services to be rendered by the tenant. An obligation on a tenant to maintain his mother (the landlord) and supply her with necessaries was sufficient to satisfy

---

33   *West Lothian D.C. v. Morrison* 1987 S.L.T. 361.
34   Gordon, *Scottish Land Law* (2nd ed.), para. 19–08.
35   Paras 4.16–4.23.
36   Gloag, *Contract* (2nd ed.), pp. 48–50; McBryde, *Contract*, para. 1–20.
37   13 *Stair Memorial Encyclopaedia*, para. 107.
38   *Sinclair v. McBeath* (1788) Hume 773; Paton and Cameron, *Landlord and Tenant*, p. 6.
39   See, *e.g.*, Minute of Agreement and Lease between Edmund Hoyle Vestey and Wester Ross Salmon Ltd, dated 6 July and 13 August 1979, and registered B.C. and S. on 21 April 1981.

the requisites of a fixed rent.[40] If the services are rendered as part of a contract of employment the services may not be a rent and the whole arrangement may not be a lease. For example, a caretaker may be provided with a flat as part of his contract of employment. This is a service occupancy which is part of the contract of employment and is not a lease.[41]

Rent is usually a fixed sum of money per month or per annum depending on the length of the lease. The parties are generally free to agree the dates upon which rent is payable but, where a lease endures for a number of years, it is common for rent to be payable in advance on the four quarter days. In Scotland these are Candlemas (28 February), Whitsunday (28 May), Lammas (28 August) and Martinmas (28 November).[42] In long leases there is usually extensive provision for review of rent to prevent the landlord's return being outstripped by inflation. In other cases the level of rent may be determined by reference to a formula, as is the case in leases of many retail premises where the rent increases when the turnover of the tenant increases.[43] In such cases it is common for there to be an additional clause making provision for a guaranteed minimum payment to the landlord so that his entitlement to an income is not wholly diminished by the tenant's lack of business success.[44]

Term

There must be a term to a lease. At common law a lease could 7.10 remain valid as a contract even if the term was indefinite or perpetual but such a right would bind only the original landlord or a subsequent landlord who novated the arrangement.[45] There was a limited utility for such leases as, unless the original landlord was a corporation, he could not live forever, and in any case the landlord might chose to alienate his land during his lifetime.

The fact that duration is not specified in a lease is not necessarily fatal because this is not the same as saying that the parties have not agreed a duration. Where parties have agreed to a lease but no period is specified the law will imply a term. This implied term will

---

40 *Farquhar v. Farquhar*, 1924 S.L.C.R. 19 at 22.
41 See, *e.g.*, *MacGregor v. Dunnett*, 1949 S.C. 510.
42 Term and Quarter Days (Scotland) Act 1990.
43 See, *e.g.*, *Smyth v. Caledonia Racing (1984), Ltd*, 1987 G.W.D. 16–612.
44 Of course if the tenant's business is ill-fated the landlord will frequently receive no payment of rent even though he is entitled to it, but that is another matter.
45 *Carruthers v. Irvine* (1717) M.15195; Rankine, *Leases*, p. 115; Paton and Cameron, *Landlord and Tenant*, p. 7.

be year to year or the shortest term which the words used will admit.[46] It is not prudent to draw up documents on this basis as in many cases the application of this rule—which is intended to implement the presumed intent of the parties—may achieve a result which no-one actually wanted. In other cases the absence of a term date will be interpreted by the courts as indicating that the parties intended the contract to be a licence and not a lease.[47]

Constitution of a Lease

7.11   With one exception, a lease should be constituted in writing.[48] The exception is where the lease is for less than one year. Defects in the constitution of a lease may be cured by the conduct of the parties such as where the tenant takes occupation and pays rent. It is always prudent for the parties to reduce their agreement to writing even if writing is not required. Nevertheless, where a written lease is not required neither party can demand that the other party enters into a written agreement except where this right is conferred by prior contractual agreement or by statute. There is special statutory provision permitting either party to an agricultural tenancy to require that the other enters into a written lease with certain minimum contents.[49] In respect of private sector assured tenancies and public sector secure tenancies all leases, of whatever duration, must be in writing.[50] If the landlord fails to have a written lease drawn up the tenant can apply to have the failure rectified.[51] Special provisions apply to the occupiers of mobile homes stationed on "protected caravan sites" so long as the occupier is occupying the mobile home as his only or main residence.[52] Where applicable, these provisions entitle the occupier to obtain from the owner of the site within three months an agreement permitting him to occupy a stance on the site and a written statement of the terms on which he does so comprising the express terms and those terms implied by statute.[53] Additional terms relating to such other matters as

---

46   *Redpath v. White* (1737) M. 15196; *Shetland Islands Council v. B.P. Petroleum Development Ltd*, 1990 S.L.T. 82; Rankine, *Leases*, p. 115; Paton and Cameron, *Landlord and Tenant*, p. 7

47   *Dunlop & Co. v. Steel Co. of Scotland Ltd* (1879) 7R. 283.

48   Requirements of Writing (Scotland) Act 1995, ss 1 and 2.

49   Agricultural Holdings (Scotland) Act 1991, s.4(1)(a).

50   Housing (Scotland) Act 1987, s.53; Housing (Scotland) Act 1988, s.30.

51   Housing (Scotland) Act 1988, s.30(2). *Cf.* Housing (Scotland) Act 1987, ss 53 and 54, which envisages only a local authority drawing up an unfair lease.

52   Mobile Homes Act 1975, s.8; Mobile Homes Act 1983; *Cooper v. Fraser*, 1987 G.W.D. 22–824; *West Lothian D.C. v. Morrison*, 1987 S.L.T. 361.

53   1983 Act, Sched. 1, Pt. I.

provision of services may be implied by the court on application of either landlord or occupier within a further six-month period.[54]

By statute it is provided that, notwithstanding any custom to the contrary, a party to a lease is to be under no obligation to pay the whole or any part of the costs of the lease incurred by any other party's solicitor unless contrary agreement has been made in writing.[55] For the purposes of these provisions "lease" includes a "sub-lease" and "costs" include fees, charges, disbursements (including stamp duty) expenses and remuneration.[56] It is very common for these provisions to be contracted out of, particularly in relation to commercial leases.

Real Right

A lease is essentially a contract between two parties—the original 7.12 landlord and the original tenant. Where assignation is permitted there may be a substitution of a new tenant in place of the old. The converse case is that of a new landlord which occurs when the landlord's interest is purchased or otherwise transferred. Such a new owner would not be bound by a mere contract unless he were to novate it but the new owner is bound by the lease provided it is a real right.

The Leases Act 1449 provides that where a property which is subject to a lease complying with certain requirements (the terms of which will be discussed later) is sold by the landlord or is otherwise transferred to a new owner then the new owner is bound by the lease. More modern statutory provision to create other leases (complying with slightly different requirements) as real rights is found in the Registration of Leases (Scotland) Act 1857, s.1, as amended, and the Land Registration (Scotland) Act 1979, s.2(1). Where a lease is made real in terms of any of these provisions the tenant can continue to exercise his rights and remain in occupation despite the transfer of the landlord's interest. In legal terms this means that the tenant under the lease obtains not only a contractual right but a real right—a right enforceable against the whole world. In particular the lease is enforceable against purchasers of the landlord's interest, the Crown as *ultimus haeres* and creditors including a heritable creditor holding a standard security over the landlord's interest unless that creditor's right was established prior to the creation of the lease and he did not consent to the grant of

---

54 1983 Act, Sched. 1, Pt. II.
55 The Costs of Leases Act 1958, s.1.
56 1958 Act, s.2.

the lease.[57] Where a lease cannot be converted into a real right in terms of any of the above statutes it remains as a contract.

Requirements of the 1449 Act

7.13   Not all leases may be converted into real rights in terms of the 1449 Act. For that to happen a lease must comply with the following:

(1) If for more than one year it must be in writing.
(2) It must be of heritage (*i.e.* land or a fixture).
(3) There must be a rent.
(4) There must be a term date.
(5) The tenant must have entered into possession.

Heritage

7.14   Although the 1449 Act refers to "landes" it applies to urban as well as rural subjects, buildings located in towns and in the country and salmon fishing rights.[58] By further statutory provision the terms of the 1449 Act have been extended to leases of freshwater fishing for not less than one year.[59] A difficult case arises in relation to shooting and sporting rights. Whilst the law here is not entirely free from doubt the matter appears to depend largely on how the lease is worded. Where the deed grants a lease in respect of the shooting rights with ancillary rights to use land or buildings to facilitate the exercise of the shooting it may not be a real right under the 1449 Act.[60] By contrast where the deed grants a lease of land for the purposes of shooting it may be a real right under the Act.[61] Whether this distinction would be applied if a case were to be decided today has been queried.[62] It is doubtful whether a real right of lease may exist in relation to something like an advertising hoarding, as it may not be capable of possession as a separate tenement, or a static wheel barrow stall in a retail complex because that would be regarded as a moveable. The rights to use these things are both probably some form of contractual licence.

---

57 *Trade Development Bank v. Warriner and Mason (Scotland) Ltd*, 1980 S.C. 74. See Chap. 11,
58 *Stephen v. L. Ad.* (1878) 6R. 282.
59 Freshwater and Salmon Fisheries (Scotland) Act 1976, s.4.
60 *Pollock, Gilmour & Co. v. Harvey* (1828) 6S. 913. *Cf. Leith v. Leith* (1862) 24D. 1059.
61 *Farquarson, Petr* (1870) 9M. 66.
62 S. Scott Robinson, *The Law of Game, Salmon and Freshwater Fishing in Scotland* (1990), pp. 35–36; 13 *Stair Memorial Encyclopaedia*, para. 297.

Rent

To qualify as a real right under the 1449 Act there must be a 7.15
definite rent. This will usually be in money but a rent in grain or
other fungibles is acceptable[63] as is a requirement to render
services.[64] The requirement of a definite rent does not mean that
there must be a fixed rent and it is acceptable for the rent to be
variable in terms of a rent review clause or ascertainable by the
application of a stated formula referring to extrinsic matters such as
the amount of a particular commodity produced from the subjects.
The latter is common where the commodity is stone or minerals and
the subjects a mine or quarry. The rent cannot be "illusory" but
there is little guidance as to what would be illusory. What can be
said is that a grassum alone is insufficient[65] but it is acceptable for a
grassum to be paid with only a requirement for a minimal rent to be
paid thereafter "if asked only". There is no need that the rent be
fair and reasonable.[66] An arrangement for rent-free accommodation cannot be a real right.[67] In rare cases the right to receive the
rent under a lease may be assigned to a third party separately from
the landlord's other interests under the lease. Such a lease would
probably not be a real right in terms of the 1449 Act[68] but the
creation of an income stream in favour of a third party is now
usually dealt with by means of an interposed lease which does create
a real right on the part of the grantee.[69]

One of the primary obligations of the tenant is to pay the rent to
the landlord on the due date.[70] Correspondingly, one of the primary
rights of the landlord is to receive the rent on that date. Subject to
statutory control, the parties may agree their own level of rent. To
protect the landlord's return from the ravages of inflation, it is
common in a commercial lease for there to be a rent review
provision. The aim of such a provision is generally to enable the
rent to be raised in cycles agreed between the parties (typically every
three to five years) to secure for the landlord a return reflecting

---

63 Bell, *Prin.*, s.1205; Rankine, *Leases*, pp. 144–145.
64 *Lundy v. Smith of Lundy* (1610) M. 15166.
65 *Mann v. Houston*, 1957 S.L.T. 89.
66 Hume, *Lectures*, Vol. IV, p. 77.
67 *Wallace v. Simmers*, 1960 S.C. 255.
68 Erskine, *Inst*, II,vi,27. This leaves open the possibility of a separate assignation of
the right to receive rents where this assignation was granted after the lease
became a real right.
69 Land Tenure Reform (Scotland) Act 1974, s.17(1); 13 *Stair Memorial
Encyclopaedia*, paras 386–388.
70 See, *e.g.*, Crofters (Scotland) Act 1993, Sched. 2, "The Statutory Conditions",
para. 1.

current market value. The relevant rent review clause requires to contain sufficient detail so that the mechanism of review is clear and the clause is not void from uncertainty.[71] During wartime or periods of high inflation, governments have sometimes resorted to general limitations on rent increases in an attempt to control the general economy. None of these general provisions is in force now but the rent review clauses employed in many commercial leases envisage the reintroduction of such provisions by stipulating for a rent review when such provisions cease to have effect. There are detailed statutory restrictions limiting the increase of rents in relation to agricultural tenancies[72] and crofts.[73] There is now only limited statutory provision to control rents in residential tenancies which are protected tenancies or short assured tenancies.[74]

Leases, particularly those relating to commercial subjects, generally contain extensive provisions relative to remedies in respect of late payment of rent. These range from interest clauses, liquidate and ascertained damages clauses, suspension of landlord's obligations to provide services and irritancy.

7.16   Leasehold casualties are a variant upon the obligation to pay rent. At their simplest they are an obligation on the tenant to pay a lump sum upon the occurrence of an event which is uncertain as regards its occurrence or timing of occurrence. A simple example is an obligation to pay one year's rent upon each transmission of the tenant's interest. In recent years the issue of leasehold casualties has come to the fore in certain areas of Scotland such as Lanarkshire and is regarded, at least by tenants, as an unacceptable relic of the past.[75] In certain cases the landlord's right to receive payment has been enforced by those whom the tenants would regard as "feudal title raiders".[76] Leasehold casualties, however, are not feudal. They will not be affected by the abolition of the feudal system of landholding.[77] Nevertheless, they have been constrained by

---

71 *City of Aberdeen Council v. Clark*, 1999 S.L.T. 613; *Crawford v. Bruce*, 1992 S.L.T. 524.
72 Agricultural Holdings (Scotland) Act 1991, s.13.
73 Crofters (Scotland) Act 1993, s.6.
74 Rent (Scotland) Act 1984, s.46; Housing (Scotland) Act 1988, ss 24 and 34; Robson and Halliday, *Residential Tenancies* (2nd ed.), Chap. 4.
75 *Crawford v. Campbell; Crawford v. Livingstone's Trs*, 1937 S.C. 596; Scot. Law Com. *Discussion Paper* No. 102 (1997); Gordon, *Scottish Land Law* (2nd ed.), para. 2–18, fn. 34 and para. 19–140.
76 See *e.g. M R S Hamilton Ltd v. Keeper of the Registers of Scotland*, 19 May 1988, case ref. LTS/LR/1997/4,5,6,7 and 8, 1998 G.W.D. 25–1267 (OH); Gretton and Reid, *Conveyancing* (2nd ed.), para. 23.06, fn. 19.
77 They were similarly unaffected by the Feudal Casualties (Scotland) Act 1914.

legislative provision. It is not lawful to stipulate for the payment of any casualty in any lease executed after 1 September 1974.[78] This provision does not prejudice the right to stipulate for review of rent or for a permanent or periodical variation of rent in accordance with any condition of or relating to the lease.[79] Legislation is proposed to abolish leasehold casualties entirely and this will probably involve some form of compensation payable to land-lords.[80] Leasehold casualties, in contrast to certain feudal casualties, do not arise from legal implication and will not be available to the landlord unless they are contracted for in the lease. As conventional stipulations, they will be enforceable according to their terms. This may cause problems where the tenant's interest is subdivided and assigned in separate portions.[81]

Term Date

To be created a real right under the 1449 Act there must be a term 7.17 date in respect of the lease.[82] Leases for a perpetual period cannot be created as real rights but, provided it does have a definite term, it does not matter how long the lease is. A particular statutory exception to the requirement that a lease shall not be for a perpetual period was contained in the Act 35 George III, c.122, s.3, enacted on 26 June 1795 to promote the granting of leases in towns and villages on the fishing coasts of Scotland. This expressly confirmed that leases granted by the British Society in certain villages in the remote parts of Scotland would be valid even though they were "renewable for ever". Although this provision is now repealed and the granting of new leases in these terms is now incompetent to create real rights it would seem that some of these leases have been granted and remain valid. Quite apart from these renewable leases, other leases with very long durations such as 999 years are still encountered in some areas.[83] In terms of the legislation abolishing

---

78 Land Tenure Reform (Scotland) Act 1974, s.16.
79 *Cf.* the view expressed on automatic uplifts on rent upon transmission: see Ross and McKichan, *Drafting and Negotiating Commercial Leases in Scotland* (2nd ed.), para. 7.7; McDonald, *Conveyancing Manual*, (6th ed.), para. 25.76.
80 Scot. Law Com., *Report on Leasehold Casualties* No. 165, April 1998). A Bill is to be introduced into the Scottish Parliament in early course.
81 *M.D. Kaye v. Mary Louise Archibald*, Hamilton Sheriff Court, case ref: A309/93: Sheriff K.L. Breslin, date of judgment 27 June 1996 (unreported); *M R S Hamilton Ltd v. Keeper of the Registers of Scotland*, 19 May 1988, case ref. LTS/LR/1997/4,5,6,7 and 8, 1998 G.W.D. 25–1267 (OH), presently on appeal.
82 18 *Stair Memorial Encyclopaedia*, para. 9(1).
83 See, *e.g.*, *M R S Hamilton Ltd v. Keeper of the Registers of Scotland, supra*; *B.G. Hamilton v. Ready Mixed Concrete (Scotland) Ltd*, 1999 S.L.T. 524.

the feudal system a maximum duration of 175 years has been imposed on leases granted on or after June 9, 2000.[84] The requirement for a definite term does not imply that the end date is to be fixed: rather it is sufficient that the lease is granted until the occurrence of an event which is bound to happen. Thus a lease for the lifetime of a person or persons can be a real right under the 1449 Act.[85]

Possession by Tenant

7.18   To acquire a real right under the 1449 Act the tenant must have entered into possession. Where possession is taken after the title of a singular successor to the landlord's right has been made real, the lease will not prevail[86] but there may be some relief with the application of the rule against "offside goals".[87] The possession of the tenant may be actual or civil, the latter being appropriate where the tenant has lawfully granted a sub-lease. The possession must be exclusive to create the real right. This may cause problems where one lease of a farm has ended and a new lease has been granted to an incoming tenant. The old tenant may retain some rights to enter the farm for the purpose of reaping crops in certain fields. In such cases the courts tend to look at the farm as a whole and not at the individual fields to determine who is in actual occupation.[88]

A difficult question may arise where the right being exercised by the tenant is not capable of exclusive possession. For example the tenant may have the right of access over adjacent land as a pertinent of his lease. It is clearly the case that the possession of such a right is likely to be intermittent, non-exclusive and in some cases desultory, yet it seems inconceivable that a tenant could find the main body of his leased subjects landlocked when the "servient" subjects burdened by the access right are sold. The nature of such a right is unclear but it must be a real right of some sort[89] and it is possible that the courts would be able to find that exclusive possession of the main body of the leasehold subjects coupled with what possession the access is capable of is sufficient to put a purchaser of the

---

84 Abolition of Feudal Tenure etc. (Scotland) Act 2000, s.67 following upon Scot. Law Com., *Report on Abolition of the Feudal System* (No.168, Dec. 1998), cl. 61 of draft bill.

85 *Thomson v. Thomson* (1896) 24R. 269.

86 *Fraser v. Laird of Pitsligo* (1611) M. 15227; *Millar v. McRobbie* 1949 S.C. 1.

87 Para. 3.30.

88 *Wight v. Earl of Hopetoun* (1863) 1M. 1074; *affd* (1864) 2M. (H.L.) 35; *Millar v. McRobbie*, 1949 S.C. 1.

89 Cusine and Paisley, *Servitudes and Rights of Way*, paras 1.18 and 2.12.

servient subject on notice and thereby cause no unfairness if the access right is regarded as a real right. Unfortunately there is a confusing body of case law relative to other rights exercised in a non-exclusive manner such as peat cutting, which contains contradictory dicta.[90] The matter requires urgent clarification but in the meantime parties wishing to create such rights would be advised to do so by means of a recorded or registered lease where there is no express requirement for possession.[91]

Requirements of Modern Registration Statutes

Leases may be created as real rights by means of registration in terms of more modern statutory provision found in the Registration of Leases (Scotland) Act 1857, s.1, as amended, and the Land Registration (Scotland) Act 1979, s.2(1). Again, as with the 1449 Act, not all leases may be converted into real rights, but the requirements to do so under the more modern statutes are different to those under the old statute. To be created as a real right in terms of these modern Acts a lease must comply with the following: 7.19

(a) the lease must be for a period of over 20 years or contain an obligation on the granter to renew it from time to time for fixed periods or upon the termination of a life or lives or otherwise so that it will endure for a period exceeding 20 years (conveniently known as a "long lease")[92];

(b) any requirement that the lease should relate to an acreage of at least 50 acres and refer to the name and extent of the lands has been repealed[93]; and

(c) outwith "operational areas" for the land registration purposes the tenant has the alternative of registering the lease in the Sasine Register to make it a real right and this is deemed to have the same effect as possession. Where the land is located within an "operational area" for the land registration system, registration of a long lease in the Land Register is obligatory to obtain a real right in respect of a registered interest.[94]

---

90 *Duncan v. Brooks* (1894) 21R. 760 per Lord Young at 764; *Campbell v. McLean* (1870) 8M. (H.L.) 40.
91 Para. 7.19.
92 Registration of Leases (Scotland) Act 1857, ss 1–2 and 15 as amended by the Land Tenure Reform (Scotland) Act 1974, ss 8–10, 18 and Sched. 6.
93 Land Tenure Reform (Scotland) Act 1974, ss 18, 23(3) and Sched. 6, para. 5, and Sched. 7 repealing Registration of Leases (Scotland) Act 1857, s.18, and amending Long Leases (Scotland) Act 1954, s.27.
94 Land Registration (Scotland) Act 1979, s.2.

Possession is insufficient in such cases. There is no express requirement in the statutory provisions that the subjects of lease shall require to be capable of exclusive possession before a leasehold right may be made real by means of registration. The matter remains decidedly obscure but this appears to leave open the possibility that certain leasehold rights can be made real by registration even though they could not be made real by possession under the 1449 Act. Possible candidates in this regard include car parking rights,[95] shooting rights[96] and access rights.

Real Conditions and Leases

7.20 The terms of a lease may contain a variety of obligations, some of which are intended to be purely contractual and bind only the original parties to the agreement. Others are intended to bind these parties and their successors. The parties are given a large measure of discretion in determining into which class the obligations are to fall but there are some constraints on which obligations may be created so as to bind the successors of the parties. For ease these may be referred to as "real" leasehold conditions as opposed to "contractual" leasehold conditions. Unfortunately the principles upon which certain purported real leasehold conditions have been rejected as such are unclear and the best that can be done present is to set out broad and somewhat speculative statements of principle together with a few illustrations.

A tripartite distinction may be made to differentiate three types of leasehold obligations as follows:

(a) Obligations binding on the tenant and enforceable by the landlord. There is a potential dominant tenement in respect of these obligations in the form of the landlord's interest. However, on one analysis the obligations are not real conditions as there is no servient property.[97] The lease has no existence independent from the conditions which it contains. The conditions bind the successor of the tenant not as real conditions but on the basis of the rule *assignatus utitur*

---

95 *Dougbar Properties Ltd v. Keeper of the Registers of Scotland*, 1999 S.C. 513; 1999 S.C.L.R. 458.
96 *Palmer's Trs v. Brown*, 1988 S.C.L.R. 499; 1989 S.L.T. 128.
97 Such conditions, however, are regarded as "land obligations" in terms of Conveyancing and Feudal Reform (Scotland) Act 1970, Pt I. See, *e.g.*, *McQuiban v. Eagle Star Insurance Co.*, 1972 S.L.T. (Lands Tr.) 38; *British Steel plc v. Kaye*, 1991 S.L.T. (Lands Tr.) 7.

jure auctoris— the assignee exercises the right of his author.[98]
The clauses relative to the essential elements in any lease—such
as the obligation to pay rent and take possession— clearly may
bind the tenant's successor under this rule. In addition to these
essential elements, what authority there is appears to indicate
that the landlord and tenant have a wide discretion to
determine such terms as they please which bind the tenant.
The matter appears to have been accepted without argument in
most cases and a landlord has been held able to enforce against
the singular successors of the initial tenant a wide array of
diverse obligations.

(b) obligations binding on the landlord and enforceable by the
tenant. These are real conditions enforceable *in personam* in
that there is a dominant tenement, the tenant's interest in the
lease, and a servient tenement, the landlord's interest which is
frequently a property right.[99] Again it would appear that
obligations directly referable to the essential elements of any
lease appear to be real conditions. So the obligations which
would qualify under this heading would include the landlord's
obligation to give full possession and maintain the tenant in
possession. Other obligations which may qualify as real
conditions may be those which can be regarded as *inter
naturalia* of the lease in question. This class extends to
obligations which are ordinarily and commonly encountered
in a particular type of lease under consideration. This would
probably cover obligations found in many leases such a
positive obligation on the landlord to put the subjects of lease
in a tenantable condition and keep the subjects of lease in
repair[1] and a negative obligation on the landlord not to carry
out activity on adjacent subjects which would derogate from
the full enjoyment of the subjects of lease.[2] It may also extend
to specific liabilities such as obligations to pay for stock in
particular leases such as agricultural leases.[3] This leaves open
the possibility that where such a clause is rarely encountered in
a particular lease it will not bind successors of the landlord but
the same obligation may bind them in other leases where it is

---

98   *Trade Development Bank v. Warriner and Mason (Scotland) Ltd*, 1980 S.C. 74; 18
     Stair Memorial Encyclopaedia, paras 349 and 660. See also K.G.C. Reid, "*Real
     Conditions in Standard Securities*", 1983 S.L.T. (News) 169 and 189.
99   18 *Stair Memorial Encyclopaedia*, para. 351.
1   *Barr v. Cochrane* (1878) 5R. 877; *Waterson v. Stewart* (1881) 9R. 155.
2   *Huber v. Ross*, 1912 S.C. 898.
3   *Gillespie v. Riddell*, 1909 S.C. (H.L.) 3.

common. Arbitration clauses are common in many forms of
lease and will probably bind successors of the landlord in most
if not all cases.[4] By contrast, options on the part of the tenant
to renew the lease or purchase the landlord's interest are
unlikely to bind successors without evidence that they are
common in the type of lease under consideration.[5] Unfortunately much of this remains speculation as authority on
particular points is in short supply and a coherent statement of
principle is lacking.[6]

(c) Obligations binding on a tenant and enforceable by another
tenant where both tenants hold of the same landlord. These
may be created in partial assignations of long leases in terms of
the Registration of Leases (Scotland) Act 1857, s.3(2)[7] or a
separate deed of conditions under the 1857 Act, s.3(5).[8] The
terms of this provision confirm that "real conditions" may be
imposed in such deeds but there are some difficulties in their
application. First, by virtue of the reference to "partial
assignations" it is limited to leasehold units originally held of
one landlord in one lease. It does not apply to two adjacent
subjects held by two separate leases from a single landlord or
two landlords.[9] Secondly, the Act declares that the conditions
in assignations shall be "as effectual against any singular
successor of the assignee in the subjects assigned as if such
assignee had been a grantee of the lease". Despite the obscure
wording employed in the section it appears to have been
assumed that the effect of the section is to facilitate part
assignations where burdens are imposed on the part of the
tenancy split off in favour of that retained or vice versa.[10]
What appears clear is that conditions created under such
statutory provisions are not conditions of the lease enforceable
by the landlord against the tenant or vice versa. They therefore
form a different category of real conditions which may have
their own rules as to content. Unfortunately these rules are

---

4   *Montgomerie v. Carrick* (1848) 10D. 1387.
5   *Bisset v. Aberdeen Mags* (1898) 1F. 87.
6   The most comprehensive analysis is contained in 13 *Stair Memorial Encyclo-
    paedia*, paras 239–243. See also McAllister, *Scottish Law of Leases*, (2nd ed.), pp.
    28–29.
7   As added by Law Reform (Misc. Prov.) (Sc.) Act 1985, s.3.
8   1857 Act, s.3(5) (as so added).
9   It is unclear whether a deed of declaration of conditions in terms of 1874 Act,
    s.32 as amended by 1979 Act, s.17, may assist with these sort of leasehold
    situations because of the definition of "land" contained in 1874 Act, s.3.
10 18 *Stair Memorial Encyclopaedia*, para. 352.

obscure as the statute contains no guidance. The common law also sheds little light on the matter although, at least on one view, it may have been competent to create rights similar to leasehold servitudes both positive and negative.[11]

Various Aspects of Leases

A lease is a very flexible device. In general the parties to a lease 7.21 are free to include in that lease whatever terms they wish provided they contain the four essentials of (a) parties, (b) subjects, (c) duration, and (d) rent, and, in addition, where the parties wish the lease to be a real right, provided the lease complies with the terms of the statute under which the lease is created as a real right. A specialty exists in relation to leases of agricultural tenancies where either party may require the other enter into a lease containing, in addition to these four essentials, provisions for insurance of buildings and harvested crops.[12]

Certain statutes also import obligations on the parties regardless of what is stated in the lease. These are largely, but not exclusively, restricted to cases in which the tenant is granted security of tenure or instances where a greater social goal is to be attained, as the following examples illustrate:

(a) The tenants of agricultural subjects are protected by four separate codes of legislation which vary according to the nature of the subjects. These are agricultural holdings,[13] small holdings,[14] statutory small tenancies[15] and crofts.[16] A detailed examination of the content of these statutory codes is beyond the confines of this book but for the sake of illustration a brief mention may be made of the effect of the statutory provisions in relation to crofts. Whatever the landlord and tenant may agree, all crofts are subject to the statutory conditions listed in the relevant legislation[17] and agreements which deprive a crofter of his statutory rights are void unless the agreement is

---

11 Cusine and Paisley, *Servitudes and Rights of Way*, paras 1.18 and 2.12.
12 Agricultural Holdings (Scotland) Act 1991, s.4 and Sched.1.
13 Agricultural Holdings (Scotland) Act 1991.
14 Crofters Holdings (Scotland) Act 1886; Small Landholders (Scotland) Act 1911; Small Landholdings and Agricultural Holdings (Scotland) Act 1931.
15 Small Landholders (Scotland) Act 1911; Small Landholdings and Agricultural Holdings (Scotland) Act 1931.
16 Crofters (Scotland) Act 1993.
17 Crofters (Scotland) Act 1993, s.5 and Sched.2.

approved by the Land Court.[18] For example, an agreement prohibiting a crofter from locating a caravan on his croft has been held void on the basis that it was unreasonable as it restricted the crofter's right to use the croft for a subsidiary or auxiliary use.[19]

(b) There is considerable statutory regulation of residential tenancies both where the landlord is a local authority and where it is a private landlord. The morass of detail on this important subject must be sought in specialist textbooks.[20] As a brief illustration only one important provision should be noted here. In residential leases for less than seven years granted on or after 3 July 1962 there is a legally implied obligation on the landlord to keep in repair the structure and installations in the house.[21] Agreements to contract out of this obligation are void unless they are determined by the sheriff to be reasonable.[22] There are no reported instances of this having occurred.[23]

(c) It is a condition of all leases granted after 1 September 1974 for a period of more than 20 years that the subjects of lease shall not be used as a private dwellinghouse.[24] Exceptions are made in the case of use as a dwellinghouse which is ancillary to the use of the remainder of the subjects of let for other purposes and it would be detrimental to the efficient exercise of the use of the remainder of the subjects if the ancillary use did not occur on that property.[25] Caravan sites, agricultural holdings, small landholdings and crofts are also exempted from the provision.[26] The main purpose of this legislation was to avoid the switch to the grant of leases imposing ground rents when the right to impose feu duties was abolished. It was accepted that long leases may still be appropriate for commercial sites.

(d) Where an employer or a "trade organisation"[27] occupies premises under a lease and is not entitled in terms of the lease to make a particular alteration to the premises to comply with

---

18 Crofters (Scotland) Act 1993, s.5(3) and Sched.2, para. 9. There are exceptions for rights under the 1993 Act, ss 12–19 and 21 and 37.
19 *Bray v. Morrison* 1973 S.L.T. (Land Ct.) 82.
20 See, *e.g.*, Robson and Halliday, *Residential Tenancies* (2nd ed.), (1998).
21 Housing (Scotland) Act 1987, Sched. 10, para. 3.
22 Housing (Scotland) Act 1987, Sched. 10, para. 5.
23 Robson and Halliday, *Residential Tenancies* (2nd ed.), paras 3.18 and 3.51.
24 Land Tenure Reform (Scotland) Act 1974, ss 8–10 as amended.
25 1974 Act, s.8(3).
26 1974 Act, s.8(2) and 8(5).
27 Defined in Disability Discrimination Act 1995, s.13.

an obligation in terms of the Disability Discrimination Act 1995, ss 6 or 15, then special provision is made in terms of the 1995 Act, s.16 in respect of obtaining the consent of the landlord to those alterations.[28] It is provided that the lease shall have effect as if it provided (i) for the tenant to be entitled to make the alteration with the written consent of the landlord, (ii) for the tenant to have to make a written application for consent if he wishes to make such alteration, (iii) if such an application is made, for the landlord not to withhold his consent unreasonably, and (iv) for the landlord to make his consent subject to reasonable conditions.

In general, however, one must consult the lease to determine the obligations and rights of the landlord and tenant in any particular case. With this caveat in mind it is useful to outline the principles of construction of leases before passing to commonly encountered aspects of leases.

Principles of Construction

Wherever a lease has been drawn up, and whether or not it employs English terminology, if it relates to heritable property in Scotland the construction of that lease will be in accordance with Scots law.[29] The principles of construction applied to a lease are more akin to those applied to contracts than those employed in relation to real conditions in dispositions. For example, the *eiusdem generis* rule is commonly employed in relation to the construction of lists.[30] There is no principle that the terms of a lease should be construed strictly[31] and there is no bias against either the landlord or the tenant except that the terms of a lease are construed *contra proferentem*—a maxim which can cut both ways depending on who relies on it.[32] The aim of the principles of construction is to give the words employed their reasonable meaning. This does not mean that the court will attempt to seek a "fair" or "equitable" result: if the parties have employed clear wording it will be given effect to even if the result is unfair. There are two limited exceptions to this at

7.22

---

28 In force 2 Dec. 1996 (S.I. 1996 No. 1474). Supplemental provisions are found in 1995 Act, Sched. 4, Pt I. The similar provisions relative to a provider of services contained in 1995 Act, s.27 are not yet in force. "Provider of services" is defined in 1995 Act, s.19(2)(b).
29 *Mackintosh v. May* (1895) 22R. 345.
30 *Admiralty v. Burns*, 1910 S.C. 531.
31 *Swan's Trs v. Muirkirk Iron Co.* (1850) 12D. 622 per Lord Mackenzie at 626.
32 *Johnston v. Gordon* (1805) Hume 822.

common law. First, the enforcement of a remedy of irritancy will be refused if it is oppressive[33] and, secondly a right of resumption may not be exercised if this constitutes a "fraud on the lease".[34] Both of these common law limitations give only slight protection to the tenant and the court will not interfere at common law just because the exercise of the right or the remedy by the landlord seems unfair.[35] As a result, there has been statutory intervention in respect of both matters to protect the interests of the tenant.[36]

Tacit Relocation

7.23   A lease does not end automatically upon the arrival of the term date (known as the "ish date"). Instead, for the lease to end there must be in addition either (a) due notice of termination given by the landlord to the tenant, or (b) circumstances showing that the parties regard the lease as ended. If due notice is not given (and such notices are easy to get wrong),[37] the lease is held to be renewed by the tacit consent of the parties. This is known as "tacit relocation". The lease is renewed from year to year if the original lease was for a year or more. The lease is renewed for the same term for which it was originally granted if the original lease was for less than a year. Tacit relocation will not operate if the parties have negotiated a new lease[38] or if the terms of the lease itself exclude tacit relocation.[39] There are special statutory rules for agricultural holdings[40] and crofts which are given special statutory protection. By and large these leases are continued perpetually by statute despite any term date stated in the written lease.

The origin of tacit relocation in the presumed intent of the parties appears to leave open the possibility of contracting out although there is surprising paucity of authority on the matter.[41] It is possible

---

33 *Stewart v. Watson* (1864) 2M. 1414; *McDouall's Trs v. MacLeod*, 1949 S.C. 593.
34 *Fotheringham v. Fotheringham*, 1987 S.L.T. (Land Ct.) 10; Gill, *Agricultural Holdings* (3rd ed.), paras 13.03–13.04.
35 For irritancy see *Dorchester Studios (Glasgow) Ltd v. Stone*, 1975 S.C. (H.L.) 56. For rights of resumption see *Stewart v. Lead* (1825) 1 W. & S. 68; *Edinburgh Corporation v. Gray*, 1948 S.C. 538 per Lord President Cooper at 545.
36 For irritancy see Law Reform (Misc. Prov.) (Sc.) Act 1985, ss 4–7 as amended by Agricultural Holdings (Scotland) Act 1991, s.88(1), Sched. 11, para. 42. For resumption see Agricultural Holdings (Scotland) Act 1991, s.21(7).
37 See, *e.g.*, *Glasgow City Council v. Torrance*, 1999 G.W.D. 35–1708.
38 *McFarlane v. Mitchell* (1900) 2F. 901.
39 *MacDougall v. Guidi*, 1992 S.C.L.R. 167. The soundness of this decision is open to criticism.
40 Agricultural Holdings (Scotland) Act 1991, s.3.
41 13 *Stair Memorial Encyclopaedia*, para. 453.

that a lease may expressly provide that when the term date arrives it will continue on a yearly basis[42] or on a shorter basis such as monthly or daily. These short express continuations are a device used by some landlords to minimise the adverse effects of failure timeously to serve a notice of termination. Their efficacy must remain questionable.

As tacit relocation is on the presumed intention only of the parties to the lease it will not extend to the liabilities of other parties such as the liability of a cautioner under a guarantee relative to the tenant's liabilities[43] unless, of course, the guarantee provides otherwise.

Assignation

The transfer of the existing tenant's interest to a new tenant is 7.24 effected by an assignation (otherwise "assignment") and not disposition. This reflects the origin of a lease as a contractual arrangement. The assignation is usually executed by the existing tenant, delivered to the assignee, and intimated to the landlord, with the real right being transferred by means of possession or recording in the Sasine Register (or the Land Register of Scotland if appropriate).[44]

The effect of assignation is normally to substitute a new tenant for the former one. Where assignation is permitted, the original tenant's right comes to an end when the assignee completes his right to the lease. His liability to the landlord will terminate upon intimation of the assignation to the landlord. Thereafter the original tenant is normally free of all obligations in the lease—other than those which accrued before the landlord was notified of the assignation. It is possible for the parties to the lease to contract otherwise and provide that notwithstanding assignation the original tenant will remain liable for the rent.[45] Such clauses are extremely onerous from the tenant's point of view and will reduce the marketability of the lease. Whilst they are not uncommon, they should be resisted strongly by a tenant's solicitor when negotiating a lease. Where assignation is not permitted, a purported assignation will be ineffective and the original tenant will remain liable for

---

42 *Barns—Graham v. Boyd*, 1998 Hous. L.R. 39 (Sh Ct).
43 Bell, *Prin.*, s. 1265.
44 Para. 3.18.
45 *Bel Investments Pension Fund Trustees v. MacTavish*, 1999 G.W.D. 27–1294 (Sh Ct).

payment of rent and the other obligations of the lease[46] and, provided the irritancy clause in the lease is suitably drafted, may involve forfeiture of the tenant's interest. The various codes of statutes conferring security of tenure on tenants in leases relating to subjects such as crofts and domestic residential property also contain provisions importing similar restrictions on assignation into the relevant leases. Each statute should be consulted for its terms.[47]

The general rule at common law is that many leases are not assignable by the tenant either during his life or on his death because of the legal rule known as *delectus personae*. This means that the landlord has made a special choice of a person with whom he wishes to contract. In general, rural leases assignable on this basis but an unfurnished urban lease is not. There are exceptions to this common law rule where the assignation is involuntary such as where the tenant is rendered insolvent and a trustee in bankruptcy is appointed to his estate. The common law has become largely irrelevant given the almost universal practice of dealing with assignation in an express clause in the lease. The lease itself may exclude, vary or confirm the common law rule and permit assignation in whole or in part. An express exclusion of assignees excludes even involuntary assignation.[48] A common form of words used in a lease is that the tenant is given right to assign "with the express consent of the landlord". This leaves unfettered the discretion of the landlord to accept or reject a new tenant.[49] There is no implied requirement in Scotland that a landlord must act reasonably in granting consent. This may be compared with the position in England where statute implies a provision into a lease that "the landlord's consent will not be unreasonably withheld" in respect of assignation.[50] Such wording may be expressly contained in a Scottish lease and, particularly in a commercial context, a tenant's solicitor would be wise to ensure that such words are revised into the draft lease if this is commercially negotiable. It is competent for a lease to contain a provision requiring that the tenant's interest be disposed of only in whole and not in parcels.[51]

---

46 *Gemmel v. Low* (1823) 2S. 563.
47 Gordon, *Scottish Land Law* (2nd. ed.), para. 19–31.
48 Bell, *Prin*, s. 1218.
49 *Lousada & Co. Ltd v. J.E. Lessel (Properties) Ltd*, 1990 S.C. 178.
50 Landlord and Tenant Act 1927, s.19.
51 See, *e.g.*, *McQuiban v. Eagle Star Insurance Co.*, 1972 S.L.T. (Lands Tr.) 39. See para. 1.28.

Sub-letting

Sub-leasing, is where the tenant carves another lease (the sub-   7.25
lease) out of his own, whilst retaining his relationship with his own
landlord. The tenant's lease then becomes known as the "head
lease". This is a term which originates in England but is now
commonly used in Scotland. The sub-lease must be for a term which
is no longer than the tenant's lease (the head lease) and frequently it
is for a lesser period.[52] A sub-lease may not relate to a greater area
than that contained in the head lease and is frequently for less. The
existing tenant remains the tenant of his existing landlord but, in
addition, becomes landlord in respect of the sub-tenant. The
existing tenant therefore continues to be liable to his landlord for all
his obligations under the lease.

The head landlord, notwithstanding the continuing relationship
with his tenant, is likely to want to control sub-letting in much the
same manner as assignation. Nevertheless, under sub-letting the
landlord has the continuing liability and covenant of the existing
tenant and may be willing to permit sub-letting where he would not
be willing to permit assignation. The general rule at common law is
that where assignation is excluded, so is sub-letting. Despite this,
the parties to a particular lease may make their own special
arrangements about sub-letting. In a sub-let, the original lease
remains in full effect. The sub-letting creates a new lease to which
the law of leases also applies. There is no contractual relationship
between the head landlord and the sub-tenant unless the former is
joined as a party to the sub-lease. The mere fact that the head
landlord consents to the granting of the sub-lease does not make
him a party to it. In some cases a landlord consents to sub-leasing
on the condition that the rent is paid directly to him to the extent of
the rent under the head lease. This does not release the original
tenant from his liability to the head landlord.

Death and Bankruptcy of the Tenant

Because leases are heritable they devolve according to the *lex loci*   7.26
situs and succession to a lease is governed by the law of Scotland
regardless of the domicile of the tenant.[53] A lease does not
automatically come to an end on the death of a tenant unless
granted only for the original tenant's lifetime. In other cases the

---

52 An exception exists in relation to interposed leases. See Land Tenure Reform
(Scotland) Act 1974, s.17(1).
53 Succession (Scotland) Act 1964, s.37(2); *Mackintosh v. May* (1895) 22R. 345.

landlord may reserve an option to terminate the lease upon the death of the original tenant. The general position is that the interest of the tenant in the lease forms part of his estate and vests for administration in the executor.[53a]

Sometimes the power to bequeath will be expressly dealt with in the lease. The lease itself may provide for succession to someone other than the tenant's successor at law. A power to assign in a lease will include a power to bequeath on death—it is simply a form of assignation. Even where a prohibition bequest exists, express or implied, where there is no valid bequest the executor may transfer the lease to any one of the persons entitled to succeed the deceased' intestate estate, or to claim legal or prior rights in or towards satisfaction of such a claim.[53b]

In some particular instances the succession to a tenant's interest is regulated or excluded by statute, as is the case with crofts and agricultural tenants. In the case of a lease of a private dwellinghouse protected by the Rent (Scotland) Act 1984[54] a statutory right of succession is given to the tenant's spouse, failing whom to any one member of the tenant's family who has been residing with him or her for six months preceding the tenant's death. This is known as a statutory tenancy and that tenancy may pass in turn to a second successor in the same way. The Housing (Scotland) Act 1988 has further restricted this.[55] A first succession is now limited to the tenant's spouse or a member of the tenant's family who has been in residence with the deceased for a two year qualifying period. In relation to assured tenancies there is a tighter regime which permits one succession only.[56] Similar statutory provision is made for succession to a tenancy of a council house or flat.[57]

At common law the bankruptcy of the tenant does not terminate the lease. The tenant's interest in the lease passes to the trustee in bankruptcy for the purposes of administration and distribution. The general practice in modern leases, however, is to insert an irritancy clause to permit the landlord to bring the lease to an end. If the tenant is a company the lease will come to an end when the company is wound up but the lease will generally contain an

---

53a Succession (Scotland) Act 1964, ss 14(1) and 16(1).
53b *ibid.*, s.16(2) as amended.
54 1984 Act, s.3 and Sched.1.
55 1988 Act, s.46 and Sched. 6; Robson and Halliday, *Residential Tenancies* (2nd ed.), p. 208.
56 Housing (Scotland) Act 1988, s.31(1)(c).
57 Housing (Scotland) Act 1987, s.52.

irritancy clause which is operative upon a liquidator, receiver or administrator being appointed.

Possession

The landlord's primary obligation is to give his tenant possession 7.27 of the subjects let on the date of entry.[58] The tenant has a converse obligation to take possession of the subjects let.[59] The nature of possession will depend on the subjects of lease. For example, a much lesser degree of possession is required for a shooting or sporting lease of a field compared to a lease of the same field for the purposes or grazing or ploughing. The period of occupation need not be continuous throughout the whole term. A lease may be granted of a holiday home for two weeks in July for a total period of 10 years.

Once possession has been taken, the landlord is obliged to maintain the tenant in undisturbed possession for the duration of the lease.[60] If the landlord grants warrandice to the tenant, this is a warranty that nothing has been done in the past and nothing will be done in the future by anyone to disturb possession. This is founded on the principle that the landlord must not derogate from the grant. Mere business competition by the landlord or another tenant of the landlord is not disturbance which will found a claim for breach of warrandice.[61] It is possible that the tenant may wish to fortify his position in relation to protection of his business by obtaining an assurance that the landlord (and none of his tenants) will set up in the same business as the original tenant. This is a restrictive covenant and will be strictly construed by the courts. They are common in relation to what are known as "anchor tenants" or specialist shops in retail arcades.

The corollary of the landlord's obligation to give possession is the tenant's obligation to take possession on the date of entry.[62] The tenant is obliged to continue in possession throughout the currency of the lease. In the absence of special stipulation the obligation of the tenant to occupy the subjects of lease will not constitute an obligation to trade from the subjects.[63] Such express obligations—

---

58 Stair, *Inst.*, I,xv,6.
59 Stair, *Inst.*, II,ix,31; Erskine, *Inst.*, II,vi,39; Bell, *Prin*, s.1222.
60 Hume, *Lectures*, Vol. II, p. 71.
61 *Craig v. Millar* (1888) 15R. 1005.
62 Stair, *Inst.*, II,ix,31; Erskine, *Inst*, II,vi,39; Bell, *Prin.*, s.1222.
63 *Whitelaw v. Fulton* (1871) 10M. 27.

known as "keep open clauses"—are common in leases of retail subjects.[64] Such provisions are particularly useful where the lease relates to an important unit in a retail centre which would suffer considerable loss of prestige if a major tenant shut up shop and left. Similar provisions are found in agricultural leases where the obligation to farm continuously is designed to retain the value of the land.

A progression on the traditional obligation to take possession and the more modern "keep open" clause is an obligation in a lease which imposes a *solus* tie or a similar obligation in a loan agreement secured by a standard security over a lease.[65] This effectively requires the tenant not only to carry out a particular trade but also to take supplies of the stock that is sold from the premises only from the landlord or another source nominated by him. Such agreements are common in relation to public houses and petrol filling stations. It may be possible for the tenant to challenge some of these agreements on the basis that they are illegal and unenforceable restraints on trade.[66]

Possession may be actual or civil but in many cases actual possession is stipulated for in particular leases.[67] In relation to crofts there is a requirement that a crofter shall by himself or his family, with or without hired labour, cultivate his croft.[68] A crofter who had moved to Canada and left the holding under the charge of a neighbour was held in breach of this condition and removed.[69] In other leases there is a requirement that the tenant resides within a certain distance of the leased subjects. For example, in relation to allotments the tenant must not live more than one mile outwith the local authority district otherwise the local authority may serve notice of termination.[70]

Use of the Subjects

7.28   The clause regulating the use of the subjects is one of the most

---

64 See, *e.g.*, *Cooperative Wholesale Society Ltd v. Saxone Ltd*, 1997 S.L.T. 1052; *Highland & Universal Properties v. Safeway Properties*, I.H., 1 February 2000 (unreported). See para. 1.2.

65 For an earlier form of security see *McIntyre v. Cleveland Petroleum Co.*, 1967 S.L.T. 95.

66 *Esso Petroleum v. Harpers Garage (Southport) Ltd* [1968] A.C. 269; MacQueen and Thomson, *Contract Law in Scotland* (2000), paras 7.16–7.20.

67 *Blair Trust Co. v. Gilbert*, 1940 S.L.T. 322.

68 Crofters (Scotland) Act 1993, s.5 and Sched.2, St. Cond. 3.

69 *Department of Agriculture v. Robertson*, 1941 S.L.C.R. 32.

70 Allotments (Scotland) Act 1892, s.8(2) as amended.

important in any lease. It is most unusual in modern practice for a lease to have no express provision relative to this matter. Nevertheless, common law makes provision in the rare cases where the lease is silent. At common law a tenant has two principal duties as regards use of the subjects. First, he must use the leased subjects in a reasonable manner so as not to cause deterioration. The import of this obligation will reflect the physical nature of the subjects of lease. For example, under an agricultural lease, a tenant will be expected to cultivate the land in accordance with the rules of good husbandry.[71] In relation to a warehouse a tenant is expected not to overload the building.[72] Secondly, he must use the premises for the purposes for which they were let and for that purpose only. This is known as the obligation not to invert possession. If the purpose of the lease is not expressly stated it will be implied from the nature of the subjects. Most modern leases do not leave the matter to implication and many leases expressly exclude particular uses such as the sale of alcoholic liquor[73] and any other activity which might constitute a nuisance to surrounding property. Particular landlords have particular preferences and some may wish to exclude everything from performing animals to sex shops. An overly strict control of use can have a deleterious impact on rent review and to counteract this the lease may allow for a change in the use with or without the landlord's consent. The latter is unlikely to be granted as the landlord will probably wish to retain some control on use so as to maintain the value of the leased subjects. As a compromise between these competing objectives the lease may sometimes permit a change of use within a limited class of uses.

Responsibility for State of Property

At common law, the tenant is entitled to take possession of 7.29 subjects which are reasonably fit for the purpose for which they are let.[74] This is not a warranty by the landlord that the subjects of lease will never need repair so the later emergence of defects will not constitute a breach of obligation by the landlord—it is only if the landlord refuses or fails to discharge his obligation of repair that this could be so.[75] If the subjects are not reasonably fit for the

---

71 Stair, *Inst.*, II,ix,31; Erskine, *Inst*, II,vi,39; *McCulloch v. Grierson* (1862) 1M. 53; Agriculture (Scotland) Act 1948, s.26 and Sched. 6.
72 *Glebe Sugar Refining Co. v. Paterson* (1900) 2 F. 615.
73 See, *e.g.*, Crofters (Scotland) Act 1993, Sched. 2, "The Statutory Conditions", para. 12.
74 See, *e.g.*, *Glebe Sugar Refining Co. v. Paterson* (1900) 2 F. 615.
75 MacQueen and Thomson, *Contract Law in Scotland* (2000), para. 3.52.

purpose of the lease the tenant may refuse to take entry.[76] The common law obligation of the landlord is sometimes circumvented by a clause in the lease requiring the tenant to accept that the premises are fit for occupation whatever their actual state. If such a clause is to be accepted it is vital that the tenant obtain a survey making it clear to him exactly what is the condition of the property he is taking on. This is particularly important where the tenant is obliged by another clause in the lease to put the subjects into full repair at the end of the lease. The combination of these clauses may impose an obligation on the tenant to upgrade the actual condition of the subjects.

At common law there is an obligation in what are known as "urban" leases which falls on the landlord to keep the property in a tenantable and habitable condition during the currency of the lease. In this context the term "urban" is a generic term which has no precise meaning. It generally means leases relating to buildings used for purposes other than agricultural uses. At common law it includes houses used for residential property. The import of the obligation is a requirement to keep the premises in a wind and water tight condition. Again, it does not import a warranty that the premises will never need repair. The landlord is liable only after the defect in the condition of the premises is drawn to his attention and he then fails to deal with the matter satisfactorily. In this regard a landlord is not liable for any of the following: (a) an act of God; (b) an act of a third party such as a neighbour; and (c) damage caused by the tenant's own negligence.

Repairs—Residential Leases

7.30   This common law position relating to urban leases has been fortified by statutory provisions to some extent. The statutory provisions do not relate to all urban leases but only to leases of houses. The landlord has only a limited freedom to contract out of these statutory provisions. Under the Housing (Scotland) Act 1987 as amended the by Housing (Scotland) Act 1988 there are two provisions as follows: (a) notwithstanding any contrary statement in a lease where the letting of a dwellinghouse is for less than three years at a low rent (this level is set from time to time by the Secretary of State (now the Scottish Ministers) by Statutory Instrument[77]) then the landlord is obliged to ensure that the house

---

76 *Brodie v. Maclachlan* (1900) 8 S.L.T. 145.
77 The Landlord's Repairing Obligations (Specified Rent) (Scotland) (No.2) Order 1988 (S.I. 1988 No. 2155).

is reasonably fit for habitation at the outset and the landlord is obliged to maintain the house in this condition throughout the let[78]; and (b) where the letting of a dwellinghouse is for less than seven years the landlord is obliged to keep the premises installations and common parts in repair and tenantable order.[79] It is not possible to contract out of the second of these provisions which may be modified only by the sheriff upon application by the landlord or the tenant.[80]

Repairs—Commercial Leases

The common law repairing obligation falling upon the landlord is 7.31 frequently contracted out of in leases relative to commercial property and it is invariably removed altogether where the lease is a full repairing and insuring lease (known as an "FRI" lease for short). The aim of the clause inserted in such leases is usually the transference to the tenant of the full burden of repairing. One particular type of defect in property which has caused difficulty in this context is the "latent and inherent" defect. This is a defect which is hidden at the time the lease is granted and is not known either to the landlord or the tenant. This tends to be most relevant in the context of new buildings where some fault in the construction is not apparent at the grant of the lease. In Scotland only very clear wording in a lease will place an obligation on a tenant to remedy this type of defect. A clause which imposed on the tenant to rebuild, reinstate and replace the premises "in the event of damage however the same shall arise" has been held to transfer the obligation to the tenant to repair and inherent defect.[81] If there is no provision in the lease for latent defects the liability of repair falls on the landlord subject to one exception—where the premises are destroyed totally or rendered wholly unusable by latent defect. In such a case the common law provides that the legal doctrine known as *rei interitus* will terminate the lease.[82] It is common for parties to FRI leases to contract out of the application of the doctrine of *rei interitus* but where this is done particular attention should be given to the obligations relative to reinstatement and insurance.

---

78 Housing (Scotland) Act 1987, Sched. 10, para. 1(2).
79 Housing (Scotland) Act 1987, Sched. 10, para. 3.
80 Housing (Scotland) Act 1987, Sched. 10, para. 5.
81 *Thorn EMI Ltd v. Taylor Woodrow Industrial Estates Ltd*, 29 October 1992, Lord Murray, Court of Session (unreported). See Ross and McKichan, *Drafting and Negotiating Commercial Leases in Scotland* (2nd ed.), paras 8.16–8.21.
82 *Cantors Properties (Scotland) v. Swear & Wells*, 1978 S.C. 310. See para. 3.41.

Repairs—Rural Leases

7.32   At common law there are obligations on the landlord and tenant
in relation to buildings and fences in the following regard: (a) the
landlord has to put buildings and fences in repair at entry; (b) the
landlord has to effect extraordinary repairs arising from natural
decay; (c) the tenant has liability for ordinary maintenance and
repairs; and (d) the tenant must leave the subjects in the same
condition as when he got them, fair wear and tear excepted. These
common law provisions may be varied in a lease. They are largely
restated and amplified for the benefit of the tenant in the
Agricultural Holdings legislation,[83] which cannot generally be
contracted out of in a lease. However it is competent to contract out
of the Agricultural Holdings provisions in what is known as a post-
lease agreement, which is an agreement entered into after the lease
has been entered into.[84]

Fixtures and Compensation for Improvements

7.33   The question of what occurs to fixtures which the tenant has
added to the property will often be addressed in the lease. In the
absence of express provision, such fixtures will belong to the
landlord unless (a) they are trade fixtures in which case they may be
removed by the tenant at the end of the lease[85] or (b) there is a right
of removal conferred by special statutory provision. For example,
at the end of his lease the tenant in an agricultural lease is entitled to
remove certain fixtures and buildings improvements.[86]

The tenant is under no obligation to improve the subjects of lease
unless there is a specific obligation to do so in the lease. In the
absence of agreement between the landlord and tenant, common
law makes no provision for compensation to a tenant in respect of
improvements which he makes to the subjects. The "Ulster" custom
to contrary effect does not apply in Scotland even though it was
introduced into the province by Scottish settlers at the time of the
Ulster Plantation.[87] This custom, broadly based on a notion of
unjustified enrichment, encouraged improvements and preserved
Ulster from starvation during the potato famine in the 1840s.[88] It is

---

83 Agricultural Holdings (Scotland) Act 1991, s.5, for leases entered into on or after
    1 November 1948.
84 Agricultural Holdings (Scotland) Act 1991, s.5(3).
85 *Cliffplant Ltd v. Kinnaird*, 1982 S.L.T. 2.
86 Agricultural Holdings (Scotland) Act 1991, s.18.
87 Wylie, *Irish Land Law*, paras 1.44–1.45.
88 Cecil Woodham Smith, *The Great Hunger: Ireland 1845–1849* (1962), p. 22.

one of Scots law's most important but least known exports. It has formed the model for almost all security of tenure statutes in America and the British Commonwealth.[89] On the Scottish mainland a tenant is presumed at common law to make improvements for his own advantage during the tenancy. This position is sometimes reinforced by a general statement in leases to the effect that the tenant will not be entitled to any compensation for improvements. This discouragement to a tenant making improvements has been removed by statute in relation to some rural leases and there are a number of instances where a statutory right to compensation has been given to the tenant where common law makes no provision. The most well known of these are contained in the Agricultural Holdings legislation[90] and the Crofting legislation.[91] These statutory rights cannot generally be contracted out of in a lease. Although common law refused the tenant any compensation for improvements made by him, it generally did not allow the landlord to increase the rent during the currency of the lease in respect of improvements which the tenant had made. The landlord could, however, increase the rent if there was a break in the lease and he would inevitably try to do so. In modern commercial leases there is usually an express statement that in relation to rent review the increase in the value of the premises caused by any improvements carried out by the tenant will be disregarded except where they have been carried out in the implement of an express obligation to the landlord.

Insurance

There is no general common law provision requiring either the 7.34 landlord or tenant to maintain insurance in respect of the subjects of lease. This position is usually altered in modern leases, particularly full repairing and insuring leases of commercial premises. In commercial leases the landlord will either require the tenant to maintain this insurance at the tenant's cost or alternatively he will maintain the insurance himself and provide that the costs may be recovered from the tenant. The clause will usually stipulate who shall determine the insurer, the amount of cover required and the risks to be insured against. Close attention should be paid to the interaction of this clause with the obligations

---

89 It was introduced throughout Ireland by Landlord and Tenant (Ireland) Act 1870.
90 Agricultural Holdings (Scotland) Act 1991, ss 33–42.
91 Crofters (Scotland) Act 1993, ss 30–33.

concerning repairs, rebuilding, abatement of rent, application of proceeds of insurance and the exclusion of the rule on *rei interitus*. There are special statutory provisions for insurance of buildings and harvested crops in relation to agricultural holdings.[92]

Landlord's Remedies

7.35 As a lease is in its origin a contract, many of the remedies of a landlord resemble those found in other contracts. There are, of course, a few specialities given that many leases are real rights and affect land. The landlord's remedies include the following:

(a) The landlord may obtain interdict where damage by the tenant is threatened or to prevent future damage. Interdict is used to prevent the tenant from doing something, and is therefore a "negative" remedy. There is considerable difficulty in obtaining interdict to make the tenant do something. For example, if a tenant is under an obligation in a lease to continue to trade, it is not possible to obtain an interdict to stop the tenant from breaching this obligation—that would be asking the court to require the tenant to trade, which is a positive remedy. Specific implement may be appropriate where the tenant has failed to carry out a positive obligation in the lease. A landlord is entitled to damages for loss resulting from the tenant's breach of contract.

(b) Where specific implement or interdict will not wholly restore the position the landlord, in appropriate cases, may be entitled to irritancy. The exercise and effect of this remedy will be further explored below.

(c) The landlord will have all the general remedies available to a creditor for recovery of debt. He may find his hand strengthened considerably if the lease is registered for execution as this will enable summary diligence.

(d) The landlord has in addition one special remedy known as the landlord's hypothec. This is a remedy for non-payment of rent but extends only to the current year. It enables the landlord to lay hands on certain moveable items of the tenant on the leased subjects and sell them to recover the rent.[93] This action involves the use of sheriff officers who must value all the items on the premises, and is consequently fairly expensive and

---

92 Agricultural Holdings (Scotland) Act 1991, Sched. 1, paras 5 and 6.
93 *Scottish & Newcastle Breweries Ltd v. City of Edinburgh D.C.*, 1979 S.L.T. (Notes) 11.

relatively rarely used. Landlord sometimes try to obtain a shorthand version of this remedy by stating in the lease that the landlord has the right to remove items affixed by the tenant in lieu of unpaid rent without necessity of court process. So far as the writer is aware this abbreviated remedy is rarely exercised and it may prove difficult to enforce where a property is constantly possessed. In a few rare cases a similar shorthand remedy is confirmed by statute. For example, the only buildings permitted on an allotment provided by the local authority are a toolhouse, shed, greenhouse, fowlhouse or pigsty and the local authority may remove and sell any other building and the proceeds of sale or disposal may be retained by the local authority towards the rent.[94]

(e) An action of removing. When all else fails the landlord may attempt to remove his tenant. There are strict statutory controls over such action, particularly where there is a form of security of tenure.[95]

Tenant's Remedies

The remedies generally available to the tenant again reflect the 7.36 contractual origins of a lease with a few specialities given the nature of the subjects and the existence of a real right. They include interdict, specific implement and damages. Two particular remedies in addition should be noted: (a) The tenant may be entitled to a reduction in the rent where the landlord is in material breach of the lease.[96] (b) The tenant may be entitled to abandon the lease on the ground that the landlord is in material breach of the lease. A lease will frequently expressly exclude these two additional remedies. Where a landlord is under an obligation to a tenant to supply certain services such as heating or water it is common for the landlord to insert a *force majeure* clause which exempts him from liability where the supply of the relevant service is disrupted by a cause beyond his control such as war or strike.[97] The effect of such a clause is to shift the risk of the eventuality to the tenant.

Arbitration

In an attempt to reduce the cost of enforcement of leases, many 7.37 leases require reference to arbitration before court procedure is

---

94 Allotments (Scotland) Act 1892, s.7(5).
95 Paras 7.1 and 7.15.
96 MacQueen and Thomson, *Contract Law in Scotland* (2000), para. 5.13.
97 MacQueen and Thomson, *Contract Law in Scotland* (2000), para. 3.75.

invoked. In other cases the reference to the court is excluded entirely.[98] It has to be said, however, that many arbitrations are as long and costly as court proceedings. There are extensive statutory provisions relative to the settlement of disputes by arbitration in relation to agricultural tenancies.[99] Each clause should be read to determine its extent and application. In some cases the arbitration clause extends to the whole subject matter of the lease and in others it is restricted to certain items such as rent review. A distinction may be made between arbitration clauses which are respectively termed "executorid" and "general". The former term denotes a clause which is inseparable from the lease and terminates with the lease with the result that a party who is in breach of the terms of the lease may not invoke it.[1] The term "general" denotes a clause which is severable and independent from the lease. It may therefore be invoked by a party in breach.[2] As there is no presumption in law as to the nature of the arbitration clause, to ascertain its nature the matter is determined by the intentions of the parties as ascertained from the provisions of the whole lease.

Termination of Tenant's Right in a Lease

7.38   The tenant's right in a lease may be terminated as follows:

(a)   Exercise of a right to break, resume or renounce a lease
(b)   Purchase by the tenant of the landlord's interest.
(c)   Irritancy.
(d)   Negative prescription.
(e)   Destruction of the Subjects of Lease—*rei interitus.*

Breaks in the Lease, Resumption and Renunciation

7.39   The tenant and landlord may agree to a voluntary renunciation by the tenant prior to the term date. Once the tenant's interest is acquired by the landlord the lease will be extinguished by the

---

98 This is subject to the possibility of a stated case being made in terms of the Administration of Justice (Scotland) Act 1972, s.3(1).
99 This is a highly specialist area. There is over two pages of entries in the index relative to arbiter and arbitration in Gill, *Agricultural Tenancies* (3rd ed., 1997), pp. 804–806.
1   *Montgomerie v. Carrick* (1848) 10D. 1387.
2   *McCosh v. Moore* (1905) 8F. 31 per Lord McLaren at 41; Gloag, *Contract* (2nd ed.), p. 596.

doctrine of *confusio*.[3] Any sub-lease will continue notwithstanding the voluntary extinction of the lease. The sub-lease will, however, be held directly from the head landlord and reference to the original lease will be made only where this is required to construe the terms of the sub-lease.

Most leases run for a single unbroken definite term. This, however, is not a requirement and a lease may provide for an option for either party to "break" the lease at prescribed intervals. Such arrangements can be of advantage to both tenant and landlord. In a rising market a landlord can use the threat to break the lease with a view to assisting a negotiation of more favourable terms. In a failing market a tenant may exercise the break clause to escape from an unduly burdensome lease. The arrangements are common in mining leases to reflect the lack of certainty that minerals will continue to be available in workable quantities throughout the duration of the lease. Break clauses are frequently encountered in commercial leases where they are linked to a rent review clause. The purpose of the clause is to provide a lifeline to a tenant who is given an opportunity to break the lease if the new revised rent is too high for his business to support.

Where a landlord exercises his option under a break clause in a lease he resumes the land which is leased. Quite apart from a break clause, a lease may make express provision for resumption in special circumstances. For example a landlord may make a provision that he can resume a field if he obtains planning permission allowing the field to be developed. There are detailed statutory provisions which regulate the resumption of agricultural tenancies[4] and crofts.[5]

A lease may provide for renunciation (otherwise known as "surrender") by the tenant in specified circumstances. In the absence of such a provision a tenant cannot renounce a lease, however burdensome, without the consent of the landlord.[6] Where a landlord does consent to a renunciation sought by the tenant he will usually do so on terms which require a payment from the tenant to compensate the landlord for loss of rent and oblige the tenant to reinstate the property. Where the renunciation is sought by the

---

3   18 *Stair Memorial Encyclopaedia*, para. 9(6); *Lord Blantyre v. Dunn* (1858) 20D. 1188. See also *B.G. Hamilton v. Ready Mixed Concrete (Scotland) Ltd*, 1999 S.L.T. 524.
4   Agricultural Holdings (Scotland) Act 1991, s.21(7) and ss 31 and 58; Gill, *Agricultural Holdings* (3rd ed.), Chap. 13.
5   Crofters (Scotland) Act 1993, ss 20–21.
6   *Salaried Staff London Loan Co. Ltd v. Swears and Wells Ltd*, 1985 S.L.T. 326.

landlord the tenant will seek payment in compensation for the loss of the use of the property for the remainder of the lease. An exceptional case arises where frustration of the lease occurs. Where there is supervening impossibility the tenant may renounce the lease unless this is expressly excluded in the lease.[7] Regardless of any provision of a lease or other rule of law, a lease which has vested in an executor may be terminated either by the executor or the landlord if the executor is satisfied that he cannot dispose of it and has informed the landlord. The lease may also be terminated if it is not disposed of within certain statutory time limits.[7a]

Acquisition of the Landlord's Interest

7.40 There is at present no general legislation in Scotland which allows a tenant to convert his lease into ownership by compelling his landlord to sell.[8] Similarly there is no general statutory right conferring a pre-emption on a tenant when a landlord wishes to dispone his interest to a third party. If a tenant wishes to obtain a property right in the subjects to his lease he must buy the right from the proprietor who will be his landlord unless his right is that of sub-tenant only. The tenant cannot compel his landlord to sell unless there is a contractual right to do so, such as may be constituted by an option to purchase clause in the lease. There are three particular exceptions to this general rule. These are tenants who are public sector tenants holding secure tenancies,[9] tenants who are crofters,[10] and (although this is probably not an instance of a tenant in a lease but another form of real right) those tenants who hold under a customary form of tenure known as a "tenancy at will".[11] In all these limited cases the tenant has a right to acquire the interest of his landlord at a price which, failing agreement, is fixed by the application of a statutory formula.

Irritancy[11a]

7.41 Irritancy is a remedy available to the landlord in certain cases of

---

7 *Mackeson v. Boyd*, 1942 S.C. 56; *Tay Salmon Fisheries Co. Ltd. v. Speedie*, 1929 S.C. 593.

7a Succession (Scotland) Act 1964, s.16(3).

8 Cf. the now expired Long Leases (Scotland) Act 1954.

9 Housing (Scotland) Act 1987, P. III, ss. 61–84.

10 Crofters (Scotland) Act 1993, ss 12–19,

11 Land Registration (Scotland) Act 1979, s.20.

11a See M. Hogg, "To Irritate or Rescind: Two Paths for the Landlord", 1999 S.L.T. (News) 1.

breach of the lease terms by the tenant. Upon its proper exercise the lease will come to an end and the tenant's right to the lease and to possession will be extinguished. The efficacy of this remedy has been circumscribed in cases where the tenant is afforded statutory security of tenure. For example in relation to assured tenancies (which relate to houses used for domestic and residential purposes) the landlord may recover possession upon a breach by the tenant of the terms of his lease only if a sheriff makes an order to that effect and then only if the statutory grounds for repossession are satisfied.[12] Upon the establishment of certain of these statutory grounds—such as three months' rent arrears[13]—the sheriff must order repossession.[14] In respect of others—such as persistent delay in rent payment, breach of obligations of tenancy and use of house for immoral purposes—the sheriff has a discretion to grant repossession.[15] There are two types of irritancy provisions—legal and conventional.

Legal Irritancies

At common law there is an implied irritancy if a tenant does not 7.42 pay his rent for two years. This is not much used in practice as very few landlords will, or can, afford to wait two years in cases of non-payment of rent.[16] Other legally implied irritancies are found in relation to agricultural or horticultural subjects. Under the agricultural holdings legislation there is an irritancy when rent is not paid for six months.[17] A crofter may also be removed for non-payment of rent for one year[18] or for breach of any of the statutory conditions.[19] In regard to allotments, a landlord may serve a notice determining the tenancy at the expiration of one month after the service of the notice if (a) a tenant is in arrears with his rent for not less than 40 days; (b) the tenant has failed to observe regulations concerning the allotment not less than three months after the commencing of the tenancy; or (c) the tenant is resident more than a mile outwith the district of the local authority.[20] There are slightly

---

12 Housing (Scotland) Act 1988, Sched. 5; Robson and Halliday, *Residential Tenancies* (2nd ed.), Chap. 5.
13 1988 Act, Sched. 5, Pt. I, Ground 8.
14 1988 Act, Sched. 5, Pt. I.
15 1988 Act, Sched. 5, Pt II, Grounds 11, 13 and 15.
16 *Nisbet v. Aikman* (1866) 4M. 284.
17 Agricultural Holdings (Scotland) Act 1991, 20.
18 Crofters (Scotland) Act 1993, s.5(2)(a) and 26(1)(a).
19 Crofters (Scotland) Act 1993, s.5(2)(b) and 26(1)(b).
20 Allotments (Scotland) Act 1892, s.8(2) as amended.

different rules for allotment gardens[21] but service of a notice of termination on the tenant is still required.[22] Legal irritancies may be purged at any time before decree—the tenant may remedy the fault and avoid loosing his lease.

Conventional Irritancies

7.43   These are expressly provided for in the lease and, subject to cases where they are disconform to statutory schemes of security of tenure,[23] they may be used to support any condition in the lease which the parties have agreed as suitable for protection in this way. This includes non-payment of rent, alteration of the use of the subjects, failure to repair, purported sub-letting or assignation without the required consent or bankruptcy of the tenant. To secure irritancy of the lease the landlord invariably proceeds with the notice procedure (outlined below) and then, in addition, he often obtains a court decree confirming that the lease has been irritated. This second stage is not a legal necessity but it occurs where the event of irritancy is disputed or where the landlord wishes some added protection. If a decree is obtained it may be exhibited to a potential new tenant to whom the landlord wishes to re-let the premises or a party who wishes to purchase the landlord's interest. If notice has been served by a landlord and he dispones his property to a successor before the process of irritancy is complete, the benefit of the notice must be assigned to the new landlord if he is to rely on it.[24] If a decree of irritancy has been obtained before a disposition of the landlord's interest is delivered, an assignation is not required because the process is complete.

A conventional irritancy is enforceable according to its terms and is not capable of being purged by the tenant as of right. A conventional irritancy may be purged at common law if there is oppression on the part of the landlord but this is difficult to establish.[25] The effect of this common law rule so undermined the value of the tenant's interest in a lease that the law was changed by the Law Reform (Miscellaneous Provisions) (Scotland) Act 1985, ss.4–7. These provisions do not apply to leases to which special

---

21 Allotments (Scotland) Act 1892, s.8(2) as amended; Allotments (Scotland) Act 1922, s.1(1)(a).
22 *Law Crescent Allotment Association v. Green* (1933) 49 Sh.Ct.Rep. 319.
23 *Royal Bank of Scotland v. Boyle* 1999 Hous L R 43 and 63.
24 *Life Association of Scotland v. Black's Leisure Group plc* 1989 SLT 674.
25 *Dorchester Studios (Glasgow) Ltd v. Stone*, 1975 S.C. (H.L.) 66; *HMV Fields Properties Ltd v. Skirt and Slack Centre of London*, 1982 S.L.T. 477. See para. 7.22.

codes of security of tenure apply such as agricultural tenancies, crofts, cottars, statutory small tenants, small holders and leases of land used mainly or wholly for residential purposes. They do apply to all other leases whether entered into before the enactment of the legislation or not and cannot be contracted out of. The provisions apply to clauses styled as "material breach" clauses as well as irritancy. The legislation provides that:

(1) for non-payment of money the landlord must serve a notice on the tenant giving at least 14 days' notice before irritancy[26];
(2) for other conditions (such as the obligation to carry out repairs) the landlord may rely on the provision only if, in all the circumstances, a fair and reasonable landlord would do so.[27]

A fair and reasonable landlord will not be precluded from taking self-interest into account. The statute requires that among the circumstances to be considered are whether a reasonable opportunity has been offered to the tenant to remedy an alleged breach which is capable of remedy within a reasonable time. Effectively, the notice must specify a reasonable time before which irritancy will be incurred.

In each case, at the end of the notice period, if the breach has not been purged, the landlord may irritate the lease.

The decision to irritate the lease upon the tenant's default rests entirely with the landlord. If the market is strong and a new tenant is readily available, the landlord will take advantage of the situation. If the market is weak and tenants are thin on the ground the landlord may prefer to use another remedy such as suing the existing tenant for the rent. An irritancy clause will not allow a tenant to unburden himself of an unwelcome lease by claiming that the event of irritancy terminates the lease *ipso facto*: rather it confers an option on the landlord to terminate the lease. Enforcement of an irritancy usually results in the loss of all real rights deriving from the lease such as standard securities created over the lease and will not normally give rise to a claim by the tenant against the landlord for unjustified enrichment.[28] Parties are free to contract to contrary effect in the lease on both these matters. Nevertheless, usually only the first point receives attention with the

---

26 1985 Act, s.4.
27 *Blythswood Investments (Scotland) Ltd v. Clydesdale Electrical Stores Ltd (in receivership)*, 1995 S.L.T. 150; *Aubrey Investments Ltd v. D.S. Crawford Ltd (in receivership)*, 1988 S.C. 21.
28 *Dollar Land (Cumbernauld) Ltd v. CIN Properties Ltd*, 1988 S.C. (H.L.) 90.

heritable creditor being given a certain limited period of time to dispose of the tenant's interest in the lease provided, in the meantime, he undertakes the tenant's obligations in the lease. Similar provisions are usually inserted in respect of receivers, liquidators and administrators where the tenant is a limited company.

Negative Prescription

7.44   Negative prescription may terminate some, but not all, leases if they have been unexercised or unenforced by the tenant for a period of 20 years. The right of a tenant under a lease which has been registered in the General Register of Sasines or the Land Register is imprescriptible.[29]

Rei Interitus

7.45   If the subjects of lease are destroyed or are damaged to such an extent that they are unfit for the purposes for which they are let the lease will terminate automatically.[30] This is known as *rei interitus*. The operation of this rule may be excluded in terms of the lease and this is invariably done in modern leases. As a matter of practice the risk of destruction is dealt with by the interaction of the provisions on repair, rent abatement and insurance.

---

29 Prescription and Limitation (Scotland) Act 1973, s.8(2) and Sched.3 (b); 18 *Stair Memorial Encyclopaedia*, para. 9(2). See para. 2.22.
30 *Duff v. Fleming* (1870) 8M. 769; *Allan v. Merkland* (1882) 10R. 383; *Cantors Properties (Scotland) Ltd v. Swears and Wells Ltd*, 1978 S.C. 310.

CHAPTER 8

SERVITUDES

Introduction

Servitudes are a class of real rights. They are burdens on one 8.1
piece of land (known as the "servient" or "burdened" tenement) in
favour of another piece of land (known as the "dominant" or
"benefited" tenement). The term "servitude" is largely synonymous
with the term "easement" which is used in common law
jurisdictions but authority from such legal systems must be treated
with caution as the applicable principles may differ considerably.
The principles applicable to servitudes in other mixed legal systems
such as South Africa,[1] Louisiana[2] or Sri Lanka[3] are more akin to
Scottish notions. Servitudes are rights which "run with the land" in
that they continue to bind the burdened land despite changes in
ownership. The original owner and his successors in title are bound.
They also benefit the original owner of the benefited tenement and
his successors in title.

Following Roman law, servitudes may be divided into "urban"
and "rural" servitudes. The former generally relate to buildings and
the latter generally relate to undeveloped land. The distinction has
no substantial practical use today except to indicate that the benefit
(or *utilitas*) of a servitude is not limited to bare land but also
includes the use thereof. Again following Roman law, servitudes are
classified as "positive" or "negative" servitudes. The former allow
the dominant proprietor to carry out some positive activity on the
servient tenement whilst the latter restrict the activity of the servient
proprietor in some way. The importance of this distinction will
diminish somewhat if anticipated legislation relative to the law of
real burdens and conditions precludes the creation of new negative

---

1 See Van der Merwe and de Waal, *The Law of Things and Servitudes.*
2 Yiannopolous, *Predial Servitudes* (2nd ed., 1997), Louisiana Civil Law Treatise,
   Vol. 4.
3 G.L. Peiris, "Servitudes and Partition", *The Law of Property in Sri Lanka*,
   (1977), Vol. 3.

servitudes and assimilates existing negative servitudes to real obligations.[4]

Enforcement and Enjoyment

8.2   Servitudes differ from most real burdens in that, at common law, real burdens are usually enforceable by the dominant proprietor only against the party who is the proprietor of the servient tenement. They are generally enforceable only *in personam*.[5] Servitudes, by contrast, are enforceable not only against the owner of the servient tenement but also against any party interfering with the exercise of the right. For example, in respect of a servitude of access the dominant proprietor may obtain interdict if it is interfered with or blocked by the proprietor of the servient tenement, his tenants, a party holding another servitude over the same route, parties purchasing the servient tenement and holding a mere contractual right under missives or even members of the general public who have no right personal or real in respect of the servient tenement.[6]

Servitudes are enforceable only by the dominant proprietor and not by tenants or any party having a subsidiary real right in respect of the dominant tenement.[7] Still less may the right be enforced by members of the public having no real right in respect of the dominant tenement. To this extent a servitude of access differs from a public right of way. Although the activity carried out in a servitude of way is similar to that encountered in a public right of way—access or passage—a servitude is a mere "private" right of way because it cannot be enforced by the general public by *actio popularis*.[8]

8.3   Enforcement must be distinguished from enjoyment.[9] A dominant proprietor may "communicate" the right to enjoy a servitude to other persons who have a legitimate connection with the dominant tenement provided always that the burden on the servient tenement is not increased beyond what is acceptable. This is most clearly observed in relation to a servitude of access. A dominant proprietor may permit the access to be exercised by those having real or statutory rights in relation to the dominant tenement

---

4   Scott. Law Com., *Discussion Paper on Real Burdens* (No. 106, Oct. 1998), paras 2.49–2.50.
5   18 *Stair Memorial Encyclopaedia*, para. 413.
6   Cusine and Paisley, *Servitudes and Rights of Way*, paras 1.06 and 12.04.
7   Cusine and Paisley, *supra*, paras 1.49–1.54.
8   *Thomson v. Murdoch* (1862) 24D. 975.
9   Cusine and Paisley, *supra*, para. 1.55.

entitling them to occupy that tenement such as proper liferenters, tenants, heritable creditors holding a standard security who have entered into lawful possession and non-entitled spouses. In addition, the access may be enjoyed by those having a personal right (however precarious or temporary) to visit or occupy the dominant tenement such as members of his family, employees, guests, those providing statutory services such as bin-men and other contractors.[10] The rights of many of these parties to enjoy the servitude may be revoked at will by the dominant proprietor, although more permanent rights may be conferred by an express licence to that effect. In any case the servient proprietor may not prevent their enjoyment of the right provided it does not exceed the capacity of the servitude.

Essentials of Servitudes

The essentials of all servitude rights are as follows: 8.4

(a) There must be two tenements in separate ownership.[11] No-one can have a servitude over his own land conform to the maxim *nemo res sua servit*.[12] Subject to the limited freedom afforded by the use of deeds of declaration of conditions, no-one may create a servitude over his own land to become effective when he disposes of it.[13] This may cause problems where a standard security is granted over part only of a greater area of land owned by a debtor with access to the secured area over the retained and unsecured land.[14] It seems more prudent in such cases to create the means of access by granting the security over a *pro indiviso* property right in the access road. A party may have a servitude over land held by him in another capacity. Thus an individual may have a servitude over land held by him as a trustee.[15] Common proprietors may be

---

10 *Hogg v. Campbell*, Lord Clyde, 2 April 1993, 1993 G.W.D. 27–1712; *Murdoch v. Carstairs* (1829) 7S. 607.
11 Stair, II,vii, preamble: Bankton, II,vii,1; Erskine, II.ix,5.
12 *Innes v. Stewart* (1542) M. 3081.
13 *Hamilton v. Elder*, 1968 S.L.T. (Sh.Ct.) 53. *Cf.* Conveyancing and Feudal Reform (Scotland) Act 1874, s.32, as amended by Land Registration (Scotland) Act 1979, s.17, applied in *Rubislaw Land Co. Ltd v. Aberdeen Construction Group Ltd*, 1999 G.W.D. 14–647. See K.G.C. Reid and G.L. Gretton, *Conveyancing 1999* (T.&T. Clark, 2000), pp. 8–9.
14 Cusine and Paisley, *Servitudes and Rights of Way*, para. 2.07; Halliday, *Conveyancing* (2nd. ed.), Vol.II, para. 51–04.
15 *Grierson v. Sandsting and Aithsting School Board* (1882) 9R. 437.

dominant proprietors in respect of a servitude over land held exclusively by one of their own number and *vice versa*.[16]

(b) The "burdened property" and the "benefited property" are usually neighbouring properties but there is no absolute requirement that they should be contiguous or adjacent.[17] The tenements, however, require to be sufficiently close so that the owner of the dominant tenement has a praedial interest to enforce the servitude. This is the requirement of *vicinitas*. The maximum distances between dominant and servient tenements for this purpose may vary from one type of servitude to another. The tenements in respect of a servitude of stillicide (discharge of water onto a neighbouring tenement) will normally be contiguous. In respect of a servitude of access they may be hundreds of metres apart—many farm lanes are well over a kilometre long and the whole of the *solum* not in single ownership. In respect of pipelines the dominant proprietor may be able to demonstrate a sufficient interest even if the tenements are hundreds of miles apart or in different jurisdictions.

(c) A servitude is derived from the right of *dominium* and not from any other subordinate real right except liferent and, in certain limited cases, from the creditor's right in a standard security.[18] In general only the owner of the servient land and not a tenant of that land can grant a servitude.[19] Similarly only the owner of the dominant land and not the tenant of that land should be the grantee in an express grant of servitude. A holder of a proper liferent may create a servitude with a maximum endurance no longer than the maximum endurance of the liferent but if he wishes to grant a servitude of longer duration he may obtain the consent of the fiar.[20] The right of a standard security holder to grant a servitude is limited.[21] In certain cases where the security subjects are sold in lots and the scheme of division requires the creation of servitudes relating to the maintenance of common property, the creditor has a limited statutory right to grant and reserve servitudes.[22] In other cases

---

16 Cusine and Paisley, *supra*, para. 2.07. *Cf. Clydesdale Bank plc v. Davidson*, 1996 S.L.T. 437. See para. 5.11.
17 Erskine, II,ix,33.
18 Cusine and Paisley, *supra*, paras 4.21–4.24.
19 *Safeway Food Stores Ltd v. Wellington Motor Co. (Ayr) Ltd*, 1976 S.L.T. 53.
20 Cusine and Paisley, *supra*, para. 2.92.
21 Cusine and Paisley, *Servitudes and Rights of Way*, paras 4.21–4.24.
22 Conveyancing (Scotland) Act 1924, s.40(2).

the power of sale may include a right to grant servitudes over unsold security subjects only where this is part of a series of intended transactions to maximise the price obtained for the whole subjects.[23] Unfortunately the matter is obscure and amending legislation is needed.

(d) A servitude may benefit and burden only heritable property. A servitude may not be created generally in favour of the assets and undertaking of an incorporated company or local authority[24]: it may, of course, be granted in favour of an item of heritable property owned by a juristic body. No-one can create a servitude over moveable property. A servitude of aqueduct and *aquaehaustus* burdens the land from which the water is abstracted and transported even though it involves the abstraction and transport of a moveable fluid. In a servitude of pasturage the right burdens the ground over which the dominant proprietor's sheep or cattle are entitled to graze. The right does not burden the grass itself when it is cut, as that grass, when separate from the ground, is moveable. A servitude of pasturage may not be granted in respect of bales of hay.[25]

(e) Servitudes impose no positive duty on the servient proprietor. The obligations they impose are *in patiendo* and not *in faciendo*.[26] For example, where a servitude of access is taken over a road, the owner of the road is not obliged to repair or maintain the road unless the obligation is created by other means such as a deed of conditions imposing a real burden or by common interest. Similarly, where a house owner has a private water supply system which runs through a field, if the pipe bursts because of frost, the owner of the field is not obliged to repair the pipe. Those repairs are the responsibility of the owner of the house who has implied rights of access to carry out the relevant repair works and to inspect the pipe from time to time to ascertain if repairs are necessary. By contrast, if the owner of the field causes damage to the pipe by some negligent act such as by ploughing the field and ripping up the pipe he will be obliged to repair the damage he has done. There are two possible exceptions to the rule excluding positive obligations on the servient proprietor. These are first that obligation to provide support does appear to involve a positive obligation on the proprietor of the servient tenement

23 Cusine and Paisley, *Servitudes and Rights of Way*, para. 4.21.
24 Cusine and Paisley, *supra*, paras 1.47 and 2.06.
25 Stair, II,i,4.
26 Stair, II,vii,6; Erskine, II,ix,1; Bankton, II,vii,7; Bell, *Prin.*, s.1003.

to do something.[27] This has led to the view that the obligation to provide support is really not a servitude at all but is a right of common interest.[28] Secondly, where the owner of the servient tenement in respect of a servitude of way installs items such as speed humps or gates and these cause the road to rut or deteriorate in other ways it appears to be the case that the obligation to repair the road to the extent of the damage caused falls on the servient proprietor.[29]

Inessentials

8.5   The following are not essential to servitude rights:

(a)   A servitude does not require to have perpetual endurance although this is the most commonly encountered form of servitude.[30] Where a servient proprietor wishes to impose a maximum duration on a servitude right he may do so by insertion of a suitably framed conventional servitude condition. Servitudes created by prescriptive exercise for 20 years will endure perpetually. In other cases the servitude may be created for a perpetual duration but under a reserved right on the part of the servient proprietor to bring it to an end short of that time. This may be framed either as a form of a resumption right or as an irritancy linked to the breach by the dominant proprietor of a particular condition of the right granted. No remedy of irritancy is implied by law in relation to servitude rights and, if the servient proprietor wishes to avail himself of this type of remedy, it must be expressly created in a deed. Given the draconian nature of such a remedy any dominant proprietor should seek to resist its incorporation.

(b)   It is not necessary that the dominant proprietor is able to exercise the facility of the servitude free of any continuing return. Servitudes differ from leases in that a rent or continuing payment is not usually charged in return for a servitude although some deeds of servitude provide for this.[31] Where a servitude relates to a water supply it is not uncommon for the dominant proprietor to pay an extra sum if the amount of water abstracted exceeds a certain volume. Where a servitude

---

27   *Dalton v. Angus* (1881) 6 App. Cas. 740.
28   See Chap. 9.
29   *Drurie v. McGarvie*, 1993 S.C. 95; Cusine and Paisley, *Servitudes and Rights of Way*, paras 12.105, 12.119–12.121. See also *Saint v. Jenner* [1973] Ch. 275.
30   Cusine and Paisley, *supra*, paras 2.88–2.96.
31   See *e.g. Stewart v. Steuart* (1877) 4R. 981.

of access is granted to a field under which minerals are located in quantities which are capable of extraction it is competent to create a servitude right in respect of which access for farming requires no payment by the dominant proprietor but if he wishes to extract minerals by the same route he will be obliged to pay a certain "royalty" per lorry load to the servient proprietor. Where a party is seeking to establish a positive servitude by prescriptive exercise it will be a factor adverse to showing that he possessed "as of right" if he has paid the proprietor of the land over which the right is claimed an annual return in exchange for the possession.[32]

(c) The tenements in servitudes need not be corporeal plots of land although they usually are. It is possible for servitude rights to benefit incorporeal rights provided they are recognised as separate tenements, such as rights of salmon fishing.[33] Because of the physical nature of these subjects it is more difficult to conceive of a positive servitude burdening an incorporeal tenement such as salmon fishings. Nonetheless there are instances where pipelines are laid across the *solum* of rivers where the party entitled to the pipeline has obtained a servitude of aqueduct not only from the owner of the *alveus* but also the owner of the salmon fishings in the river. The aim, presumably, is to prevent any claim of encroachment or nuisance in respect of the salmon fishings which may otherwise be available.

(d) It is not essential that a servitude is capable of exercise throughout its endurance at any time chosen by the dominant proprietor. Most servitudes, such as the vast majority of servitudes of access, have no set period during which they may be exercised by the dominant proprietor and it is left to him to choose when he wishes to avail himself of the right. In some cases, however, the parties may agree to restrict the time of exercise.[34] It is possible to protect the privacy and security of the servient tenement by the insertion of a servitude condition to confirm that a servitude may be used only in daylight or upon reasonable notice having been given to the servient proprietor. In cases such as access for fire escape it may be possible to limit the times of exercise to occasions of emergency or fire drill only. Where a servitude of access also confers on the dominant proprietor rights to maintain and upgrade roads

---

32 *Campbell v. Duke of Argyle* (1836) 14S. 798; 11 Fac. Dec. 672,
33 See, *e.g.*, *Middletweed v. Murray*, 1989 S.L.T. 11; Cusine and Paisley, *Servitudes and Rights of Way*, paras 1.47, 2.45 and 11.32.
34 Cusine and Paisley, *supra*, para. 2.97.

it is common for a servitude condition to require that these be carried in certain weeks or seasons when traffic on the road is lightest.

Common Occurrence

8.6   Servitudes are commonly encountered both in conveyancing transactions and in litigation. It is rare indeed for any property to exist on a separate title which does not benefit from, or is not burdened by, any servitudes. The following examples serve to illustrate the point:

(a)   Where a farmer sells off part of his land to a developer he will wish to retain servitudes of access and servitudes in respect of service media such as drains to preserve the development potential of his retained land. If such servitudes are not reserved a ransom strip situation may be created and the farmer may seek to recover damages from his solicitor on the basis that he may have been given negligent advice.[35]

(b)   Where a developer owns a tenement of flats and is selling those flats to individual purchasers he will wish to ensure that each flat has sufficient servitudes as regards services and access to render each title valid and marketable. As a result there will usually be a relatively sophisticated scheme of mutual servitudes. Central to this may be *pro indiviso* property rights to the central stairwell to each flat.[36] It may be that each separate *pro indiviso* share in that stairwell is burdened by non-exclusive servitudes of access in favour of all the other flat owners. The developer will also wish to reserve servitude rights for service media which he has installed throughout the common areas and each individually owned flat for the benefit of the remaining flats because the installation of service media may not fall within the activities permitted by the rules of normal or "ordinary" use.[37]

(c)   Where a builder sells modern self-contained houses in a residential development, he may wish to impose negative servitudes to prevent the house owner building an additional house in the garden. Servitudes of access for the purposes of carrying out repairs should be granted in respect of the fences separating the houses.[38]

---

35 See *e.g. Moffat v. Milne*, 1993 G.W.D. 8–572.
36 *WVS Office Premises Ltd v. Currie*, 1969 S.C. 170.
37 *Taylor v. Dunlop* (1872) 11M. 25. See also para. 5.6.
38 *Gray v. MacLeod*, 1979 S.L.T. (Sh.Ct.) 17.

(d) Where a farmer is selling off a redundant farm steading for conversion into a cottage he may grant a servitude right of access over the existing farm roads (with an express right to repair and upgrade them), a servitude to install pipes in connection with the use of a private water supply and a private septic tank[39] and, perhaps also, a servitude of prospect over the fields looking out over the sea. Unfortunately there is no recognised servitude which prevents the farmer from planting his fields with oil seed rape or locating a dunghill across the fence from the front garden of the cottage. Those matters require to be regulated by real conditions[40] or the law of nuisance.[41]

Content of Servitudes

It is not the case that the dominant and servient proprietors may agree that any right they consider appropriate may be created as a servitude. At common law there is a limited class of recognised servitudes which may be relaxed to some extent by future statutory reform.[42] If the activity permitted by a right agreed between the parties does not fall within the activity permitted by one of the recognised class of servitudes, the right cannot be a servitude. 8.7

This has caused some difficulty in cases where a recognised servitude has been granted but has been subjected to considerable qualification by the insertion of conventional servitude conditions.[43] For example, at common law a recognised negative servitude is an obligation not to build on a particular plot of ground. The right would still remain a servitude in the writer's view even if the servient proprietor were permitted to construct any building up to a maximum height of a stated number of metres. More difficult cases arise where the qualification is more complex. There is no known servitude which restricts the manner of design of a building, the purposes for which it may be used or the materials which may be used in its construction. This therefore must cast some doubt on the validity of a purported negative servitude which imposes an obligation on the servient proprietor not to build

---

39   *Todd v. Scoular*, 1988 G.W.D. 24–1041.
40   Chap. 9.
41   Paras 4.13–4.14.
42   Following upon Scot. Law Com., *Discussion Paper on Real Burdens* (No. 106, Oct. 1998).
43   *Braid Hills Hotel v. Manuels*, 1909 S.C. 120; Gordon, *Scottish Land Law* (2nd ed.), para. 24–25; Cusine and Paisley, *Servitudes and Rights of Way*, paras 14.12–14.13.

anything except a residential nursing home up to a maximum height of 20 metres provided always the materials used in the construction and the programme of construction is approved by the dominant proprietor. Any party wishing to create such a right would be more prudent to create it as a real condition and not a negative servitude. In any event he may be obliged to do so if negative servitudes are abolished in terms of anticipated reforms of the law of real conditions.[44]

Recognised Servitudes

8.8   Servitudes comprise a class of rights including the positive and negative rights outlined in the following paragraphs, respectively known as positive and negative servitudes. As has been outlined above, positive servitudes are "positive" in the sense that they permit the dominant proprietor to do something on the servient tenement: they are not "positive" in the sense that they require the owner of the servient tenement to do anything – that would conflict with the rule that the obligation of the servient proprietor in servitudes is *in patiendo* and not *in faciendo*.[45]

Positive Servitudes

8.9   The recognised positive servitudes include the following:

(a)   Rights of way or access, including pedestrian and vehicular traffic.[46] This servitude may also be used for the driving of loose animals if sufficient in its terms. Servitude rights of way may also extend to rights for boats over canals[47] and rights for planes to fly over land for the purpose of the inspection of pipelines. The rights may be exercisable over man-made structures such as bridges and pedestrian walkways. The Roman categories of *iter*, *actus* and *via* continue to have a limited application in Scots law. Broadly speaking, however, this application is limited to cases where the servitude is created by prescriptive exercise[48] or in a manner which does not specify the nature of the right. Where, by contrast, the servitude is created by express grant or reservation, the extent

---

44   Scot. Law Com., *Discussion Paper on Real Burdens* (No. 106, Oct. 1998).
45   Para. 8.04(e).
46   *Alvis v. Harrison*, 1991 S.L.T. 64 HL.
47   *Tennant v. Napier Smith's Trs* (1888) 15R. 671.
48   *Carstairs v. Spence*, 1924 S.C. 380.

of the right will be determined by construing the deed.[49] The
Roman concepts will have no application in such cases except,
as sometimes occurs, the actual Latin words are employed in
the deed of grant. A servitude of way need not be in a
horizontal plane. Thus it is possible to create a servitude in
respect of natural sloping ground, a staircase, a vertical access
shaft or even in respect of areas where access requires to be
taken with equipment such as lifts, ladders, conveyor belts,
overhead cables or fire escapes.

(b)   Rights to put drains or pipes in or over the ground to carry
water, sewage, oil, gas and similar matter and thereafter use the
service media installed. The authority for servitudes to convey
material other than water is surprisingly scant but this practice
is consonant with principle.[49a] Where servitudes relate to fresh
water for consumption by humans or for commercial use they
are variants of the servitude of aqueduct. A related right is the
servitude of *aquaehaustus* which is the right to abstract water
for the purposes of such consumption. Aqueduct and
aquaehaustus frequently exist together and affect a single
servient tenement but this is not necessarily the case as the
source of the water may be on a servient tenement in different
ownership from the servient tenements subjected to the pipe to
transport the water to the dominant tenement. Where a
servitude of drain is granted the terms thereof will require to be
examined to ascertain whether it may comprise the right to
discharge along natural water courses or man-made pipes and
structures. In the latter case, if the terms of the grant are
specifically extensive, the right may comprise the right to
install and use a septic tank and relative soakaways.[50]

(c)   Rights of pasturage for sheep and cattle.[51] This does not
include a right to cut hay or to plant crops. Servitudes of
pasturage continue to exist in rural areas but are now relatively
uncommon. The more common method of creating a right to
use another party's land for agricultural use is by the granting
of a lease. Such leases, however, are likely to attract security of
tenure in terms of the Agricultural Holdings legislation[52] and it
is possible that the parties may seek to utilise a servitude to

---

49   Cusine and Paisley, *Servitudes and Rights of Way*, para. 12.194.
49a See, *e.g. Fergusson v. Tennant*, 1978 S.C. (H.L.) 19 at 52 per Lord Fraser. See also
      para. 1.15.
50   *Todd v. Scoular*, 1988 G.W.D. 24–1041.
51   *Fearnan Partnership v. Grindlay*, 1988 S.L.T. 817.
52   Chap. 7.

avoid the statutory protection given to a tenant. Where such a servitude is granted subject to a limitation as to its endurance and a requirement to pay an annual monetary payment, the courts may examine it closely to ensure that the arrangement is not truly a lease.

(d) Rights to obtain fuel in the form of peat or turf from the servient tenement.[53] In general these are only found in titles relative to rural areas. The right will usually comprise various ancillary rights such as access and areas to dry and win the cut turf. Such an access may not be used for other purposes.

(e) Rights to obtain building materials from the servient tenement.[54] Depending on its terms this may extend to the extraction of sand, gravel, slate or stone. This right is now rarely used and in most cases where a party obtains a right to extract minerals from the land of another party his right will be constituted by means of a lease.[55]

(f) A right to bleach linen on the servient tenement and to a supply of water for that purpose.[56] This is very rarely used these days since the invention of modern washing machines. It is still frequently encountered in old title deeds in urban areas. It is found, for example, in the title deeds to houses in the fishing village of Footdee in Aberdeen.

(g) A right of lateral and vertical support. This is encountered not only in relation to building but also in respect of mineral strata. In modern grants of these rights in commercial developments it is common for a maximum weight restriction to be imposed. The rights are sometimes encountered where the airspace above an existing building is disponed for the purposes of facilitating a future development. In such cases the right is usually accompanied by a sophisticated scheme of servitudes and real rights enabling the dominant proprietor access to the servient tenement to carry out works (such as the removal and replacement of any existing roof on the existing building) and to install new means of support for the future building.

(h) A right to discharge water onto adjacent property from the roof of a structure with the dominant tenement. This is known as stillicide or eavesdrop. The right is much less common on modern buildings because of the particular requirements of building control legislation.

---

53 *Watson v. Sinclair*, 1966 S.L.T. (Sh.Ct.) 77.
54 *Aikman v. Duke of Hamilton and Brandon* (1832) 6 W. & Sh. 64.
55 Chap. 7. See also para. 1.16.
56 *Sinclair v. Mags of Dysart* (1779) M. 14519; (1780) 2 Pat. App. 554.

All of the above rights are known as "positive" servitudes as they 8.10
enable the holder of the right (and parties to whom the right may
lawfully be communicated) to carry on positive activity on the
servient tenement. The owner of the servient tenement is obliged to
submit to such activity but otherwise is free to use his servient
tenement. Exactly what that means will vary from case to case but
some general guidance may be offered. The servient proprietor
must not put up unreasonable obstacles to the exercise of a right of
way, although in rural areas an unlocked gate is probably allowed
in most cases.[57] The installation of a cattle grid in rural farm tracks
is probably unobjectionable unless the dominant proprietor uses the
track for the driving of loose cattle or other animals. Where the
servitude is one of aqueduct by means of water pipes located under
the ground the servient proprietor will be free to carry out
agricultural activities which do not interfere with the pipes. If,
however, he ploughs the land and damages the pipes he will be
liable to the dominant proprietor. On the analogy of the right to
erect gates in respect of servitudes of way, the servient proprietor in
respect of a servitude of aqueduct may have a power to install water
brakes within pipes or drains to slow down waterflow for the
purposes of flood prevention.

Negative Servitudes

At common law a number of rights are recognised as negative 8.11
servitudes. They enable the holder of the right to prevent activity on
the servient tenement. The recognised negative servitudes include:

(a) A right to prevent building on the servient tenement.[58] In some
   cases this may be stated to apply to all buildings or a particular
   height of building. In other cases the deed includes an
   expansive definition of building which may extend to all
   construction works including roadworks.
(b) A right to prevent obstruction of a view.[59] This right is
   frequently encountered in relation to sight lines for the
   entrance to roads leading to modern developments. The
   activity restrained generally relates to building but the terms
   of modern deeds usually ensure that this relates to all manner
   of construction including walls and fences and even the
   growing of hedges and trees.

---

57 *Wood v. Robertson*, Mar. 9, 1809, F.C.
58 *Braid Hills Hotel Co. v. Manuels*, 1909 S.C. 120.
59 *Banks & Co. v. Walker* (1874) 1R. 981.

Reforms presently being considered by the Scottish Law
Commission may result in the prohibition of the creation of
negative servitudes after the enactment of the legislation. Instead
the prohibition of building will be achieved by means of real burden
or condition.[60]

Additional or New Rights

8.12   It remains an open question whether a number of additional
rights may be added to the lists outlined above and thereby become
recognised as servitudes at common law. In reported case law there
has been some debate as to whether the right to carry out certain
recreational activities such as the playing of golf on adjacent land
can be recognised as a servitude.[61] It has been confirmed that a
right to play curling cannot be recognised as a servitude.[62] A factor
in the decision was that servitudes generally are exercisable all year
round (unless there are special terms in the grant) and curling on an
outdoor loch is capable of exercise only in winter. It has been held
that a right to install and use in a private electricity line cannot be a
servitude but the case in question has been criticised as not having
enough regard to modern social conditions.[63] There may remain
some doubt as to whether the right to park a vehicle on adjacent
land can be a servitude but the balance of the authority appears to
be moving to an acceptance of this possibility at common law.[64]

8.13   Reforms presently being considered by the Scottish Law
Commission may result in the abandonment of the recognised
categories of servitudes with the result that a much wider class of
positive activity may be carried out on a servient tenement by a
dominant proprietor in terms of a servitude.[65] It may be that the
expanded class of servitude rights will require to be created by a
recorded deed. This will effectively elide the necessity of development of the common law in this regard. Until such reforms are
enacted practice adopts a prudent course and creates any right over

---

60 Scot. Law Com., *Discussion Paper on Real Burdens* (No. 106, Oct. 1998).
61 *Mags of Earlsferry v. Malcolm* (1829) 7S. 755; (1832) 11S. 74.
62 *Harvey v. Lindsay* (1853) 15D. 768. Contrary to expectation this decision appears
    to have encouraged landowners to permit curling on their land because they
    knew that the practice would not create a real right enforceable against them and
    their successors—information kindly provided by the leading expert on the
    history of curling in Scotland, Sheriff D.B. Smith, Kilmarnock Sheriff Court.
63 *Neill v. Scobbie*, 1993 G.W.D. 8–572.
64 See *Stewart Pott & Co. v. Brown Bros* (1878) 6R. 35; *Ayr Burgh Council v. British
    Transport Commission*, 1955 S.L.T. 219; *Murrayfield Ice Rink Ltd v. Scottish
    Rugby Union*, 1973 S.L.T. 99.
65 Scot. Law Com., *Discussion Paper on Real Burdens* (No. 106, Oct. 1998).

which there is any debate as a servitude and as a real condition burdening the servient tenement usually by means of a deed of declaration of conditions.

Methods of Creation

There are various methods by which a servitude can be 8.14 constituted. A significant difference from real burdens is that servitudes may arise in ways other than creation by means of a grant or reservation in a recorded deed forming part of the title to the servient property. The more important means of creation of servitudes include:

(a) creation in a deed;
(b) implied grant and reservation;
(c) exercise for the prescriptive period;
(d) creation by statute; and
(e) acquiescence.

Creation in a Deed

Reforms presently being considered by the Scottish Law 8.15 Commission may result in a requirement that a servitude shall be constituted by a deed only if the deed is recorded (or registered as appropriate) in the title of both the dominant and servient tenement.[66] Until such reforms are enacted servitudes may be created in a variety of deeds including dispositions, deeds of declaration of conditions,[67] and separate bonds of servitude which are all valid so long as they comply with any of the following:

(a) The deed may form part of the title of the burdened land. This is known as express reservation as the servitude is usually reserved when the burdened land is first split off from a larger estate. Usually the deed is a disposition which conveys the servient tenement under reservation from the land of a list of varied servitude rights such as access, the right to use drains and a septic tank, etc. Deeds of declaration of conditions are more usually employed when imposing a scheme of servitudes and real conditions to service a new development on a modern residential or commercial site.

---

66 Scot. Law Com., *Discussion Paper on Real Burdens supra.* It may be that this requirement will be relaxed in the case of pipeline servitudes because of the practical difficulties in compliance.
67 In terms of Conveyancing (Scotland) Act 1874, s.32, as amended by Land Registration (Scotland) Act 1979, s.17.

deed may form part of the title of the benefited land. This
~~usually~~ an express grant.

~~~the~~ deed may be unrecorded and does not require to be part of
~~the~~ recorded title deeds of any land. Such deeds are easy to
~~ov~~erlook and are not recommended for practice despite their
~~v~~alidity.

Implied Grant and Reservation

8.16   Sometimes the title deeds are silent about servitudes benefiting a
plot of ground. This can lead to problems where rights are needed
to make the site usable. For example, a plot of ground may be
landlocked to the extent that it is totally enclosed by land owned by
someone else. How can the owner obtain access to the landlocked
plot? The law may intervene to grant access rights and other
servitude rights to make the plot of ground usable by virtue of the
doctrines of implied grant and implied reservation.[68] Broadly
speaking, these legal doctrines are resorted to only when someone
has made a mistake in the conveyancing process[69] or where
considerable development potential of an otherwise landlocked plot
of land can be released by breaching a ransom strip.[70]

The doctrines of implied grant and reservation generally apply
where the following conditions are complied with:

(a)   Generally speaking the law is less inclined recognise to a
servitude claimed to be reserved by implication than one
granted by implication, as the former attempts to reserve
something out of the land conveyed away and this is regarded
as giving with one hand and taking with the other. Such a
reservation would constitute a derogation from the grant and
is disapproved.[71]

(b)   The servitude claimed must generally be positive.

(c)   The servitude must be reasonably necessary for the reasonable
enjoyment of the benefited tenement.

(d)   The dominant and servient tenements must have been owned
at the same time by the same party in the same capacity ("the
common author").

(e)   The servitude must generally have been foreshadowed prior to

---

68 *Ewart v. Cochrane* (1861) 23D. (H.L.) 3.
69 See, *e.g.*, *Moffat v. Milne*, 1993 G.W.D. 8–572.
70 *Inverness Seafield Development Co. Ltd v. Macintosh*, 1999 G.W.D. 31-1497;
Bowers v. Kennedy, 1st Div., 28 June 2000, unreported but briefly noted at 2000
GWD 24–911.
71 *Wheeldon v. Burrows* (1879) L.R. 12 Ch.D. 31.

the severance by some exercise of the activity which is now claimed to be justified in terms of the servitude claimed.

(f) The terms of the deed effecting the severance of the two tenements will require to be examined to ensure that it does not exclude the implication of the grant or reservation of the servitude claimed.

(g) The common author usually requires to have both title and capacity to create the servitude at the time of the implied grant or reservation.

Although servitudes constituted by this doctrine are frequently referred to as "servitudes of necessity" the doctrine may be distinguished from those created by necessity alone. There is considerable obscurity about the latter method of creation but in the rare cases where necessity alone generates a servitude it is possible that none of the conditions outlined above needs apply.[72] 8.17

Use for the Prescriptive Period

A positive servitude may be constituted without any deed if there has been continuous use openly, peaceably and without judicial interruption for a period of 20 years. The possession may or may not follow upon the granting of a deed.[73] The general view is that negative servitudes may not be constituted in this way.[74] A common example of creation of a positive servitude occurs in relation to access. A party who owns a neighbouring farm and walks across another party's field along a definite route for 20 years every morning may acquire a servitude of access over that other party's field. Such a servitude will not be noted in the title deeds of any property. Although the servitude will be an overriding interest it may not be noted in the Title Sheet of the servient tenement or form part of the description of property in the Title Sheet relative to the dominant tenement. This has the practical consequence that a purchaser should always go to see a property if he wants to find out many of the burdens affecting it. Unfortunately if the positive servitude in question is a right to an underground drain this may not be apparent even after a site visit. The fact that the drain is concealed underground does not mean that the possession fails the 8.18

[margin note: Also, 'as if of right'.]

---

72 *Bowers v. Kennedy*, 1st Div., June 28, 2000, unreported but briefly noted at 2000 G.W.D. 24–911. Cusine and Paisley, *Servitudes and Rights of Way*, paras 11.18–11.36.

73 Prescription and Limitation (Scotland) Act 1973, s.3.

74 Gordon, *Scottish Land Law* (2nd. Ed.), para. 24–42; Cusine and Paisley, *supra*, para. 10.02.

statutory requirement to be "open" in order to create the servitude.[75]

In relation to a servitude acquired by usage the measure of the right is the actual use during the 20 years[76] conform to the maxim *tantum praescriptum quantum possessum*. As a result if a party walks over his neighbour's land for 20 years he will acquire a pedestrian right of access – he will not acquire a servitude right of access for vehicles. Similarly if a drain is used only for the discharge of fluids for the prescriptive period the dominant proprietor has no right to discharge solids down the drain.[77]

The maxim *tantum praescriptum quantum possessum* does not mean that a servitude acquired by prescriptive possession may be used only for the purpose for which it was used at the date of acquisition. The servitude acquired by prescription may be used for any lawful purpose to which the dominant tenement may be put. As a result where a servitude has been created by prescriptive possession by agricultural vehicles leading to a market garden, it remains open to the owner of the market garden to develop his site for residential housing and he may use the servitude for that purpose provided the use does not increase the burden on the servient tenement.[78]

Creation by Statute

8.19   It is possible for a servitude to be created by statutory provision. Technically creation by registration in the Land Register[79] and creation by positive prescription[80] are both examples of this. Apart from these common instances the statutory creation of a servitude is rare but it is found in some statutes relative to public works such as railways and bridges. If a servitude is created by statute the Lands Tribunal has indicated that it may not exercise its jurisdiction to vary and discharge the right even though there is no specific exception to that effect in the relevant statute.[81] This comment

75 *Buchan v. Hunter*, Peterhead Sheriff Court, case ref: A250/90, Sheriff Keiran A. McLernan, date of judgment 12 February 1993 (unreported); Cusine and Paisley, *Servitudes and Rights of Way*, para. 10.16.
76 *Carstairs v. Spence*, 1924 S.C. 380.
77 *Kerr v. Brown*, 1939 S.C. 140.
78 *Carstairs v. Spence*, 1924 S.C. 380.
79 Para. 3.14.
80 Para. 3.13.
81 Conveyancing and Feudal Reform (Scotland) Act 1970, P I and Sched.1; *MacDonald, Applicant*, 1973 S.L.T (Lands Tr.) 26; Gordon, *Scottish Land Law*, (2nd. ed.), para. 25–06; Cusine and Paisley, *supra*, paras 11.01, 12.76 and 15.11.

clearly does not relate to creation by prescriptive exercise and registration in the Land Register; otherwise the vast majority of servitudes would be incapable of variation and discharge.

Acquiescence

A servitude may be constituted by acquiescence where the 8.20 dominant proprietor has openly carried out works at some cost to himself with the knowledge of the servient proprietor who has not objected. An example may be where the dominant proprietor has built a house on a field and has taken access over a lane (which he has specially made up at his cost) for some time both during the construction phase and thereafter. The failure of the servient proprietor to object may lead to the creation of a servitude by acquiescence. The doctrine is resorted to where none of the other grounds for creation of a servitude may apply. It is a doctrine of last resort. Having said that there are a number of cases in which it has been successfully pled.[82]

Clarity and Precision of Words

To create a servitude in a deed it is important to use words which 8.21 are clear and precise. A number of rules in this regard may be identified:

(a) Just like real burdens, no special technical words are required to create a servitude but it has to be clearly shown that the right is intended to affect the property and the successive owners of the property and not just the original grantee. It is obviously easier to come to the conclusion that a right is a servitude if the deed expressly states that the obligation concerned is a "servitude" and uses that very word. If that word is not used and the creation of a servitude is not otherwise excluded the courts will look at the nature of the right for guidance. If the right created in the deed purports to permit activity which falls within the activities recognised in the general law as servitudes then the right in the deed will be treated as a servitude. So if a deed grants a right to drive a car across a road but does not use the word "servitude" it is likely

---

82 Cusine and Paisley, *Servitudes and Rights of Way*, paras 11.37–11.46; *George Jobson Forbes Fyfie v. J. Ross Morrison and Yvonne Morrison*, Arbroath Sheriff Court, Sheriff Principal R A Dunlop, Q.C. 30 May 2000, case ref: A155/98 (unreported). The author thanks Professor George Gretton for drawing his attention to this decision and to Sheriff K. Veal for producing a copy.

that the right is still a servitude because access is a recognised servitude. Conversely, if the deed requires the grantee to do something which is beyond the recognised servitudes (such as a right to play bagpipes on an adjacent field on Bannockburn day) this will not be regarded as a servitude.

(b)   Just like the law in relation to real burdens, there requires to be precision in the drafting employed because the words used will be strictly construed by the courts. The words are construed *contra proferentem* (against the interests of the party relying on them). There is, however, a slightly more lax approach with servitudes than real burdens because servitudes are rights which are generally recognised by the law. As a result some general phrases constituting servitudes may be upheld where they would fail if the right were a real burden.[83]

(c)   Not all aspects of the right require to be spelled out in the deed of constitution. For example, where a deed clearly creates a servitude of access there will be implied various ancillary rights necessary to keep the main right of passage in existence. These ancillary rights will include rights to repair and maintain the roadway over which the servitude is granted.[84] Similarly the right of access to carry out repairs to pipes will be implied in respect of servitudes of aqueduct.[85]

Exercise

8.22   Unless there is contrary provision in a deed, the exercise of every servitude is governed by three implied rules as follows:

(a)   The servitude can be used only for the dominant tenement.[86] In a deed of constitution this means the plot of land described in the deed as the dominant tenement. Where the servitude is created by prescription the extent of use is examined to determine the dominant tenement. If the dominant proprietor buys the field next door to the dominant tenement he cannot take access to the new field by the servitude of access which existed for the old and existing field. This is a problem in relation to what is known as "site assembly" where a developer is acquiring different plots of ground to build up a viable site

---

83   *McLean v. Marwhirn Developments Ltd*, 1976 S.L.T. (Notes) 47; *Axis West Developments Ltd v. Chartwell Land Investments Ltd*, 1999 S.L.T. 1416.
84   *Wimpey Homes Holdings Ltd v. Collins*, 1999 S.L.T. (Sh.Ct.) 16.
85   *Middleton v. Town of Old Aberdeen* (1765) 3 Brown's Supp 904.
86   *Irvine Knitters Ltd v. North Ayrshire Co-operative Society Ltd*, 1978 S.C. 109.

but the servitude of access benefits only one part of his intended site.

(b) The servitude must be exercised *civiliter* which means that it must be exercised only in such manner as is least burdensome to the servient tenement consonant always with a full exercise of the servitude. This rule means different things in different contexts. If a property owner acquires a servitude through a road running through an established residential area for the purpose of taking access to his house he will not be able to abuse this right by driving a muddy tractor along the road and causing damage to the tarmac on the road. By contrast if the lane over which access is taken is a farm lane the driving of a tractor would be perfectly acceptable even if some mud were left on the road unless this were excessive amounts.

(c) The servitude must be exercised in such manner as will not increase the burden on the servient tenement beyond that which was originally anticipated. If a property owner grants a servitude to a neighbouring proprietor to allow him to take access to a new cottage he is building, the neighbour could not demolish the cottage and, instead, mine the minerals under the site and cart the material in large lorries along the lane. If, however, the servitude was originally granted for the purposes of taking access to an existing quarry it would not be an increase in the burden to take access by means of quarry trucks.[87]

One theory categorises these three rules as legally implied servitude conditions enforceable by the servient proprietor against the dominant proprietor.[88] They apply to all servitudes in the absence of contrary statement. Whilst their application may be modified to some extent by the terms of a deed, it seems that they may not be excluded altogether.

Conventional Servitude Conditions

Where a servitude is created by a deed (whether by grant or reservation) then it is important to read the deed. The reason is that the terms of the deed will govern the extent of the right. This may be illustrated by reference to a servitude of access. The deed may place

8.23

---

87 *Lovie v. Kirkmyres Sand & Gravel Ltd*, 9 January, 9 and 24 October and 5 November 1991, Peterhead Sheriff Court, case ref. A572/90 (unreported).
88 Cusine and Paisley, *Servitudes and Rights of Way*, Chaps 13 and 14.

a number of conventional servitude conditions on the access right as follows:

(a)   The right may be limited to vehicular access by trucks and lorries of a maximum width and axle weight. This is particularly useful where there are culverts under the road which would otherwise be crushed. The servient proprietor may reserve the right to insert a height barrier to prevent access over the road by caravans.

(b)   The traffic may have a maximum speed limit placed on it and there may be a single direction traffic system where appropriate.

(c)   The purpose of the access may be limited to facilitating the carrying out of a particular business on the dominant tenement such as agriculture or horticulture. Alternatively, the servitude may expressly permit the road to be used for whatever purpose the holder of the servitude wishes including all future development of the dominant tenement. If a servitude is expressly limited to one purpose it cannot be used for anything else.[89] If the deed of servitude grants a general right of access without specifying any purpose for which it may be used it is now accepted that the access right may be used for any lawful purpose for which the dominant tenement may be put.[90]

(d)   The owner of the servient tenement may reserve the right to install traffic-calming measures such as speed humps or signs and traffic lights.

(e)   The owner of the servient tenement may reserve the right to re-route the servitude if he wishes to develop his land at a future date. Such a clause should include provisions for notice and a specification of the standard of the new road.

(f)   The owner of the servient tenement may reserve the right to install pipes and wires underneath the road to service development on adjacent sites.

(g)   The owner of the servient tenement may reserve the right to terminate the servitude if the holder of the servitude does not comply with the conditions of grant. This is very like an irritancy clause but is not controlled by statutory provisions.[91] Alternatively he may wish to reserve the right to suspend exercise of the servitude during periods of non-compliance with servitude conditions by the dominant proprietor.

---

89   *Cronin v. Sutherland* (1899) 2F. 217.
90   *Alvis v. Harrison*, 1991 S.L.T. 64 HL.
91   For irritancy clauses in leases see paras 7.41–7.43.

Enforcement and Remedies

As a real right a servitude may be enforced against any party 8.24 infringing it although it is most common for the right to be enforced against the servient proprietor. The remedies available to a party wishing to enforce a servitude include a personal action against the party infringing the right for interdict or damages. Similar remedies are available to the servient proprietor who may enforce his real right of property against any person exceeding the extent of the servitude. The remedies available to a proprietor are examined in greater detail in Chapter 4. A person wishing to enforce a servitude must have (a) a title to enforce and (b) an interest to enforce. In this regard the law is similar to the law relating to real burdens.[92] Only the dominant proprietor (and not those holding subordinate real rights such as a tenant of the dominant proprietor) has a title to enforce a servitude. As regards sufficient interest to enforce the interest must be praedial (*utilitas*) and not merely personal. It is generally accepted that a close location of the dominant and servient tenements (*vicinitas*) is a major factor in demonstrating praedial interest to enforce on the part of the proprietor of the dominant tenement. The carrying out of a business on the dominant tenement may qualify as a sufficient praedial interest[93] although it should be remembered that the servitude is created in favour of the land used for the business and not in favour of the business alone.

Extinction

Servitudes may be extinguished by various means. The most 8.25 commonly encountered of these include:

(a) Express or implied discharge. Express discharge by formal deed granted by the dominant proprietor is preferable. The discharge should be recorded in the titles of both tenements and this is likely to become a requirement in terms of statutory reform of the law of title conditions.[94]

(b) Abandonment. This may occur where non-use is accompanied by some additional factor indicating that the servitude right has been given up. An example in relation to a servitude right of way might be the erection of a stone wall across the route without objection for a period of time.[95] This may result in

---

92 Chap. 9.
93 Cusine and Paisley, *Servitudes and Rights of Way*, paras 2.51 and 12.163.
94 Scot. Law Com., *Discussion Paper on Real Burdens* (No. 106, Oct. 1998).
95 *Hogg v. Campbell*, Lord Clyde, 2 April 1993, 1993 G.W.D. 27–1712.

extinction of the servitude short of the 20-year period of negative prescription.

(c) Destruction of either tenement.[96] A servitude of access to a particular dominant tenement will not be extinguished by the demolition of a particular building thereon unless the grant confirms that the right existed only for that building.[97] Nevertheless, if the area of ground is destroyed by falling into the sea the servitude will be extinguished. Less dramatic events may constitute destruction in respect of other servitudes. A servitude of peat cutting may be extinguished when the peat bank is worked out.

(d) *Confusio.* Where the dominant and servient tenements come into the ownership of one party the servitude may not be enforced. Where the ownership of the tenements is again split the issue of revival of the servitude arises. The law on this matter is unclear[98] and may be clarified in future statutory reform in relation to real burdens.[99] Until such reform is enacted it is prudent to reconstitute servitudes upon the splitting of the tenements.

(e) Negative prescription. A servitude will be extinguished by non-use for the prescriptive period of 20 years.[1]

(f) Discharge by reference to the Lands Tribunal. As a land obligation a servitude may be discharged by reference to the Lands Tribunal.[2] This will be addressed more fully in Chapter Nine.

(g) Acquisition of the servient tenement by means of compulsory purchase powers. In certain cases these expressly provide for the extinction of servitudes and in other cases the extinction is implied because the exercise of the servitude might frustrate the statutory purpose of the acquisitions.[3]

---

96 Cusine and Paisley, *supra*, para. 17.21.
97 *Irvine Knitters Ltd v. North Ayrshire Co-operative Society Ltd*, 1978 S.C. 109.
98 See, e.g., Erskine, *Inst*, II,ix,37; Bell, *Prin.*, s.997; *Preston's Trs v. Preston* (1866) 16 Sc. Jur. 433; *Union Bank of Scotland Ltd v. The Daily Record (Glasgow) Ltd* (1902) 11 S.L.T. 71; Cusine and Paisley, *Servitudes and Rights of Way*, paras 17.22–17.31.
99 Scot. law Com., *Discussion Paper on Real Burdens* (No. 106, Oct. 1998), paras 5.53–5.59.
1 Prescription and Limitation (Scotland) Act 1973, s.8.
2 Conveyancing and Feudal Reform (Scotland) Act 1970, P I.
3 See the similar position in relation to real burdens noted in para. 9.26.

CHAPTER 9

REAL BURDENS AND CONDITIONS, AND COMMON INTEREST

Introduction

Any analysis of the law relative to real burdens and conditions is 9.1 hampered by semantics and so it is best to start with a few definitions. Real burdens form a class of obligations and rights otherwise known as "real conditions" (in the narrow sense of that term) and as "obligations which run with the lands". This terminology indicates that the obligations continue to bind the burdened land even though it changes hands and the owner and his successors in title are bound. They also benefit the original owner of the benefited tenement and his successors in title. The rights form part of the wider family group of "real conditions" (in the wider sense of that term) to which rights of common interest, servitudes (and perhaps real conditions in leases, proper liferents and conditions in standard securities) also belong. The Scottish Law Commission has invited views on the term "real burden" and its suitability but, despite its old fashioned nature, it is difficult to see how renaming the device, by itself, will greatly improve Scots law except for presentation to non-lawyers.[1]

Reform

The law relative to real conditions is soon to be the subject of a 9.2 root and branch reform following upon years of work of the Scottish Law Commission. Not only is there to be provision for the abolition of the type of real conditions enforceable by feudal superiors (known as "feudal real conditions"),[2] but also the law

---

1 Scot. Law Com., *Discussion Paper on Real Burdens* (No. 168, Oct. 1998), para. 9.16.
2 Abolition of Feudal Tenure etc. (Scotland) Act 2000, Pt 4.

relative to real conditions enforceable by neighbouring proprietors is to be restated and brought up to date.[3] In addition to this, the role of common interest in the context of the law of the tenement will be recast considerably.[4] Much of what is stated in this chapter will require to be re-examined when the relevant legislation is enacted. It would be true to say that there are few areas of land law in relation to which more systematic reform is expected in the next 10 years.

Types of Real Conditions

9.3   Two types of real conditions burdening property rights are recognised at common law in the modern era of Scots law. These are:

(a)   Feudal real conditions usually enforceable by a feudal superior against the vassal and, rarely, by a vassal against a superior. The dominant and servient tenements are the *dominium utile* and the *dominium directum*, interests in the same thing, a single piece of land. These feudal real conditions are to be abolished as part of the abolition of the feudal system of landholding although in some cases the obligations may be preserved in a different form.[5] The obligation on a feudal vassal to pay to his superior a monetary return known as "feu duty" is not a feudal land obligation but, instead, is part of the *reddendo* (the feudal return) originally inherent in feudal tenure. It too will be abolished in terms of feudal reform with some limited provision for compensation available to superiors and the distinction with feudal land obligations will become of historic significance only.[6] It shall not be considered further in this book.

(b)   Real conditions enforceable by the proprietor of one plot of land in respect of another plot of land. There is no generally used generic name for these burdens but for ease of analysis they can be sub-classified into two types.[7] First, a class of rights may be termed "neighbour burdens" where they benefit one plot of land and burden a neighbouring plot of land. For example, the owner of a plot of land may be restricted from

---

3   Scot. Law Com., *Discussion Paper on Real Burdens, supra*; Scot. Law Com., *Thirty Fourth Annual Report 1998–1999* (No. 179), paras 2.50–2.62.
4   Scot. Law Com., *Report on the Law of the Tenement* (No. 162, 1998).
5   Paras 9.7–9.8.
6   See Abolition of Feudal Tenure etc. (Scotland) Act 2000, Pt 3.
7   Gretton and Reid, *Conveyancing* (2nd ed.), para. 13.03.

building a factory and the restriction is enforceable by the neighbour. Secondly, another class may be known as "community burdens" where the burden is reciprocal. For example, the titles to all the units within a particular industrial estate may restrict use to light industrial use and this restriction may be declared to be enforceable by proprietors of all the units *inter se*. It is possible to some extent to regard common interest as a real condition arising by implication of law which falls into this latter category. There are, however, specialities relating to rights of common interest which do not arise in relation to real conditions and this book shall treat them as a separate type of real condition.

Other obligations which, at least on one view, may more broadly be regarded as real conditions, such as obligations in assignations of leases,[8] in proper liferents[8a] and standard conditions in standard securities,[9] are dealt with elsewhere. This chapter will limit its attention to real conditions burdening property rights and benefitting other property rights.

Differences to Other Real Conditions

With the exception of servitudes, which are enforceable *in rem*, the vast majority of real conditions are enforceable only *in personam*—whilst they are enforceable against the servient proprietor and his successors in title they are not generally enforceable directly against those holding subsidiary real rights in the servient tenement. The consequences of this distinction have already been noted in Chapter 2.[10] The reader should note, however, that the dividing line between servitudes and real conditions and the enforceability of real conditions is likely to be altered in terms of the legislation to reform real conditions.[11]   9.4

Statutory Agreements and Obligations

Scots common law does not generally recognise real conditions as being enforceable by a person or a legal entity who does not own a separate tenement. This is summed up in the maxim *praedium non*   9.5

---

8   Para. 7.19.
8a See para. 6.7.
9   Chap. 11.
10 Para. 2.18.
11 Scot. Law Com., *Discussion Paper on Real Burdens* (No. 168, Oct. 1998).

servit personam.[12] Various statutes have conferred on certain parties the power to create a type of real condition which burdens the owner of a servient tenement and his successors in title and which are enforceable not by the successive owners of a dominant tenement but by a particular benefited person or juristic body and, possibly also, by a limited class of assignees permitted under the relevant statute.[13] Typically, these obligations are created by agreement between the entitled body and the owner of the servient tenement which binds the owner when entered into and his successors in title when recorded in the General Register of Sasines (or registered in the Land Register of Scotland as appropriate). In some cases there is a statutory restatement of the "offside goals" rule[14] (albeit in a negative way) to the effect that such an agreement is not enforceable against a party who in good faith and for value has acquired an interest in the land prior to the agreement being recorded or registered.[15]

The more commonly encountered of these agreements include:

(a) agreements with planning authorities[16];
(b) access agreements with Scottish Natural Heritage and planning authorities[17],
(c) management agreements with Scottish Natural Heritage and planning authorities[18];
(d) forestry dedication agreements[19];
(e) agreements with the roads authority restricting the use of land near a road[20];

---

12 See the opinion of Lord Meadowbank in the *Burntisland* case quoted in *Home v Young or Gray* (1846) 9D. 286 per Lord Cunninghame at 294.

13 *Cf.* agreements with the sewerage authority in terms of Sewerage (Scotland) Act 1968, s.8(1), which are enforceable against the authority by the owner or occupier of the premises for the time being; 25 *Stair Memorial Encyclopaedia* para. 438.

14 Para. 3.30.

15 Countryside (Scotland) Act 1967, s.16(5), proviso, and s.49A(9), as amended by Natural Heritage (Scotland) Act 1991, Sched. 3, para. 6 and Sched. 10, para 4(3); Town and Country Planning (Scotland) Act 1997, s.75(4); Forestry Act 1967, s.5(3), proviso; Roads (Scotland) Act 1984, s.53(4).

16 Town and Country Planning (Scotland) Act 1997, s.75; Gordon, *Scottish Land Law* (2nd ed.), paras 21–25 and 28–39; McDonald, *Conveyancing Manual* (6th ed.), para. 19.34. See generally Rowan-Robinson and Young, *Planning by Agreement in Scotland* (1989).

17 Countryside (Scotland) Act 1967, ss 13 and 16 as amended.

18 Countryside (Scotland) Act 1967, s.49A.

19 Forestry Act 1967, s.5; Gordon, *Scottish Land Law* (2nd ed.), para. 27–23.

20 Roads (Scotland) Act 1984, s.53; 20 *Stair Memorial Encyclopaedia*, para. 674.

f) agreements relative to ancient monuments[21];
g) conservation burdens[22]; and
h) maritime burdens.[23]

The nature of many of these obligations is not clearly expressed in the relevant statutes but, subject to exceptional provision in the statute, they generally appear to be real obligations enforceable *in personam* only against the proprietor and those deriving right therefrom[24] and not *in rem* against the rest of the world at large.[25] Apart from these statutory exceptions Scots law does not readily permit parties to agree to create restrictions on land which perpetually bind the proprietor and his successors in land and which benefit a party not having ownership of a plot of land. Because there is no dominant tenement such obligations cannot be varied or discharged by the Lands Tribunal in terms of the Conveyancing and Feudal Reform (Scotland) Act 1970, Pt I,[26] unless there is an express statutory exception. Conservation and maritime burdens created in terms of feudal reform will be capable of variation and discharge by the Lands Tribunal[27] and it is likely that the proposed legislation relative to title conditions reform will continue the provision for conservation and maritime burdens created in subsequent years.

---

1 Ancient Monuments and Archaeological Areas Act 1979, s.17.
2 Abolition of Feudal Tenure etc. (Scotland) Act 2000, ss 26–32. There are likely to be further provisions in the legislation relative to reform of the law concerning title conditions following upon Scot. Law Com., *Discussion Paper on Real Burdens* (No. 168, Oct. 1998). These will probably supersede the agreements in favour of the National Trust which are competent under private legislation relative to that body.
3 Abolition of Feudal Tenure etc. (Scotland) Act 2000, s.60. There are likely to be further provisions in the legislation relative to reform of the law concerning title conditions following upon Scot. Law Com., *Discussion Paper on Real Burdens, supra.*
4 See, *e.g.*, Countryside (Scotland) Act 1967, ss13(7) and 16(5) as amended by Natural Heritage (Scotland) Act 1991, Sched. 3, para. 6; Ancient Monuments and Archaeological Areas Act 1979, s.17(5) and (6).
5 There appears to be no express requirement that conservation or maritime burdens preserved after feudal reform should be enforceable only *in personam* (2000 Act, ss 27(2) and 60(1)) but the matter may be altered in terms of the legislation relative to title conditions.
6 There is express confirmation of non-waivability in some statutes: see, *e.g.*, Ancient Monuments and Archaeological Areas Act 1979, s.17(7)(b).
7 Conveyancing and Feudal Reform (Scotland) Act 1970, s.1(2), as amended by 2000 Act, Sched. 12, para. 30(2)(a)(iv).

Statutory Orders and Obligations

9.6   In some cases restrictions on land may be created in a statutor
order made by the entitled body. The more commonly encountere
orders include:

(a)   confirmed tree preservation orders made by planning autho
rities or the Scottish Ministers[28];
(b)   access orders.[29]

Provided the relevant statute is sufficiently worded these order
appear capable to create rights enforceable *in rem* and not just *i.
personam*. Thus it is an offence for "any person" to breach th
provisions of a tree preservation order.[30] Most of the conditions i
these orders impose negative restraints but it seems theoreticall
possible that they might impose positive obligations. Although i
some cases these orders may be recorded in the Sasine Register o
Land Register, the effect of recording is not necessarily the same a
regards the agreements noted in the preceding paragraph. Fo
example in relation to tree preservation orders the obligations ar
enforceable when the order is made or confirmed as the case ma
be. Although there is an obligation on the authority to record th
order as soon as possible after the making of the order, there is n
stated sanction for failure to so record.[31] In short, the recording i
intended to augment the notice already given to the public in term
of statutory or regulatory requirements but is not a prerequisite fo
validity and enforceability. In other cases such as access order
recording appears to be a prerequisite for enforcement agains
parties other than the signatories.[32] The law is simply consisten
and each statute must be examined individually.

Feudal Reform

9.7   Subject to four exceptions noted below,[33] all feudal rea
conditions are to be abolished on the "appointed day"[34]—a da

---

28   Town and Country Planning (Scotland) Act 1997, ss 160, 161, 164, 167, 168 an
171; Gordon, *Scottish Land Law* (2nd ed.), paras 21–25, 27–39 and 28–2
McDonald, *Conveyancing Manual* (6th ed.), para. 19.38.
29   Countryside (Scotland) Act 1967, s.14.
30   Town and Country Planning (Scotland) Act 1997, s.171.
31   Town and Country Planning (Scotland) Act 1997, s.161(1) and (2).
32   Countryside (Scotland) Act 1967, s.16(5), as amended by Natural Herita
(Scotland) Act 1991, Sched. 3, para. 6.
33   Para. 9.8.
34   Abolition of Feudal Tenure etc. (Scotland) Act 2000, s.17.

to be appointed by the Scottish Ministers.[35] The reforms outlined below are yet to come into force either on the "appointed day" or another day to be appointed by order of the Scottish Ministers.[36] Where at present a feudal restriction is enforceable by a superior and, in addition, by co-vassals or any-one else to whom a right of enforcement has been given, the right of the superior to enforce will cease but the separate right of the others to enforce will continue.[37] Fortunately, where a real burden has been created in a feudal deed there is no implication that any land owned by a superior in the vicinity is a dominant tenement.[38] Even where a feudal real burden cannot be perpetuated in a non-feudal form in terms of one of the exceptional cases there is limited provision for a superior to register a notice to reserve the right to claim compensation where that feudal burden reserves any development value of the land. These are termed "development value burdens".[39] If the superior does not record the notice then he has no reserved right to compensation. If the superior does record a notice reserving his right to claim compensation then the compensation will be payable only if during a period of 20 years occurring after the appointed day an act takes place which would have been in breach of the real burden if it had not been extinguished.[40]

Four Exceptional Cases

The four exceptional cases where feudal restrictions may be   9.8 perpetuated in another form are as follows:

(a) Maritime burdens. These are feudal real burdens affecting the seabed or foreshore and enforceable by the Crown as superior. After the appointed day they will continue to be enforceable by the Crown without reference to any interest in land.[41] The right to enforce is not subsequently assignable.

(b) Conservation burdens. These are feudal real conditions which are enforceable by a "conservation body" and the purpose of this is to preserve or protect, for the public benefit, the architectural, historical or other special interest of the servient

---

35 Abolition of Feudal Tenure etc. (Scotland) Act 2000, s.71.
36 2000 Act, s.77.
37 2000 Act, s.17(1)(b).
38 2000 Act, s.48.
39 2000 Act, ss 33–40.
40 2000 Act, s.35(2)(c)(ii).
41 2000 Act, s.60.

tenement or any buildings thereon.[42] Most feudal restrictions
which require alteration to buildings to be carried out only
with the superior's consent will be incapable of transformation
into conservation burdens as they are clearly imposed for the
private benefit of the superior and not principally for the
benefit of the public. Where a burden qualifies as a
conservation burden the conservation body is entitled before
the "appointed day" to record a special notice in the Register
of Sasines or the Land Register of Scotland which converts the
feudal real condition into a conservation burden.[43] "Conservation body" means a body which is nominated as such by
the Secretary of State (the Scottish Ministers) by regulation.
The power is limited in its application in that only juristic
bodies such as limited companies, trusts, local authorities or
other corporations can be conservation bodies. Natural
persons are excluded. Not all juristic bodies can be conservation bodies but, instead, only those bodies which include
among their objects the preservation or protection, for the
benefit of the public, of the architectural, historical or other
special interest of land or other buildings. Conservation
burdens cannot be assigned to any body which is not a
conservation body[44] and will be extinguished if the body ceases
to be a conservation body.[45]

(c)   Common facility burdens.[46] A "common facility burden" is
defined as a feudal real burden regulating the maintenance,
management, reinstatement or use of property which constitutes (and is intended to constitute) a facility for other
property. Examples are feudal real conditions which regulate
the maintenance of a common part of a tenement, a common
area for recreation, a private road, private sewerage and a
boundary wall.[47] After the appointed day this real burden will
continue to be enforceable by (a) the owner or owners of that
facility and (b) the owner or owners of any other property
benefited by that facility.[48] This is one of the rare cases where
the number of parties entitled to enforce a real condition will
increase because of feudal reform. In the example of the

---

42   2000 Act, s.26.
43   2000 Act, s.27.
44   2000 Act, s.29.
45   2000 Act, s.31.
46   2000 Act, s.23.
47   2000 Act, s.23(4).
48   2000 Act, s.23(1).

common access road, where there was only one superior who could enforce the real conditions, he will be replaced by a class of persons consisting of the owner of the servient tenement and, in addition, by the owners of all the dominant tenements, without any arbitrary limitation as to their number. Broadly speaking this may be regarded as a statutory form of common interest because it deals with feudal real burdens regulating the use or maintenance of common facilities.

(d)   Reallotted burdens.[49] There is a limited provision permitting feudal superiors to nominate a new dominant tenement for feudal burdens. This provision is designed to enable these real conditions to remain in force not as feudal burdens but as real conditions enforceable by a proprietor of a new plot of land. Prior to the "appointed day" the superior may execute and register in the General Register of Sasines or the Land Register a notice nominating the other land as the dominant tenement.[50] To avoid a mere transfer of all feudal burdens there are some limitations as to the type of burdens which can be transferred and the type of new dominant tenement. The superior can transfer the feudal burdens only to a tenement of which he is the sole proprietor. This excludes tenements owned by his friends, family members or, if the superior is a company, companies in the same group. It also excludes tenements in respect of which the superior is a co-proprietor, unless of course the superiority is co-owned by the same parties. One of three further conditions must be satisfied as follows:

(i)   the proposed dominant tenement has on it a permanent building which is in use wholly or mainly as a place of human habitation or resort, and that building is, at some point, within 100 metres (measuring along a horizontal plane) of the land which would be the servient tenement— thus a transfer to a grass verge or a minerals reservation is excluded;

(ii)   the real burden comprises a right to enter, or otherwise make use of, the servient tenement, or is a right of pre-emption or redemption[50a]; and

(iii)   the proposed dominant tenement comprises minerals or salmon fishings or other incorporeal property and it is

---

49   2000 Act, ss 18–22.
50   2000 Act, s.18.
50a   See para. 4.5.

apparent from the terms of the real burden that it was
created for the benefit of that tenement.

As an alternative to the unilateral reallottment of the feudal
burden by means of notice a superior may enter into a registered
agreement with the vassal to reallott the burden to benefit another
plot of ground.[51] This is simply a specialised form of deed of
declaration of conditions. Where a vassal declines to enter into such
an agreement the superior may apply to the Lands Tribunal to have
the burden reallocated to a new tenement.[52] Where a burden is
reallotted to a new tenement by agreement or by the Lands
Tribunal there is no maximum distance between the tenements
proscribed by statute but the common law principles requiring
interest would continue to impose limitations in this regard.[53]

Occurrence of Real Conditions

9.9   Where a proprietor conveys land he will often want to protect
various interests and a scheme of real conditions is a flexible device
to achieve this. They comprise three types of obligation as may be
illustrated by the following examples:

(a)   Where a property company has constructed a new tenement of
       flats and is selling off those flats to various owners, the
       company will wish to impose conditions concerning regular
       painting of each flat by the owner thereof and payment for
       mutual repairs in relation to common parts such as the roof
       etc. These are positive obligations imposed on the servient
       proprietor. In terms of the obligations the servient owner is
       required to do something. In this respect the content of real
       burdens and conditions differs from servitudes in that the
       obligation may be *in faciendo—i.e.* require the servient
       proprietor to do something.[54] As part of their reform of the
       law of real burdens the Scottish Law Commission is presently
       considering proposals which introduce a system of rudimen-
       tary management rules which would apply to a development
       unless contrary provision is made. These might empower the
       majority of the owners of the various units within a
       development (i) to carry out maintenance in accordance with

---

51 2000 Act, s.19. It is not immediately obvious why a vassal would volunteer to
    enter into such an agreement.
52 2000 Act, s.20.
53 Paras 9.15 and 9.16.
54 *Cf.* the position with servitudes noted at paras 8.4 and 8.8.

any maintenance burdens, (ii) to appoint a factor/manager; and (iii) to discharge any real burdens, whether for an individual unit or the whole community within the development.[55]

(b) Where a building firm sells houses in a new residential development, the firm usually wishes to impose conditions to preserve the amenity of the housing development. Commonly encountered examples are restrictions declaring that the houses cannot be used for industrial or business purposes and an obligation not to carry out any activity which might constitute a nuisance to neighbours. These are negative obligations and the servient owner is required to desist from some activity. Again a distinction with servitudes may be noted in that with negative servitudes the activity which is restricted is generally building works only.[56] With the reform of the law of real conditions it is likely that the type of negative obligation contained in the existing negative servitudes will be capable of creation only as a real condition.[57]

(c) Where a farmer wishes to sell off a part of his field and retain the development potential of his remaining ground he may reserve the right to construct a road and service media through the plot sold off.[58] This type of reservation permits the dominant proprietor to enter upon the servient tenement and do something on it, and the servient owner is bound to submit to it. This form of right is frequently coupled with a servitude permitting the dominant proprietor to use the road or the service media after they have been built. These rights bear a close resemblance to positive servitudes in that they probably also extend to permitting the dominant proprietor to carry out other activity within the servient tenement such as the laying of electricity cables and other service media and parking. At common law it may be the case that these rights are enforceable *in rem* and not simply *in personam* but there is a dearth of authority on the matter.[59] It is probable that the reform of the law of real conditions may reclassify these rights

---

55 Scot Law Com., *Thirty Fourth Annual Report 1998–1999*, No. 179), para. 2.57.
56 Para. 8.11.
57 Scot. Law Com., *Discussion Paper on Real Burdens* (No. 168, Oct. 1998), paras 2.49–2.50.
58 *B and C Group Management Ltd, Haren & Wood, Petrs.*, Dec. 4, 1992, Lord Cullen, O.H. (unreported).
59 Cusine and Paisley, *Servitudes and Rights of Way*, para. 1.06.

as servitudes with the result that they may be created only as such.[60] A minor overlap between servitudes and real conditions may remain where there is imposed on the servient proprietor a real condition requiring him to maintain a structure such as a fence and there is reserved to the dominant proprietor the remedy to enter property and carry out requisite works upon failure by the servient proprietor.

General Requirements as to Content

9.10   Proprietors are given a large measure of freedom as to the content of real conditions with the result that in recent years they have been used in a widespread manner. In contrast to the categories of servitudes recognised at common law there are no fixed types of obligation which can be created as a real burden or condition. That is not to say that there are no rules as to content of a real condition: not every obligation can be constituted as a real burden. What can be said, however, is that the rules of requisite content are much more flexible in relation to real conditions as compared to servitudes.

Two general rules as to content may be noted and it is likely that the proposed reform of the law relative to real conditions following upon the work of the Scottish Law Commission will not greatly vary these general requirements:

(a)   There must be a praedial burden. The obligation sought to be imposed must relate to land or the buildings and other fixtures thereon or the use of land or buildings and fixtures.[61] For example, a real burden may require the owner of a plot of land to maintain a lawn in front of his house, trim the hedges bounding his garden and to paint the front door of his house regularly. Such obligations relate to the use and appearance of land, fixtures and buildings. By contrast, a real burden may not oblige the proprietor of land to wash himself or herself, educate his or her children or comb their hair every day. Those obligations relate to the bodies of the owners and their family and not to the land which they occupy. There are, however, instances where the distinction between personal and praedial burdens is not so clearcut. It is probably impossible to impose an obligation by means of real condition that the owner of a

---

60   Scot. Law Com., *Discussion Paper on Real Burdens* (No. 168, Oct. 1998), para. 7.66.
61   *Earl of Zetland v. Hislop* (1882) 9R. (H.L.) 40; 18 *Stair Memorial Encyclopaedia*, para. 391.

plot of ground must eat only vegetarian food because this relates to his personal behaviour. Nevertheless, in some cases it may be possible to impose an obligation that the owner will not cook strong smelling curries or fried fish to such an extent that will annoy neighbours. This latter form of restriction may be appropriate in a tenement flat because in that context it protects the amenity of the neighbouring flats.

(b)   There must be a praedial benefit. This is known as *utilitas*. The burden must be for the utility of the dominant tenement and not the mere benefit of an individual. In most cases this will be a requirement which is easy to satisfy and only extreme cases will fail. The overloading of floors in a tenement flat can be prevented by real condition so a flat owner can be prevented from collecting tons of law reports in his flat to the extent that it risks a collapse of the floors into the flat below. By contrast, a landowner, having a liking for Scottish literature, cannot impose a real condition obliging his neighbour to recite Burns poetry in his garden every evening. However, in some cases the distinction between personal and praedial utility is difficult to make. Difficult cases have been linked to religious belief. It may be possible in some cases to protect a neighbourhood by imposing a real condition precluding certain activities on a Sunday.[62] Such restrictions are common in parts of former glebes sold off by churches particularly where the area sold off is located beside the church. Nevertheless the courts are not likely to regard respect for religious beliefs as an open door to religious bigotry. In one case a real burden the enforcement of a burden to exclude the erection of a Roman Catholic chapel was rejected as lacking praedial interest on the part of a neighbour who alleged potential damage to his business on the basis that if the chapel had not been built houses would have been erected and this would have increased the pool of his potential clients.[63] It is submitted that in some cases the prevention of buildings being used for religious purposes could be a legitimate praedial interest as the owner of the dominant tenement may wish to be free from the problems associated with the large numbers of persons they might attract. In this regard a religious building is no different from temples of pleasure such as dance halls and football stadia which might

---

62   *Cf. Marsden v. Craighelen Lawn Tennis and Squash Club*, 1999 G.W.D. 37–1820 (Sh Ct).
63   *Maguire v. Burges*, 1909 S.C. 1283. See 18 *Stair Memorial Encyclopaedia*, para. 407.

cause a similar amount of temporary congestion in the neighbourhood. At common law there is some uncertainty about benefit to commerce on the dominant tenement but the relevant cases appear to indicate that protection for a business on a dominant tenement is acceptable provided (a) the properties are sufficiently close to satisfy requirements of *vicinitas*[64] and (b) there is no attempt to create a commercial monopoly.[65] The common law is unsatisfactory and unresponsive to modern commercial needs and is likely to be reformed.[66]

Detailed Rules as to Content

9.11   In addition to the general limitations there are a number of more detailed restrictions on the permissible content of real conditions. These were identified by Lord Corehouse giving the opinion of the court in *Incorporation of Tailors of Aberdeen v. Coutts*[67] where it was confirmed that a real burden must comply with the following requirements:

(a)   It must not be contrary to law. For example, a real burden cannot require a proprietor to do something which is illegal. This has two meanings. First, certain statutory provisions declare certain requirements as null and void.[68] Secondly, a landowner cannot be required to carry out activities which would amount to a criminal offence. Statutory reform of the law of title conditions is not likely to alter this latter aspect of the requirement but its content will alter from time to time as the more general criminal law renders certain matters now legal to be illegal or declares certain activities which are presently illegal to be legal.

(b)   It must not be contrary to public policy. In this context, the common law has regarded certain restrictions which purport to

---

64   This means that the properties must not be so far apart that the dominant tenement cannot benefit from the compliance with the real burden. See *Aberdeen Varieties Ltd v. James F. Donald (Aberdeen Cinemas) Ltd*, 1940 S.C. (H.L.) 52.
65   *Co-operative Wholesale Society Ltd v. Ushers Brewery*, 1975 S.L.T. (Lands Tr.) 9. Cf. *Phillips v. Lavery*, 1962 S.L.T. (Sh.Ct.) 57. See para. 9.11.
66   Scot. Law Com., *Discussion Paper on Real Burdens* (No. 168, Oct. 1998), paras 7.58–7.63.
67   (1840) 1 Robin. 296.
68   See, *e.g.*, Conveyancing (Scotland) Act 1874, s.22 (superiors and law agents). Future restrictions may preclude the servient proprietor from being obliged to submit to activity by the dominant proprietor on the servient tenement unless a servitude is created.

create trade monopolies impeding the commerce of land as contrary to public policy.[69] It is difficult to say with certainty exactly what this means. The rule does not preclude simple restrictions which prevent the use of property for something like a public house[70] or industrial purposes[71] where such restrictions are imposed to protect the amenity of surrounding subjects. As has been noted above in relation to praedial benefit,[72] it may, however, render invalid a restriction against the use of a plot of ground for a public house where the purpose of the restriction is not to enhance amenity but merely to protect the trade of another public house next door.[73] This will probably not preclude the obligation frequently found in a deed of conditions in modern retail developments which seeks to ensure a mix of users by prohibiting more than one type of shop. Modern businessmen and investors require more certainty and do not take well to the use of the word "probably" in reports on title in respect of a matter which is essential to their new commercial venture. As noted above it is likely that reform will reflect commercial reality and permit restraints of trade to a greater extent.[74]

(c) It must not be "vexatious" or "useless". In one sense all restrictions on land are vexatious but this is not what this requirement means. Generally, an obligation which is imposed for no real benefit and is simply imposed to make life miserable for the owner will not be enforced. For example, an obligation which requires a proprietor to paint his house a different colour every day would fail by virtue of this rule. The anticipated statutory reform is not likely to alter this requirement and it can probably be regarded as an aspect of the requirement of praedial utility or *utilitas* in any event.

(d) A real burden must not be "inconsistent with the nature of the species of property".[74a] This phrase has two broad elements. First, it requires that a real burden must not purport to remove

---

69 *Aberdeen Varieties Ltd v. James F. Donald (Aberdeen Cinemas) Ltd*, 1940 S.C. (H.L.) 52; 1939 S.C. 788.

70 *Scot v. Cairns* (1830) 9S. 246.

71 *Finnie v. Andrew Usher & Co.* (1891) 29 S.L.R. 273.

72 Para. 9.10.

73 *Aberdeen Varieties Ltd v. James F. Donald (Aberdeen Cinemas) Ltd Co-operative Wholesale Society Ltd v. Ushers Brewery*, 1975 S.L.T. (Lands Tr.) 9. *Cf. Phillips v. Lavery*, 1962 S.L.T. (Sh.Ct.) 57. See para. 9.10.

74 Para. 9.10.

74a After feudal reform there will be only one species of property—ownership. Abolition of Feudal Tenure, etc. (Scotland) Act 2000, s.2(1).

from the servient proprietor the right to use and possess his property to an undue extent. Secondly, a real burden must not preclude the exercise of juristic acts. The extent of the first of these elements is rather vague because all real conditions do deprive the servient proprietor of his rights freely to use his property to some extent. Extensive restrictions are sometimes acceptable. For example, an obligation not to use the property except for an ice rink has been regarded as valid.[75] Nevertheless it is more likely that a real burden will be inconsistent with property where it allows the dominant proprietor to carry out activity within the servient tenement. Where real conditions purport to arrogate to the dominant proprietor the exclusive right to use the servient tenement for shooting[76] or social occasions[77] they have been regarded as invalid. The dividing line between what is acceptable and what is too invasive is not easy to draw. The impact of this restriction on the content of real conditions is likely to be reduced considerably if the right to carry out activity on the servient tenement is reclassified as a servitude in terms of statutory reform.[78] The focus of attention in this regard will then shift to servitudes and the case law relative to real conditions will continue to be relevant in any assessment of whether a new servitude permitting activity on the servient tenement is inconsistent with the right of property. As regards the second element concerning juristic acts, it has been noted already that a real condition cannot absolutely remove the right of a proprietor to dispone land, lease it or grant securities over it.[79] Nevertheless, it is possible to limit (rather than remove totally) the exercise of these rights by means of real condition. Thus rights known as rights of pre-emption are competent[80] (subject to statutory limitations which may be augmented in the course of expected statutory reform) as they are rights not to have the servient tenement divided in certain circumstances.[81]

---

75 *Cumbernauld Development Corporation v. County Properties and Developments Ltd*, 1996 S.L.T. 1106.
76 *Beckett v. Bissett*, 1921 2 S.L.T. 33. *Cf. Harper v. Flaws*, 1940 S.L.T. 150. See discussion in Scot. Law Comm. *Report on the Abolition of the Feudal System* (No. 169, Feb. 1999), paras 6.30–6.35.
77 *Kirkintilloch Kirk Session v. Kirkintilloch School Board*, 1911 S.C. 1127; *Scott v. Howard* (1881) 8R. (H.L.) 59.
78 Para. 2.23.
79 Paras 4.4–4.6.
80 See, *e.g.*, *Mathieson v. Tinney*, 1989 S.L.T. 535. See para. 4.5.
81 Para. 4.6.

Document of Constitution

Real burdens may be distinguished from servitudes in the manner 9.12
of their creation. Real burdens cannot arise by use alone even if that
use continues for the prescriptive period of 20 years, nor can they
arise by virtue of grant or reservation implied from the
circumstances surrounding a conveyance. At common law all real
burdens require to be created in a conveyance of the servient
tenement but this has been expanded by statute to include a deed of
declaration of conditions[82] which forms part of the title of the
burdened land. Deeds of declaration of conditions (generally
known as "deeds of conditions") are commonly, if not invariably,
found in modern developments. There is no statutory form of a
deed of conditions—nor does a deed require to state *in gremio* that
it is a deed of conditions[83]—but recognised styles have evolved in
practice and these usually contain a narrative explaining the
purpose of the deed and confirming that it is a deed of conditions in
terms of the appropriate statutory provision. At common law it is
clear that writing is required to constitute a real condition and the
deed must affect the title of the servient tenement by being recorded
in the General Register of Sasines or registered in the Land Register
of Scotland. In terms of reforms presently being considered by the
Scottish Law Commission it will probably be necessary to record
(or register as appropriate) the deed of constitution in the titles of
both the dominant and servient tenements.[84]

Clarity and Precision of Words Used

The general position may be briefly stated. To create a real 9.13
burden it is essential to use words which are clear, unambiguous
and precise. A number of subsidiary rules in this regard may be
identified:

(a) No special technical words (*voces signatae*) are required to
    create a real burden but it has to be clearly shown that the
    obligation is intended to affect the property and the successive
    owners of the property and not just the original grantee. It is
    more likely that the parties to a deed intended that the
    obligation imposed should be a real burden if the deed

---

82 Conveyancing (Scotland) Act 1874, s.32, as amended by Land Registration
   (Scotland) Act 1979, s.17.
83 *Cf.* the special requirements in Abolition of Feudal Tenure etc. (Scotland) Act
   2000, s.19(3)(a).
84 Scot. Law Com., *Discussion Paper on Real Burdens* (No. 106, Oct. 1998).

expressly states that the obligation concerned is a "real burden" or a "real condition" and uses those exact words. A declaration that the obligation is to be repeated in future transmissions of the servient tenement will also assist in reaching the conclusion that the obligation is intended to be a real burden.[85] If those words are not used or if such a declaration is not inserted in the deed the courts will look at the nature of the obligation for guidance. If the obligation is capable of performance by a single act (such as an obligation to erect a fence or a house) there is a presumption—but only a presumption—that it is not a real burden but simply a contractual obligation affecting the original grantee.[86] Conversely, obligations to maintain a fence or to keep in good repair the walls of a house are obligations which require repeated acts or a series of acts over a period time and these are likely to be regarded as real burdens. The Scottish Law Commission have suggested that a condition should not be effective as a real burden unless the words "real burden", "community burden" or "neighbour burden" are used in the constitutive deed.[86a]

(b)   At present the full text of the real burden must be included in the deed which is registered or recorded. Extrinsic evidence is not generally admissible and it is not competent to refer to an unrecorded deed for greater detail. If the full text of the restriction is not set out in the recorded or registered deed the purported real condition will be invalid as such but may survive as a contract between the original parties. Thus an obligation to comply with a statute or Act of Parliament cannot be created a real burden if all the draftsman does is to refer to the statute.[87] Should the draftsman wish to incorporate the provisions of the statute into the restrictions he wishes to impose, the full text of the statutory provision must be repeated at length in the deed. Similarly, it is not competent to refer to an unrecorded list of estate conditions which can be examined at the office of the estate factor. These conditions should be added as a schedule to the deed. This requirement may, of course, be relaxed by statute. There is one commonly

---

85 *Nicholson v. Glasgow Asylum for the Blind* 1911 S.C. 391.

86 *Edinburgh Mags v. Begg* (1883) 11R. 352.

86a Scot. Law Comm., *Discussion Paper on Real Burdens* (No. 106, Oct. 1998), para. 7.18.

87 *Aberdeen Varieties Ltd v. James F. Donald (Aberdeen Cinemas) Ltd*, 1940 S.C. (H.L.) 52; 1939 S.C. 788.

encountered example of such a relaxation in existing legislation and two more in proposed or anticipated legislation. First, where a tenement is registered in the Land Register for Scotland the Keeper may enter therein a real right pertaining to the interest or subsisting real burden or condition affecting the interest or a summary thereof and where a summary only is entered it shall be presumed to be a correct statement of the terms of the right burden or condition.[88] In practice this appears to be used only in relation to burdens or conditions affecting the servient tenement and, in the writer's experience, summaries of the right to enforce burdens affecting other tenements are not frequently encountered.[89] Secondly, in terms of the proposed reform of the law of the tenement it will be competent in a deed of conditions to refer to and incorporate (subject to variations if appropriate) a management scheme set out in a Schedule to the relevant statute.[90] In terms of reforms presently being considered by the Scottish Law Commission in respect of the law of real conditions it is proposed that a real burden should not be unenforceable only because it incorporates information which is contained in an Act of Parliament or statutory instrument, public register, public records or other document in Scotland which is available to the general public.[91] This is intended to render enforceable maintenance obligations which refer to matters such as valuation rolls to allocate fractions of liability.

Presumption in Favour of Freedom

The Scottish Law Commission has proposed that provisions imposing real burdens should be interpreted in the same manner as other provisions in deeds relating to land and intended for registration.[92] Until such reform is enacted the common law will apply. At common law any words used in the clause imposing a real burden will be strictly construed by the courts. They are also to be construed *contra proferentem*. In other words, they are construed

9.14

---

88 Land Registration (Scotland) Act 1979, s.6(2).
89 To be real in any event these burdens would require to be registered in the title of the servient tenement anyway.
90 Scot. Law Com., *Report on the Law of the Tenement* (No. 162, Mar. 1998), Pts 5 and 6, Draft Bill, ss 5 and 6 and Scheds 1 and 2. See also Scot. Law Com., *Discussion Paper on Real Burdens* (No. 106, Oct. 1998), paras 7.85–7.88 ("Model Management Scheme").
91 Scot. Law Com., *Discussion Paper on Real Burdens, supra*, para. 7.70.
92 Scot. Law Com., *Discussion Paper on Real Burdens, supra*, para. 4.37.

against the interests of the party wishing to rely on them. This results from a presumption in Scots law that land should be free from restrictions. If there is an ambiguity it is resolved always in favour of freedom. This a multi-faceted presumption with various aspects as follows:

(a) The servient tenement must be exactly defined.[93] This is not to say that a particular description or a bounding description of the servient tenement is required.

(b) The clause must impose an obligation and not merely express a wish.[94]

(c) Where the burden relates to the paying of a sum of money it must be a definite amount and it must be payable to an identified creditor. This rule has led to some debate. It is common in tenemental situations to find provisions burdening each flat with a share of the costs of repairs of the common parts such as the roof. For example, if there are six flats in a tenement it is common for each share to be a one-sixth share. It is generally accepted that such a precise division is enforceable. By contrast, an obligation which states that each flat owner will be liable for "an equitable share" or "a fair share" or some other share calculated by other equally vague phraseology is generally regarded as too vague for enforcement. As noted above in terms of reforms presently being considered by the Scottish Law Commission it will become competent to refer to the valuation roll to allocate fractions of liability.[95]

(d) Words will be given their normal meaning and not an over-extended or benevolent meaning. For example, an obligation to build a house or a building will not be construed as an obligation to maintain the house in all time coming.[96] Unfortunately the word "maintain" itself has several meanings ranging from (a) retain in a single location to (b) keep in a state of repair. To avoid unenforceability it is best to specify which is intended.[97]

(e) Real conditions are usually intended to be perpetual and endure for so long as the property right endures. The parties, may, however, by express clause restrict the endurance of a real

---

93 *Anderson v. Dickie*, 1915 S.C. (H.L.) 74.
94 *Kemp v. Largs Mags*, 1939 S.C. (H.L.) 6.
95 Scot. Law Com., *Discussion Paper on Real Burdens* (No. 106, Oct. 1998), para. 7.70.
96 *Kemp v. Largs Mags, supra Peter Walker and Son (Edinburgh) v. Church of Scotland General Trs*, 1967 S.L.T. 297.
97 See, *e.g.*, *Heritage Fisheries Ltd v. Duke of Roxburghe*, 1999 G.W.D. 24–1161.

condition to a limited period of time terminating either upon the happening of an event which must happen[98] or which may happen. If, however, there is no express time limitation and no inference to that effect which readily arises from the deed the presumption for freedom may not be used to terminate the real condition ahead of perpetuity. This results in many titles being burdened by real conditions which are manifestly out of date. At present the solution to the problem is to seek variation and discharge by application to the Lands Tribunal.[99] The problem of obsolete real conditions has been considered by the Scottish Law Commission and future legislation is likely to provide for mechanisms which terminate the endurance of real conditions after a set period of time with limited provisions for extension.[1] This will probably involve a "sunset" rule whereby a burdened proprietor may trigger the application of rules to terminate the burden by service of notice on the dominant proprietor.[2]

Enforcement of Real Conditions

A person wishing to enforce a real burden must have (a) a title to 9.15 enforce and (b) an interest to enforce.

(a) Title to enforce.

The proprietor for the time being of the dominant tenement (the benefited property) has a title to enforce a real burden. This means that the original creator of the burden and his successors in title as owner of the dominant tenement have a title to enforce the burden. An exceptional case at common law sometimes permits neighbouring proprietors to enforce a title restriction in a deed to which they were not a party. This is known in Scotland as the rule of *ius quaesitum tertio*—the rule of third party rights. This is examined below.[3]

(b) Interest to enforce.

A party wishing to enforce a real burden must show that he has an interest to enforce it at the time he wishes to enforce. Such interest is

---

98 *E.g.* the time limitation seen in the deed examined in *Palmer's Trs v. Brown*, 1989 S.L.T. 129. See further Cusine and Paisley, *Servitudes and Rights of Way*, paras 2.91–2.93.
99 Paras 9.31–9.38.
1   Scot. Law Com., *Discussion Paper on Real Burdens* (No. 106, Oct. 1998), pt 7.
2   Scot. Law Com., *Thirty Fourth Annual Report 1998–1999* (No. 179), para. 2.62.
3   Para. 9.17.

also needed at the time of creation for the burden to be validly created. This interest (otherwise known as "*utilitas*") must relate to the land and not merely to the personal circumstances of the owner for the time being. The general rule is preserved in terms of feudal reform legislation[4] and there is no presumption of interest on the part of a dominant proprietor where the real burden has been created in a disposition or deed of conditions but, as an exception to the general rule, that legislation provides that the Crown's interest to enforce a maritime burden[5] and a conservation body's interest to enforce a conservation burden[6] are presumed. The proposed legislation relative to the reform of real burdens is likely to contain similar provisions for subsequently created conservation and maritime burdens.

9.16   In the determination of whether a sufficient interest exists a major factor will be the distance between the dominant and servient tenement. There is no fixed rule as to a maximum distance beyond which no interest will be deemed to exist[7] and the distance will certainly vary according to the nature of the particular obligation, its purpose and the nature of the dominant and servient tenements. If a particular obligation is intended to preserve visual aspect then it may be the case that there will be sufficient praedial interest from any point within the dominant tenement from which there is a clear view of the servient tenement, and where the obligation relates to the avoidance of a nuisance such as a smell there may be sufficient praedial interest at a point where the smell materially affects the enjoyment of the dominant tenement.[8] In rural areas a much wider area may be regarded as falling within the interested area whereas a smaller area in a city may qualify.[9] It is difficult to see how the *vicinitas* requirement can apply in relation to rights of pre-emption.

Ius Quaesitum Tertio

9.17   At common law neighbouring proprietors are sometimes

---

4   2000 Act, s.24.
5   2000 Act, s.60(1)(b).
6   2000 Act, s.28(2).
7   *Cf.* the new rules relative to reallocated burdens in feudal reform noted in para. 9.8 and the proposed limitation on *ius quaesitum tertio* noted in para. 9.18.
8   *Mannofield Residents Property Co. Ltd v. Roy Thomson*, case ref. A980/81, June 1982, Sheriff Douglas Risk. Earlier proceedings are reported at 1983 S.L.T. (Sh.Ct.) 71.
9   *Aberdeen Varieties Ltd v. James F. Donald (Aberdeen Cinemas) Ltd*, 1940 S.C. (H.L.) 52. See also the notion of "neighbourhood" in terms of Conveyancing and Feudal Reform (Scotland) Act 1970, s.1(3)(a). See para. 9.36.

permitted to enforce a title restriction created in a deed to which they were not parties. This is known in Scotland as the rule of *ius quaesitum tertio*.[10] The right of the third party may be granted expressly and this is common in modern deeds of conditions.[11] If there is no express grant of the right to third parties it may in some cases be granted by implication. Although the classification of the first of these cases outlined below as *ius quaesitum tertio* is not entirely free from controversy,[12] it is generally accepted that such an implication arises in two distinct types of cases. Prior to abolition of the feudal system these two cases can also arise in relation to conveyances in feudal form[13]—and such neighbourhood rights created thereby may survive feudal reform although the right of the superior to enforce will be extinguished[14]—but for simplicity's sake this paragraph will concentrate on non-feudal deeds. The implied right of enforcement may be expressly excluded or excluded by inference as would be the case where the disponer reserves the right to deal with his remaining estates and to waive existing burdens on such terms as he sees fit.[15]

The two cases for creation of third party rights by implication are set out below but it should be remembered that the cases may overlap where one plot of ground which is part of a series of plots subject to similar burdens is subsequently subdivided. Contrary to some earlier judicial indications the area concerned in each case does not require to be large. In each case the burdens in each title do not require to be absolutely identical but must be substantially identical or equivalent.[16] It is an unanswered question whether all or most of the burdens in each title must pass this test or whether it is sufficient for the actual burdens sought to be enforced. The two cases are as follows:

(a) First, "single disposition followed by subdivision"—where there is a single disposition of an area of ground which is later subdivided. This creates a body of co-disponees receiving title from a common author. The burdens in the original single

---

10 A.J. McDonald, *"Enforcement of Title Conditions"*, in D.J. Cusine (ed.), *Scots Conveyancing Miscellany: Essays in Honour of Professor J.M. Halliday.*

11 18 *Stair Memorial Encyclopaedia*, para. 405.

12 18 *Stair Memorial Encyclopaedia*, paras 402 and 404.

13 18 *Stair Memorial Encyclopaedia*, paras 399–402.

14 Subject to the exceptions noted at para. 9.8.

15 *Thomson v. Alley and Maclellan* (1883) 10R. 433.

16 *Botanic Gardens Picture House Ltd v. Adamson* 1924 S.C. 549 per L.P. Clyde at 563.

disposition are enforceable by the co-disponees *inter se*.[17] The burdens remain dormant and unenforceable until the tenement is divided. The *ius quaesitium tertio* may be extinguished or varied in the deed by which the tenement is divided.

(b) Secondly, "successive grants"—where a proprietor dispones off a series of plots of ground in similar terms in one neighbourhood. If the terms of the series of dispositions are sufficiently similar and sufficient notice is given to the co-disponees of the intent to create a common scheme of conditions, this is regarded as sufficient to give rise to an implication that the neighbours can enforce the relevant obligation amongst themselves for the benefit of the neighbourhood.[18] Sufficient notice of intention to create a common scheme of real conditions may be given to each disponee by two means. First, each disposition may contain an obligation on the disponer to impose similar or equivalent conditions in subsequent grants.[19] This is rarely found with the use of modern deeds of conditions but the deed of conditions will itself satisfy the second requirement now to be noted. Secondly, there is clear evidence of a common plan for the development. This does not mean the attaching of a plan or map to each deed; rather it implies an indication from the disponer that each plot is part of a greater area to be disponed off with uniformity in the burdens affecting each plot. The matter is complex but, unfortunately, the whole picture is confused further by the application of the rule that land reserved to a disponer may form an implied dominant tenement for any real burdens created in a disposition.[20] The interaction of the rules may lead to an incomprehensible overlay of rights of enforcement.

9.18 The implied enforcement rights which arise from the existence of third party rights may cause considerable conveyancing problems if strict attention were paid to them in practice. At worst it could be argued that a purchaser seeking a waiver of an obligation to maintain a town house in a situation such as the Edinburgh old town should be obliged to approach an uncertain class of persons which may comprise dozens of dominant proprietors. It seems to be the case that many of such rights have been overlooked. The law

---

17 *Lees v. North East Fife Dist. C.* 1987 S.L.T. 769.
18 *Hislop v. MacRitchie's Trs* (1881) 8R. (H.L.) 95.
19 *McGibbon v. Rankin* (1871) 9M. 423.
20 *J. A. MacTaggart & Co. v. Harrower* (1906) 8F. 1101.

may now be reformed to bring it more into line with practice or, at least, to make it more manageable and comprehensible. The Scottish Law Commission may take the view that implied rights should be abolished subject to a number of limited exceptions. They are considering whether, where a number of properties are subject to identical or equivalent burdens, *i.e.* "a common scheme", the general rule should be that such burdens should be enforceable against immediate neighbours who are within a four-metre radius. This would be restricted to cases where the burdens are currently enforceable by those neighbours. The Scottish Law Commission are likely to recommend a saving for burdens which regulate the maintenance and use of common facilities and services. The burdens would be enforceable by all those who take benefit from them whether or not they already hold implied rights. In addition, The Scottish Law Commission are likely to recommend the creation of a mechanism to extinguish neighbour burdens involving the registration of a statutory notice.[21]

Remedies for breach of Real Conditions

The remedies available to a party wishing to enforce a real 9.19 burden or condition include a personal action for specific implement, interdict or damages. A clause providing for liquidate damages is competent but is likely to be difficult to frame because of the ravages of inflation and the changes in ownership of the dominant tenement.[22] Damages of £100 for not building a house may have been adequate compensation in respect of a high amenity square in Aberdeen in 1840 but would be a trifle now.[23] Where buildings are in the course of erection in contravention of a real condition the dominant proprietor may also seek demolition of the buildings. The courts, however, have a discretion to refuse this remedy where any benefit would far exceed the hardship to the servient proprietor[24] or where the dominant proprietor has personally barred himself by allowing the buildings to be constructed. There is some doubt as to whether a remedy of irritancy is competent in a disposition but in any event it is likely that the Scottish Law Commission will recommend the abolition of

---

21 Scot. Law Com., *Thirty Fourth Annual Report 1998–1999* (No. 179), paras 2.59–2.61.
22 *Dalrymple v. Herdman* (1878) 5R. 847.
23 *Tailors of Aberdeen v. Coutts* (1840) 1 Robin. 296 at 315 per Lord Corehouse.
24 *Alexander v. Stobo* (1871) 9M. 599; Paisley, *Development Sites, Interdicts and the Risks of Adverse Title Conditions*, 1997 S.L.P.Q. 249–273.

all existing rights of irritancy in favour of disponers and a prohibition on their future creation.[25]

Extinction

9.20   Real burdens may be extinguished in various ways which include the following:

(a)   express discharge by the servient proprietor;
(b)   implied discharge;
(c)   loss of interest to enforce;
(d)   negative prescription;
(e)   *confusio*;
(f)   compulsory purchase;
(g)   failure to appear in the Land Register; and
(h)   variation and discharge by the Lands Tribunal.[26]

Express Discharge

9.21   The dominant proprietor has the right to grant a discharge of a real condition. Legislation may extend this right to a heritable creditor in possession of the dominant tenement.[27] The deed effecting the discharge is generally known as a minute of waiver. Discharges of real conditions are frequently sought upon a sale of the servient tenement when the purchaser wishes to develop the site. He will not wish to be obliged to pay for the site until he can be certain that he may use it for the desired purpose. The legal device used to reconcile the interests of the parties to the sale is a suitably drafted suspensive condition in the contract of purchase. A waiver or discharge should be executed in the same manner as a deed of conditions.[28] Usually a sum of money is expected in exchange for an express discharge although the introduction of the Lands Tribunal jurisdiction (introduced in 1970) has tended to keep the amount within reasonable bounds[29] especially as the Tribunal may award expenses against a dominant proprietor who has acted particularly unreasonably.[30] Once the deed of discharge is granted it should be registered in the General Register of Sasines or the Land

---

25   Scot. Law Com., *Discussion Paper on Real Burdens* (No. 106, Oct. 1998), para. 4.41.
26   See paras 9.31–9.38.
27   Scot. Law Com., *Discussion Paper on Real Burdens* (No. 106, Oct. 1998), para. 5.32.
28   Requirements of Writing (Scotland) Act 1995, s.1(2)(b) and 1(7).
29   Paras 9.31–9.38.
30   *Harris v. Dunglass*, 1993 S.L.T. (Lands Tr.) 56.

Register of Scotland and it then becomes binding upon the granter of the discharge and his successors in title in the dominant tenement.[31] In terms of reforms presently being considered by the Scottish Law Commission it is likely that legislation will require that to be effective against singular successors a discharge will require to be recorded in the Sasine Register (or registered in the Land Register of Scotland) in respect of both the dominant and servient tenements.[32]

Implied Discharge

In some situations a dominant proprietor will be deemed to have 9.22 granted a discharge not by granting a deed but by his actions or inaction.[33] To establish implied discharge it must be shown, first, that the dominant proprietor or his agent knew of the breach of the real condition and did nothing and, secondly, that the servient proprietor has relied on this inaction and it would cause him considerable prejudice if the obligation were now to be enforced. The most obvious case is where a house has been built in contravention of a real condition without protest.

Loss of Interest to Enforce

Loss of interest to enforce a real condition may occur where such 9.23 a change of circumstances has occurred that there is no point in enforcing the burden. Loss of interest may occur without any act on the part of the dominant proprietor—he may simply be outflanked by events. It would seem, however, there is no single reported case in which the principle has been applied to extinguish a burden. The high standard of the law was exemplified in *Howard de Walden Estates Ltd v. Bowmaker Ltd*[34] in which interest to enforce a restriction requiring a property to be used only as a dwellinghouse would be lost only if the whole residential character of the neighbourhood had disappeared. It was not sufficient for there to be changes in a considerable number of the plots in the area. As a result this doctrine is not of much use to a servient proprietor seeking freedom from a burden and it has largely been superseded by the operation of the powers of the Lands Tribunal.[35]

---

31 Land Registration (Scotland) Act 1979, s.18.
32 Scot. Law Com., *Discussion Paper on Real Burdens, supra*, para. 5.32.
33 18 *Stair Memorial Encyclopaedia*, paras 427–429. See also Halliday, "Acquiescence and the Baby Linnet", 1977 J.R. 89.
34 1965 S.C. 163.
35 Paras 9.31–9.38.

Prescription

9.24   A failure to enforce a real condition in the face of a contravention for a period of 20 years will render the land obligation unenforceable. This gives rise to practical problems of proof. The result is that the law of prescription is rarely resorted to in practice. The Scottish Law Commission may recommend that the period of prescription is to be reduced to five years.[36]

Consolidation

9.25   A real condition will be extinguished if the dominant and servient tenements come into single ownership. There is some doubt as to whether the real condition is re-established when the ownership of the two plots is split at a later date. The safest course is to re-impose the real condition. The Scottish Law Commission has suggested that a real burden should not be extinguished only because the dominant and servient tenements are owned by the same person in the same capacity.[37]

Compulsory Purchase

9.26   Real conditions may be extinguished when the plot of ground which they affect is compulsorily purchased but there has always been doubt as to whether the extinction was limited to those real conditions which were inconsistent with the purposes for which the compulsory purchase was made. The Scottish Law Commission has suggested that the doubt be removed and real burdens should be extinguished in all time coming on the acquisition of land following upon a confirmed compulsory purchase order.[38]

Failure to Appear in the Land Register

9.27   The mere fact that a real burden appears in the Land Register is not a guarantee of its enforceability. By contrast, where a real burden fails to be entered or summarised on the Title Sheet of a registered interest in land it will be extinguished.[39] In some cases the Keeper may be willing to take a view with little prompting that a burden is no longer subsisting and he will delete it. In other cases he

---

36 Scot. Law Com., *Discussion Paper on Real Burdens* (No. 106, Oct. 1998), para. 5.47.
37 Scottish Law Commission, *Discussion Paper on Real Burdens, supra*, para. 5.59.
38 Scot. Law Com., *Discussion Paper on Real Burdens* (No. 106, Oct. 1998), para. 5.62.
39 Land Registration (Scotland) Act 1979, s.3(1)(a).

may require the party seeking deletion to obtain declarator that the burden is unenforceable whereupon he will remove the burden as part of the process of rectification.[40]

Common Interest

Common interest is a form of right (with a correlative obligation) 9.28 which arises by implication of law. Although there is some debate as to whether it is competent to create the right by provision in a deed[41] it is likely that this will be clarified in statutory reform. With a view to ensuring that rights of common interest are not used to avoid the new restrictions on the creation of real conditions it is likely that the express creation of rights of common interest will be rendered incompetent in future legislation. Common interest may be discharged by express or implied provision in a deed and arises only in a "default" situation, that is, where there is no alternative provision in the form of real conditions and servitudes. In respect of tenement buildings the Scottish Law Commission has recommended the introduction of a statutory framework of rights and obligations which would apply in the absence of alternative express provision.[42] If such a recommendation is enacted it will constrain the application of common interest in that context. This is not intended to affect common interest in other contexts. Common interest may be regarded as a form of legally implied real condition which is enforceable *in personam* against the proprietor of the burdened tenement by the benefited proprietor. In general, no liability falls on tenants in the burdened tenement nor can the obligation be enforced by tenants in the benefited tenement. It has been held, however, that the right may be enforced by a proper liferenter in the dominant tenement, a decision which is justifiable on the basis that such a party is an interim *dominus*.[43] As we shall see, the content of common interest is very flexible and depending on the geographical context may impose restrictions on the servient proprietor, require him to carry out some act or permit the dominant proprietor to use the servient tenement. This resembled the tripartite distinction which can be made in respect of real

---

40 *Brookfield Developments Ltd v. Keeper of the Registers of Scotland*, 1989 S.C.L.R. 435.
41 *Cf. Fearnan Partnership v. Grindlay*, 1992 S.L.T. 460 per Lord Jauncey at 463. See para. 5.3.
42 Scot. Law Com., *Report on the Law of the Tenement* (No. 162, Mar. 1998).
43 *Cyril Newton v. Agnes Godfrey*, June 19, 2000, Stranraer Sheriff Court, Sheriff J.R. Smith, case ref. A118/98 (unreported). See para. 6.2.

conditions at common law.[44] Whilst there is little authority on, or analysis of, the subject it would seem that there is a possibility that rights of common interest falling into the third of these categories may be enforceable *in rem* like a servitude. Common interest may be expressly discharged and will fall into abeyance upon a material alteration in the geographical or topographical make-up of a site which originally generated the right.

Tenement Situations

9.29   In the context of tenement buildings the mix of rights created by rights of property and rights of common interest is known as "the law of the tenement". The titles of each tenement are unique and must be examined for their terms. In many cases the flat owners have rights of common property in the common access and a number of express servitude rights relative to service media. In addition, each proprietor of the various flats usually has a right of common interest in those parts of the building which he does not own. In this context common interest includes the following rights:

(a)   The right to support. The lower flats must bear the weight of the upper flats.[45] A lower flat owner may be restrained by interdict from carrying out building operations which would prejudice the support of the upper flats.[46] There is a corresponding obligation on the upper flats not materially to increase the weight on the lower flats.

(b)   The right to shelter. The owner of the roof must maintain it in a wind and water tight condition and not allow water ingress.[47] As this places a considerable burden on upper flat proprietors and renders them unattractive to some purchasers the obligation is commonly varied in deeds of conditions. Where a client wishes to purchase an upper flat and the obligation is unchanged it is important to ascertain that the roof is in good condition—a surveyor should be specifically instructed to check this—and that insurance cover for defects is available on reasonable terms. Where the whole tenement is destroyed this obligation of shelter is extinguished but may be recreated upon reconstruction.[48]

(c)   The right to light. This exists in respect of any garden ground

---

44 Para. 2.23.
45 Stair, *Institutions*, II,vii,6.
46 *Fergusson v. Marjoribanks*, 12 Nov. 1816 F.C.
47 *Luke v. Dundass* (1695) 4 Brown's Supp. 258.
48 *Thomson v. St Cuthbert's Co-operative Society Ltd*, 1958 S.C. 380.

attached to the tenement.[49] The right is not sufficiently extensive to protect a view or general amenity.

Other Contexts

Common interest may also exist in other contexts of which the following are the most commonly encountered: 9.30

(a) Where boundary walls or mutual gables are owned by neighbours up to the mid-line each has a common interest in the other half of the wall entitling them to support by the other half of the wall.[50] Not only may the servient proprietor be restrained from any actions which might prejudice the stability of the wall[51] but he may be required to carry out repairs to preserve its stability failing which the dominant proprietor may enter the servient subjects and carry out such repairs and thereafter recover the costs from the servient proprietor.[52] It would not be wise to do this without judicial sanction as the servient proprietor may resist.

(b) Where private gardens serving two or more properties are in common ownership (such as an ornamental square surrounded by houses) there is a view that each of the co-proprietors has a right of common interest in the garden.[53] The ambit of the right in such cases is slightly obscure but a right of common interest may in such cases permit the storing of necessary items such as mowers, garden tools and grass cuttings.

(c) In respect of non-tidal lochs each proprietor of a part of the loch has a right to use all of the loch for boating, sailing and fishing.[54]

(d) A proprietor of land naturally located above other land has a right to the natural drainage of water from his land and the inferior proprietor has an obligation to receive that water.[55]

Land Obligations

The term "land obligation" is not used in Scottish common law but was borrowed from English law and was originally first used in   9.31

---

49   *Heron v. Gray* (1880) 8R. 155.
50   *Crisp v. McCutcheon*, 1963 S.L.T. (Sh.Ct.) 4.
51   *Thom v. Hetherington*, 1988 S.L.T. 724.
52   *Cyril Newton v. Agnes Godfrey*, June 19, 2000, Stranraer Sheriff Court, Sheriff J.R. Smith, case ref. A118/98 (unreported).
53   *Grant v. Heriot's Trust* (1906) 8F. 647.
54   *Montgomery v. Watson* (1861) 23D. 635.
55   Erskine, *Inst.*, II,ix,ii.

Scotland as part of the Conveyancing and Feudal Reform (Scotland) Act 1970.[56] In a manner similar to the wide meaning of "real conditions"[57] the expression describes a family or group of various rights affecting land.

The term "land obligation" is defined in the 1970 Act[58] as an obligation which:

(a) relates to land—the term "land" includes buildings on land;
(b) is enforceable by a proprietor of an "interest in land" (another defined term) by virtue of his being such a proprietor and his successors in title; and
(c) is binding upon a proprietor of another interest in that land or of an interest in another land by virtue of being such proprietor and his successors in title.

The term "interest in land" means any estate or interest in land which is capable of being owned or held as a separate interest and to which a title may be recorded in the Register of Sasines or Land Register of Scotland.[59] The land burdened by the land obligation is known as the "burdened land" or "burdened tenement" or "servient tenement". The land benefited by the obligation is known as the "benefited land" or "benefited tenement" or "dominant tenement".

9.32   Obligations included in the definition of "land obligation" are as follows:

(a) Restrictions in "long leases" (which endure for 20 years or more) enforceable by the landlord against the tenant—this does not include restrictions in short leases (endurance of under 20 years) as these leases cannot be recorded in the General Register of Sasines or registered in the Land Register of Scotland. These are dealt with in the context of leases which are examined in Chapter 7.[60]
(b) Restrictions in a feudal grant enforceable by a superior against the vassal ("feudal real burdens").[61]
(c) Servitudes. These are dealt with in Chapter 8.

---

56 Conveyancing and Feudal Reform (Scotland) Act 1970.
57 Para. 9.1.
58 Conveyancing and Feudal Reform (Scotland) Act 1970, ss 1 and 2.
59 This will be amended in terms of Abolition of Feudal Tenure etc. (Scotland) Act 2000, s.76(1) and Sched. 12, para. 30(2)–(3).
60 Para. 7.20.
61 Abolition of Feudal Tenure etc. (Scotland) Act 2000 following upon Scot. Law Com., *Report on Abolition of the Feudal System* (No. 168, Feb. 1999).

(d) Real burdens and conditions enforceable by one neighbour against another.[62]
(e) Rights of common interest.[63]
(f) It probably also includes obligations in proper liferents enforceable by the fiar against the liferenter and vice versa.[63a]

The term "land obligation" does not include public rights of way or other public rights as these benefit not a piece of land but the general public.[64]

Variation and Discharge by Lands Tribunal

The Lands Tribunal for Scotland has power on application by 9.33 the servient proprietor to grant an order varying or discharging a land obligation.[65] The terms "discharge" and "variation" are not defined but the former is taken to mean that the obligation is removed in full whilst the latter "variation" means that only part of the obligation is removed or that the obligation is altered in some way with a view to its relaxation and not its extension. The order of the Tribunal is binding on all parties having interest when an extract thereof is registered in the General Register of Sasines (or the Land Register of Scotland as the case may be).[66]

The jurisdiction and powers of the Lands Tribunal in relation to the discharge and variation of land obligations may be considerably expanded in terms of legislation to implement reforms presently being considered by the Scottish Law Commission.[67] At present the Lands Tribunal has no power to issue a declarator of enforceability of a real condition.

Excluded Land Obligations

The Lands Tribunal can vary or discharge most land obligations 9.34 but not all. These excluded land obligations include[68]:

(a) obligations relating to the right to work minerals;
(b) obligations imposed on behalf of the Crown to protect any royal park, garden or palace;

---

62 See para. 9.3.
63 See paras 9.28–9.30.
63a See para. 6.7.
64 See Chap. 10.
65 Conveyancing and Feudal Reform (Scotland) Act 1970 ("the 1970 Act").
66 1970 Act, s.2(4).
67 Scot. Law Com., *Discussion Paper on Real Burdens* (No. 106, Oct. 1998), Pt 6.
68 1970 Act, Sched. 1.

(c) obligations imposed for naval, military or air force purposes; and

(d) obligations imposed in any agricultural tenancy or croft.

Land obligations (whatever their purpose or content) cannot be varied within two years of their creation.[69] Some of the particular exceptions, particularly that of royal parks, seem to have little relevance to Scotland and the exceptional cases are likely to be amended in terms of the anticipated reform of the jurisdiction of the Lands Tribunal.

Grounds for Variation or Discharge

9.35   The Lands Tribunal may exercise its power to vary or discharge only where it is satisfied in all the circumstances that one or more of three grounds for waiver set out in the Conveyancing and Feudal Reform (Scotland) Act 1970 has been established. The establishing of any one of the grounds is sufficient to permit the Tribunal to exercise its discretion but it still retains this discretion even if all or any one of the grounds is established. It is likely that the anticipated reform of the jurisdiction of the Lands Tribunal will consolidate the three grounds into a single ground permitting variation and discharge where this is considered by the Tribunal to be reasonable and allowing the Tribunal to take different factors into consideration in reaching its view.[69a] In the meantime the three separate grounds continue to exist and many applicants making an application simply refer to all three. The three statutory grounds for variation and discharge are as follows[70]:

(a) that by reason of changes in the character of the servient tenement or the neighbourhood thereof or other circumstances which the Tribunal may deem material, the obligation is or has become unreasonable or inappropriate;

(b) that the obligation is unduly burdensome compared to any benefit resulting or which would result from its performance;

(c) that the existence of the obligation impedes some reasonable use of the servient tenement.

---

69 1970 Act, s.2(5). This period may be extended in proposed reforms.
69a Scot. Law Comm., *Discussion Paper on Real Burdens* (No. 106, Oct. 1998), para. 6.41.
70 1970 Act, s.1(3).

Application of the Three Grounds

To a considerable extent each application will turn on its own 9.36
facts and circumstances and the results of a Lands Tribunal
application can be notoriously difficult to predict. Nevertheless
there are certain principles which can be extracted from the decided
cases to date. In general where the application is sought to ratify
work which has been carried out already the Tribunal has indicated
that it will not have its hand forced and will decide the issue as if the
work had not yet started.[71] As regards the separate grounds for
variation one may comment as follows:

(a) The obligation has become unreasonable or inappropriate in
the light of changes. There are two parts to this ground. First,
there may be changes in the servient land itself. This ground
has been interpreted as dealing with cases where the land has
become useless for the very purpose or purposes which the
obligation was designed to support. For example, if the land
obligation consisted of a real condition imposing an obligation
on the servient proprietor to build a retail complex or a factory
unit within a fixed period of time and the land has become
permanently flooded the obligation may be discharged.
Changes which have been brought about by the applicant
himself in breach of the condition which he seeks to have
varied are not to be considered.[72] Secondly there may be
changes in the neighbourhood. If there is an obligation to
maintain a house for residential purposes on the servient
ground and not build any commercial premises such as a
factory or office on that ground there may a justification for
variation if a large proportion of properties in the neighbourhood have already been converted into factories and other
commercial buildings. Small building alterations having no
effect on the character of the neighbourhood will be ignored.[73]
It may be a rather difficult issue to define exactly what
geographical area of ground is comprised within the "neighbourhood" as this will differ from place to place. In rural areas
the neighbourhood may comprise a whole village[74] but in a
larger town or city it may be limited to a housing estate or to
one single ornamental square.[75] The reference to "other

---

71 *Harris v. Douglas; Erskine v. Douglas*, 1993 S.L.T. (Lands Tr.) 56.
72 *North East Fife D. C. v. Lees*, 1989 S.L.T. (Lands Tr.) 30.
73 *Stoddart v. Glendinning*, 1993 S.L.T. (Lands Tr.) 12.
74 See, *e.g.*, *Main v. Doune* 1972 S.L.T. (Lands Tr.) 14.
75 *Manz v. Butter's Trs*, 1973 S.L.T. (Lands Tr.) 2.

circumstances" may be used to allow the Tribunal to refer to changes in the wider economy such as an alteration in levels of tourism[76] or a decline in domestic service.[77] A mere decline in the business success of the applicant will not suffice.

(b) Obligation unduly burdensome. The Tribunal is required to balance the interests of the burdened and benefited proprietors, particularly those affected by the performance of the obligation. The interests concerned, however, are not the personal circumstances of the parties but their interests in the maintenance or variation of the obligation as a permanent burden on the land. Consequently the prospect of the dominant proprietor charging a fee for the grant of a minute of waiver is ignored. Similarly the personal disability of the applicant is ignored.[78] This ground is frequently resorted to where the applicant wishes to change the existing use of all or part of the land burdened by the land obligation. An example frequently encountered is where a developer enters into missives to purchase a plot of ground with a view to building a housing development. The developer may conduct site investigations and find that this development plan is frustrated because one of the neighbouring proprietors has a servitude of drainage running through the site. The negotiations for a minute of waiver may be difficult unless the developer can show that the owner of the site could readily obtain a discharge by application to the Lands Tribunal. If the developer can show that he can provide suitable alternative drainage or that the drain is never really used and closing up the drain would not prejudice the neighbour, the Tribunal may exercise its discretion to discharge it on the basis that the existing obligation is unduly burdensome. It should be noted, however, that the developer will not become the burdened proprietor until he acquires the property right in the site. Missives should make provision for the seller to make the application to the Lands Tribunal subject, of course, to suitable indemnities as to costs.

(c) Obligation impeding reasonable use. This is the provision most commonly relied on in a developmental context where there are proposed changes. This ground for variation looks to the future and attempts to see what the proprietor of the servient

---

76 *Owen v. Mackenzie* 1974 S.L.T. (Lands Tr.) 11.
77 *Morris v. Feuars of Waverley Park*, 1973 S.L.T. (Lands Tr.) 6.
78 *Stoddart v. Glendinning*, 1993 S.L.T. (Lands Tr.) 12.

tenement wishes to do with the ground. It is clear that some proposed new use is required and that the applicant must not be wishing to use the application to achieve a completely different purpose.[79] If the new use is reasonable and it is impeded by the existing obligation then the ground is established. In assessing whether a proposed use is reasonable the fact that planning permission or another statutory licence such as under the Licensing (Scotland) Acts has been obtained will be a favourable factor. But the obtaining of such a licence or consent is not conclusive as the concerns of the planning authority and the relevant licensing body do not necessarily coincide with those of the Tribunal. Where, however, the land obligations are imposed and are enforceable by a local authority as a form of planning control, the fact that planning permission for a development has been obtained will be given considerable weight.[80]

Payment of Compensation

A dominant proprietor is not guaranteed a payment of compensation for the variation or discharge of a land obligation but the requirement to pay compensation is again a matter for the discretion of the Tribunal. In exchange for the Lands Tribunal granting a variation or discharge, the servient proprietor may be directed to pay to the dominant proprietor compensation. This compensation may be paid only under one of two heads of claim.[81] These are either: (a) a sum to compensate for any substantial loss or disadvantage resulting from the order. The loss or disadvantage must be substantial but there is no minimum sum for compensation. On more than one occasion no compensation whatsoever has been awarded. It is possible, however, that where there is a very substantial loss or disadvantage this might be a reason for refusing a variation or discharge. Or (b) a sum to make up for any substantial loss or disadvantage resulting from the order or a sum to make up for any effect which the land obligation produced, at the time when it was first imposed, in reducing the consideration paid for the servient tenement. A common situation is where land is sold off by a proprietor to a local authority on the basis that it will

9.37

79 *Spafford v. Bryden*, 1991 S.L.T. (Lands Tr.) 49.
80 *British Bakeries (Scotland) Ltd v. City of Edinburgh D. C.*, 1990 S.L.T. (Lands Tr.) 33 at 34 H-L.
81 1970 Act, s.1(4).

be permanently used for public purposes.[82] This obligation is inserted in the titles by means of a land obligation. The price for the land is substantially less than would have been obtained if the land were sold on the open market. Years later the public use ceases and the purchaser wishes to develop the land for a retail use such as a public house. The party entitled to enforce the land obligation is unwilling to discharge the land obligation without payment of a sum of money in exchange That party is entitled to receive some compensation given the original reduced consideration for the plot. There is no ground upon which the person entitled to enforce the land obligation is entitled to what is known as "a cut of the action"—a share of the development value of land. So if a party entitled to enforce a real condition wishes to grant a minute of waiver only in exchange for a share of the increased development value of the land his claim for compensation will be rejected by the Lands Tribunal.[83]

Substitute Provisions

9.38   The Lands Tribunal has a power to impose substitute land obligations as appear to the Lands Tribunal to be reasonable as a result of the variation or discharge of the original burden provided these are accepted by the servient proprietor.[84] As a result the servient proprietor may veto the use of this power but if he does so the variation or discharge for which he has applied may not be granted. This power has been used in a number of cases to allow variations which might otherwise not have been granted, for example, by permitting building subject to conditions such as the installation of sound insulation to prevent the drifting of music, the operation of fans to remove smells of food, or of the planting of screening by trees to protect privacy.[85] Whilst there is little authority on the matter it is submitted that the obligations which can be so imposed must comply with the rules of content relative to real conditions or servitudes as the case may be.

---

82 *Gorrie & Banks Ltd v. Musselburgh Town Council*, 1974 S.L.T. (Lands Tr.) 5.
83 *Robertson v. Church of Scotland General Trs*, 1976 S.L.T. (Lands Tr.) 11; *Keith v. Texaco Ltd*, 1977 S.L.T. (Lands Tr.) 16.
84 1970 Act, s.1(5).
85 See, *e.g.*, *Crombie v. George Heriot's Trust*, 1972 S.L.T. (Lands Tr.) 40.

Chapter 10

PUBLIC AND STATUTORY RIGHTS

Public Rights—Introduction

The most important of the public rights in Scotland are public 10.1
rights of way and public rights in the tidal rivers, lochs and
foreshore in respect of matters such as navigation and fishing.

Public Rights of Way

A public right of way entitles the public to a right of passage from 10.2
one public place to another over a defined route between those
public places. Public rights of way are encountered comparatively
rarely in conveyancing practice but this does not accurately
represent their importance to the public at large. For some they
represent touchstones of freedom. In a few cases their exercise may
be accompanied by scarcely concealed hostility on the part of the
landowner and unbridled enthusiasm on the part of the parties
exercising the right. It is an explosive mix which can lead to actual
battles on the ground. Fortunately the tradition of tolerated access
to public places in Scotland is long established and is generally
accepted as conducive to the common good. Most landowners and
members of the public in Scotland have an enlightened and
responsible attitude to public access (which may be favourably
contrasted with the situation in other jurisdictions) and the exercise
of most public rights of way in Scotland creates no difficulty at all.

Essentials of Public Rights of Way

A public right of way is one of the real rights recognised by the 10.3
law of Scotland but a landowner or any other party may not simply
take it upon themselves to declare that a public right of way exists
in any given circumstances that they think fit. Instead the law of
Scotland requires that certain essential pre-requisites exist before a
public right of way may exist. Most of the judicial statements of the
essentials of a public right of way appear to conflate two separate
issues: (i) the essentials of the right, and (ii) the requirements for

creation of a public right of way by prescriptive exercise.[1] Whilst this may be justified on the basis that very few public rights of way are created by any means other than exercise for the prescriptive period, the two issues are severable. In this book these two issues will be dealt with separately.

The essentials of a public right of way, however created, appear to be:

(a) A public place at either end—public *termini*.
(b) A defined line for the public passage across land between the public places.
(c) The activity conducted must be passage only.
(d) The right must be enforceable by the general public and, in theory also, by the Crown.
(e) Public rights of way must be created by human intervention.

These shall be examined in order in the immediately following paragraphs. It should be noted that these essentials do not apply to the creation by a local authority of a public path by agreement or order.[2] Such paths are essentially different legal creatures and the nature of rights so created have been discussed in Chapter 9.

Public Places

10.4   Public rights of way cannot exist in all locations. They are limited to linking public places. What constitutes a public place for the purposes of a public right of way is not an easy issue to resolve. In the abstract a public place may be defined as a place to which the public have resort but this does little to assist a determination of any particular case. Some limited assistance may be got by reference to particular examples. The following have been held to be public places for the purposes of a public right of way: a churchyard of the Church of Scotland,[3] a small town or village[4] and a public harbour.[5] Some of these examples are rather difficult to apply in modern practice. It is manifestly the case that not all parts of a small town or village or a public harbour are public places. They usually comprise buildings such as private houses and offices which

---

1   See, *e.g.*, *Rhins District Committee v. Cuninghame* 1917 2 S.L.T. 169 per Lord Sands at 170. See also Cusine and Paisley, *Servitudes and Rights of Way*, para. 20.01.
2   Countryside (Scotland) Act 1967, ss 30 and 31; Cusine and Paisley, *Servitudes and Rights of Way*, para. 19.05.
3   *Smith v. Saxton* 1927 S.N. 98.
4   *Duncan v. Lees* (1870) 9M. 855 per Lord President Inglis at 856.
5   *Cuthbertson v. Young* (1851) 14D. 300.

are clearly restricted areas as far as the public are concerned and from which the public may be wholly excluded. It may be that the decided cases may be taken as indicating little more than a public right of way may lead to a town or village or public harbour and one may assume that when the public right of way reaches the relevant place it then joins with another public right of way or a public road where the public are entitled to be. It is clear that a public road is a public place.[6] The following have been held not to be public places: a sub-post office in private property[7] and a rock forming a local landmark.[8] It has been doubted whether a market place open only on certain days of the week could constitute a public place.[9] Early cases had indicated that a public right of way could not be created if members of the public merely wished to carry out recreational activity on the public place. It is now clear that what members of the public do when they reach the public place is irrelevant provided it is lawful.[10] It is doubtful if any declaration or statement in a deed may *ipso facto* create a place as a public place and some actual public resort to the place, *i.e.* actual use, will be required in addition. This, however, is not to require that public exercise is required to make a public right of way a real right where a deed declares that such a right exists between two established public places.[11]

From the above it is clear that a public place is invariably heritable. A moveable object cannot itself be a public "place". Thus members of the public cannot demand to have access to a famous painting wherever it is, on the basis of an alleged public right of way. An art gallery does not become a public place simply because it contains an art treasure owned by the State. This of course does not prevent a fixture, such as a significant house or church, becoming a public place by virtue of public resort to that place over a period of time.

The Burdened Ground

It is self-evident that the burdened ground in a right of way is 10.5 always heritable and it is difficult to conceive of a situation in which the public could claim to have a right of way across a moveable

Jenkins v. Murray (1866) 4M. 1046 per Lord Deas at 1052.
Love-Lee v. Cameron 1991 S.C.L.R. 61.
Duncan v. Lees (1870) 9M. 274.
Ayr Burgh Council v. British Transport Commission 1955 S.L.T. 219.
0 *Cumbernauld and Kilsyth D. C. v. Dollar Land (Cumbernauld) Ltd*, 1993 S.C. (H.L.) 44; Cusine and Paisley, *Servitudes and Rights of Way*, para. 20.03.
1 Para. 3.25.

item. This does not preclude a public right of way across land or through airspace by means of a structure which has become a fixture.[12] For example, a public right of way may cross a bridge. There is no requirement that the land burdened by a public right of way is "privately" owned and such a right may exist over land owned by a public trust, a public authority or other governmental organisation. The right of property in the *solum* rests with the owner of the burdened property[13] and he will, in theory, be one of the parties entitled to enforce the public right of way. Whilst his ownership of the burdened property subsists that will never occur but his right to enforce the public right of way will revive and become enforceable upon his disposal of the property. It has never been decided whether a grant of warrandice in unqualified terms would preclude a seller from subsequently exercising or seeking to enforce an existing right of way against the party to whom he has sold the land. Such enjoyment and enforcement seems unobjectionable but prudent conveyancers acting for such a seller will wish to exclude the public right of way from warrandice. The raising of proceedings by a former proprietor to have new public right of way declared may be a different matter.

A public right of way entitles members of the public to a right of passage from one public place to another over a defined route over the land situated between those public places. The requirement of a defined route does not imply that there must always be a visible track[14] but merely that the right does not confer upon the public the privilege of strolling or wandering about on any unenclosed land located between two public places.[15] Nevertheless, as a matter of practicality, where there is no visible track it is generally more likely that a landowner, particularly a new purchaser, will deny that a right exists at all. Much of the difficulty with public rights of way is that they are not often created by a deed and there may be little or no documentary evidence to determine the extent of the right. Needless to say, the burdened landowners and the parties wishing to exercise the right often disagree on this point. Where a

---

12 *Cumbernauld and Kilsyth D.C. v. Dollar Land (Cumbernauld) Ltd*, 1993 S.C. (H.L.) 44.
13 *Galbreath v. Armour* (1845) 4 Bell 374 per L.C. Campbell at 380 and Lord Brougham at 389; *Marquis of Breadalbane v. McGregor* (1848) 7 Bell 43 per L.C. Campbell at 60; *McRobert v. Reid* 1914 S.C. 833 per Lord Skerrington at 648; Cusine and Paisley, *Servitudes and Rights of Way*, para. 18.06.
14 *Rhins District Committee of Wigtownshire County Council v Cunninghame*, 1917 2 S.L.T. 168 per Lord Sands at 171; 18 *Stair Memorial Encyclopaedia*, para. 497.
15 *Mackintosh v. Moir* (1871) 9M. 574 per L. P. Inglis at 575; Cusine and Paisley, *Servitudes and Rights of Way*, paras 20.32–20.35.

landowner substitutes a route for an existing path any possession relative to the old route and the new route may be added together for the purposes of determining whether a public right of way has been created by prescriptive exercise.[16] The servient proprietor has a statutory right to apply to the planning authority for diversion of the right.[17]

Passage

Passage is the activity which the members of the general public 10.6 are entitled to carry out on a public right of way. The passage is, in theory, only passage from end to end,[18] but as we shall see,[19] a relaxation of this strict theoretical position is recognised in Scots law as regards access to properties abutting the right of way. Despite the relaxation, the activity permitted is still only passage or access. Pasturage on stances along the way is excluded.[20] A public right of way may, however, include a right to erect direction signs[21] and possibly also some other aids to passage.[22] In this respect a public right of way may be distinguished from servitudes. Whilst positive servitudes may permit the carrying out of other activities such as aqueduct, *aquaehaustus* and pasturage,[23] there are no equivalent public rights.[23a] A public right of way comprises a right to passage and is not a right to carry out other activity such as the laying of service media. It is possible, however, that the right includes rights which are ancillary to the taking of access such as the laying of drains to take surface water off the track. As we shall see below,[24] however, it is possible that some activities on the part of members of the public other than passage may be justified on the basis of certain community rights.

In respect of a public right of way the passage may be exercised by humans on foot, on horseback, accompanied by animals such as farm animals or pet dogs or in vehicles. The extent of the public

---

16 *Hozier v. Hawthorne* (1884) 11R. 766.
17 Countryside (Scotland) Act 1967, s.35(1) as amended.
18 *Mann v. Brodie* (1885) 12R. (H.L.) 52 per Lord Watson at 59; Cusine and Paisley, *Supra*, paras 20.23 and 20.29.
19 Para. 10.7.
20 *Marquis of Breadalbane v. Macgregor* (1848) 7 Bell 43 rev'd (1846) 9D. 210.
21 Cusine and Paisley, *Supra*, para. 21.18.
22 *Cf.* the installation of seats mentioned (but not decided) in *Milne v. Inveresk Parish Landward Association* (1899) 2F. 283.
23 These categories may be extended by statute see para. 8.13.
23a Although as we shall see in para. 10.15 there may be equivalent community rights.
24 Para. 10.15.

right will depend on the terms of any deed creating it (which is rare) or, more likely, where the right is created by prescriptive possession on the extent of the possession during the prescriptive period conform to the maxim *tantum praescriptum tantum possessum*.[25] As mentioned above where a public right of way is created by a deed the terms of the deed will govern the nature of the right and a right of "vehicular" passage will be regarded as exactly that and may exclude pedestrians or driven animals. Where, however, the right is created by prescriptive exercise the greater right will include the lesser so that a right for vehicles will include pedestrians and riders on horseback.[26] A deed creating a public right of way may limit the exercise of the right to certain types of vehicles; such niceties are not implied where the public right of way is created by prescriptive exercise.[27] A public right of way created by prescriptive exercise for pedestrians only may be used by cyclists because bicycles, at least in their traditional form, are regarded not as vehicles but as a device to facilitate the individual's own muscle power.[28] The same principle would apply to wheelchairs propelled by the muscle power of a disabled person but this leaves doubt as regards wheelchairs powered by batteries.

As mentioned above, a public right of passage may include ancillary activities. An activity is more likely to be regarded as an ancillary activity if it clearly tends to promote and foster the primary right, passage itself. Chief amongst the ancillary activities which are inherent in a public right of way are maintenance and repairs. As a result, whilst their right may not extend to upgrading or improving the public right of way, the public have a right to maintain and repair the surface of the way.[29] Access to carry out the repairs is generally to be taken over the route of the public right of way and not over adjacent ground. Planning authorities have statutory powers to repair and maintain any public rights other than a public road or footpath at the side of a road[30] and powers to convert roads used by vehicles into footpaths or bridleways and

---

25 Prescription and Limitation (Scotland) Act 1973, s.3(3); Gordon, *Scottish Land Law* (2nd ed.), para. 24–141; Cusine and Paisley, *Servitudes and Rights of Way*, para. 20.31.

26 *Forbes v. Forbes* (1829) 7S. 441; (1829) 4 Fac. Dec. 563; *Mackenzie v. Bankes* (1868) 6M. 936.

27 *Oswald v. Lawrie* (1828) 5 Mur. 6.

28 *Aberdeenshire County Council v. Lord Glentanar* (decided Dec. 10, 1931), 1999 S.L.T. 1456.

29 Cusine and Paisley, *Supra*, paras 21.11–21.16; Gordon, *supra*, para. 24–138.

30 Countryside (Scotland) Act 1967, s.46, as amended by Countryside (Scotland) Act 1981, s.7, and Local Government etc. (Scotland) Act 1994, Sched. 13.

place such objects or structures on the road as are deemed to improve the amenity of the area or benefit the public.[31]

As he retains a right of ownership in the *solum* of the property, the burdened proprietor may exercise his rights in any manner which is not inconsistent with the public right of way. He may erect stiles and gates on a footway provided these do not materially interfere with the exercise of the right. Statutory provision has supplemented the common law by imposing certain additional restrictions on the landowner in relation to activities which might restrict the exercise of the public right. Such activities include ploughing[32] and the allowing of bulls to be at large in a field through which the public right of way runs.[33] In addition a public right of way comes within the definition of "road" in the Roads (Scotland) Act 1984[34] which creates various offences in relation to obstruction of a public right of way.[35] The obligation of the proprietor of the *solum* is *in patiendo* only and not *in faciendo*. Subject to special provision in a deed, there is no duty of maintenance of a public right of way falling upon the owner of the *solum* but he may be interdicted from carrying out any act which would destroy the route or render passage materially more difficult. Delictual liability may, however, arise in appropriate cases.[36]

The Benefited Parties

A public right of way is enforceable by members of the general public by means of *actio popularis*. There is no authority as to whether a proprietor wishing to create a public right of way by means of a deed could expressly exclude enforcement by certain named individuals whom he regards as undesirable or limit its enjoyment to a restricted class of parties. The matter appears to be one of degree—whilst a number of limited exceptions may not materially alter the nature of the right a multiplicity of limitations on enforcement may deprive the right of its essential public character. Quite separate from, and in addition to, the public right of enforcement is a right of enforcement, at least in theory, on the part of the Crown or its delegate. There is no reported instance of

10.7

---

31 Town and Country Planning (Scotland) Act 1997, s.201.
32 Countryside (Scotland) Act 1967, s.43.
33 Countryside (Scotland) Act 1967, s.44
34 1984 Act, s.151(1).
35 1984 Act, ss 57–59, 85–91 and 93.
36 *Johnstone v. Sweeney* 1985 S.L.T. (Sh.Ct.) 2; *McGeown v. Northern Ireland Housing Executive* [1995] 1 A.C. 233.

the Crown having enforced a public right of way. A statutory right
and duty to assert public rights of way has been conferred on local
authorities.[37] In most cases local authorities consider that there are
many other activities which are to be given priority in relation to
resources. Whilst this may cause disappointment to enthusiasts for
public access it is understandable in the context of competing claims
on limited resources. When faced with a potential dispute relative to
a public right of way many authorities wisely try to defuse the issue
to avoid wasteful and costly litigation.

A public right of way is distinguishable from a servitude of access
in that a public right of way is not a pertinent of a dominant
tenement but the two may exist in respect of the same route.[38] A
public right of way is to be used by members of the general public
proceeding from one end of the way to another but this does not
preclude the use of the right as a means of access from one end of
the way to properties located at a point along the route.[39] Although
one terminus of a former public right of way is closed this does not,
of itself, result in a right of access to intermediate places being
lost.[40] The nature of this surviving right of access to the intervening
properties is unclear but it may be that it could be regarded as a
form of servitude. Having said that, most conveyancers would not
be prepared to accept a title to a property as "valid and
marketable" if the only access to that property was an alleged
public right of way at least until that right was judicially declared or
was so notorious that the matter could not realistically be disputed.
There is no absolute rule on this matter and this phenomenon
merely appears to be a product of a general practice of those
practitioners who feel more comfortable with rights created in deeds
than rights created by other means such as prescriptive exercise.

Methods of Creation

10.8   Public rights of way are not "tacit" rights which arise out of the
physical nature of a location. Before a public right of way exists
something needs to be done in the form of physical or juristic acts
by the landowner or members of the public. Although it is
competent for the proprietor of land to create a public right of way

---

37 Countryside (Scotland) Act 1967, s.46, as amended by Countryside (Scotland)
    Act 1981.
38 *Smith v. Saxton*, 1927 S.N. 98.
39 *McRobert v. Reid*, 1914 S.C. 633; Cusine and Paisley, *Servitudes and Rights of
    Way*, para. 20.29.
40 *Lord Burton v. MacKay*, 1995 S.L.T. 507.

by express grant, in practice public rights of way are almost without exception created by public exercise for the prescriptive period of 20 years.[41] This has three important consequences:

(a) First, in the vast majority of cases the Sasine title deeds to the burdened land will not disclose the existence or extent of the right. The same applies to a Land Certificate and a public right of way is a mere "overriding interest".[42]

(b) Secondly, the rights and obligations relating to a public right of way are implied by law and do not generally require the interpretation of written agreements entered into by the landowner. That is not to say that the public are free to exercise a right of way created by prescription in whatever manner they see fit—the public are required to exercise the right *civiliter*, that is to say, in a reasonable manner.

(c) Thirdly, just because a landowner creates a road on his property linking two public points does not, *ipso facto*, create a public right of way. It is *a fortiori* the case that the indication of the existence of a path or road on the Ordnance Survey map does not create a public right of way: the map merely indicates a factual state of affairs—the physical existence of the path or road— and in no way confirms the existence of any legal rights in relation to that path or road.

Creation by Prescription

The Prescription and Limitation (Scotland) Act 1973, s.3(3), 10.9 provides that where a public right of way over land has been possessed by the public for a continuous period of 20 years openly, peaceably and without judicial interruption, then, as from the expiration of that period, the existence of the right of way as so possessed shall be exempt from challenge.

The provision largely speaks for itself but the following matters require comment:

(a) Use must be by the public. The use by parties who may have their use attributable to other rights or tolerance must be ignored. Thus, use by employees or dependants of the

---

41 Prescription and Limitation (Scotland) Act 1973, s.3(3); *Richardson v. Cromarty Petroleum Co. Ltd*, 1982 S.L.T. 237; *The City of Aberdeen D. C. v. Camphill Rudolf Steiner Estates Ltd*, Sheriff Meston, Aberdeen Sheriff Court, 1996, case ref. A1286/95 (unreported); Gordon, *Scottish Land Law* (2nd ed.), para. 24–132; Cusine and Paisley, *Supra*, para. 20.48.

42 Land Registration (Scotland) Act 1979, s.28(1).

proprietor is excluded.[43] The use of many "privileged" parties such as doctors and clergymen may be ignored on the basis of customary tolerance as will the use by those exercising public functions such as policemen.[44]

(b) Use must be "as of right" although this is not expressly stated in the statute. The public right of way is not created until after the public have used the route for 20 years. This requirement therefore does not mean that the public must have a right to use the route (because that could indefinitely delay the acquisition of the right)[45] but they must use it *as if* they had a right to do so. In determining this issue it is easier to hold that use has been as of right where the use is substantial. Clearly what is substantial will vary from area to area and much less in the way of volume of traffic may be accepted to create a public right of way in remote rural places than in urban areas.[46]

Methods of Extinction

10.10   Public rights of way may be extinguished in the following ways:

(a) Agreement. In theory a public right of way could be extinguished by an agreement with all parties entitled to enforce it or someone, such as the Crown, representing the public interest.[47] For obvious practical reasons this is never attempted in practice. An agreement entered into with a single party, such as the Scottish Rights of Way Society Limited, or a group of such parties who are not entitled to represent the public, runs the risk that a member of the public who is not a party to the deed will not be bound by it. This is a commercial risk which may be acceptable in particular circumstances.[48]

(b) Prescription. This is probably the most frequently encountered method of extinction. A public right of way will be extinguished by non-use for a period of 20 years.[49] There may be partial loss of the right as where a public right of way

---

43 Rankine, *Landownership*, p. 331.
44 *Norrie v. Mags of Kirriemuir*, 1945 S.C. 302.
45 *Richardson v. Cromarty Petroleum Co. Ltd*, 1982 S.L.T. 237.
46 *MacPherson v. Scottish Rights of Way and Recreation Society Ltd* (1887) 14R. 875 at 880 per Lord Kinnear; *Strathclyde (Hyndland) Housing Society Ltd v. Cowie*, 1983 S.L.T. (Sh.Ct.) 61.
47 Gordon, *Scottish Land Law* (2nd Ed.), para. 24–148.
48 Cusine and Paisley, *Servitudes and Rights of Way*, para. 24.02.
49 Prescription and Limitation (Scotland) Act 1973, s.8; Gordon, *Scottish Land Law* (2nd ed.), para. 24–149.

originally created as a route for vehicles is used only for pedestrians for the prescriptive period; the extent of the right may be reduced to a pedestrian right.[50]

(c) Acquiesence. Where the owner of the *solum* does something, such as totally obliterating the route or building a solid wall across it, which is inconsistent with the existence of the servitude and this is accepted by the public then the public right of way may be extinguished before a period of 20 years, non-use has elapsed.[51] The same principle applies where the owner of the *solum* diverts the route of an existing public right of way but only to the extent of extinguishing the public right of way over the old route.[52]

(d) Destruction. A public right of way may be extinguished where one of the public *termini* is permanently destroyed. If the public right of way is exercised over a man-made structure and this is destroyed without the possibility of reinstatement the right will be extinguished.[53]

(e) Statutory powers. Certain statutory procedures may be invoked to close public rights of way.[54] The extent of the powers given is a matter of statutory interpretation. Where the land subject to the public right of way is compulsorily acquired under statutory powers and the continued exercise of the servitude would be incompatible with the purpose of the acquisition the public right of way will be extinguished.

Public Navigation

The public right of navigation in a non-tidal river is not a public right of way but is a different real right recognised by Scots law. The right is essentially one of passage and does not extend to any right of ownership in the river bed to which it applies.[55] Consequently it does not include a right to moor permanently on the river bed but temporary moorings may be permissible.[56] It does   10.11

---

50 *Macfarlane v. Morrison* (865) 4M. 257.
51 Rankine, *Landownership*, pp. 336–337; Cusine and Paisley, *Supra*, para. 24.06.
52 *Hozier v. Hawthorne* (1884) 11R. 766; *Kinloch's Trs v. Young*, 1911 S.C. (H.L.) 1.
53 Cusine and Paisley, *Supra*, para. 24.07.
54 Countryside (Scotland) Act 1967 and 1981, s.34; Roads (Scotland) Act 1984, s.68; Gordon, *Supra*, para. 24–154.
55 *Orr Ewing v. Colquhoun's Trs* (1877) 4R. (H.L.) 116 at 126 per Lord Blackburn.
56 *Will's Trs v. Cairngorm Canoeing and Sailing School Ltd*, 1976 S.C. (H.L.) 30; *Campbell's Trs v. Sweeney*, 1911 S.C. 1319; *Leith- Buchana v. Hogg*, 1931 S.C. 204; *Burton's Trs v. Scottish Sports Council*, 1983 S.L.T. 418; *Scammell v. Scottish Sports Council*, 1983 S.L.T. 462.

not extend to a right to fish[57] or a right to shoot game.[58] The right of navigation does not require to be taken over a route between two public places. Unlike a servitude or a public right of way, it is not extinguished by non-use for the period of long negative prescription.[59] The measure of the public right of navigation is the physical capacity of the river and is not limited by evidence of past user.[60] Until recently there were two views as to its acquisition. The first approach maintained that, unlike a public right of way, a public right of navigation did not require to be positively acquired. Instead, this approach asserted that it was a tacit right which arose automatically provided it could be shown that the river in question was physically navigable. The second view asserted that physical navigability required to be coupled with evidence of actual use by the public. The second view has been upheld by the House of Lords and it is now settled that a river may not be regarded as "navigable" unless there is evidence that it has been regularly and habitually used by the public for navigation since time immemorial— customarily reckoned as 40 years.[61] The right exists only in respect of natural rivers and watercourses and does not extend to man-made inland canals.[62] It is an unsettled question as to whether a right of public navigation could be created by a deed over a man-made watercourse.

Public Roads

10.12   Common law recognises the public rights of highway over roads in the countryside and passage over streets within towns. These are rights to traverse the surface of the road and street and closely resemble public rights of way in that they are enforceable by members of the public by means of an *actio popularis*.

In some senses, however, a public right of passage on a road or street is a much stronger right than a mere public right of way. For example, styles or other openable gates may be erected on a public

---

57 *Grant v. Henry* (1894) 1 S.L.T. 448; Gordon, *supra* para. 8–135.
58 *Colquhoun's Trs v. Lee*, 1957 S.L.T. (Sh.Ct.) 50.
59 *Will's Trs v. Cairngorm Canoeing and Sailing School Ltd*, 1976 S.C. (H.L.) 30; 1976 S.L.T. 162; 18 *Stair Memorial Encyclopaedia*, paras 497 and 523.
60 *Will's Trs v. Cairngorm Canoeing and Sailing School Ltd*, 1976 S.C. (H.L.) 30 at 169; 1976 S.L.T. 162 at 216 per Lord Fraser.
61 *Will's Trs v. Cairngorm Canoeing and Sailing School Ltd*, 1976 S.C. (H.L.) 30 at 165; 1976 S.L.T. 162 at 212–213 per Lord Fraser.
62 *Anderson v. The Union Canal Co.* (1839) 11Sc. Jur. 409 at 410 per counsel for the pursuer; *Macdonnell v. Caledonian Canal Commissioners* (1830) 8S. 881.

right of way[63] by the owner of the *solum* but no obstruction at all is permitted on a public road or street.[64] A public right of way is limited to a right of passage and does not include a right to fish in an adjacent river[65] or shoot game from the route of the public right of way[66] but, at common law, the public appear to have possessed a right to shoot game on the highway.[67] Most of these distinctions have little relevance due to the obscuring of the common law by the vast overlay of statutes relative to public roads, but a number of incidents retain a relevance for modern conveyancing and property law as follows:

(a) First, a public right of way is extinguished by negative prescription but a public right of road is probably imprescriptible except in cases where the land subject to the rights has been altered to such an extent that physical exercise of the right is impossible.[68] This is an issue which still arises where a stopping-up order has not been issued or it cannot be ascertained whether one has been issued.[69] The public right of passage does not necessarily cease upon the issuing of a stopping-up order. Only where the road has been stopped up on the basis that it is dangerous is that the case. Where the road is stopped up on the basis that it is unnecessary the public right of passage will continue until the road is actually unnecessary as a matter of fact.[70] The requirement of necessity is not expressly restricted to considerations of access for public purposes and it would seem that access to a plot of land for private purposes would suffice. Thus a single proprietor may be able to rely on the public right of passage even if the stopping-up order has been issued and the road is not shown on the property enquiry certificate as a public road and there is no need to rely on a doctrine that pre-existing servitudes of

---

63 *Kirkpatrick v. Murray* (1856) 19D. 91.
64 *Sutherland v. Thomson* (1876) 3R. 485 at 490 per Lord Neaves and at 493 per Lord Ormidale; 18 *Stair Memorial Encyclopaedia*, para. 495. See also Roads (Scotland) Act 1984, s.59.
65 *Fergusson v. Shireff* (1844) 16 Sc. Jur. 580.
66 *Colt v. Webb* (1898) 1F. (J) 7.
67 *Simon v. Reid* (1879) 4 Coup. 220 noted in *Hope v. Bennewith* (1904) 6F. 1004.
68 Gordon, *Scottish Land Law* (2nd ed.), para. 24–149; *Will's Trs v. Cairngorm Canoeing and Sailing School Ltd*, 1976 S.C. (H.L.) 30 at 168–169 per Lord Fraser (opinion reserved), referring to *Waddell v. Earl of Buchan* (1868) 6M. 690. Quite apart from prescription such a public right may be regarded as abandoned in such circumstances.
69 Roads (Scotland) Act 1984, ss 68 and 115.
70 Roads (Scotland) Act 1984, s.68.

access will revive to protect his interests.[71] This, however, is an unusual situation which will probably not be expressly dealt with in missives relative to a normal domestic property.[72] It may, however, be difficult to convince a purchaser that there is a valid and marketable title where the property enquiry certificate indicates that the road *ex adverso* the property is not a public road. Lastly, where a road is stopped up on the basis that the road is unnecessary the stopping-up order may reserve a means of passage along the road for pedestrians, or cyclists or both.[73] This reserved right will be akin to a public right of passage rather than a servitude unless the reservation relates to passage to and from a particular property along the road or part of it.

(b) Secondly, it is clear that public streets[74] and roads[75] are regarded as *res publicae* and *inter regalia* at common law, indicating that the right of passage over them is enforceable by the Crown in addition to enforcement by members of the general public. The link with the Crown in relation to public rights of way does exist but, as has been noted above,[76] the Crown as a matter of fact took less to do with the enforcement of public rights of way and this is reflected in the rarity of *dicta* confirming that public rights of way are *inter regalia*.[77] In sharp distinction to public rights of way, members of the public rarely if ever enforced their right of passage along public streets or roads in recent years. Instead, the Crown's right of enforcement has been developed as the primary means of securing the public interest in streets and roads with the right

---

71 *Cf.* South African law where any pre-existing servitudes of access revive: *Malherbe v. Van Rensberg*, 1970 4 S.A. 78 (C).

72 Gretton and Reid, *Conveyancing* (2nd ed.), paras 4.12–4.13.

73 1984 Act, s.68(4).

74 *Town of Linlithgow v. Fleshers of Edinburgh*, 15 Nov. 1621 M. 10886; *City of Glasgow Union Railway Co. v. Hunter* (1870) 8 Macq. (H.L.) 56; *Scott v. Orphan Hospital* (1835) 14S. 18; *Mags of Edinburgh v. N.B. Railway* (1904) 6F. 620 at 639 per Lord Kinnear.

75 Erskine, *Inst.*, II,vi,17; Duff, *Deeds*, para. 49(1); *Waddell v. Earl of Buchan* (1868) 6M. 690 at 699 per Lord Curriehill; *Galbreath v. Armour* (1845) 4 Bell's App. 374 at 380–381 per Lord Campbell; *Sutherland v. Thomson* (1876) 3R. 485 at 492 per Lord Ormidale; *Shetland Salmon Farmers Association (Special Case)*, 1990 S.C.L.R. 484 per Lord Murray at 499.

76 Para. 10.7.

77 See, *e.g.*, *Fergusson v. Shireff* (1844) 16 Sc. Jur. 580 at 582 per Lord Moncreiff. For a view that public rights of way are held directly by the public see 18 *Stair Memorial Encyclopaedia*, para. 494. See also Napier, *Prescription*, p. 270, disapproved in *Mann v. Brodie* (1885) 12R. (H.L.) 52 at 57 per Lord Watson.

being delegated to successive bodies in increasingly comprehensive statutory regulation culminating in the Roads (Scotland) Act 1984. The reason for this is obvious: roads have a much greater economic and strategic value to the State than public rights of way.

(c) Thirdly, a public right of way is limited to passage and may in some cases be restricted to pedestrians. By contrast a public road or street at common law is open to all vehicles and in relation to public streets the public right extends beyond passage to other rights and purposes "municipal, sanitary and economic"[78] including purposes such as markets and meeting—"for conveying water and gas to the houses—for a paved way between the houses . . ."[79] It probably extends in such locations to a right to light.[80] The public right to install apparatus under a public road[81] or projections over a road is now severely curtailed and regulated by statute to the extent that it cannot be exercised at all without the consent of the roads authority.[82]

(d) Fourthly, in the past the public right of passage over many public roads and streets was created by prescriptive exercise in the same way as public rights of way are still constituted. In recent years, however, the overlay of statutory control and stricter planning of roads proposals has resulted in roads being created not by prescriptive exercise but by adoption under statutory process. Once adopted the public have a right of passage over the road and the roads authority have a duty to maintain it.[83] This is a process which should not be abused and the decision to adopt an area of ground as a road may be subject to judicial review.[84]

(e) Lastly, one should note that the definition of a "road" in the

---

78 *George Donald & Sons Ltd v. Esslemont & MacIntosh Ltd*, 1923 S.C. 122 per the Lord President at 131.

79 *Threshie v. Mags of Annan* (1845) 8D. 286 at 280 per Lord Mackenzie, at 281 per L.P. Boyle, and at 282 per Lord Fullerton.

80 *Cf.* 18 *Stair Memorial Encyclopaedia*, para. 359(7), where this is regarded as right of common interest.

81 Roads (Scotland) Act 1984, s.61; 20 *Stair Memorial Encyclopaedia*, para. 687.

82 Roads (Scotland) Act 1984, ss 90–93; 20 *Stair Memorial Encyclopaedia*, para. 693.

83 Roads (Scotland) Act 1984, s.1; 20 *Stair Memorial Encyclopaedia*, paras 611–613.

84 See, *e.g.*, *MacKinnon v. Argyll and Bute Council*, O.H., Lord Osborne, Mar. 8, 2000 G.W.D. 11–371; *Elmford Ltd, Petrs*, Lord Clarke, September 12, 2000, unreported.

Roads (Scotland) Act 1984 is a way over which there is a public right of passage (by whatever means).[85] A public right of passage may fall far short of a public right of way, highway or street recognised at common law and may comprise a mere licence by the proprietor of the *solum*. If the public right of passage is of a precarious nature the route will cease to be a road in terms of the statute when the right terminates.[86]

Other Services

10.13   At common law there is no public right recognised in relation to supply of services to property such as public sewerage, water supply, electricity telecommunications and gas. All of these services are essential for modern living and cannot be ignored by a conveyancer when purchasing a house.[87] The matter of rights in relation to these matters is extensively regulated by statute. Broadly speaking the provider of these services has a statutory right to install the media whereby these services are transmitted or conveyed through private land and the customer has a statutory right to be connected in the mains services upon certain terms. There is generally no right directly enforceable by the customer against the landowner except where additional rights are created by servitudes or real conditions. The reader is referred to other textbooks for further details.[88]

Foreshore, Seabed and Territorial Sea

10.14   The general public have certain rights in and to the foreshore, sea and territorial sea. The rights comprise the right to use the foreshore and territorial sea for whitefishing (all floating fish other than salmon),[89] recreation and navigation. The foreshore may also be used for passage along the foreshore. As regards navigation the use of the foreshore may extend to "casting anchors, disloading of goods, taking in of ballast, or water rising in fountains there, drying of nets, erecting of tents, and the like".[90] It probably does not

---

85 Roads (Scotland) Act 1984, s.151.
86 *Viewpoint Housing Association Ltd v. Lothian R. C.*, 1993 S.L.T. 921; Cusine and Paisley, *Servitudes and Rights of Way*, para. 14.22.
87 Gretton and Reid, *Conveyancing* (2nd ed.), paras 4.14 and 4.15.
88 See, *e.g.*, Gordon, *Scottish Land Law* (2nd ed.), paras 7–70–7–72 (sewerage); 7–73–7–76 (water supply).
89 The right appears to exist at common law and be confirmed by statute: see *Bowie v Marquis of Ailsa* (1887) 14R. 649; Fisheries Act 1705.
90 Stair, II,i,5.

permit the taking away of sand and pebbles even for ballast.[91] These are real rights recognised by the law of Scotland and can be enforced *in rem*.[92] They are part of the *regalia majora*[93] and may be enforced separately by the Crown[94] and by members of the public by means of an *actio popularis*.[95] The party against whom they are usually enforced is the proprietor of the foreshore who may wish to carry out activities in contravention of the rights, but it may include other parties who infringe the rights.

It is probably the case that the rights of navigation and whitefishing are tacit rights and arise by operation of law.[96] A greater element of uncertainty exists in relation to the public right of recreation but the modern judicial dicta tend to regard it as tacit also.[97] The right of enforcement may be constrained or removed by statute.[98] The public rights of navigation may also be extinguished by physical impossibility of exercise as may be the case if a navigable channel in a river silts up.

Community Rights

In or around the locations of some old Royal and other burghs 10.15 there may be located land or other property such as a loch owned by the local authority or third parties over which the local community have certain rights recognised at common law.[99] These rights, usually of ancient origin, vary from case to case depending on the nature of the property but the activity permitted on such property has comprised activities as diverse as recreation[1] and fishing other than for salmon.[2] The rights are enforceable by the Crown,[3] its delegate (probably the relevant local authority) and members of the community by means of an *actio popularis*.[4] The

---

91   *Carswell v. Nith Navigation Commissioners* (1878) 6R. 60.
92   18 *Stair Memorial Encyclopaedia*, paras 5, 318 and 494.
93   18 *Stair Memorial Encyclopaedia*, para. 514.
94   *Crown Estate Commissioners v. Fairlie Yacht Slip Ltd*, 1979 S.C. 156 at 178 per L.P. Emslie.
95   *Walford v. David*, 1989 S.L.T. 876; *Walford v. Crown Estate Commissioners*, 1988 S.C.L.R. 113.
96   18 *Stair Memorial Encyclopaedia*, paras 494 and 524.
97   *Nicol v. Bliakie* (1859) 22D. 335.
98   Offshore Petroleum Development (Scotland) Act 1975, s.5(3).
99   Cusine and Paisley, *Servitudes and Rights of Way*, para. 1.14.
1   *Paterson v. Mags of St. Andrews* (1881) 8R. (HL) 117 per Lord Blackburn at 123 and Lord Watson at 125.
2   *Beck v. Mags of Lochmaben* (1839) 1D. 1212; (1841) 4D. 16.
3   *Phin v. Mags of Auchtermuchty* (1827) 5S. 690.
4   *Grahame v. Mags of Kirkcaldy* (1882) 9R. (H.L.) 91 per Lord Watson at 93.

determination of the identity of the persons falling within this class of persons has been rendered virtually impossible by the periodic reorganisations of local government. The manner of creation of the rights is obscure but it is submitted that they are acquired rights rather than tacit rights because their existence appears to depend on the special function or utility they have for a particular community. They therefore require to be created by some form of dedication to that community or prescriptive possession by that community. The matter, however, remains decidedly obscure. Statutory provisions have been enacted to allow the free disposal of local authority land which would otherwise be subject to these rights.[5] In some particular instances local statutes have created rights in favour of communities, such as fishing, over local reservoirs.[5a]

Rights in Graves

10.16   A lair certificate may evidence or constitute a contractual right to carry out burials in a particular plot of ground.[6] The property right in graveyards is not transferred by a lair certificate nor in most modern forms does it usually comprise a right to require the owner to grant a conveyance of the property right in a particular plot, nor would such a right be implied.[7] It is of course possible to provide otherwise in relation to an obligation to convey and some old lair certificates confer upon the grantee a right to obtain a disposition of the grave plot.[8] That, however, is not the modern fashion.

The nature of the surviving relative's right in and to the plot of ground in which his deceased relative is interred has been long obscured by feudal notions but the following now appears to be clear. The surviving relatives each have the rights[9]:

(a)   To prevent desecration of the grave by reasonable acts such as erecting a low wall and to repair the surrounds of the grave. It was observed in one case that this does not necessarily extend to a right to adorn the grave with a tombstone[10] but this is frequently tolerated out of custom and may be required as a matter of contract.

---

5   Para 1.26.
5a   Discussed in *Kilsyth Fish Protection Association v. McFarlane*, 1937 S.L.T. 562; *Falkirk and Larbert Water Trs v. Forbes*, 1893 1 S.L.T. 290.
6   *Black v. McCallum* (1924) 11 Sh.Ct.Rep. 108.
7   *Cunningham v. Edmiston* (1871) 9M. 869.
8   For examples of such dispositions see para. 1.28(c).
9   *Hill v. Wood* (1863) 1 Macq. 360.
10   *Cunninghams v. Cunningham* (1778) 5 B.S. 415

(b) To take access to the grave and remove obstructions to the taking of that access. The quality of access in rural kirkyards does not require to be high.[11]
(c) To carry out future burials. This appears to be capable of regulation in terms of the lair certificate.
(d) To petition for a disinterment of the deceased[12] or the body of a non-relative mistakenly buried in the grave of a relative.[13]

In principle the rights would arise immediately upon the carrying out of the interment and not by prescriptive exercise.[14] It may be possible to regard the interment as the public act by which existing personal rights are transformed into real rights.[15] The rights endure at least for so long as the interred body is capable of reverence[16] but some dicta indicate they are perpetual.[17] The rights are not servitudes as the relatives are entitled to enforce them without reference to a dominant tenement. The rights appear to belong to the relatives simply by virtue of their being related to the deceased and they may not be capable of alienation to other parties. This is not to say that the enjoyment of the rights could not be communicated temporarily to a third party as might be the case where a surviving relative takes a friend along to visit a grave. The extent of the class of entitled relatives has received little comprehensive analysis and the courts have been content with general observations indicating that the rights are not enforceable by the public at large or the occupants of a nearby town.[18] To qualify for entitlement the surviving relative need not be alive at the same time as the interred was alive. A genealogist may therefore visit the grave of his deceased great-great-grandfather. The nature of the action to enforce the rights may be a form of *actio popularis* as the relatives form a section of the public. The Crown also has an independent right to ensure that graves are not descecrated[19] and

---

11 *Mcbean v. Young* (1859) 21D. 314.
12 See, *e.g.*, *Solheim, Petr*, 1947 S.C. 243. For the costs of doing so where the body has been buried by mistake see *Blandford v. Corsock Church of Scotland* (1950) S.L.T. (Sh.Ct.) 37.
13 *Paterson, Petr*, July 14, 2000, O.H., Lord Penrose (unreported).
14 Despite some contrary *dicta* see, *e.g.*, *Hill v. Wood* (1863) 1 Macq. 360 at 373 per Lord Barcaple.
15 See the publicity principle discussed at paras 3.18–3.22.
16 Erskine, *Inst*, II,i,8.
17 See, *e.g.*, *Earl of Mansfield v. Wright* (1824) 2S. 104 at 108 per L.J-C. Boyle.
18 *Earl of Mansfield v. Wright* (1824) 2S. 104. See also Church of Scotland (Property and Endowments) Act 1925, s.33.
19 See *Bowie, Petirs.*, 1967 S.C. 36 where the petition was served on the Lord Advocate for the public interest.

may also have a right to exercise the other rights of the relatives except for that relating to additional burials. This pattern of entitlement to enforce gives rise to the hint, but only the hint, of a resemblance with other public and regalian rights.

10.17 Graveyards are not *extra commercium* or *res religiosa*.[20] In general the rights of the relatives impose limitations not on the juristic acts which the owner may carry out (although the matter may be otherwise if the ground is held in trust for the relatives and the purposes of burial) but on the physical acts which the proprietor may carry out. The proprietor of the graveyard is precluded from carrying out any act which interferes with the full exercise of these rights of the relatives. He is probably entitled to cut trees[21] and the grass[22] but he cannot plough the ground[23] or use it as the site of a rock festival or carnival. He may, however, repair the walls around the graveyard[24] put up memorials to persons not buried in the graveyard[25] and even work the strata of minerals far below the graves.[26] The proprietor of land has a title to petition for disinterment.[27] The court will order disinterment only if it considers it appropriate to do so in the circumstances taking into account both the private interests of the landowner and the surviving relatives and, in addition, the public interest. The rights of the relatives may be terminated or limited by statutory provision.[28] Not being land obligations they cannot be varied or discharged by reference to the Lands Tribunal.[29]

Statutory Rights—Introduction

10.18 A variety of statutes create rights which have certain of the characteristics of real rights. Other statutes confer power on the courts or certain parties to create rights which have a similar nature. These rights affect land even without a specific reference to the relevant statutes in the title deeds or Land Certificate relative to the burdened land. Where these statutory rights benefit an individual

---

20 Para. 1.24.
21 *Ure v. Ramsay and Johnstone* (1828) 6S. 916 at 920 per Lord Alloway.
22 *Mags of Greenock v. Shaw Stewart* (1777) 2 Hailes 758.
23 *Robert v. Ewart* (1778) 2 Hailes 799.
24 *Fraser v. Turner and Landale* (1893) 21R. 278.
25 *Paterson v. Beattie* (1845) 7D. 561.
26 *Welsh v. MacDonald* (1896) 3 S.L.T. 304.
27 See, *e.g.*, *Sister Jarlath, Petr.* 1980 S.L.T. (Sh.Ct.) 72.
28 See, *e.g.*, Aberdeen University (Buildings Extension) Act 1893 (56 & 57 Vict.), c.clxxvii.
29 Paras 9.31–9.38.

rather than the successive owners of a plot of ground they do not constitute "land obligations" and cannot be varied in the Lands Tribunal.[30] The proper exercise of the rights may constitute a sufficient defence to a claim based on trespass. If a landowner seeks ejection and interdict in respect of a particular activity which is justified by reference to a statutory right, the terms of the order sought will be regarded as too wide and will be refused as being capable of denying the defender of the possibility of exercising a statutory right.[31]

There is a multiplicity of these rights and a mere sample will be noted here. These are as follows:

(a) A statutory right of occupation may be conferred by a local authority where it makes a control order in respect of a house in multiple occupancy: it may create an interest in the nature of a contractual licence or, alternatively, an interest which "as near as may be, has the incidents of a lease".[32]

(b) Drainage rights for agricultural land may be created in terms of the Land Drainage (Scotland) Acts 1930 and 1958.[33]

(c) Fishermen have statutory rights to use the foreshore and the land above the foreshore.[34] Every person employed in the British white herring fisheries may use the shore and the forelands in Great Britain below the highest high-water mark and also waste and uncultivated land for 100 yards inland, for purposes connected with fishing, without payment.[35] What amounts to "waste or uncultivated" land is a question of fact in every case[36] but it does not include ground enclosed for a boat building.[37] In addition, white herring fishers are entitled to the free use of all natural ports and harbours.[38] This does not extend to harbours and piers which have been built or artificially made with the permission of the Crown.[39]

(d) In terms of the Mines (Working Facilities and Support) Act 1966 and subsequent amending Acts rights may be obtained

---

30 *ibid.*
31 *Captain Robert Alexander Montgomerie v. John Thomson Mearns*, Kilmarnock Sheriff Court, case ref. A1380/1975. (unreported).
32 Housing (Scotland) Act 1987, s.179(2); Gordon, *Scottish Land Law* (2nd. ed.), para. 19–17.
33 These are discussed at para. 2.08. See also Gordon, *Supra*, paras. 7–64–7–66.
34 Gordon, *Supra*, para 8–08.
35 White Herring Fisheries Act 1771, s.11.
36 *Stephen v. Aiton* (1875) 2R. 470; *affd.* (1876) 3R. (H.L.) 4.
37 *Campbelltown Shipbuilding Co. v. Robertson* (1898) 25R. 922.
38 White Herring Fisheries Act 1771, ss 11 and 12.
39 *Earl of Stair v. Austin* (1880) 8R. 183.

upon petition to the sheriff to enable working of the minerals and access over the surface.

(e) In terms of the Civic Government (Scotland) Act 1982, ss 88, 90 and 91 proprietors of "buildings" may petition the court to obtain rights to install cables, ducts, lights and other service media in other parts of the building. The classic case is a tenemental building. It does not relate to undeveloped land. It probably does not allow ventilation for commercial purposes.

(f) In terms of the Sewerage (Scotland) Act 1968, ss.3 and 3A, a party may be authorised to construct sewers in land owned by other parties. This may benefit development sites. It probably also extends to surface water drainage.

(g) In terms of the Matrimonial Homes (Family Protection)(Scotland) Act 1981 as amended a non-entitled spouse may obtain occupancy rights in respect of the matrimonial home.[40]

---

40 See para. 2.9.

CHAPTER 11

SECURITIES OVER LAND

Introduction

Debts are personal obligations owed by debtors to creditors and may be enforced by personal actions in the normal way. This may prove unsatisfactory for some creditors as a particular debtor may have many existing debts and may continue to incur new debts. A creditor who does not wish to compete with other creditors on the same terms may seek to enhance his position by obtaining a right in heritable property owned by the debtor in security of his debt. A heritable security (otherwise known as *debitim fundi*) improves the position of the creditor by conferring upon him additional remedies and an advantageous position in a situation where the debtor becomes insolvent.[1] This is possible because the creditor is given certain advantages to recover the sums due to him in respect of an item of the debtor's heritable property which, to a considerable extent, is "ring fenced" for the purposes of the favoured creditor. In theory, the underlying personal obligation of the debtor to pay the creditor, usually in the form of a loan contract, and the security conferring additional rights on the creditor are quite distinct. It is simple, however, to allow the two devices to become confused and the Scottish legislation relevant to standard securities[2] does not observe the distinction completely in all its provisions.[3]

11.1

---

1 Scott C. Styles, "Rights in Security" in A.D.M. Forte (ed.), *Scots Commercial Law* (1997), Chap. 6, p. 179.
2 Conveyancing and Feudal Reform (Scotland) Act 1970 ("the 1970 Act").
3 Gretton and Reid, *Conveyancing* (2nd ed.), para. 20.03.

Types of Heritable Securities in Scotland

11.2   More than one form of heritable security is presently competent
in Scotland. The heritable securities which are commonly encountered in modern Scots law are all creatures of statute.[4] They are:

(a)   Standard security.[5]
(b)   Floating charge.[6]
(c)   Charging orders.[7]
(d)   The *debitum fundi* in respect of the redemption sum for feu
      duty redeemed upon the transfer of land[8] and the pecuniary
      real burden capable of reservation in terms of the Housing
      (Scotland) Act 1987, s.72(7).

Since November 29, 1970 the standard security has been the
primary form of fixed security which may be created over an
"interest in land".[9] There remains the historical anomaly of
securities over entailed lands, which will disappear upon feudal
reform.[10] The last of these securities noted at (d) above is a relic of
the past and, apart from the deliberate statutory retention in the
context of feu duty, remains technically competent merely because
of a statutory oversight.[11] Fortunately the oversight has not
encouraged use and examples in practice are rare. Apart from the
theoretical possibility of reservation in a disposition,[12] the security
is created involuntarily and then only in respect of a particular type
of debt – the redemption sum for feu duty. As regards feu duty it
will cease to exist upon the appointed day in terms of the feudal

---

4   One may argue, however, that the concept of pecuniary real burden, in so far as
    still valid, is a creature of common law recognised by particular statutes. For an
    argument that it is possible to have a lien over land in Scotland see A. Steven
    Ph.D. thesis, Edinburgh University, *Pledge and Lien in Scots Law*, p. 199, para.
    170 and p. 208, para. 175. See also *Binning v. Brotherstones* (1676) M. 13401.
5   Paras 11.3–11.24.
6   Paras 11.25–11.31.
7   Para. 11.32.
8   Land Tenure Reform (Scotland) Act 1974, s.5(5).
9   1970 Act, s.9(3). For older forms of security see Gretton and Reid, *Conveyancing*
    (2nd ed.), para. 20.01–20.03.
10 1970 Act, s.9(8)(b), definition of "interest in land" to be amended by Abolition
    of feudal Tenure etc. (Scotland) Act 2000, s.76(1) and Sched. 12, para. 30(6). This
    anomaly will disappear with the disentailing of all remaining entailed land in
    terms of Abolition of Feudal Tenure etc. (Scotland) Act 2000, s.50.
11 1970 Act, s.9(3) failed to abolish creation of securities by reservation. See 18 *Stair
    Memorial Encyclopaedia*, para. 383.
12 Presupposed as still competent in terms of the Housing (Scotland) Act 1987,
    s.72(7).

reform legislation[13] and as regards other contexts will probably be abolished generally as part of the reform of the law of real conditions proposed by the Scottish Law Commission.[14] The charging order is a fixed charge like the standard security, whereas a floating charge is not a fixed charge when created but it becomes a fixed charge when it "attaches" or "crystallizes"[15] by liquidation[16] or receivership.[17] Standard securities, floating charges and charging orders will be examined in order in this chapter. For completeness it should be noted that the method of constituting a security over a lease which is not a recordable lease (a "short" lease) remains an assignation in security.[18] This device is encountered relatively rarely in practice as it has the effect of imposing the obligations of the tenant on the creditor. As a result, a short lease is a relatively unattractive asset for the purposes of raising secured finance from a bank or other lender.

Standard Securities

A standard security is the primary form of heritable security in Scotland and, by far, is the most frequently encountered in practice. Standard securities did not exist at common law and have been competent only since 1970.[19] Very few securities in the older forms created prior to that date remain undischarged and they shall not be discussed in this book. The standard security is a "fixed" security but this term is intended to denote the fact that it relates to a particular secured plot of land and not the fact that it is inflexible.

The flexibility of a standard security may be seen in the range of obligations which it may secure. A standard security is a multi-purpose form of security which can secure obligations to pay money

11.3

---

13 Abolition of Feudal Tenure etc. (Scotland) Act 2000, s.13(2).

14 Chap. 9.

15 The two terms have identical meanings. The first term is used in statute but the latter is widely used. See 4 *Stair Memorial Encyclopaedia*, para. 659; Gretton and Reid, *supra* para. 28.09.

16 Companies Act 1985 (c.6), s.463(1), prospectively amended by Companies Act 1989 (c.40), s.140(1) from a day to be appointed under s.215(2). See 4 *Stair Memorial Encyclopaedia*, para. 659.

17 Insolvency Act 1986, s.53(7); *Forth & Clyde Construction Co. Ltd v. Trinity Timber & Plywood Co. Ltd*, 1984 S.C. 1 per Lord President Emslie at 10; *National Commercial Bank of Scotland Ltd v. Telford Grier Mackay & Co. Ltd Liquidators*, 1969 S.C. 181.

18 Registration of Leases (Scotland) Act 1857, s.4; 20 *Stair Memorial Encyclopaedia*, paras 256–262.

19 Conveyancing and Feudal Reform (Scotland) Act 1970 ("the 1970 Act").

and obligations *ad factum praestandum*.[20] There is no specific statutory reference to an obligation to refrain from doing something. The debt secured may be a present, future or contingent debt[21] and may be the debt of the granter of the security or of a third party.[22] The security may be for a fixed amount, an amount calculated according to a statutory formula[23] or, as is more common in practice, for all sums due or to become due.[24] Because a standard security is so flexible and may cover all these debts it is vital to ensure that the documentation governing the extent and nature of the debt secured is accurately drawn failing which arguments are inevitable.[25] Unlike a floating charge its competency is not limited by reference to the nature of the granter, and it is not limited to corporate borrowers.[26] Where, however, a standard security is granted by a company there are additional requirements as regards registration in the Companies Charges Register to be completed to ensure validity of the charge.[27]

A standard security is limited by reference to the nature of the security subjects—it may be used to create a security only over heritage, or more precisely only over an "interest in land". For the purposes of the Conveyancing and Feudal Reform (Scotland) Act 1970 ("the 1970 Act"), an "interest in land" is defined as meaning any estate or interest in land . . . which is capable of being owned or held as a separate interest and to which a title may be recorded in the Register of Sasines.[28] This definition will be updated in the light of feudal reform.[29] A standard security may be constituted over a right of property, a proper liferent, a standard security,[30] a

---

20 1970 Act, s.9(8)(c), definition of "debt". Many of the remedies afforded to a creditor are not well suited to a standard security in respect of the latter type of obligation.

21 An example of a security for a contingent debt is discount standard security in terms of Housing (Scotland) Act 1987, ss 72 and 73. See Cusine, *Standard Securities*, paras 4.41 and 10.06; Gretton and Reid, *Conveyancing* (2nd ed.), para. 30.12.

22 Gretton and Reid, *supra*, para. 20.05.

23 See, *e.g.*, Housing (Scotland) Act 1987, s.72(3).

24 Gretton and Reid, *supra*, para. 20.05.

25 See, *e.g. Societe General S.A. v. Lloyds TSB Bank plc*, 1999 G.W.D. 37–1822.

26 Para. 2.29.

27 Para. 3.20.

28 1970 Act, ss 9(8)(b) and 30(1).

29 Abolition of Feudal Reform (Scotland) Act 2000, s.76(1) and Sched. 12, para. 30(6)(d)(ii) and 30(16).

30 Cusine, *Standard Securities*, para. 4.03; Gretton and Reid, *Conveyancing* (2nd ed.), para. 20.16.

recordable lease (a "long" lease)[31] and a servitude but not separately from the dominant tenement.[32] It may not be created over a short lease.[33]

A standard security is a real right, but not of ownership. The granter of the security remains the owner of the secured subjects until either (a) he grants a voluntary conveyance to a disponee and it is recorded, (b) a disposition is recorded in favour of a purchaser acquiring from a creditor exercising a power of sale, or (c) a decree of foreclosure in favour of the creditor is recorded.[33a] Until he voluntarily acquires from the debtor by means of disposition or completes the process of foreclosure the secured creditor has a mere *ius in re aliena* and not a right of *dominium*. This has the advantage for the creditor in that he is not liable for the burdens of ownership except insofar as these have been imposed on him by virtue of statute.[34] By the same token the debtor retains all the liabilities and powers of owner except insofar as these are limited by the standard security or the statutory provisions governing standard securities.

Form of Standard Security

The deed creating the security cannot be in any form which the 11.4 debtor and creditor agree but it must be in one of the two prescribed forms, A and B, set out in Schedule 2 to the 1970 Act.[35] Precise adherence to the actual words of the prescribed forms is not absolutely essential.[36] Unfortunately the degree of permitted deviation is not made clear in the statute.[37] It is likely, however, that the words "standard security" will be regarded as essential in any clause of grant of a deed which purports to be a standard

---

31 These are generally leases for a period exceeding 20 years – Registration of Leases (Scotland) Act 1857, s.1. See, *e.g. Trade Development Bank v. Warriner and Mason (Scotland) Ltd*, 1980 S.C. 74; 1980 S.L.T. 223.
32 Halliday, *Conveyancing* (2nd ed.), Vol.2, para. 51–05(3); Cusine and Paisley, *Servitudes and Rights of Way*, para. 1.24.
33 A lease of a period up to and including 20 years.
33a The creditor may also become owner by proceeding with a course of action also open to unsecured creditors, an action of adjudication. See 18 *Stair Memorial Encyclopaedia*, para. 664(3).
34 1970 Act, s.20(5)(b). See paras 2.24 and 11.21.
35 1970 Act, s.9(2) and Sched.2.
36 1970 Act, s.53(1); Halliday, *Conveyancing Law and Practice* (2nd ed., 1997), Vol.2, para. 52–31; Gretton and Reid, *supra*, para. 20–03.
37 *Royal Bank of Scotland v. William and George Marshall*, Glasgow Sheriff Court, Sheriff Gerald Gordon, Q.C. (unreported); Begg, *The Conveyancing Code*, p. 48; Cusine, *Standard Securities*, paras 4.36 and 8.10.

security. A particular description of the secured subjects is no longer an essential.[38]

Form A is a combined personal obligation to repay the debt and a grant of security. Form B is a grant of security used where the personal obligation to repay is constituted in a separate deed. Form B is used more frequently in commercial situations[39] because the loan contract is not recorded in any public register and the parties may retain a degree of confidentiality about their dealings.[40]

Standard Conditions

11.5   Both statutory forms of standard security are admirably short. This is possible because 1970 Act, Sched. 3, sets out standard conditions that are automatically imported into any standard security unless altered or varied.[41] Express provision is made to adapt the statutory standard conditions where the debtor is not proprietor of the security subjects.[42]

It has been stated that the idea behind the statutory standard conditions is to provide "a sort of ready made contract to save people the bother of making their own".[43] To this extent they can be compared with the standard form of articles of association in company law or the management scheme comprised in the reform of the law of the tenement proposed by the Scottish Law Commission.[44] If, however, the aim of the statutory standard conditions was to save paper it has signally failed. In practice in all cases where a standard security is granted and quite regardless of whether the statutory standard conditions are wholly unvaried or varied beyond recognition, a copy of the statutory standard conditions is delivered by the creditor to the borrower (and granter if different). The aim here is to deny any possibility that the debtor or other granter can argue he did not know the nature of the arrangement into which he was entering. Indeed, some banks insert into their loan instructions a specific requirement that their

---

38 Abolition of Feudal Tenure etc. (Scotland) Act 2000, s.77(3) and Sched. 12, para. 30(23)(a), reversing *Bennett v. Beneficial Bank*, 1995 S.L.T. 1105; 1995 S.C.L.R. 284; *Beneficial Bank v. McConnachie*, 1996 S.L.T. 413; 1996 S.C.L.R. 438.

39 Gretton and Reid, *Conveyancing*, para. 20.03.

40 Paisley, "*Development Sites, Interdicts and the Risks of Adverse Title Conditions*", 1997 S.L.P.Q. 249–273 at 267.

41 1970 Act, s.11(2).

42 1970 Act, Sched. 3, "Interpretation".

43 Gretton and Reid, *supra*, p. 311.

44 Scot. Law Com., *Report on the Law of the Tenement* (No.162, Mar. 1998). See Chap. 9.

solicitors confirm prior to drawdown that a copy has been handed to the borrower and require sight of a receipt from the borrower to this effect. One reason may be the fear that the statutory standard conditions and those varied in so far as permitted by statute are a complete code governing the legal relationship between the debtor and creditor. The legal profession have clearly adopted the "safety first" approach.[44a]

Functions of Standard Conditions

Broadly speaking the statutory standard conditions can be 11.6 divided into two classes according to their function. These are:

(a) the maintenance of the value of the security subjects prior to enforcement of the security; and
(b) the realisation of the value of the security subjects upon enforcement of the security and the freeing of the creditor of expenses.

Conditions Relevant to Maintenance of Value

Into the first class falls standard conditions 1–6 which contain the 11.7 practical obligations on the proprietor to maintain the security subjects and to refrain from activity which might destroy it. They also require the proprietor to comply with certain legal obligations such as title conditions and to refrain from exercising certain legal powers (such as the granting of leases) which might diminish the value of the security subjects. In summary these are as follows:

(a) Standard condition 1 places obligations on the debtor to maintain the security subjects in good and sufficient repair to the reasonable satisfaction of the creditor. The debtor is obliged to permit the creditor or his agent to enter upon the security subjects at all reasonable times to examine their condition. The creditor is obliged to give seven clear days' notice in writing. The repairs and maintenance must be carried out within such reasonable period as the creditor may by notice in writing require.
(b) Standard condition 2 requires the debtor to complete as soon as practicable any uncompleted buildings and works to the reasonable satisfaction of the creditor. Normally where a creditor lends on the security of uncompleted subjects there

---

44a *Hambros Bank Ltd v. Lloyds Bank plc*, 1998 S.L.T. 49; *Trade Development Bank v. Warriner and Mason (Scotland) Limited*, 1990 S.C. 74 at 107 *per* Lord Kissen.

will be a provision in the loan documentation to permit staged drawdowns upon certification of the works having been properly carried out. The debtor is obliged not to demolish or alter any existing buildings without the prior written consent of the creditor. The debtor is also required to obtain any statutory consent or licence appropriate to such demolition, alteration or addition and exhibit them to the creditor. There is no such express requirement to exhibit consents or licences relative to the completion of uncompleted buildings or works but the creditor will be able to insist on this as part of the general requirement to complete the buildings and works to his reasonable satisfaction. Frequently the standard condition is varied to this effect and the variation extends to an obligation not to apply for any statutory licence or consent without the consent of the creditor.

(c) Standard condition 3 obliges the debtor to comply with any condition or perform any obligation in respect of the security subjects lawfully binding on him in relation to the security subjects. This extends to compliance with all relevant real conditions and servitudes. The debtor must make due and punctual payment of all rates, taxes and other public burdens and other payments exigible in respect of the security subjects. He must also comply with any requirement imposed on him in relation to the security subjects by virtue of any enactment.

(d) Standard condition 4 relates to notices or orders under the Town and Country Planning (Scotland) legislation and proposals thereof received by the debtor. It obliges the debtor to give the creditor a copy of any such notice within 14 days of receipt of a copy. The debtor is obliged to comply with such notice or, as the case may be, to object thereto. The debtor is obliged to object or join with the creditor in objecting to any such notice if required by the creditor and to make representations if required by the creditor. The standard condition applies not only to planning notices etc. but also "any other notice or document affecting or likely to affect the security subjects". In commercial situations this condition is frequently amended to include a specific reference to notices under other statutes relating to matters as diverse as fire precautions and health and safety at work.

(e) Standard condition 5 obliges the debtor to insure the security subjects or to permit the creditor to insure it in the names of the creditor and the debtor to the extent of the "market value" thereof against the risk of fire and such other risks as the creditor may reasonably require. Frequently this is varied to require the debtor to insure for the reinstatement value. Where the security subjects include items of a special nature such as salmon fishings, the risks insured against will be varied to include matters such as water pollution rather than destruction by fire. The condition contains detailed provisions concerning the deposit of the insurance policy with the creditor, payment of any insurance premium by the debtor, intimation of claims, compliance with the requirements of the creditor as regards the application of sums received in respect of a claim, and a general obligation on the debtor to refrain from any act or omission which would invalidate the policy. Despite the detail in the statutory form of the condition, the common practice in modern secured lending is to delete this condition altogether and for the creditor to substitute a lengthy clause relative to insurance. As a standard security is not a security over moveables the standard conditions do not impose any requirement to insure the contents of a house or other building: that is a matter for the debtor.

(f)   Standard condition 6 requires the proprietor of the security subjects not to let or agree to let the security subjects without the consent of the heritable creditor. There is no requirement that the consent should not be unreasonably withheld. In practice this is commonly extended in deeds of variation to exclude the sharing of occupancy. Where a company is the borrower there is often a relaxation to permit leasing to companies within the same group as the borrower provided the terms of the lease are approved by the creditor. After the creation of the standard security if the proprietor of the security subjects grants a lease without the consent of the heritable creditor that lease may be reduced by the heritable creditor.[45] A particularly difficult issue arises in relation to grants of assured tenancies without the consent of the heritable creditor. In terms of the legislation conferring security of tenure on the tenant in such a tenancy[46] (and such legislation significantly post-dates the 1970 Act) the sheriff shall not make an order for possession of a house let on an assured tenancy except on one or more of grounds set out in the legislation.[47]

---

45 *Trade Development Bank v. Warriner and Mason (Scotland) Ltd*, 1980 S.C. 74; *Trade Development Bank v. David W. Haig (Bellshill) Ltd*, 1983 S.L.T. 510; *Trade Development bank v. Crittall Windows Ltd*, 1983 S.L.T. 510.

46 Housing (Scotland) Act 1988, s.18.

47 1988 Act, Sched. 5.

One of the grounds set out in the legislation is that a tenant may be removed where there is a pre-existing standard security which is being enforced and the tenant had advance notice of its existence. In practice, where a debtor does not seek the consent of the creditor to the lease he will not bother to apprise the prospective tenant of the existence of the security. Although the standard security is recorded in a public register it does not appear to be sufficient for the tenant to be deemed to have knowledge of the contents of that register.[48] A tenant who has not received such notice may be granted interim interdict against the creditor preventing eviction[49] but the matter has not yet been fully litigated.

Conditions Relevant to Enforcement of Security

11.8 Into the second class fall the conditions about the various remedies available to the creditor such as power of sale, power of lease, power to maintain the security subjects, etc. These are standard conditions 7–11. Standard condition 12 cannot readily be classified in this group as it relates to the extent of sums secured. Nevertheless, as standard condition 12 makes provision, *inter alia*, for the securing of expenses incurred by the creditor in relation to a number of matters including creation and realisation of the standard security it may conveniently be dealt with here. In summary these are as follows:

(a) Standard condition 7 confers on the creditor a general power to perform obligations imposed on the debtor in terms of the standard conditions on the failure of the debtor and to charge the debtor for the costs in so doing. Where necessary for the performance of any such obligation the creditor may enter upon the security subjects at all reasonable times after giving seven clear days' notice in writing to the debtor. Unusually this standard condition does not refer specifically to the right of entry being capable of exercise by the creditor's agent (and in this regard there is an inconsistency with standard condition 1(b)) but the rights of the creditor to have his agents enter the subjects for this purpose is generally taken to be implied. In any event the matter is usually addressed in lengthy variations

---

48 *Cf.* the deemed intimation to a landlord where an assignation of a lease is recorded in the Sasine Register or registered in the Land Register of Scotland see para. 3.18.

49 *Tamroui v. Clydesdale Bank plc*, 1996 S.C.L.R. 732n; 1997 S.L.T. (Sh.Ct.) 20; *Cameron v. Abbey National plc*, 1999 Hous. L.R. 19 (Sh.Ct.).

of the standard condition which are common in modern practice. The right of the creditor to recover from the debtor all expenses and charges incurred (including interest thereon) is preserved by this condition and such sums are deemed to be secured by the standard security.

(b) Standard condition 8 entitles the creditor to call up the security in conformity with the statutory procedure and any require-ments of law in the manner prescribed in the 1970 Act.[50]

(c) Standard condition 9 sets out the circumstances in which a debtor will be in default. They include (i) where a calling-up notice has been served in respect of the security subjects and not complied with; (ii) where there has been a failure to comply with any other requirement arising out of the security; and (iii) where the proprietor of the security subjects has become insolvent.

(d) Standard condition 10 lists some of the rights of the creditor on default. These include sale, entry into possession and uplifiting of rents, leasing of the security subjects, management of the security subjects, effecting repairs, and application for a decree of foreclosure. These will be examined more fully later in this chapter.

(e) Standard condition 11 governs the exercise by the debtor of a right of redemption. This shall be outlined below.[51]

(f) Standard condition 12 renders the debtor personally liable to the creditor for the whole expenses of the preparation and execution of the standard security and any variation, restric-tion and discharge thereof and the recording dues of any deeds, all expenses reasonably incurred in calling up the security and exercising the powers conferred on the creditor in the security.[52]

Variation of the Standard Conditions

"Variation" in relation to real burdens and contracts has a 11.9 number of meanings. The most common meaning denotes some-thing which frequently occurs after the parties have entered into a contract or real condition. Where parties to a contract or a real condition agree to the terms thereof those terms cannot be altered without mutual consent unless one party reserves the right to vary all or part thereof. In rare cases this meaning of variation has

---

50 Para. 11.17.
51 Para. 11.23.
52 See *Clydesdale Bank plc v. Mowbray*, 1999 G.W.D. 40–1951.

relevance to standard conditions in a standard security where the creditor inserts an additional standard condition reserving to itself the right to vary the terms of the agreement entered into with the debtor. Such a clause appears to be competent (within its terms) and is commonly found in relation to the particular issue of the rate of interest chargeable on a loan but it may be dangerous for a debtor to accept such a clause which applies generally in that it would confer on the creditor a right to re-write the whole deal. In the context of standard conditions, however, the term "variation" generally denotes something more fundamental but less dangerous to the debtor. The term relates to the terms upon which the law will allow the parties to contract. The limitations on variation restrict the permissible alterations which the creditor and debtor can make, even if they agree, to the standard conditions in a standard security whether at the time of initial grant or any time thereafter. In short, the "variation" of standard conditions generally relates to limitations on permissible content of standard conditions and it is in that sense that the term is used in the 1970 Act.

It was recognised from the outset that untrammeled variation of the standard conditions would act to the prejudice of many debtors. This would be particularly the case in relation to many purchasers of residential property as they are in a relatively poor negotiating position compared to the lender. A bank does not usually ask the borrower for suggestions as to what should be included in the contract of loan or the security documentation. "The borrower is . . . presented with a contract of adhesion – take it or leave it. In the context of residential conveyancing there is virtually no possibility of negotiation of terms".[53] The danger to borrowers is that the parties are free to vary, supplement or exclude this statutory code of standard conditions as they wish except in certain respects and this leaves open the possibility that the bank or other lender will prepare a lengthy document loaded in its favour.

11.10   There may be one implied limitation on conventional variation in that it may be argued that any new standard conditions inserted by variation must resemble the content of the statutory standard conditions. That, however, is a nebulous idea which has not prevented the enthusiasm of lenders in recent years to overload deeds of variation with a multiplicity of new standard conditions. One would surmise, however, that to be valid as a standard condition it would require to relate to the security subjects, the maintenance of value thereof and the realisation of that value and

---

53 Gretton and Reid, *Conveyancing* (2nd ed.), para. 20.04

not irrelevant matters such as the personal behaviour of the debtor.[54] The generality of the restriction offers little guidance, but there are indications that conventional variations to standard conditions may impose greater restrictions on juristic acts than are permissible in real burdens. Statutory standard condition 6 is frequently expanded to prohibit grants of leases, servitudes and other subordinate real rights. To protect borrowers from the worst effects of freedom of contract certain standard conditions are declared by statute to be incapable of variation. Freedom of contract, however, is essential to protect the flexibility of a standard security and where a standard condition is not stated to be incapable of variation it remains variable. The invariable conditions are as follows:

(a) The statutory standard conditions relative to sale and foreclosure of the subjects may not be varied[55] nor may any other standard condition be varied to conflict with these standard conditions in their unvaried form and any such purported variation is void and unenforceable.[56] It may be possible that the standard conditions relating to sale and foreclosure can be altered in a way that is more favourable to the debtor or proprietor.[57] So far as is known no bank or other major lender has taken this step.[58]

(b) A more general limitation on the power of variation of the standard conditions is the provision that the power of variation is subject to the provisions of Part II of the 1970 Act.[59] This provision creates a wider class of standard conditions which cannot be varied and the exact limits of the class can be difficult to ascertain. Certainly this would render null any attempt to vary the standard conditions so that a creditor in lawful possession has a power to lease the security subjects for more than seven years without the consent of the court.[60]

(c) Originally the standard condition relative to procedure on

---

54 *Cf.* the limitations on the content of real conditions burdening land in favour of a neighbouring plot of land discussed in paras 9.10 and 9.11.

55 1970 Act, s.11(3).

56 1970 Act, s.11(4)(b).

57 Halliday, *The Conveyancing and Feudal Reform (Scotland) Act 1970* (2nd ed.), para. 8–07; Halliday, *Conveyancing Law and Practice* (2nd ed.), para. 53–06.

58 Cusine, *Standard Securities* (1991), para. 5.02.

59 1970 Act, s.11(3).

60 This would conflict with 1970 Act, s.20(3). See para. 11.22.

redemption could not be varied.[61] This caused difficulty in the lending market and has been altered on two occasions with the result that this standard condition may be varied[62] except in relation to a standard security executed after September 1, 1974 over security subjects used as or as part of a private dwellinghouse.[63] In the case of securities over private dwellinghouses executed after that date no variation may exclude the right of the debtor to redeem the security in exchange for a sum not exceeding a figure calculated according to a statutory formula upon giving two months' notice at any time not less than 20 years after the execution of the security.[64] Although this exception is most frequently to be encountered in the domestic purchase situation the statutory provisions are not limited to domestic lending: rather they apply where the property is used for residential purposes. Thus they will apply where the lender is funding a party who in turn lets out the property for residential use such as a commercial residential home, student accommodation or a tenement let out to families.

Ranking

11.11   A standard security is a real right affecting an "interest in land". It is possible for there to be more than one heritable security affecting the one "interest in land".[65] Frequently the standard conditions are varied so that the proprietor is prohibited from granting a second security over the subjects without the creditor's prior written consent. If the proprietor breaches this condition he will be in default and the creditor may call up the loan. In addition it is possible that the second security may be set aside by the creditor in the first security.[66]

Where more than one security is granted over the same property the issue of ranking arises. The starting position is the common law rule governing all real rights *prior tempore potior jure* meaning

---

61 1970 Act, s.11(3).
62 1970 Act, s.18(1A), added by Redemption of Standard Securities (Scotland) Act 1971, s.1.
63 Conveyancing and Feudal Reform (Scotland) Act 1974, ss 11 and 24(2).
64 1974 Act, s.11(2).
65 Paras 2.11 and 2.12.
66 The matter remains somewhat obscure: see Gretton and Reid, *Conveyancing* (2nd ed.), para. 20.08, fn. 23 where the whole area of law is described as "very difficult". *Cf. Trade Development Bank v. Warriner and Mason (Scotland) Ltd*, 1980 S.C. 74.

earlier by time, stronger by right.[67] In a competition between standard securities an earlier recording date gives a priority of ranking.[68] The debtor and creditors may make such alternative provision as to ranking as they think fit by means of a ranking agreement.[69] They may even reverse the common law provision entirely and agree that a security created second will rank prior to the first security. In some cases, such as discount standard securities, statute makes special provision for ranking.[70]

A potential problem exists if the first security is a security granted   11.12 not for a fixed sum but for all sums due or to become due and after the second security is granted the first creditor lends further sums. If the first security had an unlimited priority in such a case the loan of the further sums could render the second security worthless if they, together with the sums already loaned by the first creditor, added up to the whole valuation of the property. Protection against this possibility is given to the second security holder by statute.[71] Where the creditor in the first standard security receives notice[72] of the creation of a subsequent security over the same interest in land or part thereof the preference in ranking of the security shall be restricted to security for:

(a) his present advances;
(b) future advances which he may be required to make under the contract to which the security relates;
(c) interest present or future on such present or future advances (including any such interest which has accrued or may accrue); and
(d) any expenses or outlays (including interest thereon) which may be, or may have been, reasonably incurred in the exercise of any power conferred on any creditor by the deed expressing the existing security.

There remains some controversy about the position of a first security holder who makes a further advance after receiving notice of the creation of a second security. There is no clear answer as to whether the further advance is wholly unsecured or, alternatively, is

---

67 Para. 3.17.
68 Gretton and Reid, *supra*, para. 20.21.
69 1970 Act, s.13(3)(b); Cusine, *Standard Securities*, para. 7.03.
70 Housing (Scotland) Act 1987, s.72(5) and (6).
71 1970 Act, s.13.
72 The notice required is actual knowledge, and constructive knowledge arising from the recording of the second security in a public register is insufficient. There is no statutory form of such notice.

secured but ranks after the second security.[73] In practice, the creditor who makes the new advance will seek a new security to be created in his favour.

Ranking and Floating Charges

11.13   Where an item of heritable property is subject to a standard security and a floating charge the creditors and the company borrower may make provision as to ranking in a ranking agreement. Failing the existence of a ranking agreement, in a competition with a floating charge, a standard security will prevail provided it has been "constituted as a real right" before the crystallisation of the floating charge.[74] A floating charge may contain a prohibition or restriction, known as a "negative pledge", on creating a fixed security or other floating charge.[75] In such a case the creditor obtaining a standard security will seek the consent of the creditor in the floating charge to the creation of the standard security but such consent merely waives the negative pledge and does not, *per se*, constitute a ranking agreement to the effect of giving the standard security priority over the floating charge.[76]

Drafting Postponed Securities

11.14   A postponed standard security will rank according to the rules discussed above.[77] Statute provides that where a postponed standard security is granted it should refer to the prior security and repeat this statement in the warrandice clause.[78] Such a provision is useful where the two securities are being granted at the one time as it then does not matter whether the two securities are registered on the same day or whether the postponed security is registered first. The exception from warrandice also protects the

---

73 G.L. Gretton, "*Ranking of Heritable Creditors*", 1980 J.L.S.S. 275; J.M. Halliday, "*Ranking of Heritable Creditors*", 1981 J.L.S.S. 26 and 31; G.L. Gretton, "*Ranking of Heritable Creditors*", 1991 J.L.S.S. 280; Gretton and Reid, *Conveyancing* (2nd ed.), para. 20.21.

74 Companies Act 1985, s.484(3), (4)(b).

75 Companies Act 1985, s.464(1) and (1A) prospectively added by the Companies Act 1989, s.140(4); *AIB Finance Ltd v. Bank of Scotland*, 1993 S.C. 588; 1995 S.L.T. 2; Gretton and Reid, *supra*, para. 28.12.

76 *Bank of Scotland v. Bass Brewers Ltd*, June 1, 2000, Lord Macfadyen, O.H. (unreported); *Griffith and Powdill, Petrs.*, Nov. 13, 1998, Lord Cameron of Lochbroom, O.H. (unreported).

77 Paras 11.11–11.12.

78 1970 Act, Sched. 2, n. 5.

proprietor from a claim by the postponed creditor that his position has been diminished by the existence of the prior ranking security.

Land Obligations

The 1970 Act had two basic purposes. The First Part of the Act 11.15 conferred on the Lands Tribunal a right to vary and discharge "land obligations".[79] The Second Part created the device of standard security. The interaction between the two parts of the statute is rarely examined but, at least in theory, the First Part of the statute has a direct impact upon the Second. The definition of a "land obligation" contained in the Act is a broad one.[80] It is commonly recognised that this definition comprises real conditions created in leases, feu dispositions, and servitudes[81] but it is less commonly recognised that the definition may also extend to standard conditions in standard securities.[82] A standard condition may be viewed as a form of real condition enforceable by the creditor in the standard security and his successors who are entitled to the creditor's rights. It is also enforceable against the proprietor and his successors in title. It may therefore fall within the definition of "land obligation" and may be varied by the Lands Tribunal in terms of 1970 Act, Pt I.[83] This matter is rendered largely academic by the fact that many standard securities state that the loan is payable "on demand". This clause may be at variance with what clients understand to be the case and lenders who use this clause do not normally mean to rely on it.[84] In any event, if the lender is using a Form A (a security which contains the loan contract), such a clause will be implied unless excluded.[85] If a borrower were to attempt to have any of the standard conditions varied by reference to the Lands Tribunal the lender would probably respond by calling up the loan.

---

79 Chap. 9.
80 1970 Act, s.1(2).
81 Para. 9.32.
82 18 *Stair Memorial Encyclopaedia*, para. 351.
83 For details see *Trade Development Bank v. Warriner and Mason (Scotland) Ltd*, 1980 S.C. 74 at 107; K.G.C. Reid, *Real Conditions in Standard Securities*, 1983 S.L.T. (News) 169 and 189.
84 Gretton and Reid, *Conveyancing* (2nd ed.), para. 20.09.
85 1970 Act, s.10.

Contractual Rights

11.16   A standard security is not only a security, but is also a contract
between the debtor and proprietor. To this extent the document is
similar to a disposition the terms of which may create real rights but
also constitute a contract between the parties.[86] The contractual
rights arise when the deed is executed and delivered. The real right
in a standard security arises only when the security is recorded in
the General Register of Sasines or registered in the Land Register of
Scotland as the case may be.[87] This gives rise to the possibility of
the application of the "offside goals" rule if a second standard
security is granted after the first standard security and is recorded
before it.[88] The application of this rule to standard conditions is still
developing but a small body of recently decided case law indicates
that the rule is not to be applied to rescue the position of the holder
of the standard security granted first but recorded second.[89] In the
light of this it is vital that a standard security is recorded as swiftly
as practicable and certainly within the time-limit of any letter of
obligation granted by the debtor's solicitor.[90]

In some cases a creditor may be perfectly satisfied with a
contractual remedy against the debtor knowing that it is not a real
obligation provided the underlying security is a real right. The
reason for this is that it is relatively unusual for the debtor or
creditor's interest to be transferred whilst the standard security is
extant. The creditor may be prepared to insert into a variation of
the standard conditions a right which clearly could not be a real
condition but which may be extremely useful whilst the debtor
remains solvent and has not been sequestrated (or, if a company,
subject to the appointment of a receiver, liquidator or administrator). Examples of this which have become very common in
modern practice are the following two types of clauses:

(a)   A statement in a deed of variation of standard conditions that
the creditor shall have a power to dispose of any moveables in
the security subjects.[91] Not being heritable, these objects are

---

86   18 *Stair Memorial Encyclopaedia*, para. 392.
87   Paras 3.17–3.20.
88   Para. 3.30. Similar problems arise with a floating charge granted after the
delivery of the standard security but before its recording.
89   *Scotlife Home Loans (No.2) Ltd v. Muir*, 1994 S.C.L.R. 791 (Sh Ct); *Scotlife
Home Loans (No.2) Ltd v. A. J. Bruce*, Sh.P. J.J. Maguire Q.C., Sept. 4, 1994
(unreported), overruling the sheriff's judgment of 17 June 1994 (Dunfermline
Sheriff Court unreported). See also *Leslie v. McIndoe's Trs* (1824) 3 S. 48.
90   Paras 3.27 and 3.28.
91   Cusine, *Standard Securities*, para. 5.25.

clearly not part of the security subjects and cannot be sold by
the creditor as part of his power of sale.[92] The creditor will not,
however, wish the sale price obtainable for the security subjects
to be depressed by the presence of large amounts of useless
stock, rubbish or furniture within the security subjects nor will
he wish to have to store the material and call upon the debtor
to remove it. In recent years debtors have sought to use the
method of disposal of moveables as a ground to sue the
creditor. A well-drafted clause may assist the creditor in
avoiding becoming embroiled in such litigation which, for
them, is largely a waste of time.[93]

b) The "agency" clause which has crept into many modern deeds
of variation of standard conditions. This confers on the
creditor an "irrevocable power of attorney" to do all things
including legal acts which the debtor might competently do.
Clearly this includes a power of sale and to the extent that it
purports to vary the standard condition on sale it is invalid. To
the extent that it contravenes statutory limitations it is
probably invalid both as a contract and a real obligation but
insofar as it remains valid it may be very useful and assist in
filling the gaps between the various specific obligations created
in the standard conditions and the variations. In short, it is
used as a "sweeper" power to deal with unexpected issues.

Default

In respect of a standard security a debtor will be deemed to be in   11.17
default in three situations. These are (a) where a calling-up notice
has been served but not complied with; (b) where there has been a
failure to comply with any other requirement arising out of the
security; and (c) where the proprietor of the security subjects
becomes insolvent.[94] Where a debtor is in default a court has no
option but to grant warrant to the creditor to exercise the remedies

---

[92] A power of sale may be obtained if the creditor has resorted to the diligence of
poinding of the ground but this is rare in domestic situations. It may be
worthwhile in commercial situations where the heritable subjects are occupied by
a business such as a farm or pub with a lot of stock.

[93] See, *e.g.*, *Gemmell v. Bank of Scotland*, 1998 S.C.L.R. 144; *Harris v. Abbey
National*, 1996 Hous. L.R. 100.

[94] 1970 Act, Sched.3, S.C. 9(1).

in standard condition 10.[95] It may be, however, that the heritable creditor may be directed in the manner of sale by the court but not prevented from selling.[96]

Remedies on Default

11.18   There are a number of different remedies open to a creditor in a standard security on the debtor's default but many of these remedies are rarely encountered in practice and are of theoretical interest only. In the vast majority of cases the creditor will simply wish to enter into possession and sell.[97] In addition there is some inconsistency in the 1970 Act as standard condition 10 gives a variety of powers stated to arise "where the debtor is in default" this is contradicted by the body of the Act which does not allow all of these powers on default.[98] In addition the Act uses the word "default" in different ways and there is some controversy about exactly what it is supposed to mean in different contexts.[99] Where there is more than one security extant over the subjects the exercise of the remedies under any of the securities may be restricted by a creditors' agreement entered into between the various creditors. Such an agreement is not intended to augment or vary the rights of the debtor but is restricted to regulating the rights of the creditors *inter se*. It may have more radical effects than a ranking agreement. Provided the creditors' agreement is suitably drafted a particular creditor may find that he is precluded from exercising certain remedies without the consent of the other or, at best, restricted in exercising those remedies until he has consulted with or given notice to the other creditor. There is no statutory form for such an agreement but certain styles are recognised in practice.

---

95 *United Dominion Trust Ltd v. Site Preparations Ltd (No.1)*, 1978 S.L.T. (Sh.Ct.) 14; Jamieson "*Creditors' Remedies under a Standard Security*", 1989 S.L.T. (News) 201; Parker Hood, "*The Duties of the Standard Security Holder*" (1994) 39 J.L.S.S. 257; Guthrie, "*Controlling Creditors' Rights under Standard Securities*", 1994 S.L.T. (News) 93; Urquhart, "*Enforcing Standard Securities*", 1995 40 J.L.S.S. 400. *Cf. Armstrong, Petr.*, 1988 S.L.T. 255. See the discussion in Cusine, *Standard Securities*, para. 8.25.

96 Cusine, *Standard Securities*, para. 8.25 on the authority of *Beveridge v. Wilson* (1829) 7S. 279.

97 Gretton and Reid, *Conveyancing* (2nd ed.), para. 20.28.

98 Gretton and Reid, *supra*, para. 20.29, fn. 70.

99 Cusine, *Standard Securities*, para. 8.14; Gretton and Reid, *supra*, para. 20.29.

Power of Sale

The creditor's primary remedy is the power to sell the security 11.19
subjects.[1] The creditor may obtain a power of sale by three different
routes. These are (a) calling up; (b) notice of default; and (c)
section-24 application. Sale may be by private bargain or by
exposure to sale by means of public roup (auction). However he
obtains the power of sale the creditor is under an obligation to take
all reasonable steps to ensure that the price at which all or any of
the subjects are sold is the best that can be reasonably obtained.[2]
For the details of the procedures leading to a power of sale and
consequences of the best price obligation on conveyancing practice
the reader is directed to the undernoted textbooks.[3]

The aim of selling is clearly that the creditor should be able to lay
his hands on the proceeds of sale and put them towards satisfaction
of the debt due to him. In the vast majority of cases in a forced sale,
the proceeds of sale will not cover the whole debt which will remain
outstanding but unsecured. The debtor remains liable for that
balance. Where a standard security is granted in respect of an
obligation *ad factum praestandum* (such as the obligation to sell
land to a creditor who has exercised an option to purchase land) it
is not clear, should there be default, how the proceeds of sale are to
be applied by the creditor in satisfaction of the obligation which has
been breached. The most convincing explanation appears to be that
the proceeds of sale may be used to satisfy the contingent monetary
debt comprising the claim for damages which arises from the
default.[4] The distribution of the proceeds of sale is dealt with in
statute and this provides as follows.[5] The creditor holds the
proceeds in trust for payment in the following order:

(a)   to pay all expenses properly incurred by the creditor in
      connection with the sale or any attempted sale;

(b)   to pay the whole amount due under any prior security to which
      the sale is not made subject;

(c)   to pay the whole amount due under the standard security and
      to pay, in due proportion, the whole amount due under a duly

---

1   1970 Act, Sched. 3, S.C. 10(2).
2   1970 Act, s.25; *Bisset v. Standard Property Investment plc*, 1999 G.W.D. 26–1253.
3   Cusine, *Standard Securities*, Chap. 8; Gretton and Reid, *supra*, paras 20.28–
    20.31.
4   G. Gretton, *"The concept of a Security"* in *A Scots Conveyancing Miscellany:
    Essays in Honour of Professor J M Halliday*, 126–151 at 129; Cusine, *Standard
    Securities*, para. 4.04; Gretton and Reid *Conveyancing*, (2nd ed.), para. 20.05.
5   1970 Act, s.27.

recorded security, if any, ranking pari passu with the securit
in respect of which the power of sale is exercised;

(d) to pay amounts due under postponed ranking securitie
according to their ranking; and

(e) to pay the residue to the person entitled to the security subjects

11.20 Despite its apparent clarity this provision is not easy to apply i
practice.[6] In complex cases many creditors will resort to an actio
of multiple poinding to determine the proper distribution of th
funds.

Entering into Possession

11.21   The remedy of entering into possession is available to a creditor i
(a) a calling-up notice has not been complied with or (b) the debto
is in default by reason of failure to comply with some othe
requirement arising from the security and the court has grante
warrant to the creditor to enter into possession.[7] The power to ente
into possession of the security subjects is the second most importan
remedy of the heritable creditor.[8] When a creditor has entered int
possession he has effective control of the subjects and does not ru
the risk of a debtor in possession causing deterioration to th
subjects or putting off potential purchasers by difficult behaviour
Entering into possession is the precondition for the exercise of tw
additional remedies, namely, the power to let the security subjects
and the right to uplift rents in any extant leases of the securit
subjects.[10] Entering into possession is not a precondition of th
power to effect repairs and making good defects as are necessary t
maintain the security subjects in good and sufficient repair or t
carry out such reconstruction, alteration and improvement on th
subjects as would be expected of a prudent proprietor to maintai
the market value of the subjects. In respect of these matters th
creditor has a separate power to enter on the subjects at al
reasonable times.[11] Nevertheless if the works required are extensiv
it is difficult to see a creditor wishing to carry them out withou
entering into possession. In many cases a creditor will enter int

---

6   See, *e.g.*, *Halifax Building Society v. Smith*, 1985 S.L.T. (Sh.Ct.) 25; *Bas.
     Breweries Ltd v. Humberclyde Finance Group Ltd*, 1996 G.W.D. 19–1076.
7   *Abbey National plc v. Arthur*, 2000 S.L.T. 103.
8   1970 Act, Sched. 3, S.C. 10(3).
9   1970 Act, s.20(3) and Sched. 3, S.C. 10(4).
10   1970 Act, Sched. 3, S.C. 10(5). See *UCB Bank plc v. Hire Foulis Ltd*, 1999 S.C
     250.
11   1970 Act, Sched. 3, S.C. 10(6).

possession by arrangement with the debtor (and the powers of the creditor in such case may be restricted by any agreement then entered into) but in a small minority of cases it will be necessary to take proceedings to dispossess the debtor.[12] The potential for liability arising from real conditions may discourage the heritable creditor from entering into possession.[13] Where a title to security subjects is burdened by real conditions requiring the building to be maintained in a good state of repair but it is in obvious disrepair, a lender may wish to assess his potential liability by instructing a survey before entering into possession. It is an open question whether the mere ejection of the borrower, the changing of the locks, the putting up of "for sale" signs and the accompanying of potential purchasers around the subjects as part of the marketing of the subjects amounts to the entering into of lawful possession.

Other Remedies

The creditor's other remedies include: 11.22

(a) once possession has been obtained, the power to let the security subjects. Leases over seven years' endurance require the sanction of the court[14];

(b) once possession has been obtained, the right to uplift rents in any extant leases of the security subjects[15];

(c) the power to effect repairs to the security subjects[16];

(d) the power to apply to the court for a decree of foreclosure[17]. This is a remedy which is not frequently exercised.[18] The remedy of foreclosure enables a creditor who has failed to find a purchaser for the security subjects at a price sufficient to cover the amount due to the creditor to take title to the security subjects rather than sell them at a lower price. The right may be exercised only where the creditor has exposed the security subjects for sale by public roup at a price not exceeding the sum due under the security and any prior ranking security or one ranking *pari passu* and has failed to find a purchaser. The

---

12 *Clydesdale Bank plc v. Davidson*, 1996 S.L.T. 437.
13 1970 Act, s.20(5)(b); *David Watson Property Management Ltd v. Woolwich Equitable Building Society*, 1992 S.C. (H.L.) 21.
14 1970 Act, Sched. 3, S.C. 10(4).
15 1970 Act, s.20(3) and Sched. 3, S.C. 10(5).
16 1970 Act, Sched. 3, S.C. 10(6).
17 1970 Act, s.28 and Sched. 3, S.C. 10(7).
18 It is stated to be "extremely rare" in Gretton and Reid, *Conveyancing* (2nd ed.), para. 20.31

sale of a part of the security subjects for less than this price will not prevent the exercise of foreclosure in respect of the remainder. An attempt to achieve a private bargain is insufficient. Two months must have elapsed from the first exposure to sale. The recording or registration of the extract of the decree of foreclosure has four effects. First, it extinguishes any right of redemption. Secondly, it vests the security subjects in the creditor—he becomes the proprietor in place of the proprietor granting the security.[19] Thirdly, it disburdens the subjects of the standard security and all postponed securities and diligences. Fourthly, it gives the creditor the same right as the debtor to redeem prior or *pari passu* ranking securities. The personal obligation of the debtor remains in full force to the extent of any excess still owing over and above the value at which the property is deemed to be taken over[20];

(e)   all remedies available to the debtor arising from the contract of loan.[21]

Redemption

11.23   The debtor and the proprietor of the security subjects, if different, each has a right to redeem the standard security upon giving two months notice in a statutory form.[22] This right is subject to "any agreement to the contrary".[23] The parties to the security may agree that the loan will subsist for a fixed period or that there should be a different period of notice.[24] The creditor may waive the necessity for notice or agree to a period of notice less than that to which he is entitled.[25] If the creditor has not waived notice, or agreed to a shorter period of notice, he cannot be obliged to accept redemption other than in terms of the standard security and loan agreement.[26] Such an agreement may contain a penalty clause which may be enforceable if it is reasonable.[27] However the procedure for redemption cannot be varied.[28] A special right of

---

19   1970 Act, s.28(6)(a); Gretton and Reid, *Conveyancing* (2nd ed.), para. 20.31.
20   1970 Act, s.28(7).
21   1970 Act, s.20(1).
22   1970 Act, s.18(1), Sched. 3, S.C. 11 and Sched. 5, Form A.
23   1970 Act, s.18(1); Redemption of Standard Securities (Scotland) Act 1971 (c.45), s.1.
24   Cusine, *Standard Securities*, para. 10.11.
25   1970 Act, Sched. 3, S.C. 11(2).
26   For a similar position in relation to a bond and disposition in security see *Ashburton v. Escombe* (1893) 20R. 107; Cusine, *Standard Securities*, para. 10.12.
27   Cusine, *Standard Securities*, para. 10.14.
28   Cusine, *Standard Securities*, para. 10.12.

redemption exists in relation to a standard security over security subjects used as a private dwellinghouse[29] after 20 years have elapsed since the security was constituted.[30]

When the notice of default procedure is used to initiate the creditor's power of sale in a standard security, the debtor and the proprietor each has the right to redeem the standard security without giving notice at any time up to the conclusion of missives between the heritable creditor exercising a power of sale and a purchaser.[31] This right is subject to "any agreement to the contrary" so it may be limited or excluded altogether.[32] There is no parallel provision for the other two routes to sale and in such cases the debtors may require to serve a notice of redemption.[33]

Discharge of Standard Securities

A security is distinguishable from the underlying obligation 11.24 which it secures. Nevertheless, when the underlying obligation, whether one requiring payment or *ad factum praestandum*, is performed in full, the security will also be discharged.[34] Nevertheless, with a view to regularising the position shown on the public registers, a formal discharge is usually obtained. Where the underlying obligation is contingent upon the happening of a certain event within a certain time-limit and that period has expired without the contingency occurring, the security will be discharged. An example of this occurs in relation to standard securities obtained by local authorities to secure the repayment of a discount on the purchase of a local authority house in terms of the "right to buy" legislation. No discount is repayable where the purchaser does not sell the property within a three-year period. In such a case practice has accepted that no discharge needs to be put on the register.[35]

A standard security may be discharged by the recording of a

---

29 The term is not defined in the 1974 Act. For the use of the term in other contexts see *Airdrie, Coatbridge and District Water Trs v. Flanagan* (1906) 8F. 942 per Lord Low at 946; *Gordon v. Kirkcaldy D. C.* 1990 S.L.T. 644.

30 Land Tenure Reform (Scotland) Act 1974, s.11; Cusine, *Standard Securities*, para. 10.13.

31 1970 Act, s.23(3).

32 *Cf.* the view that this right of redemption cannot be varied by the standard conditions see Cusine, *Standard Securities*, para. 10.15.

33 *Forbes v. Armstrong*, 1993 S.C.L.R. 204. See Gretton and Reid, *Conveyancing* (2nd ed.), para. 20.32.

34 *Cameron v. Williamson* (1895) 22R. 393; Cusine, *Standard Securities*, para. 10.03.

35 Cusine, *Standard Securities*, para. 10.06.

discharge in statutory form granted by the creditor.[36] Where a debtor has exercised a right to redeem and has made payment of the whole amount due or performed the whole obligations of the debtor under the contract to which the security relates the creditor is obliged to grant a discharge in statutory form.[37] Where a discharge by the creditor cannot be obtained due to the death or absence of the creditor or any other cause, a standard security may be discharged by the recording of a certificate in statutory form confirming either that the redemption sums have been consigned or the court has declared that the whole obligations under the contract to which the security relates have been performed.[38]

Floating Charges

11.25   A floating charge is a method of obtaining security over both the heritage and moveables of incorporated companies and a limited number of other juristic bodies.[39] This book will deal only with the charge insofar as it relates to heritage. It is a creature of statute but, unfortunately, there is no comprehensive statutory definition of what a floating charge is.[40] This may cause some difficulty in determining whether some forms of security used outwith the United Kingdom of Great Britain and Northern Ireland would be regarded as a floating charge.[41] Until 1972 a Scottish floating charge required to be in a statutory form.[42] Now a floating charge may be in any form provided it satisfies the following three requirements:

(a)   It must be in writing.[43] This is implied in the whole regime of registration of company charges but is required in any event by the Requirements of Writing (Scotland) Act 1995.[44] Although a floating charge does not create a real right until attachment

---

36   1970 Act, s.17 and Sched. 4, Form F.
37   1970 Act, Sched. 3, S.C. 11(5).
38   1970 Act, s.18(2)–(4) and Sched. 5, Form D; Cusine, *Standard Securities*, para. 10.05.
39   Companies Act 1985, s.462(1). See para. 2.29.
40   The nearest approximation to such a statement is Companies Act 1985, s.462 See 4 *Stair Memorial Encyclopaedia*, para. 652.
41   4 *Stair Memorial Encyclopaedia*, para. 652.
42   Companies (Floating Charges) (Scotland) Act 1961 (c.46), s.2 and Sched. 1 repealed by Companies (Floating Charges and Receivers)(Scotland) Act 1972 (c.67), s.30(1).
43   Companies Act 1985, s.462(2), as amended and substituted; 4 *Stair Memorial Encyclopaedia*, para. 655.
44   1995 Act, s.1. See further Reid, *Requirements of Writing (Scotland) Act 1995* p. 6.

(which may never happen), such a real right could not be created unless the original charge were granted in written form. In addition, the appointment of the receiver by the holder of the charge must be by a validly executed instrument "in writing".[45]

(b) It must be granted "for the purpose of securing any debt or other obligation (including a cautionary obligation) incurred or to be incurred by, or binding upon, the company or any other person".[46] This quotation clearly indicates that the secured obligation need not be a monetary obligation[47] and there is no doubt that this includes obligations *ad factum praestandum* and obligations to desist from doing something.[48]

(c) It must be over "all or any part of the property (including uncalled capital) which may from time to time be comprised in . . . [the granting company's] . . . property and undertaking".[49] This reflects the general limitation of the power to grant floating charges to incorporated companies.[50]

It is not essential for the constitution of a Scottish floating charge that the deed creating the charge uses the term "floating charge"[51], nor is it now essential for the document to "purport" to create a floating charge although it once appears to have been so essential.[52] Clearly the use of the term "floating charge" is desirable to avoid confusion. To ensure validity of the charge it is of course necessary for it to be registered in the Companies Charges Register within 21 days of creation but this does not impose any specific obligations as to form.[53]

---

45 Insolvency Act 1986, s.53(1).
46 Companies Act 1985, s.462.
47 4 *Stair Memorial Encyclopaedia*, para. 654.
48 *Cf.* standard securities noted at para. 11.3.
49 Companies Act 1985, s.462.
50 Companies Act 1985, s.462(1).
51 4 *Stair Memorial Encyclopaedia*, para. 652.
52 Companies Act 1985, s.462(2). This requirement was omitted in later amendment to legislation: see Companies Act 1989, s.130(7) and Sched. 17, para. 8 later repealed by Law Reform (Misc. Prov.)(Scot.) Act 1990, s.74 and Sched. 8, para. 33(6) and Sched. 9. See also Companies Act 1985, s.36B as inserted by Companies Act 1989, s.130 and substituted by Requirements of Writing (Scotland) Act 1995, s.14(1) and Sched. 4, para. 51; 4 *Stair Memorial Encyclopaedia*, para. 655.
53 Companies Act 1985, ss 410 and 420. McBryde and Allan, "The Registration of Charges", 1982 S.L.T. (News) 177. See paras 3.20 and 3.23.

Disposal of Land

11.26   Until the floating charge attaches, the statutory provisions clearly imply that the company is to be free to dispose of the assets covered by the charge without the consent of the holder of the floating charge.[54] Once the charge has attached the clear inference is that the company acting through the directors is not free to dispose of the assets. For a purchaser of land it is therefore essential that he is able to determine that any relevant charge has not attached or crystallised. As crystallisation may occur without a public act[55] the best that can be done in practice is for a warranty or certificate of non-crystallisation to be obtained, usually from the creditor in the floating charge. The modern styles of such letter incorporate an express release of the property concerned from the charge where the letter is sought in the context of a sale to a third party. Where the letter is granted in the context of the grant of a subsequent security such a release is inappropriate but the parties may wish to consider a ranking provision.[56] Where the letter is issued in the context of a grant of a lease or other derivative real right it may contain a consent to the grant. Whatever its content this is generally known as a "letter of non-crystallisation". There is no statutory form of such letter but acceptable forms have developed in practice.

Attachment

11.27   A floating charge is not a fixed charge when it is created but it becomes a fixed charge or the equivalent of a fixed charge when it "attaches" or "crystallises".[57] In *Sharp v. Thomson*[58] it was observed that when a floating charge attaches to heritage it has the immediate effect of a recorded standard security. This is inaccurate as the creditor in an attached floating charge does not have the same remedies as are available to the creditor in a standard security. The statute merely indicates that the floating charge attaches to the relevant property "*as if* the charge were a fixed security over the property to which it has attached [emphasis

---

54 4 *Stair Memorial Encyclopaedia*, para. 652.

55 Para 3.23 and 11.27.

56 *Bank of Scotland v Bass Brewers Ltd*, June 1, 2000, Lord Macfadyen, O.H. (unreported); *Griffith and Powdill, Petirs.*, Nov. 3, 1998, Lord Cameron of Lochbroom, O.H. (unreported).

57 The two terms have identical meanings. The first term is used in statute but the latter is widely used. See 4 *Stair Memorial Encyclopaedia*, para. 659; Gretton and Reid, *Conveyancing* (2nd ed.), para. 28.09.

58 1997 S.L.T. 636 at 639 per Lord Jauncey and at 644–645 per Lord Clyde.

added]"[59]. It may be argued that this is not to state that the creditor actually has a fixed security. Whatever the niceties of the matter the fixed security analogy cannot be taken too far. Although the floating charge holder will be entitled to a ranking in relation to the separate assets comprised in the charge as if it held the appropriate form of fixed security (whatever that is—and there is more than one type) constituted in its favour at the date upon which the floating charge attached,[60] it is provided by statute that certain categories of creditor shall rank in priority to the floating charge holder. In addition the only mechanism for enforcing the floating charge is through the appointment of a receiver to ingather the assets, convert them into cash and distribute the money realised.[61] Such a party is unknown in relation to other fixed securities. It is the receiver and not the charge holder who has various powers to realise the value of the assets subject to the security even though the receiver has no real right in those assets.[62] The effective right of the creditor holding the attached floating charge is to require the receiver to carry out his duties and to refuse to discharge the attached charge until the creditor receives the payment to which he is entitled. The holder of an attached floating charge may act in a more pro-active manner than the holder of some of the statutory charging orders. He does not merely require to act as a dog in the manger in respect of a particular asset waiting to be paid off when the owner wishes to carry out juristic acts, but can require (by personal action if necessary) the co-operation of someone within the company (the receiver) taking it to bits for his benefit.

A floating charge attaches when the company goes into liquidation[63] or a receiver is appointed to the company under the floating charge.[64] The latter is largely a private act because the appointment of the receiver does not date from intimation of his

---

59 Companies Act 1985 (c.6), s.463(2); Insolvency Act 1986 (c.45), ss 53(7), 54(6).
60 *Forth and Clyde Construction Co. Ltd v. Trinity Timber and Plywood Co. Ltd,* 1984 S.C. 1; 1984 S.L.T. 94.
61 Insolvency Act 1986, s.60; *Myles J. Callaghan Ltd v. City of Glasgow D. C.,* 1987 S.C.L.R. 627; 1988 S.L.T. 227. Gretton and Reid, *Conveyancing* (2nd ed.), para. 29.06.
62 Gretton and Reid, *supra,* para. 29.06.
63 Companies Act 1985 (c.6), s.463(1) prospectively amended by Companies Act 1989 (c.40), s.140(1) from a day to be appointed under s.215(2). See 4 *Stair Memorial Encyclopaedia,* para. 659; *National Commercial Bank of Scotland Ltd v. Telford Grier Mackay & Co. Ltd Liquidators,* 1969 S.C. 181.
64 Insolvency Act 1986, (c.45), ss 53(7) and 54(6); *Forth & Clyde Construction Co. Ltd v. Trinity Timber & Plywood Co. Ltd,* 1984 S.C. 1 per Lord President Emslie at 10.

appointment in the Company Charges Register but is deemed to be when he receives his written instrument of appointment although it is conditional on timeous acceptance thereof.[65] A docquet, so signed, is conclusive evidence of when the receiver received the instrument of appointment and determines the date of his appointment.[66] A copy of the instrument of appointment must be delivered to the Registrar of Companies within seven days but failure incurs a fine and not invalidation.[67] A floating charge does not crystallise because of the appointment of a receiver under another floating charge. It is not competent for the parties to provide in the floating charge or any other contract to expand the circumstances in which the floating charge may attach.[68] Nevertheless it is competent for the parties to a floating charge to provide that the creditor may appoint a receiver on any ground specified in the instrument creating the charge under which the appointment was made. The parties to a floating charge may therefore specify that the appointment of a receiver under another floating charge may give the creditor in the first floating charge a right to appoint a receiver under the first floating charge.[69]

When a floating charge attaches on the company going into liquidation the property attached is "the property then comprised in the company's property and undertaking or, as the case may be, in part of that property and undertaking" (that is the part comprised in the floating charge).[70] When a floating charge attaches by virtue of the appointment of a receiver, the property attached is "the property then subject to the charge". The difference in wording does not appear to indicate a distinction in the consequences of attachment[71] except for *acquirenda* (property acquired by the company after the floating charge has attached). If the charge is so worded as to include *acquirenda*, receivership will not prevent the charge catching this but liquidation will prevent it.[72] This distinction is anomalous. Not all property to which the

---

65 Insolvency Act 1986, s.53(6)(b). See para. 3.23.
66 Insolvency Act 1986, s.53(6)(b); *Secretary of State for Trade and Industry v. Houston*, 1994 S.L.T. 775, OH.
67 Insolvency Act 1986, s.53(2).
68 4 *Stair Memorial Encyclopaedia*, para. 659. The position is otherwise in England: see *Re Brightlife Ltd* [1987] Ch. 200; [1986] 3 All E.R. 673; *Re Permanent Houses (Holdings) Ltd* (1989) 5 B.C.C. 151.
69 Insolvency Act 1986, s.52(1); 4 *Stair Memorial Encyclopaedia*, para. 659.
70 Companies Act 1985 (c.6), s.463(1).
71 4 *Stair Memorial Encyclopaedia*, para. 660.
72 *Ross v. Taylor*, 1985 S.C. 156; 1985 S.L.T. 387; 4 *Stair Memorial Encyclopaedia*, paras 661 and 662.

company has title is attached by the floating charge on the appointment of a receiver. Excluded property extends to property held by the company subject to a valid trust in favour of a third party[73] and property held by the company subject to a beneficial interest in favour of a purchaser holding a delivered disposition as yet unrecorded.[74]

Ranking of Floating Charges

Irrespective of any ranking provisions contained in a floating 11.28 charge, it will always rank after a fixed security arising by operation of law.[75] There is some debate as to what this class of security may comprise particularly in relation to a landlord's hypothec, but the better view appears to be that the landlord's hypothec would fall within such a classification.[76] It is clear that this will include the *debitum fundi* to secure the redemption sum for feuduty upon voluntary transfer of a feu for valuable consideration.[77]

A floating charge may contain provisions which prohibit or restrict the creation of any fixed security or any floating charge having priority over or ranking *pari passu* with it. It may also contain ranking provisions.[78] These provisions may regulate the order in which the floating charge is to rank with:

(a) any other subsisting floating charges or fixed securities over any of the property comprised in it provided always the consent is obtained of the holder of any subsisting floating charge or fixed security which would be adversely affected; and

---

73 *Tay Valley Joinery Ltd v. C. F. Financial Services Ltd*, 1987 S.C.L.R. 117; 1987 S.L.T. 207. For difficulties with the case see K.G.C. Reid, "*Trusts and Floating Charges*", 1987 S.L.T. (News) 113. See also 4 *Stair Memorial Encyclopaedia*, para 660.

74 *Sharp v. Thomson*, 1997 S.C. (H.L.) 66; 1997 S.L.T. 636; 1997 S.C.L.R. 328. For difficulties with this case see Scott C. Styles, "Rights in Security" in A.D.M. Forte (ed.), *Scots Commercial Law* (1997), Chap. 6, p. 196; Gretton and Reid, *Conveyancing* (2nd ed.), paras 11.31 and 28.09.

75 Companies Act 1985 (c.6), s.464(2).

76 *Grampian R. C. v. Drill Stem (Inspection Services) Ltd (in receivership)*, 1994 S.C.L.R. 36, Sh.Ct.; *Cumbernauld Development Corporation v. Mustone*, 1983 S.L.T. (Sh.Ct) 55; G.L. Gretton "*Receivership and Sequestration for Rent*", 1983 S.L.T. (News) 277; 4 *Stair Memorial Encyclopaedia*, para. 665.

77 Land Tenure Reform (Scotland) Act 1974, s.5(5). See para. 11.02.

78 Companies Act 1985 (c.6), s.464(1), (1A) respectively amended and added by the Companies Act 1989 (c.40), s.140(3),(4). The provisions of 1989 Act, s.140 and 178 come into force on a day to be appointed under s.215(2). See 4 *Stair Memorial Encyclopaedia*, para. 664.

    (b)   future floating charges or fixed securities over any of the property comprised in it.

11.29   In the absence of express restrictive provisions or ranking provisions the following rules apply[79]:

    (a)   a fixed security the right to which has been constituted as a real right before the floating charge has attached has priority of ranking over the floating charge[80];

    (b)   floating charges rank with one another according to the time of their registration in the Company Charges Register; and

    (c)   floating charges which have been received by the Registrar of Companies for registration by the same postal delivery rank with one another equally.

Where the holder of a floating charge which has been duly registered has received intimation in writing of the subsequent registration of another floating charge over the same property or any part of it, the preference in ranking of the first charge is restricted to a security for[81]:

    (a)   the holder's present advances;

    (b)   future advances which he may be required to make under the instrument creating the charge or under any ancillary documentation;

    (c)   interest due or to become due on all such advances;

    (d)   any expenses or outlays which may reasonably be incurred by the holder; and

    (e)   in the case of a floating charge to secure a contingent liability other than a liability arising under any further advances made from time to time the maximum, sum to which that contingent liability is capable of amounting,[82] whether or not it is contractually limited.

Complex and unresolved problems arise in relation to the situation where further advances are made under the first floating charge following the intimation of the creation of a second floating charge.

---

79 Companies Act 1985, s.464(4)(a)–(c).

80 *AIB Finance Ltd v. Bank of Scotland*, 1995 S.L.T. 2.

81 Companies Act 1985, s.464(5)(a)–(e)(s.464(5)(e) being added by the Companies Act 1989, s.140(6).

82 G.L. Gretton "*Ranking of Heritable Creditors*" (1980) 25 J.L.S.S. 275; 4 *Stair Memorial Encyclopaedia*, para. 667. *Cf.* Conveyancing and Feudal Reform (Scotland) Act 1970 (c.35), s.13(1). See para. 11.11.

Receivers, their Functions and Powers[83]

Broadly speaking, a receiver is the party appointed to realise the   11.30
assets of the company for the purposes of paying the debt secured
by the floating charge. A receiver may not be a body corporate, an
undischarged bankrupt or a firm according to the law of
Scotland.[84] There is no express statutory provsions to the effect
that the creditor should not also act as receiver but this is implicit in
the nature of a receiver's office and obligations. A receiver may be
appointed by the charge holder[85] or by the court upon petition.[86]
The former is more common by far.

The principal function of the receiver is to seek enforcement of
the obligation secured by the floating charge. To do this he will
usually realise the assets of the company to the extent required and
distribute the money received in accordance with the statutory
order of ranking. In carrying out his functions a receiver is deemed
to be the agent of the company in relation to the property attached
by the floating charge.[87] In relation to the property attached by the
floating charge a receiver has all the powers given to him in the
instrument creating the floating charge[88] and, in addition, so far as
they are not inconsistent with any provision of the floating charge,
the powers conferred upon him by statute.[89] These are much more
extensive and flexible than the powers available to a creditor in a
standard security. They include the following powers which have
direct relevance to heritable property:

(1)   power to take possession of the property from the company or
      a liquidator or any other person, and for that purpose to take
      such proceedings as may seem to the receiver expedient;
(2)   power to sell or otherwise dispose of the property;
(3)   power to borrow and grant securities;
(4)   power to appoint a solicitor or accountant, etc. to assist him;
(5)   power to bring or defend legal proceedings;
(6)   power to do all acts and to execute in the name and on behalf
      of the company any deed, receipt or other document; and
(7)   power to do all other things incidental to the exercise of the

---

83   See generally Greene and Fletcher, *The Law and Practice of Receivorship in
     Scotland* (2nd ed., 1992).
84   Insolvency Act 1986, s.51(3)(a)–(c); 4 *Stair Memorial Encyclopaedia*, para. 671.
85   4 *Stair Memorial Encyclopaedia*, para. 674.
86   4 *Stair Memorial Encyclopaedia*, para. 675.
87   Insolvency Act 1986 (c.45), s.57(1); 4 *Stair Memorial Encyclopaedia*, para. 676.
88   Insolvency Act 1986 (c.45), s.55(1).
89   Insolvency Act 1986, s.55(2) and Sched.2.

powers conferred upon the receiver by the instrument creating the floating charge or any of the statutory powers.

The exercise by the receiver of his powers is subject to the rights of any person who holds a fixed security or floating charge having priority over, or ranking *pari passu* with,[90] the floating charge by virtue of which the receiver was appointed.[91]

The Receiver's Duties

11.31   The position of the receiver is somewhat anomalous in that, although he is deemed by statute to be the agent of the company in respect of whose property he is appointed,[92] he is primarily responsible to his appointer for the efficient realisation of the assets secured by the charge and the repayment of the debt secured by it. The receiver also owes a duty of care to the company itself which may be enforced by the directors or by a liquidator.

Charging Orders

11.32   Charging orders are sometimes referred to as "statutory" charges.[93] Whilst this phraseology is undoubtedly correct it tends to indicate that, as compared to other heritable securities, there is something different about charging orders in relation to their origin. As we have seen, however, the most important heritable securities encountered in modern Scots law, except for assignations in security, are statutory creatures.

Under certain statutory procedures it is competent for a local authority or other authorised creditor to impose a statutory form of fixed security known as "a charging order" on an "interest in land". These orders are intended to secure payment of a debt to the local authority or the particular creditor in terms of certain statutes or statutory instruments where the debtor has been unwilling or unable to pay. The order is executed and recorded in the General Register of Sasines (or registered in the Land Register of Scotland if appropriate) by the local authority or other entitled creditor and not by the debtor. The underlying debt may relate only to the type

---

90   *Forth and Clyde Construction Co. Ltd v. Trinity Timber and Plywood Co. Ltd*, 1984 S.C. 1 per Lord President Emslie at 11; R.J. Reed, *"Aspects of the Law of Receivers in Scotland"*, 1983 S.L.T. (News) 261; 4 *Stair Memorial Encyclopaedia*, para. 693.
91   Insolvency Act 1986, s.55(3)(a) and (b).
92   Insolvency Act 1986 (c.45), s.57(1).
93   Gordon, *Scottish Land Law* (2nd ed.), paras 20–227–20–241.

of debt stated in the relevant statute but these comprise an array of matters as diverse as sums due in respect of legal aid,[94] residential accommodation[95] and the costs of repairing and demolishing buildings.[96] The nature and effect of the charge is not uniform and depends on the provisions in the relevant statutes. In some cases the legislature has attempted to strengthen the position of the creditor by grafting additional rights on to the security and in one case the statutory provisions relative to standard securities are applied to charging orders subject to some important exceptions and variations. This has an unfortunate consequence as the provisions relaxing the requirement to impose a particular description in the security are inapplicable to such charging orders with the result that one may presume that such a requirement still exists in relation to these charging orders.[97] Furthermore, in that case the statutory notes provided to guide the completion of the charging order specifically require the insertion of a particular description.[98] It is possible that charging orders which have been completed not in conformity with these requirements are invalid.[99] In most cases, however, the remedies of the creditor are more restricted than those available to the holders of floating charges or standard securities. Charging orders are generally a non-aggressive form of security in that many of the teeth of the creditors in other securities are not available. The aim of charging orders is generally to obtain

---

94 The Civil Legal Aid (Scotland) Regulations 1987 (SI. 1987 No. 381), reg. 40 and Sched. 4, Form 1, as amended by the Civil Legal Aid (Scotland) Amendment (No.2) Regulations 1991 (S.I. 1991 No. 1904), reg. 9.

95 Charging Orders (Residential Accommodation) (Scotland) Order (S.I. 1993 No. 1516) made in terms of Health and Social Services and Social Security Adjudications Act 1983, s.23(5) and (6).

96 The Building (Forms) (Scotland) Regulations 1991 (S.I. 1991 No. 160), Form 26, made in terms of Building (Scotland) Act 1959, ss.10, 11, 13 and 24(1)(a), Sched. 6; Housing (Scotland) Act 1969, s.25(4) and Sched. 2 (repealed by Housing (Scotland) Act 1987, Sched. 24); Housing (Scotland) Act 1987, ss.109(5), 131, 164(4), Sched. 9 and Sched. 11, Pt IV; Civic Government (Scotland) Act 1982, s.108 as amended by Housing (Scotland) Act 1987, s.339 and Sched. 23. See Gretton and Reid, *Conveyancing* (2nd ed.), para. 4.17; McDonald, *Conveyancing Manual*, (6th ed.), paras 19.49 and 19.52; *County Council of Moray and Petrs.*, 1962 S.C. 601; *Lindsay v. Glasgow D.C.*, 1998 Hous. L.R. 4.

97 Abolition of Feudal Tenure etc. (Scotland) Act 2000, s.75(3) and Sched. 10, para. 32(23)(a).

98 See, *e.g.* Charging Orders (Residential Accommodation) (Scotland) Order (S.I. 1993 No.1516), Art. 3 and Sched., Form 1.

99 *Cf. Beneficial Bank plc v. Bennett*, 1995 S.C.L.R. 284; *Beneficial Bank plc v. McConnachie* 1996 S.C. 119; *Beneficial Bank plc v. Wardle* 1996 G.W.D. 30–1825; Gretton and Reid, *Conveyancing* (2nd ed.), para. 12.23; McDonald, *Conveyancing Manual* (6th ed.), para. 8.11.

payment "on the drip" over a period of time by methods such as a long term annuity or to encourage payment upon transfer of the burdened interest simply by being there and preventing a seller from granting a clear title. One additional method of achieving this is to vary the rule of ranking according to the general principle *prior tempore potior jure*[1] to ensure that the charging order has a ranking ahead of any voluntarily created security such as a standard security, but the statutory provisions are not consistent to this effect.[2]

---

1 Para. 3.17.
2 *Sowman v. City of Glasgow D. C.*, 1985 S.L.T. 65; Cusine, *Standard Securities*, para. 7.22; Gordon, *Scottish Land Law* (2nd ed.), para. 20–227.

INDEX